Affect, Archive, Archipelago

RETHINKING THE ISLAND

The Rethinking the Island series seeks to unsettle assumptions by comprehensively investigating the range of topological and topographical characteristics that lie at the heart of the idea of "islandness."

Series Editors:

Elaine Stratford, professor in the Institute for the Study of Social Change, University of Tasmania, Australia

Godfrey Baldacchino, professor of sociology and pro-rector at the University of Malta, UNESCO co-chair in Island Studies and Sustainability

Elizabeth McMahon, associate professor in the School of the Arts and Media, University of New South Wales, Australia

Titles in the Series

Theorizing Literary Islands: The Island Trope in Contemporary Robinsonade Narratives by Ian Kinane

Island Genres, Genre Islands: Conceptualization and Representation in Popular Fiction by Ralph Crane and Lisa Fletcher

Postcolonial Nations, Islands, and Tourism: Reading Real and Imagined Spaces by Helen Kapstein

Caribbean Island Movements: Culebra's Trans-Insularities by Carlo A. Cubero

Poetry and Islands: Materiality and the Creative Imagination by Rajeev S. Patke

Contemporary Archipelagic Thinking: Towards New Comparative Methodologies and Disciplinary Formations edited by Michelle Stephens and Yolanda Martínez-San Miguel

The Notion of Near Islands: The Croatian Archipelago edited by Nenad Starc

Atolls of the Maldives: Nissology and Geography edited by Stefano Malatesta, Marcella Schmidt di Friedberg, Shahida Zubair, David Bowen, and Mizna Mohamed

An Introduction to Island Studies by James Randall

Affect, Archive, Archipelago: Puerto Rico's Sovereign Caribbean Lives by Beatriz Llenín-Figueroa

Ecocriticism and the Island: Readings from the British-Irish Archipelago by Pippa Marland (forthcoming)

Affect, Archive, Archipelago

Puerto Rico's Sovereign Caribbean Lives

Beatriz Llenín-Figueroa

ROWMAN & LITTLEFIELD
Lanham • Boulder • New York • London

Published by Rowman & Littlefield
An imprint of The Rowman & Littlefield Publishing Group, Inc.
4501 Forbes Boulevard, Suite 200, Lanham, Maryland 20706
www.rowman.com

86-90 Paul Street, London EC2A 4NE

Copyright © 2022 by The Rowman & Littlefield Publishing Group, Inc.

All rights reserved. No part of this book may be reproduced in any form or by any electronic or mechanical means, including information storage and retrieval systems, without written permission from the publisher, except by a reviewer who may quote passages in a review.

British Library Cataloguing in Publication Information Available

Library of Congress Cataloging-in-Publication Data
Names: Llenín-Figueroa, Beatriz, author.
Title: Affect, archive, archipelago : Puerto Rico's sovereign Caribbean lives / Beatriz Llenín-Figueroa.
Description: Lanham : Rowman & Littlefield Publishers, [2022] | Series: Rethinking the island | Includes bibliographical references and index. | Summary: "This timely book presents the contexts and perspectives needed for imagining possible decolonial futures for twenty-first century Puerto Rico"— Provided by publisher.
Identifiers: LCCN 2021060031 (print) | LCCN 2021060032 (ebook) | ISBN 9781538151440 (cloth) | ISBN 9781538151457 (ebook)
Subjects: LCSH: Sovereignty—Puerto Rico—History—21st century. | Archipelagoes—Puerto Rico—History—21st century. | Decolonization—Puerto Rico—History—21st century.
Classification: LCC JC327 .L583 2022 (print) | LCC JC327 (ebook) | DDC 320.1/5097295—dc23/eng/20220125
LC record available at https://lccn.loc.gov/2021060031
LC ebook record available at https://lccn.loc.gov/2021060032

∞™ The paper used in this publication meets the minimum requirements of American National Standard for Information Sciences—Permanence of Paper for Printed Library Materials, ANSI/NISO Z39.48-1992.

*To lives and loves submerged,
breathing in our midst.*

Being conscious of oneself as part of a small literature imposes the tone.

—Marta Aponte Alsina, "Principio estrella"

I was made at sea
The sea made me like this

—Alegría Rampante, "El recipiente"

Island sighting.
Disembark your heart,
your chords polished by the unexpected
adversity of each cardinal point.
Your eyes, two compasses
stuttering, dampened by the sting
of salt and pounding water. What else is an island
if not a bastion of simulated securities,
where to walk steadily is to maneuver turns,
to stumble upon the previous footprint on the sand . . .

—Claudia Becerra, "12," *Versión del viaje*

[T]he smallest area one envisages, island or village, prominent ridge or buried valley, flatland or heartland, is charged immediately with the openness of imagination, and the longest chain of sovereign territories one sees is ultimately no stronger than its weakest and most obscure connecting link.

—Wilson Harris, "Tradition and the West Indian Novel"

Contents

Note of Gratitude	ix
Note on the Text	xi
List of Illustrations	xiii
Prelude: An Unsheltered Walk-Swim of a Book, or For the Love of Us	xv
The Call	xxi
Introduction: Waters Coming Ashore, Affects Creating Archives, Islands Touching Each Other	1

PART I: PERFORMATIVE POLITICS IN PUERTO RICO'S AFFECTIVE ARCHIVE OF CARIBBEAN RELATIONS — 41

1. Feeling the Archipelagic Confederation: Ramón Emeterio Betances and the *Confederación Antillana* — 43
   Hunted Flesh — 66

2. Embodying Oceanic Sovereignties: Luisa Capetillo and the *Tribuna* on the Street — 75
   Subversive Walk — 96

3. Commanding the Islands' Liberation: Pedro Albizu Campos and the *Partido Nacionalista* — 105
   Resounding Voice — 128

PART II: POLITICAL PERFORMANCES IN PUERTO RICO'S AFFECTIVE ARCHIVE OF CARIBBEAN RELATIONS — 139

4 Tidal Relations of Art, Struggle, and Liberation: *Agua, Sol y Sereno, Amigxs del MAR, Comuna Caribe, Mujeres que Abrazan la Mar,* and *Coalición 8M* — 141

Embracing Coast — 171

5 Sea, Salt, Survive: Teresa Hernández's Multitudinously Small Art — 181

Overflowing Sea — 211

Coda: The Liquid Homeland of Our Reparative and Sovereign Relations, or, For the Love of Us — 219

Bibliography — 227

Index — 257

About the Author — 275

Note of Gratitude

We have come to this moment together, over the course of many years. I mention your names here as an intimation of the other, ineffable life you live and allow me to live, every day, in our common walk holding each other. Thank you. Forever.

No turn of words could possibly encompass my gratitude to you, Lissette, beloved of beloveds, my most committed reader, *compañera* of lives, loves, and worlds. Your love, brilliance, patience, generosity, and faith have seen me through so many tears and fears and sleepless nights. With you, too, I have known true joy and the always possible impossible. Thank you, my love, my home.

My friends, *compañeres*, comrades, fellow walkers-swimmers-mammals-artists-writers, have been the constant embrace of love and confidence, light and laughter, invention and risk. Several of you read, commented, and then reread drafts, portions, or the entirety of this book. Some of you have been such steady, deep, and transformative company that the book should bear your names next to mine. Thank you forever, as well as your partners and children (if you have them), and the dogs and cats with whom you share your lives (if you do). Thank you, Ana Rodríguez, Anayra Santory, Ángela Figueroa, Ariadna Godreau, Christopher Powers, Claudia Becerra, Eury Orsini, Guillermo Rebollo, Jocelyn Géliga, Kairiana Núñez, Mabel Rodríguez, Mari Mari, Marta Aponte, Michelle Koerner, Pelé Sánchez, Rima Brusi, Sandra Soto, Sofía Cardona, Sofía Gallisá, Teresa Hernández, Toño Ramos, Vanessa Vilches, and Zuleira Soto.

Affect, Archive, Archipelago also became a pretext to meet—or deepen my relation with—extraordinary Puerto Rican artists and activists alongside whom we live a common, "sovereign life." Thank you Cristina Vives, Hilda Guerrero, Pedro Adorno, Vanesa Contreras, and Vanessa Uriarte.

Both my family and Lissette's have been a constant source of support and love. Thank you, *mami*, *papi*, Gaby, José, *tías y tíos*, Lourdes, Dilia, and all your spouses and beloved children.

Now that I am no longer amid my University of Puerto Rico (UPR) students, I reiterate my gratitude to them for unyieldingly reminding me that our islands are not what the powers that be say they are. I am especially indebted to a group of students who helped me over the years with tasks that ultimately made this book possible. Thank you, Diego López, María Fernanda Ortiz, Nashaly Cima, Nicole Ruiz, Nicole Talavera, and Paola González. For the intensity of her assistance, Paola Egipciaco deserves a word of heartfelt gratitude of her own.

The *Rethinking the Island* series editors, as well as the book's editors, Katelyn Turner, Haley White, and Madeline Kogler, have been most welcoming in their generosity and patience. I am particularly grateful to Godfrey Baldacchino, whom I met at a conference in Aruba in 2019, where he invited me to submit to Rowman & Littlefield what was then very far from a finished manuscript. Thank you.

Nothing at all would be possible if it were not for the existence of all that is not human. I am eternally grateful—and declare myself their humble apprentice—to Andre, the dog; Clara, the cat; and all living creatures, most especially, dogs, cats, trees, birds, bees, flowers, fungi, forest and mangrove paths, sands, coasts, corals, crabs, shells, turtles, fish, the sea . . . and the exuberantly green and red, minuscule *San Pedritos* I have learned to listen for and love.

Note on the Text

Previous versions of some portions of this book were published in the academic journals *Discourse, Caribbean Studies, Shima, Voces del Caribe,* and *Visitas al Patio,* as well as in the digital arts and culture magazines *80grados* and *PREE*.

List of Illustrations

CHAPTER 1

1.1 *Betances in the Streets* at the Puerto Rican March for Black Lives, Harlem, New York, 2020. Courtesy of Molly Crabapple.   64

CHAPTER 2

2.1 *Luisa, café sobre hilo.* Courtesy of Editora Educación Emergente (EEE), Art by Zuleira Soto-Román for EEE's 2022 Commemorative Series on the Centenary of Luisa Capetillo's Death, Mixed Media, 2021.   90

CHAPTER 3

3.1 Pedro Albizu Campos at the Partido Nacionalista *Tribuna*. Courtesy of the Ruth M. Reynolds Papers 1915–1989 at the Archives of the Puerto Rican Diaspora, Center for Puerto Rican Studies, Hunter College, City University of New York.   126

CHAPTER 4

4.1 *Agua, Sol y Sereno*'s *Marea alta, marea baja* (promotional material). Courtesy of Pedro Adorno.   145

4.2	*Amigxs del MAR, Coalición Playas Pa'l Pueblo*, and *Agua, Sol y Sereno* Celebrate Their Triumph in Carolina, 2019. Courtesy of Luis López.	152
4.3	*Comuna Caribe* logo. Courtesy of Hilda Guerrero.	160
4.4	*Comuna Caribe* and *Mujeres que Abrazan la Mar* Handwoven Solidarity Banner. Courtesy of Hilda Guerrero.	160
4.5	*Mujeres que Abrazan la Mar* 2014 Calendar for Haiti. Courtesy of Yvette Pérez Álvarez.	164
4.6	*Mujeres que Abrazan la Mar* 2016 Calendar for Ivania Zayas Ortiz. Courtesy of Ernesto Robles.	164
4.7	*Amigxs del MAR, Mujeres que Abrazan la Mar*, and Members of *Coalición 8M* Demand Public Access to Beaches at the Ocean Park Beach, San Juan, 2020. Courtesy of Vanesa Contreras Capó.	166

CHAPTER 5

5.1	*La mujer del cuchillo* Climbs the Colonial Wall, *bravata: el comienzo de un comienzo*, Fortín Conde Mirasol, Vieques, 2019. Courtesy of Rafael Orejuela.	183
5.2	*La mujer de la cola* with the Heart Pierced by 23 Nails, *(a)parecer*, Plaza Colón, San Juan. Courtesy of Antonio Ramírez Aponte.	193
5.3	Vieques and Culebra Made of Salt, *inciertas-espectáculo erosionado*, Arriví Theater, Santurce, 2020. Courtesy of Teresa Hernández.	206
5.4	*La mujer del sillón* in an Abandoned Cultural Center in Loíza, *inciertas-espectáculo erosionado*, 2020. Courtesy of María del Mar Rosario.	207
5.5	*La erizada*, the Sea, and the Theater's Empty Seats, *inciertas-espectáculo erosionado*, Arriví Theater, Santurce, 2020. Courtesy of Teresa Hernández.	208

Prelude

An Unsheltered Walk-Swim of a Book, or For the Love of Us

> Let us move closer, yes, as soon as possible, to the entrails of life.
>
> —Anayra Santory Jorge, *Nada es igual: Bocetos del país que nos acontece*, 2018, 201[1]

A dense relation of love, at once fraught and light, whole and broken, bonds my body to our archipelagos. In my wildest flights, by "our archipelagos" I mean the entire planet, as water surrounds all lands and connects them, deeply, under its surface. In my more proximate stirrings, I mean the Caribbean, the recurring dream of our common horizons, of our touching each other every single second our waters come ashore over there, yes, where you and I are now, and over here, yes, where you and I are now, too. In my most immediate sensations, "our archipelagos" mean "Puerto Rico"—*Borikén*—this most unusual yet paradigmatic place, where everything—including that which is defined as impossible per se, a "free colony"—seems to have been enacted by power.

Affect, Archive, Archipelago: Puerto Rico's Sovereign Caribbean Lives emerges from such love. It is nothing if not affect, deep, expansive. It comes from nothing if not from feeling affected, *all the time*.[2] Its writing is that of an ex-adjunct faculty turned "independent writer," attempting to navigate the increasing entrapment of nets thrown at us, liquid, mammal[3] creatures, hunted for our persistence by power's ever more ruthless, annihilating command.

As such, although this book is certainly an academic intellectual exercise, it is not, and cannot be, of the sort born of enclosed rooms and ruminations. Rather, as it "wants to move closer to the entrails of life," it feels more like a love letter, an imaginative sandcastle, ephemeral and fragile, both land and water, crafted in the open, a walk-swim of a book.[4] I have written significant portions of it while engaging in a conscious practice of daily walking-witnessing in ever more adverse collective conditions.[5] Each chapter is thus followed by a written walk-swim. Those in part I emerged from imaginative flights with the chapters' protagonists, who have all transitioned, in Puerto Rican coasts they traversed or might have. Those in part II are the result of live encounters with some of the artists and activists included in the chapters, in littorals they chose or are salient in this book. These maritime-terrestrial transits want to trace and further submarine relations of care, love, creation, and liberation. And they want to do it bodily, that is, before and beyond the word.

While this is a rather undisciplined book, it has certainly found nourishment from many practices learned at institutions we call "academic." I am grateful, deeply, for having been taught valuable lessons on how to read, think, conceptualize, imagine, investigate, and make of myself a nerd who is proud of and dignified by that name. "In but not of," as Fred Moten and Stefano Harney describe the undercommons' relation to the university,[6] *Affect, Archive, Archipelago* aspires to be of the school Alexis Pauline Gumbs learns from dolphins:

> I know that what scientists mean when they call groups of dolphins "schools" is not exactly what I usually mean when I, Black feminist book nerd say "school," but these dolphin schools are organizational structures for learning, nurturance, and survival, both intergenerationally and within generations. . . . What if school, as we used it on a daily basis, signaled not the name of a process or institution through which we could be indoctrinated, not a structure through which social capital was grasped and policed, but something more organic, like a scale of care. *What if school was the scale at which we could care for each other and move together. In my view, at this moment in history, that is really what we need to learn most urgently.* (*Undrowned* 2020, 55–56, emphasis added)

One of the ways in which *Affect, Archive, Archipelago* is of the dolphin schools rather than the university is in its copious quotation practice, our "echolocation."[7] The book's proposal itself, its aspiration to archive becoming, and the rainbows of materials it relates with, all demand a decentering of the writing "voice," the "I" of the author. Whatever "I" stand for is the constant remade result of a common encounter with, a being affected by, all living beings, and, in the specific context of this book, every "I" that traverses it. This is a many-bodied book echolocating with Édouard Glissant's *Rélation*, Marta Aponte Alsina's *patria líquida*, Ramón Emeterio Betances's *Confederación Antillana*, Luisa Capetillo's transg/dressing, Pedro Albizu

Campos's liberation, *Agua, Sol y Sereno*'s tidal theater, *Amigxs del MAR*'s *las playas son del pueblo*, *Comuna Caribe*'s and *Mujeres que Abrazan la Mar*'s *la mar sana*, *Coalición 8M*'s *animalista* consciousness, and Teresa Hernández's swelling *bravatas*, to name a few. And so, we all come to you, "quoting-bouncing" our traces, sounds, moves, words . . .

An amalgam of relations within a daily attempt at living a present, intentional life in these archipelagos surrounded by rising sea levels, this book walks-swims in the care and companionship of other queer mammals and fellow creatures who struggle and love, create and disrupt, in and despite of impossible conditions. It is an offering, or, rather, an aspiration to become one. Will you take it in your trembling hands that were wings, that were fins, and consider it a gift? Its entrails carry no hidden poison. This book is not out to kill. Rather, with Chris Finley, it desires and is aroused by "a deep way of being together," where "we see the brokenness as a method of relatedness."[8] It wants to walk-swim with you, and you, and you, and innumerable Puerto Rican and Caribbean dreamers of liberation, wherever they are, of many generations, upbringings, skills, practices, archives, who gave/give us many kinds of love offerings that live on, even when met with killing sprees.

Despite not being able to visit—let alone, live in—most of the archipelagos that compose the region we call "Caribbean," there are many ways in which I sense, feel, and embody myself a Caribbean creature. Defining this with precise terms is notoriously fraught,[9] but elusiveness does not preclude the real, as art unceasingly teaches us. The stories that run deep in this book, those that will not be readily available, nor even visible, have mostly to do with this simultaneous, apparently impossible, sensation: a here that feels an elsewhere, an elsewhere that feels a here, a walk-swim in waters and submerged mountain ridges that comes ashore on our shared islands.

Most intensely, these stories have to do with countering Puerto Rico's continuous political-institutional refusal to recognize its *archipelagic condition* and to *imagine itself Caribbean*.[10] The time has indeed come for a reckoning with such negation, which necessarily entails rummaging for, tuning in with, and otherwise encountering and mobilizing for the present moment, our subtler, affective archive of Caribbean relations, a fundamental concept-poetics to which I devote a section in this book's Introduction. Decidedly situated in Puerto Rico's contemporary struggles for decolonization, this project responds to such necessity, felt, at once, as collective and personal, political and imaginative, abstract and embodied. Here, decolonization is understood, with Denise Ferreira da Silva, as "the demand for nothing less than the return of the total value expropriated from and yielded by the productive capacity of Native lands and slave bodies,"[11] which entails reparatory justice, as well as the defense of our multiple sovereignties within a deep, relational, Caribbean consciousness.

Affect, Archive, Archipelago gathers its life from the conceptual-poetic-imaginative world that Caribbean philosophical literature and literary philosophy have gifted us. In particular, the book's overarching argument responds to my encounter with Édouard Glissant's and Marta Aponte Alsina's critical-creative thought-sensation. Without ambitioning the exhaustive—since "being conscious of oneself as part of a small literature imposes the tone"[12]—*Affect, Archive, Archipelago* threads various richly entangled forms, both of the word and the body, both apparently more sweeping (part I) and seemingly more delimited (part II), liberation projects of Puerto Rico's affective archive of Caribbean relations, from the nineteenth century to the present. Historical legacies, political and activist thought and action, performance and live arts pieces, interventions, objects, materialities, and texts traverse this book as areas of praxis and imagination more intimately connected than what might appear at first glance. The same premise applies to the ways in which Puerto Rican historical figures of immense consequence—Ramón Emeterio Betances (chapter 1), Luisa Capetillo (chapter 2), and Pedro Albizu Campos (chapter 3)—are reconsidered and compared in this book's first part.

Commentaries on political manifestos, letters, essays, philosophical-literary texts of various kinds, performative writing, live arts pieces, objects, costumes, materialities, political/activist actions as performative interventions, and performative interventions as political/activist actions, are all confluenced and confluencing in this book. The latter instances in the previous enumeration constitute the second part of *Affect, Archive, Archipelago*, which sets the stage for an encounter with the work of the live arts collective *Agua, Sol y Sereno*, the political/activist work of *Amigxs del MAR*, *Comuna Caribe*, *Mujeres que Abrazan la Mar*, and *Coalición 8M* (chapter 4), and Teresa Hernández's transdisciplinary artistic trajectory (chapter 5). This deep dive into Puerto Rico's affective archive of Caribbean relations comparatively considers how decolonization, the archipelagic, the sea, Caribbean regionalism, and various forms and practices of sovereignty have been envisioned in Puerto Rico's tradition and imagination from the nineteenth century through the twenty-first.

Finally, stemming from the offerings explored throughout the book and the immediate historical-political-affective context of the *Verano Boricua* (Puerto Rico's summer 2019 rebellion), the Coda offers some reflections and proposals for furthering decolonial, sovereign, and archipelagic horizons for Puerto Rico.[13] In particular, it addresses the enduring question of the nation-state and the extent to which it could or could not embody an emancipatory and archipelagic horizon; it argues for the inclusion of Puerto Rico in the Caribbean struggle for reparations, offering some concrete proposals in that direction; and it suggests possible nurturing links between Puerto Rico's communitarian-artistic-bodily sovereignties, as discussed in the book, and other radical emancipatory efforts across the Global South.

NOTES

1. In this book, all translations from materials originally in Spanish are mine.
2. "Affectability" in Denise Ferreira da Silva's sense: "the condition of being subjected to both natural (in the scientific and lay sense) conditions and to other's power" (*Toward a Global Idea of Race*, 2007, xv). For the "subjects of affectability," "universal reason remains an exterior ruler," while for the subjects of power, whom Ferreira da Silva calls "the subject of transparency"—an echo of Glissant's thought, as we will see in the Introduction—"universal reason is an interior guide" (xxxix). "Feeling affected, all the time," then, means "being subjected to other's power," that is, to the "exterior rule" of "universal reason," for which the below-the-surface sovereign lives in these archipelagos—what this book is made of—make no sense at all. This holds a connection with Tiffany Lethabo King, Jenell Navarro, and Andrea Smith's attention to shared "affective dispositions" (*Otherwise Worlds*, 2020, 13).
3. Thank you, Alexis Pauline Gumbs, for the book *Undrowned*, and Karen Langevin for the performance *MAMÍFERAsola*.
4. "The book is an expression of a physiology. In too many works, one perceives the bent, seated, stooped, shrunken body. The body that walks is upright and tense like an arc: open to ample spaces as the flower to the sun" (Gros 2015, 15–16).
5. The deliberate opposition to capitalist acceleration that walking entails has been beautifully defended by Franco Cassano in his *Pensamiento meridiano* (2004), which, coincidentally, argues from the Mediterranean for the emancipatory epistemology enabled by coastal lives in a common sea.
6. "In the face of these conditions one can only sneak into the university and steal what one can. To abuse its hospitality, to spite its mission, to join its refugee colony, its gypsy encampment, to be in but not of—this is the path of the subversive intellectual in the modern university" (2013, 26).
7. "How does echolocation, the practice many marine mammals use to navigate the world through bouncing sounds, change our understandings of 'vision' and visionary action?" (Gumbs 2020, 15).
8. Chris Finley, "Building Maroon Intellectual Communities," in *Otherwise Worlds: Against Settler Colonialism and Anti-Blackness*, edited by Tiffany Lethabo King, Jenell Navarro, and Andrea Smith (Durham, NC: Duke University Press, 2020), 368.
9. See, for instance, Antonio Gaztambide Géigel's "La invención del Caribe" (2006) and Pedro L. San Miguel's "Visiones históricas del Caribe" (2004). Yolanda Martínez-San Miguel, for her part, has summarized the diverse proposals to define "the Caribbean geographic zone" put forth by Caribbean intellectuals and artists. In "Cartografías pancaribeñas" (1998), she explains that these have been based on *mestizaje*, music, creolization, the plantation system, the common experience of

enslavement, colonialism and imperialism, or strict geography. Specifically with respect to discourses on Caribbean creolization and its critique, I know of no better place to start than Michaeline A. Chrichlow's *Globalization and the Post-Creole Imagination* (2009).

10. Considering Puerto Rico's scarce "official relations" with the Caribbean after 1952, Efraín Vázquez Vera's "Las relaciones oficiales de Puerto Rico con el Caribe" (2005) concludes that only governmental administrations led by the pro–status quo *Partido Popular Democrático* have attempted—with little success—to establish "an autonomous foreign policy" in connection with the Caribbean region, since those controlled by the pro–US annexation *Partido Nuevo Progresista* have only engaged in "external actions" as per "the North American government's instruction" (1). See the Introduction for a historical panorama of Puerto Rico's twentieth-century history, including commentaries on its two dominant political parties, to which I also return briefly in chapter 1.

11. Denise Ferreira da Silva, "Reading the Dead: A Feminist Black Critique of Global Capital," in *Otherwise Worlds: Against Settler Colonialism and Anti-Blackness*, edited by Tiffany Lethabo King, Jenell Navarro, and Andrea Smith (Durham, NC: Duke University Press, 2020), 40–41.

12. Marta Aponte Alsina, "Principio estrella," May 1, 2021, www.angelicafuriosa.blogspot.com/2021/.

13. Some of the most significant reflections to date on this historical sequence of events can be found in books published within Editora Educación Emergente's series *reVolucionA*. See also the profuse materials compiled by the *Puerto Rico Syllabus*, as well as the forum, *The Decolonial Geographies of Puerto Rico's 2019 Summer Protests*, co-organized by Joaquín Villanueva and Marisol LeBrón.

The Call

The island presumes other islands. Antilles. The giant call of the earth's horizon is unknown to us. We could not wander without end to the ever withdrawn limits. But we forage. Our role will be to convene. The island is an amphitheater with ocean stands, where representation is temptation: of the world.

—Édouard Glissant, *Poetic Intention*, [1969]–2010

How to fall into temptation?
That is to say,
how to touch and let ourselves be touched
by, from and for,
the other islands presumed by mine,
and yours?

—On clear days, we can see our silhouettes, elevated above the surface, a miracle!—

Such proximity an invitation
to graze us with corals
to salt us in mutual preservation.

I aspire to read for the horizon,
but the master has raised walls

. . . on the water.

And they blind us.

Wo-andering on the s-land,
I open my flesh with our amphitheater's injection,
Édouard, Marta, Ramón, Luisa, Pedro, Hilda, Vanessa, Vanesa, Teresa, and all beloveds,

I convene.

And let myself be convened.

> Facing a coastal landscape, like witnessing the appearance of bees and spilling the honey at the same time, the mouth can achieve saline condensation, a mine multiplying, excess. My body walks smelling of cave, river, limestone, and sea.
>
> —Elizabeth Magaly Robles, "Notas II: De(s)generar," 2021

Bring down the imperial wall
with a kitchen knife.

Held by the smallness of a mouth-body-island
that does nothing else

but walk on the sands
smelling of cave, river, limestone, and sea

but tidal, nonhuman-becoming art

but fierce beach defending

but healing sea embracing

—which is the same as saying, that does it all—

—which is the same as saying, that survives, in spite of it all—

—which is the same as saying, that opens passages through which we, the islands, touch each other—

Like a spider in its oh-so-subtle exercise of making itself a home,
from which hang drops of morning dew,
presuming the ocean.

And within which
there will never, ever, be a wall—or an empire—to speak of.

Introduction

Waters Coming Ashore, Affects Creating Archives, Islands Touching Each Other

> Faced with this systematic onslaught in which the economy is the method, but the target is the soul, we must practice solidarity as though it were a religion.
>
> —Anayra Santory Jorge, *Nada es igual*, 2018, 89

> And to trust that all water touches all water everywhere.
>
> —Alexis Pauline Gumbs, *Undrowned*, 2020, 40

Walking along our coasts' "exploding spray"—their "only power," according to Derek Walcott's *Tiepolo's Hound* (2000, 162)—, this introduction performs a cartographical exercise. Yet, instead of overseeing, as cartography's foundational impulse for mastery does, this introductory map aspires to help me-us *undersee* the conceptual, imaginative, historical, political, and bodily "bases" orienting my-our walk-swim in the archipelago of Puerto Rico.[1] The tracing work below is not meant to be comprehensive. Rather, it brings together the lifelines—many encountered haphazardly, with no predetermined plan—that have become essential in my wonderstruck, uncertain, and ever more determined attempt to "practice solidarity as though it were a religion," which, in the context of this book, means to love Puerto Rico and the Caribbean differently, and to trust that, yes, we are/will be free because "all water touches all water everywhere."

A LIQUID HOMELAND IN RELATION

As much as this walk-swim of a book became possible in the wake of the relational emphases I learned years ago when first encountering comparative literature and cultural studies, it is also informed by more recent scholarly transformations, among which island and archipelago studies and ecological humanities stand out. Within island and archipelago studies, the work published in *Shima* and *Island Studies Journal* has been seminal. Specifically, for this book to become imaginable, both thematically and methodologically, the 2011 call divulged in the latter journal by Elaine Stratford, Godfrey Baldacchino, Elizabeth McMahon, Carol Farbotko, and Andrew Harwood toward a focus on the archipelago has been nothing short of essential. As they argue:

> presumptions about *how* archipelagic relations manifest, operate or circulate are to be avoided . . . Rather, their possibility may provide novel opportunities to unsettle certain tropes: singularity, isolation, dependency and peripherality; perhaps even islandness and insularity. Tracing the existence, implications and affect of archipelagic relations will also demand and expect various theoretical, methodological and empirical innovations if island scholars and colleagues in allied fields are to understand how this "world of islands" (Baldacchino, 2007) might be experienced in terms of networks, assemblages, filaments, connective tissue, mobilities and multiplicities. This tracing of archipelagic relations may constitute a form of counter-mapping, which DeLoughrey (2007) has termed *archipelagraphy*: a re-presentation of identity, interaction, space and place that comes across in different combinations of affect, materiality, performance, things.[2]

In the astonishing breadth and scope of Elizabeth M. DeLoughrey's urgent scholarship, moreover, I find the most illuminating connections between archipelagic and ecological thinking and praxis, as can be corroborated in her multiple essays, as well as in the books *Routes and Roots* (2007) and the more recent *Allegories of the Anthropocene* (2019). Approaching my more immediate Puerto Rican context from the perspective of archipelago studies, recent work by Yolanda Martínez-San Miguel, who is also the co-editor, with Michelle Stephens, of the landmark collection, *Contemporary Archipelagic Thinking*, has been particularly inspiring, as the rest of this book will show.[3]

However, the original thrust for *Affect, Archive, Archipelago*, as signaled in the prelude, emerged from a passionate engagement with Caribbean literatures and philosophies. In particular, this book's most fundamental conceptual-poetic-imaginative scaffolding responds to the work of Édouard Glissant and Marta Aponte Alsina, who redress the enduring and large-scale assault of our Caribbean imagination and thought through a poetics, an art, and an embodied experience resolutely situated within our archipelagic region.[4]

Glissant's life-long oeuvre constitutes, simultaneously, a denouncement of the "myth of the continent's" (Lewis and Wigen 1997, XX) imaginative and conceptual onslaught, as well as an impassioned defense for the need to think, imagine, and create from within, according to our small, archipelagic scale. Glissant's work achieves this double movement by a method of generous observation, description, and analysis of Caribbean lived experience:

> *It is against this double hegemony of a History with a capital H and a Literature consecrated by the absolute power of the written sign that the peoples who until now inhabited the hidden side of the earth fought, at the same time they were fighting for food and freedom.* . . . *we should let the weight of lived experience "slip in."* . . . We must reflect on a new relationship between history and literature. *We need to live it differently.* (*Caribbean Discourse* 1989, 77, emphasis added)

"Living it differently" defends smallness and insularity as mediums of *Rélation* (Relation), a concept that emerges from the writer's close attention to the colonized islanders' nonutilitarian, nonexploitative experience along the coast and the sea ("it is impossible to use the sea" [*Poetic Intention* [1969] 2010, 230]).[5] Moreover, Glissant's Relation encodes the sea itself in its spiraling movement, as well as in its primary role as both the source of life and of the latter's constant movement and displacement.[6] By refusing insularist ideology's tendency to figure the sea as an isolating, hostile, and featureless, yet exploitable, expanse,[7] Glissant argues for the archipelagic coasts as opening the way for Relation, interconnection, and the transformation of History's brutal and bloody legacies.

As anyone familiar with Glissant's work would agree, in light of his texts' interwoven intensity and peculiarly anomalous coherence, the difficulty of choosing passages and breaking them off in quotes cannot be overstated. For the purpose of presenting Glissant's thought-imagination in connection with Aponte Alsina's as the conceptual-poetic sustenance of this book, I focus primarily on some passages from *Poetics of Relation* ([1990] 1997), a book composed of five main parts with four sections each.[8] Its opening, middle, and end sections are explicitly situated on the shore and built around the Caribbean's lived experience. *Affect, Archive, Archipelago* is especially echolocating with *Poetics of Relation*'s first section of part I, fourth section of part III, and last section of part V, from which I offer here only a few portions:

> Whenever a fleet of ships gave chase to slave ships, it was easiest just to lighten the boat by throwing cargo overboard, weighing it down with balls and chains.

These underwater signposts mark the course between the Gold Coast and the Leeward Islands . . . *the entire ocean, the entire sea gently collapsing in the end into the pleasures of sand, make one vast beginning, but a beginning whose time is marked by these balls and chains gone green* . . . *their ordeal did not die; it quickened into this continuous/discontinuous thing: the panic of the new land, the haunting of the former land, finally the alliance with the imposed land, suffered and redeemed. The unconscious memory of the abyss served as the alluvium for these metamorphoses.* . . . *The land-beyond turned into land-in-itself.* (Part I, "Approaches," Section 1, "The Open Boat," 5–8, emphasis added)[9]

The beach at Le Diamant on the southern coast of Martinique has a subterranean, cyclical life. . . . Brown seaweed piled there by the invisible assault buries the line between sand and soil. . . . *The edge of the sea thus represents the alternation (but one that is illegible) between order and chaos.* . . . *The movement of the beach, this rhythmic rhetoric of a shore, do not seem to me gratuitous.* . . . This is where I first saw a ghostly young man go by; his tireless wandering traced a frontier between the land and water as invisible as floodtide at night. . . . He refused to speak and no longer admitted the possibility of any language. . . . *I thought of the people struggling within this speck of the world against silence and obliteration.* . . . *Then, in this circularity I haunt, I turned my efforts toward seeing the beach's backwash into the nearby eddying void as the equivalent of the circling of this man completely withdrawn into his motor forces; tried to relate them, and myself as well, to this rhythm of the world that we consent to without being able to measure or control its course.* . . . *I wondered whether, in little countries such as ours ("I believe in the future of little countries"), economic prospects (their inspiration) ought now to be more like the beach at Le Diamant*: cyclical, changeable, mutating, running through an economy of disorder whose detail would be meticulously calculated but whose comprehensive view would change rapidly depending on different circumstances. (Part III, "Paths," Section 4, "The Black Beach," 121–26, emphasis added)

I catch the quivering of this beach by surprise, this beach where visitors exclaim how beautiful! how typical! and I see that it is burning. . . . This tie between beach and island, which allows us to take off like maroons, far from the permanent tourist spots, is thus tied into the dis-appearance—a dis-appearing—in which the depths of the volcano circulate. I have always imagined *these depths navigate a path beneath the sea* in the west and the ocean in the east and that, though we are separated, each in our own Plantation, *the now green balls and chains have rolled beneath from one island to the next, weaving shared rivers that we shall open up when it is our time and where we shall take our boats.* . . . The man who walks [the same man from "The Black Beach"] (because that's who it is) has soon come down from the hills; once again he is making sense of the beach. . . . Distant reader . . . *Imagine him . . . he will not leave you. The shadow he throws from a distance is cast close by you.* . . . No one could be content with this enclosed errantry, this circular nomadism—but one with no *goal or end or recommencing. The absent man who walks exhausts no territory . . . This man who walks is an echo-monde.* (Part V, "Poetics," Section 4, "The Burning Beach," 205–09, emphasis added)

Relation is, thus, an archipelagic, coastal poetics; it entails walking along the edge of land and sea, where the "line" between "sand and soil" is "buried." It emerges from the lived experience—affective archives—of Caribbean peoples: the submerged histories of a "beginning" whose markers are the underwater "chains and balls gone green." These histories inaugurate the transformation from "land-beyond to land-in-itself"—that is, our "little countries" as experienced from *within*. The beach at Le Diamant, alternating between order and chaos, its "subterranean life" that "burns," communicates in a language that is recognizable yet "illegible," "invisible," just as that of the young man who walks. *Poetics of Relation*'s reflection-spine (opening, middle, end) thus proposes the following equation, according to our small island scale: sea (enslavement's echo) = beach (in "burning" connections "beneath the sea") = coastal walking ("bare outline of a movement that precedes all language") = "economy of disorder" that responds to our archipelagic "shared rivers."

Moreover, in the words of *Poetics of Relation*'s first few sections, Relation names a movement inspired by that of the waves and tides, a both-and process rather than an either-or system. In stark contrast with what Glissant calls the "arrowlike" movement of "atavistic" cultures, Relation is the sand, the rhizome, and the spiral, both water and land, chaos and order, history and imagination (art, poetics).

Like Aponte Alsina's *patria líquida* (liquid homeland), to which I turn below, Relation names an understanding of the centuries-old encounters in the Caribbean archipelagos as a never-ending spiral with neither definitive, rooted origins nor endings. These smaller histories, as against continental history, are those of chaotic mixture—the "underwater signposts," the land-beyond becoming land-in-itself, the walking man's withdrawal (his "right to opacity"), the submerged connection between beach, volcano, rivers, and boats. Therefore, they must be *imagined*. They require a *poetics* (Ferreira da Silva's method of "intuition and imagination," addressed below) rather than an empirical science. Thus, Glissant's repeated and direct address to the reader's imagination.

Significantly, in *Treatise of the Tout-Monde*, Glissant relates "The Sands"—that is, the coastal position embodied by the young man that "will not leave you"—as "the trace's" (Relation) "fertile" land: "We know that it is the trace that puts us all, wherever we may come from, in Relation. . . . *The trace goes through the land, which will never again be territory. The trace is an opaque form of learning from the branch and the wind: to be oneself, but derived from the other. It is the sand in authentic disorder of utopia*" ([1990] 1997, 15–23, my translation).¹⁰ The sands are, consequently, Relation's geological apotheosis.

As we will see throughout this book, Puerto Rico's affective archive of Caribbean relations is overwhelmingly situated on our littorals' sands, where all signs are necessarily opaque *traces*. These must be underseen, intuited, imagined, according to a small, archipelagic poetics, rather than approached as transparent territorial systems to be deciphered in the terms of the West's rationalist tradition.¹¹ Indeed, *Affect, Archive, Archipelago* mobilizes the poetic imagination, while walking-swimming on our sands, across generations and forms of political and artistic creation, to weave together diverse traces of Puerto Rico's affective archive of Caribbean relations. These traces are here understood as Glissant's "histories"—Aponte Alsina calls them *historias íntimas* (intimate histories)—against "History," a premise in *Poetics of Relation* to which I now turn.¹²

"The Open Boat" section lyrically recounts the slave trade's ineffably violent embodiment on the ships as fundamentally maritime and thus continuously "alive."¹³ Inasmuch as this section opens *Poetics of Relation*, the text suggests that the slave trade both inaugurates and is the necessary and urgent touchstone of the poetics of Relation. It is, at once, a "womb" and an "abyss." The history retold in the book's opening section unfolds by directly asking the reader to position/imagine herself inside the excruciating slave ship. Glissant had already proclaimed—in a brief, italicized section entitled "Imaginary," situated after the Walcott and Brathwaite epigraphs to his book—the imagination's supreme importance, equated there with the poetics of a people: "Thinking thought usually amounts to withdrawing into a dimensionless place in which the idea of thought alone persists. But thought in reality spaces itself out into the world. It informs the imaginary of peoples, their varied poetics, which it then transforms, meaning, *in them its risk becomes realized*" ([1990] 1997, 1, emphasis added). In other words, only by activating the imagination, a poetics, can thought appear. Only then can its "risk" become realized, and the devastating history of slavery and colonization can be encountered.

Notice that we are called on to apprehend the history of slavery recounted in "The Open Boat" through the metaphorization of the "balls and chains" turned "underwater signposts." Only a poetics (literature, art, orality)—as opposed to (continental) History—can affirm the validity for thought of "underwater signposts." The latter are *there*, somewhere in the depths of the sea, but the fact that they may be physically irretrievable (as "illegible" as the alternation of the beach at Le Diamant, and as "invisible" as the walking man's gesture) does not preclude them from being markers for (historical) thought. In other words, rather than representing the sea as a featureless image in our hegemonic maps,[14] Relation names a sea saturated with histories whose traces it is recalcitrant to yield by means of any conventional "historical" register or overseeing map we may be accustomed to. In contrast with History's territorializing operation and its complicity with the "myth of the continent," the sea of Relation works as a mnemonic device whose unyielding movement echoes the Caribbean peoples' histories. These move from a deterritorialized (or *detoured*) "birth"—the quintessentially deterritorializing slave trade as inauguration—to the reterritorialization (or *retour*) of "new shores"—that is, the constantly reterritorializing *métissage* of Relation.[15]

Glissant's homage to the ocean in "The Open Boat" beautifully condenses this detour-retour movement: "'*Je te salue, vieil Océan*!' You still preserve on your crests the silent boat of our births, your chasms are our own unconscious, furrowed with fugitive memories. Then you lay out these new shores, where we hook our tar-streaked wounds, our reddened mouths and stifled outcries" ([1990] 1997, 7). Relation comes out of the Historical tragedy, echoed in what Glissant considers the walking man's "recreation of the Plantation," but refuses to be capsized by its overwhelming logic, since, as Glissant concludes in "The Burning Beach," the man is always fleeing, detouring (208). Again, the sea is not an agent of isolation. Immanently experienced in the Caribbean, the sea produces "new shores" and "metamorphoses": "The unconscious memory of the abyss served as the alluvium for these metamorphoses [from 'the panic of the new land,' to 'the haunting of the former land,' and 'finally the alliance with the imposed land, suffered and redeemed']" (7).

On another equally important question, Relation, as a concept that implies the encounters precipitated by Western colonization, represents an alternative to "acculturation." In fact, Glissant insists on the people's (as much as the sea's) "right to opacity" and "detour," which was anticipated in the discussion concerning the walking man in *Poetics of Relation*. Frequently repeating this demand in texts such as *Poetic Intention*, *Poetics of Relation*, and *Treatise of the Tout-Monde*, Glissant claims the right to opacity in opposition to the "transparency"—remember Ferreira da Silva's (2007) argument concerning transparency and power, quoted in this book's Prelude—of cultural traits demanded by the acculturation model. "I ask for everyone," writes Glissant, "the right to opacity, which is not the same as enclosure. . . . I do not need to 'understand' anyone, be it an individual, a community, a people, nor do I need to 'make it mine' by asphyxiating it, by provoking that it loses itself" (*Tratado del Todo-Mundo*, [1997] 2006, 31).[16] There is a mystery, an unknowability, in people as much as in the sea, that must be defended, Glissant argues, and that is immanent and necessary to Relation. Indeed, Puerto Rico's "right to opacity," our constant "detour" from "transparent," juridico-political Western outcomes and creative outpours, runs through this book's underwater entrails.

Echoing Derek Walcott's impassioned call for a literature that is not kidnapped by "revenge" or "remorse,"[17] Glissant wants us to imagine and represent the Caribbean according to our own archipelagic scale, which has always been an "open boat" to Relation. The generosity and modesty of such openness comes, once more, from the lived, affective experience of Caribbean peoples: "Peoples who have been to the abyss do not brag of being chosen. They do not believe they are giving birth to any modern force. They live Relation and clear the way for it, to the extent that the oblivion of the abyss comes to them and that, consequently, their memory intensifies" (*Poetics of Relation*, 8). The experience of the abyss, for the "original victim" an "exception," "became something shared and made us, the descendants, one people among others" (*Poetics of Relation*, 8). Because we affirm "this Relation made of storms and profound moments of peace" (*Poetics of Relation*, [1990] 1997, 8–9), explains Glissant, we "stay with poetry . . . we cry our cry of poetry" (9).

In closing the first section and opening the rest of *Poetics of Relation* with the line, "Our boats are open, and we sail them for everyone" (9), Glissant connects once again Caribbean people's lives and loves with the coast and the sea. But this link, we should recall, is "open," and "for everyone." Thus, it is in absolute opposition to the closed, individualist, and exploitative relationship implied in coming ashore and taking possession of/abandoning the land. As I further discuss below, such are the two actions recurrently performed by power, which has historically approached "the island" as a "no-place."[18] It is only fitting, then, that Glissant would insist more than once on this apparently simple premise celebrating the Caribbean archipelagos' smallness: "I believe in the future of 'small countries'" (*Caribbean Discourse*, 1989, 255). As we saw, he quotes himself on this in *Poetics of Relation* (125), and had already established it in the earlier *Poetic Intention*: "One returns to one's island. And then: *in the gigantic world we dare to have a limited experience of the sea, a challenge of smallness and concentration, an enclosed perfectibility of humanity*. I believe in small countries" (147).

In resolute communion, *Affect, Archive, Archipelago* offers an archipelagic archive of Puerto Rico's Caribbean relations because it believes in our small countries. To nurture a decolonial imagination and politics that will ensure all forms of sovereignty and liberation, we must abandon the "myth of the continent" and "return to [our] island," which demands that we respond to the "challenge of smallness and concentration." The Antilles must be "imagined" immanently (they are already "there"), on their own terms: those of smallness and concentration, but also, and at the same time, those of a "multiple body" (*Poetic Intention*, [1969] 2010, 147)—that is, the archipelagic.

To be clear, the archipelagic, Relational thought and practice proposed by Glissant, does not sanitize, or deny the region's (neo)colonial devastation. Rather, with Aponte Alsina, it transforms it into "stanzas of beauty" that we can wield as "weapons against terror and inhumanity." Lingering exclusively on an apocalyptic perspective concerning Caribbean History will only yield ever more intense repetitions of the continent's "myth" as the only possible "real": the "confirmation" of the lacks, impotence, impossibilities, and dead ends that, according to insularist ideology, are "characteristic" of islands (see the following section). Indeed, Glissant implores us *not* to "make use of the real": "If the solution seems difficult, perhaps even impractical, don't go crying out of the blue that it is false. Don't make use of the real to justify your lack. Realize instead your dreams in order to earn your reality" (*Poetic Intention*, [1969] 2010, 228). And immediately afterward: "Exalt the heat, fortify yourself by it. Your thought will be searing" (229). What else can be said of/for the archipelagic Caribbean's own, immanent qualities? Such is the conceptual-poetic imagination igniting this book's archipelagic and decolonial approach to Puerto Rico's affective archive of Caribbean relations.

Glissant's Martinique and Marta Aponte Alsina's Puerto Rico echolocate loudly. Several poetic essays by the Puerto Rican writer show, from their very titles, her interest in archiving and honoring the networks of innumerable, inherently cosmopolitan, and sometimes improbable connections between circum-Caribbean histories and narrations: "Caminos de la sorpresa" (2005), "Historias íntimas, cuentos dispersos: palabras, tramas e identidades" (2007), "The Secret Island: A Literary Reading of Puerto Rico" (2008), "La patria líquida" (2010), "La metáfora madre" (2013), and "Madre del fuego: La identidad caribeña de William Carlos Williams" (2014).[19] Most recently, in response to the visual arts exhibition *One Month after Being Known in That Island: Caribbean Art Today* (2020), Aponte Alsina's essay "The Pocket of a Migrant" (2020) carries similar vibrations. Indeed, the writer has explained in personal communication with me that, "In what I have written so far, I notice a uniting vocation, a will for confluence, for breaking off limits, for crafting a literature of connections."

Weaving urgent plots beyond the Hispanic (and hispanophile) literary and intellectual traditions dominating Puerto Rico's anticolonial left,[20] Aponte Alsina's reflections on insularity, the sea, a small scale, and a "literature of connections" and "intimate" narrations/histories, amplify the context within which to approach and feel Puerto Rico and its literature. Her work thus asks us to be at sea, recognizing, too, that "our unity is submarine," and sensing, affectively, an archive of insular loves. The Puerto Rican writer's thought and poetics, as much as Glissant's, offer us an affirmative reconceptualization of the small, insular scale of our archipelagos, a register of the submarine histories that unite us, and the affirmation of our archipelagic multiplicity. If transformed according to "the small island, close to our human scale" ("Caminos de la sorpresa," 2005), our vision becomes able to notice that our archipelagos, far from being individual spaces of asphyxiating isolation, are diverse and complex myceliums of mélanges. We must deepen the Caribbean's multifarious archipelagic connections, described by Aponte Alsina as our *patria líquida* (liquid homeland), noticing, laying bare, and connecting our *historias íntimas* (intimate histories) against the univocal and continental History. These histories, the writer continues, are a distinctive trait of "Caribbean creatures," for whom "the vocation of *tránsfuga* (transfugitive) is . . . unavoidable" ("Caminos de la sorpresa," 2005). Only by honoring and remaining alert to such relations will we be able to imagine an *other* Puerto Rico in these times of deep sorrow. Such is *Affect, Archive, Archipelago*'s underseeing methodological cartography.

Further echoing Glissant's work discussed above, Aponte Alsina celebrates the Caribbean poetics capable of transforming Historical horror into poetic beauty. She does so while offering us the concept *liquid homeland*, an incomparable image to capture the sea's primacy as an element of Caribbean Relation instead of isolation—that is, as a subversion of the landbound, dividing logic of power:

> That sort of liquid homeland, forged according to the empires' swaying, gave birth to, however, a legacy whose unifying thread consists of the transformation of phenomena as abominable as slavery and the wars of conquest into stanzas of beauty. Beauty as a precipitate of cruelty may seem, to evoke Adorno, detestable in itself. But since it is the expression of an anarchist desire, of an undrowned joy, it constitutes a weapon against terror and inhumanity. As a result, the Caribbean extends as amply as the boisterous cartography of those who imagine it, in maps whose mutable demarcating lines have not only anchored in the US South and the coastlines of Central and South America, but also, in a certain way, replicate themselves in the Mississippi's black mirrors and traverse the streets of Harlem, where the Jamaican Marcus Garvey inspired an entire renaissance. ("Caminos de la sorpresa," 2005)[21]

Remaining an essential quality for Aponte Alsina, "liquid" has come to activate in her writing an even more intensely *embodied* thought: "Caribbean artists use their bodies in their creative processes to explore non-European theoretical frameworks. 'Liquid' readings and writings, which overflow customary senses, generate enriching connections. These actions seek to transcend restricted, solid, political, and cultural divisions between countries" ("The Pocket of a Migrant," 2020, 31). This exact premise may very well be applied to all the instances of Puerto Rico's affective archive of Caribbean relations included in this book.

Aponte Alsina's essays reiterate in diverse ways the pressing necessity of a method capable of perceiving, with its retrained, insular eye, "closer to our human scale," the Caribbean inter-insular connections, Glissantian Relation or, in her words, our liquid homeland. The method entails, as we also saw with Glissant's coastal walker, situating ourselves within our Puerto Rican/Caribbean lived experience, and remaining ever alert to small stories of eclipsed characters in official history, or of characters so excessively storied that they have become woefully onedimensional. Beyond the macro-historical connections within the Caribbean region, noticing submarine bonds between "intimate histories" amounts to walking on the island's "secret expanses" (Aponte Alsina, "Madre del fuego," 2014), whose opacity and mystery are honored by Aponte Alsina and Glissant alike. This book is a heartfelt and embodied—that is, at once clear and intractable—attempt at walking with, and swimming between, multiple, small, "intimate histories" of Puerto Rico's affective archive of Caribbean relations, both of little- and of ostensibly well-known political and artistic figures and collectives. In doing so, *Affect, Archive, Archipelago* will elaborate and hopefully prove that there can be no politics truly *beyond* colonization, extraction, and exploitation if we do not transform our poetics into an affirmation and an embodiment of our archipelago's smallness and multiplicity, as well as its Caribbean senses and sensibilities.

As a result, this book is not only transdisciplinary, but also, perhaps, impossibly eclectic for any given academic quarter. To that, I respond with Aponte Alsina: "the Caribbean was always one of the most open and infected world regions" ("Caminos de la sorpresa," 2005). "We have the right," she continues, "to eclecticism as our aesthetic," which I read as an echo of Glissant's "detour" and "right to opacity." Our method, aesthetic, and, of course, poetics (in Glissant's terms) will only adequately sense that which is from "here" if approached from the Martinican thinker's "open boat:" "I have attempted to ground myself in my country eccentrically, with my ear elsewhere" (Alsina, "Caminos de la sorpresa," 2005).

This kind of thought-practice demands of us, moreover, that we relationally reflect about "tradition," a matter that Aponte Alsina considers, with special attention, in the essays "Historias íntimas" (2007) and "La patria líquida" (2011). As she writes in the former, tradition means an interweaving of histories and stories, foundational characteristics of humanity, which "connect themselves underground." In the latter, she adds that tradition must be engaged with "generous and risky readings . . . more ludic, more liquid," rather than with stiff reverence.

One of the "more liquid" forms emphasized by Aponte Alsina is rewriting, a common engagement with tradition in the Caribbean and other colonized regions. Rewriting is a reappropriation and a resignification—as is the Caribbean itself—that "betrays the tradition it honors" ("La patria líquida," 2011). The argument becomes forcefully evident in "Madre del fuego" ("Mother of Fire," 2014), where Aponte Alsina reflects on her own creative process to write her 2015 novel *La muerte feliz de William Carlos Williams* (*The Happy Death of William Carlos Williams*). The novel revolves around Raquel Elena Hoheb Williams, who was the mother, from Mayagüez, Puerto Rico, and the eastern Caribbean, of the US poet William Carlos Williams. Aponte Alsina describes Raquel's genealogy and her own novelistic project as forged within the Sargasso Sea, one of the richest and most persistent metaphors of confluence and rewriting in the Caribbean. The following quote about the sea that inspired one of the Caribbean's most memorable and enduring rewritings—Jean Rhys's novel *Wide Sargasso Sea*—shows the inherent connection that Aponte Alsina perceives, along with Glissant, between the imaginative realm and a reconceptualized sea that does not isolate. Rather, the Sargasso Sea constitutes a "place where the waters mingle"; its center is "without pretenses of dominion":

> It is apparently the only sea without coasts, an enormous body that, from our position, might seem an Atlantic extension of the Caribbean. Its frontiers, as much as those of every sea, have something of caprice. Those demarcating limits reveal something of invention and madness, generally accepted more by force of convention than evidence. Because, who can trace without smiling the frontier of something that is always moving? The Sargasso Sea is a sea without coasts that draws near San Juan's trench, extends to the north from the Chesapeake Bay, close to Maryland and Virginia, to the Rock of Gibraltar on the north of Africa, and to the south, it moves from Haiti to Dakar, Senegal's capital, on the east of Africa. Columbus gave it its name, as in the notes of his first voyage he described the waters where "packs of very green herbs" floated. Towards its still, windless center, higher than its perimeter, the waves form a whirlpool that spins clockwise. Towards this marine eye of deep waters, live creatures from various latitudes move, dragged by north and south currents. Stuck in the algae, they adapt to the laws of a sea apparently without bottom. The plants that take centuries to arrive at the absolute stillness of the center acquire immortality. It is, or was, said that some of the live herbs that flower today might be the same that Columbus and his mariners saw. A floating center without pretenses of dominion. A place of irregular limits whose shipwreck legends have a great presence in literature. ("Madre del fuego," 2014)[22]

Exemplifying Glissant's "detour" and "retour," *La muerte feliz de William Carlos Williams* rewrites the biography of a canonical poet in US literature, turning it into a series of "mobile" and "intimate" stories that converge "apparently without bottom." They do so in Relation, as they "avoid the straight, closed paths," and are "alien to cause and effect":

> The poetry of William Carlos Williams, the poet who, after his death, has come to represent one of the "heights" of US poetry . . . refers . . . to the imagination of that chatty, provincial, and Parisian . . . mother, who was born here [in Puerto Rico]. It is not that it makes sense to claim that a Puerto Rican is the mother of a parcel of US twentieth-century poetry, although it would be licit to do so (after all, identity is a gift from that other, opposed and inseparable). It is about a movement alien to cause and effect, more analogous to the turbine of the Sargasso Sea and other places spoiled by the imagination, which avoid straight, closed paths. ("Madre del fuego," 2014)

Likewise, Aponte Alsina understands tradition as "writings that vibrate according to a common tone," between which there are no "influences, but, rather, reverberations" ("Historias íntimas," 2007). Indeed, in the same essay she intimates her desire to read texts "from a vision of time that transcends unilateral influences and chronologies." Fittingly, in her writing we find reverberations with—and the identification of reverberations between— Caribbean and American (in the ample sense) writers, such as Édouard Glissant, Derek Walcott, William Faulkner, Luis Palés Matos, Ana Lydia Vega, Jean Rhys, Alejandro Tapia y Rivera, Edgardo Rodríguez Juliá, and William Carlos Williams, among others. At the same time, stories reverberate, too, as is the case with Raquel, a "Caribbean creature" ("Madre del fuego," 2014), whose opaque trace can be found in the archives, but has not been narrated from the immanent and relational perspective characterizing Glissant's and Aponte Alsina's passions.

Finally, "La metáfora madre" (2013) more explicitly confronts the concept of island. Here, Aponte Alsina documents some of the most powerful insular metaphors specifically in the Puerto Rican tradition of the nineteenth and twentieth centuries, among which I highlight the following: "the corpse of a society yet to be born" (Jacinto Salas Quiroga); "the damsel island" (José Gautier Benítez); the tapeworm exhibited in alcohol by the pharmacist in the grey and opaque town of a Luis Palés Matos's poem; the voyage as extirpation and uprooting; and the illness ("La metáfora madre," 2013). Note that these metaphors reproduce the hegemonic version of the island-as-negation, to which I turn in the following section: death, vulnerability, illness, loss, lack. Against this, Aponte Alsina prefers the "experimental island" metaphor, "a paranoic excess that suppurates novels such as [her] *Sexto sueño* and others" ("La metáfora madre," 2013), among which, as we saw, one must situate the later *La muerte feliz de William Carlos Williams* (2015).

In contrast with the metaphors of death and vulnerability, in the experimental island, "the laboratory rat that feels observed, classified, and annotated, *returns the gaze*" ("La metáfora madre," 2013, emphasis added). As we saw, in "La patria líquida" (2011) Aponte Alsina argued that rewriting has immense importance in Caribbean literatures, as the island and the insular subject position themselves relationally: they "betray and honor," recognizing the dominant, colonial discourse *and* crafting, to subvert its oppression, a counter-discourse of their own. As we will see throughout this book, Puerto Rico's affective archive of Caribbean relations is all about liberating forms of experimentation, mobilizing Aponte Alsina's "experimental island" metaphor to powerfully counteract the continuing legacy of History's horrors.

In terms of Glissant's poetics, this experimental practice amounts to the immanent affirmation of the insular land ("the land beyond turned into the land within"), that is, of our sovereignty. The island and the insular subject thus reclaim their agency to their own land- and seascape, their thought-sensing, their writing and their art. Aponte Alsina, like Glissant, is unambiguous when defending the necessity of a transformed poetics, of imagination, if we are to materialize our immanent, sovereign claim: "In order to appreciate the beauty of such places [the "uncommunicated worlds," "secret" and "occult"] one would have to imagine them; to imagine them, they must surprise us, and voices and things must attract us. The predicament of conceiving a relation, a community, or the plot of a novel, is lived in the imagination" ("Madre del fuego," 2014). Further, "the place where one is born . . . stops being [accidental] when it installs itself in the imagination" ("Madre del fuego," 2014). In Puerto Rico we must continue imaginatively unearthing, rewriting, relating, embodying, and echolocating with the "intimate histories" from our "small, secret islands," from our "liquid homeland," irreducibly connected with the rest of the Caribbean archipelagos, where "the beach that burns" (Glissant [1990] 1997, 205) continually reminds us of the beauty and political potency of our common, submarine palpitations, those of our affective archive of Caribbean relations. Such is the inspiration for this book's staging of what might seem impossibly disparate texts, bodies, and thoughts-sensations.

THE ISLAND AS LABORATORY OF/FOR POWER

In the first section of my study *Imagined Islands: A Caribbean Tidalectics* (2012), I explore some of the uses and abuses of global islands in the dominant, modern Western tradition, as well as in its imaginary and historical record.[23] These uses and abuses, which might appear diverse, ultimately respond to the same fabricated equivalence between insular geography and negation, privation, lack, and isolation—a phenomenon I call insularist ideology.[24] Within this framework, islands, understood as antithetical to continents despite the fact that all planetary landforms are entirely surrounded by water, are conceived primarily as laboratories of and for power, where the latter tests possibilities to solve its varied crises, both material and immaterial:

1. disciplinary-ideological: islands' primary use in the arts, anthropology, archaeology, geography, and cartography, among other disciplines;
2. mythical-existential: the exploration of the "I" in a "desert island"; the islands-monsters that produce, through negation, the respectable, rational, male subject preferred by the Western tradition; the touristic happiness machine;
3. juridical, or related to the law: islands used as "states/spaces of exception," prisons, places for forced banishment and torture machines for all kinds of social "undesirables";
4. political: wars waged for and on islands, as well as their longstanding use in territorializing oceans;
5. identitarian: islands as brutally feminized sites to "discover," "penetrate," "explore"; islands as "pure," differentiated places to develop or discard gendered and racialized, among other, identities; and
6. climatic: islands as *marginalia* facing the worst effects of the climate emergency produced by capitalist and imperial powers; islands as objects of study on disappearing ecosystems and species as a result of human actions.[25]

Considering the extent of this panorama's reach, one cannot help but take long, deep breaths, whispering in agreement with Guillermo Rebollo Gil: "So much depends on the island-place. And what the island-place is about, meaning its historical character. And what others have done to the island-place along its history" (2018, 17–18). Caribbean insularity, in particular, has been thought of and designed explicitly as a laboratory for the consolidation and expansion of capitalist-patriarchal-racist-coloniality, which in this book I simply call "power."[26] To begin with, power itself was symbolically figured in terms of insularity:

> It is important in this respect to reflect on the shift from the fundamentally anti-expansionist insularism of classical and medieval Europe to the post sixteenth-century elevation of "the motif of the island" into what [Diana] Loxley describes

as "the theme of colonialism." If, as Christian Jacob has argued, islands formally highlight the link between represented space and the inscription of the toponym, they inevitably also foreground the toponym's association with claims "of precedence and of symbolic ownership, analogous to the political and colonial mastery suggested by the name of the sovereign." In Rod Edmond and Vanessa Smith's related argument, colonial desire is quite literally the engine that mobilizes the cartographical vision of islands in the era of maritime colonialism: to the extent that islands "look like property" (that is to say, to the extent that their small size appears to invite their capture by a synoptic gaze), they are likely to appear not merely as ideal states but also as "ideal colonies," bite-size parcels of territory that stir fantasies of symbolic possession. (Balasopoulos 2008, 11)

In material terms, as Sidney Mintz shows in *Sweetness and Power* (1986), the insular Caribbean was exploited as laboratory to perfect and expand mercantilist capitalism, associated with the classic imperial models of Western Europe, and, at the same time, to foster the development of industrial capitalism, with the plantation system as its primordial axis. Mintz describes the plantations as "precocious cases of industrialization" (59).[27] The plantation, as a system, acquired and, indeed, fomented, many of the later characteristics associated with industrial capitalism: the regulation of bodies and time for work, the organization of a massive spatial concentration of the labor force, the notable use of machinery, the separation of production from consumption, the alienation of workers from the tools of their work (50–52). At the same time, the plantation retained characteristics of mercantilist capitalism, especially the use of enslaved or indentured labor, and the fact of it being a fundamentally agrarian enterprise, even if highly mechanized (56–59).

Mintz insists, moreover, on the industrial character of the plantation when considering consumption, as the introduction of Caribbean sugar in the metropolis "nourished certain capitalist classes at home *as they were becoming more* capitalistic" (61). In contrast with its previous primary consumption by elites, sugar became a phenomenon of mass consumption in Europe precisely because it was turned into a crucial source of calories for industrial workers, now subjected to a more exploitative work regime (146). Thus, sugar was turned into a form of "legitimized population control," whose primary target—as is logical for patriarchy—were women and girls, "with the costly protein foods being largely monopolized by the adult male, and the sucrose being eaten in larger proportion by the wife and children" (149). From the plantation system hinging between mercantilist and industrial capitalism, the exploitation of the insular Caribbean was extended to its use as laboratory for industrialization "by invitation"—a matter I return to below—and, later, to the transition from industrial to the current postindustrial (financial or neoliberal) capitalism. In the Caribbean, the latter is characterized by mass tourism, dependent and service economies, working-class "flexibilization," land/seascapes of toxic, industrial abandonment and ruin, and "fiscal paradises," as Aarón Gamaliel Ramos shows in *Islas migajas* (2016).²⁸

Furthermore, to enable power's exploitation and subjection of the Caribbean, the systematic and deliberate fragmentation of inter-insular connections characterizing the archipelagic region before the European empires' irruption has been of the essence. This rupturing process, which included linguistic fragmentations and varied legal conscriptions concerning gender and racial "contact," was spread through a territorialization of the ocean that turned it into an abyss of enslavement and genocide.²⁹ Over the long and enduring era of colonial subjection, almost every calamity experienced in the Caribbean has *come ashore*, a profoundly traumatic legacy that I return to in chapter 4.

Today, Caribbean peoples experience banishment even from *the vision* of the sea, as Puerto Rican writer Ana Lydia Vega deplores:

> The harsh truth is that the coastal tragedy is limitlessly reproduced. . . . in every corner graced by the waves' perpetual rolling, we are being unabashedly robbed of the sea. Soon we will have to rent balconies in luxury condominiums or pay for rides on motorboats to remember the wave's infinitude or the spatter's taste on the skin. The seascape's systematic concealment constitutes a crime against humanity. One of the most gratifying activities that islanders can engage in is the contemplation of the ocean. The play of light and color subverts the concrete's grey empire. Amid urban hustle and bustle, the waves' hypnotic rumor provokes a supremely relaxing, meditative state. With such a colossal instrument of peace at our disposal, having allowed, with our indolence, the privatization of our main natural resource is inconceivable. (23–24)³⁰

The current exploitation of the sea for tourists and foreigners—echoes of colonial masters, as Olive Senior's poem, "Meditation on Yellow" (2005) and Reinaldo Funes Monzote's essay "El Gran Caribe. De las plantaciones al turismo" (2013) make abundantly clear—constitutes the latest manifestation of a series of colonial relations that have produced the "inward-looking islander" that insularist ideology ontologically assigns to peoples born on islands. This image conveniently buttresses the ideologues' sense of superiority by virtue of its contrast with respect to the non-islanders' supposed "openness," "cosmopolitanism," and "uprootedness."

The legacy of colonial fragmentation in the Caribbean is also characterized by racism's (and racial capitalism's) multifarious effects, as an ideology used and spread in the region to justify the genocidal enslavement of Black bodies by western European and North American empires, as well as to replicate forms of White supremacy.³¹ It includes, too, the increasing dismantling of economic relations between Caribbean countries, as they are set against each other in competition over neoliberal treaties decided and designed to benefit North America, as well as the restrictions to regional collaborations that result from neocolonial models of governance in the Caribbean.[32] Within such a historical and present scenario, it comes as no surprise that Caribbean populations up to the present have a distressing, and often deeply traumatic, relation to the sea and to insularity itself, and that both formal—such as the *Confederación Antillana* and the West Indies Federation—and informal efforts toward Caribbean integration have had limited and fraught material success.[33]

Puerto Rico as a Paradigmatic Case

The case of Puerto Rico is paradigmatic of insularity's exploitation for the development, transformation, and expansion of power.[34] After the US invasion of the archipelago and the imposition of a military government in 1898, the juridical debate associated with the *Insular Cases* during the first few years of the twentieth century marked the conceptual and political standard of Puerto Rico as island-laboratory.[35] As Efrén Rivera Ramos (1998) and José Atiles-Osoria (2016) show, the result of such legal-colonial experimentation ("Puerto Rico is a property of, but not part of, the US") constituted an unprecedented formulation serving two insidious purposes at once: on the one hand, when considered in the international arena, Puerto Rico's official "status" evaded the imperial-colonial "relation" Puerto Rico–US, while on the other, it produced a highly "juridified" zone within which all posterior political resistance to US colonialism in Puerto Rico would be understood.[36]

Moreover, and in tandem with the archipelago's increasing militarization through the construction of multiple bases during the twentieth century's first few decades (including in the island municipalities of Vieques and Culebra),[37] Puerto Rico was forced to move from mercantilist capitalism hinging on industrialization (Spanish sugar plantations), to the industrialized monopoly of US absentee sugar industries, themselves sisters of other US companies controlling Latin American markets, such as the United Fruit Company. At the same time, and during the transition toward the colonial-legal experiment that is the ELA (*Estado Libre Asociado*, or "Commonwealth") itself (see below), the United States imposed on Puerto Rico eugenic experimentations for "racial purity" and the control of women's bodies as well as the overall size of the population. As Ana María García shows in the documentary *La operación* (1982), starting in the mid-1940s and extending for over two decades, a forced sterilization campaign was conducted in the archipelago. As is customary in the power regime (see, especially, Silvia Federici's *Caliban and the Witch*, 2004), the institutional violence was unleashed primarily against the most vulnerable of the colony's women, using them as laboratory objects for the pharmaceutical industry to experiment with sterilization processes and the contraceptive pill while "improving the race."[38]

These eugenic initiatives found in local *criollo* elites a favorable ideological context, as the Western discourse feminizing the island had climaxed in the *Generación del 30* and, particularly, in the editorial orientation that Antonio S. Pedreira had given to its main communicative organ, the *Índice* journal, and in his 1934 book, *Insularismo*. While evaluating Pedreira's thought in tandem with that of José Lezama Lima, Édouard Glissant, and Rosario Ferré, Ben Heller reminds us of one of the most relevant—yet scarcely discussed—passages in *Insularismo*:

> Our landscape possesses a measured sense and harmonizes with geography and ethnography. There is no strength, uproar or magnitude. . . . Its predominant tone is the lyric: it is a tender, bland, bridge, crystalline landscape. Samuel Gili Gaya captured it well when he said that it "is far from being imposing. Everything adopts a soft, flattering, kind and profoundly feminine air. The mountains are no more than hills dressed in light green, where a cow grazes but does not attack." (1996, 41)

In contemporary hurricane- and earthquake-ravaged Puerto Rico, Gili Gaya's last imperialist declaration, approvingly reproduced by Pedreira, is even more disquieting: "'We miss the poisonous serpents and cannot believe in the hurricanes and earthquakes that they say occur'" (1934, 41). In his analysis of this passage, Heller correctly points out that:

> Gili Gaya (and Pedreira as well) does not disguise his disdain for the feminine, i.e., "unmanly," landscape. . . . This figuration of the landscape uses the feminine as symbolic vector of lack, a lack of "virility" . . . that conditions and contaminates the Puerto Rican character. Just as Pedreira erects his vision of the nation upon a racist typology, where blacks are the "inferior race" and racial mixing a "confusion" that leads to passivity, he also creates a national image where the feminine is a noxious influence. . . . The elite must create a culture that can raise them (phallically) above it [the "feminine landscape"], into a more spiritual realm. (1996, 395)

This is what Pedreira calls "the vertical expansion" of "virile ideas and sentiments" that Puerto Rico must nurture, since (obviously to Pedreira's dismay) "we cannot reduce the number of births, nor can we advance towards the sea in order to expand our territory" (1934, 43). In *Insularismo*, then, we find an epitome of insularist ideology, seeking to convince us that Puerto Rico's problems, as much as those of the rest of the Caribbean, are, fundamentally, its geography and its apparent "overpopulation," a phenomenon muddily argued to exist in direct connection with insularity.[39]

Insularismo seals the ideological pact that symbiotically conceives women and insularity by feminizing the latter even more profoundly as a negative value, since, as Heller suggests, Pedreira represents the sea as the "womb" from which the country is born and, at the same time, as the "belt" that oppresses it. What is more, Puerto Rico's status in Pedreira's thought as the "go-between" in the "great intercontinental debate" (Heller 1996, 396), constitutes a *celestina* position associated with infertility. Thus, the island is represented at once as a closure upon itself (a tomb enclosed by the separating sea), and as a woman whose reproductive capacities are impossible to control for "virile" development, either because they are excessive or nonexistent. The island, in a word, is "destined by nature" to only one, undesirable, unmanageable, condition: the same of women in the patriarchal regime.

As a result, the imperial and colonial eugenic politics that pursued, through the control of women's bodies, an "advancement" of the development of Puerto Rico from the 1940s through the 1960s, understood our islands, too, as women's bodies, precisely because "nature" was the cause of our "backwardness."[40] In today's Puerto Rico, it is evident that such an ideological panorama continues to be a breeding ground for measures of population control and displacement that use "the crisis" as justification and, most especially, the consequences of recent political and natural disasters, including the PROMESA law, to which I return below.[41]

The multifarious forms of ideological, material, and bodily exploitation sketched above were compounded by an economic phenomenon initiated in the 1950s and extended over the next few decades. With the consent and complicity of the ascending *Partido Popular Democrático*, its leader Luis Muñoz Marín (the first Puerto Rican governor of Puerto Rico), and its neocolonial *Estado Libre Asociado* (ELA) platform (formally adopted through the 1952 Constitution), the US empire imposed on the archipelago an experimental form of industrialization "by invitation"—that is, tax exemptions—characterized by enterprises of little or no desirability, toxic execution, and even scanter success. The exemplary case was that of petrochemical plants, whose rusted ruins of highly toxic material continue to contaminate multiple coastal zones to this day. The economic success of some factories—in particular, pharmaceuticals—has been primarily for their owners, since the—as it ultimately turned out, temporary—employment of Puerto Ricans does not entail the strengthening of a local production economy.[42]

Once these experiments were abandoned—although their nefarious effects are very much with us—the country moved to the 1990s postindustrial era of the end of "Section 936"[43] and, with it, the flight of most of the "successful" factories, as well as rampant privatization, uncontrolled indebtedness, and the approval of massive economic incentives to the most powerful local and imperial classes.⁴⁴ The contemporary crisis in Puerto Rico is the direct result of an unprecedented acceleration of this regressive neoliberal dynamic, enabled by the archipelago's status as a colony of the United States.

The crassest expression of Puerto Rico's colonial subjugation in the present moment is undoubtedly the Barack Obama–era 2016 PROMESA law, with its Fiscal Oversight and Management Board (FOMB), *La Junta*.⁴⁵ As the *de facto* government since then, in attending to its priorities *La Junta* enjoys the tacit or overt complicity and obedience of most of the members of the Puerto Rican executive, legislative, and judicial branches. Without any audit process and while shielding all responsible elite parties from responsibility, *La Junta* imposes draconian austerity measures, squeezing every remaining public good toward repayment and the "return" of Puerto Rico to the financial market's "confidence," which ultimately means furthering the debt spiral. In fact, as recently as June 2021, five years after PROMESA's imposition, Deepak Lamba-Nieves, Sergio M. Marxuach, and Rosanna Torres, from Puerto Rico's *Centro para una Nueva Economía*, published a detailed analysis of the law's trajectory, only to conclude that:

> it has failed to accomplish most of the objectives set forth by its authors. . . . five years in, about 2/3 of the bonded debt has not been restructured; no critical projects for economic development have been approved; audited financial statements are still three years in arrears; the shift to budgeting on a modified accrual accounting basis is a work in progress; and the government's budget is still out of balance. . . . In sum, PROMESA has been, in the words of Judge Torruella, "Congress's fourth try at cutting through the Puerto Rican Gordian knot in its interminable attempt to colonially rule Puerto Rico and its people" and, in our opinion, it has failed. (2021)

Moreover, as Ariadna Godreau Aubert rightfully explains in *Las propias* (2018), this criminal extraction machine makes Puerto Rico's most marginalized and vulnerable populations responsible for repaying the system that ensured—and continues to ensure—their own precarity:

> [P]overty is traditionally linked to lack of economic resources. But this definition is incomplete. More than economic deprivation, [poverty] refers to lack of political and social power, and to the progressive erosion of human dignity. . . . Austerity increases poverty and, with it, inequality and economic, social, and political precarity. Neither austerity nor poverty are natural or accidental. Both concepts, linked to prejudices related to class, race, and gender, refer to political and economic systems systematically imposed on certain persons, groups, or identities. (41–42)

Thus, while guaranteeing our "recovery from the crisis," *La Junta* only deepens it, and does so by design.[46] For instance, *La Junta* has (1) spearheaded an assault on the University of Puerto Rico, which is experiencing a reduction of over half of its operating budget, while students confront disproportionate tuition hikes; (2) taken measures to protect and expand tax exemptions for private corporations; (3) encouraged, with the local government's collaboration, a so-called labor reform that brings the country back to labor conditions akin to those in the nineteenth century; (4) taken decisions to undermine local credit unions in favor of commercial banks; (5) supported the dismantling of the public education system by means of charter schools, the closure of hundreds of schools, and the gutting of resources for direly needed special education; (6) stimulated the flexibilization of environmental laws; and (7) supported the privatization of public corporations, such as the public energy corporation.

Not even the string of recent catastrophes—beyond the 2017 hurricanes, an earthquake sequence in 2020 and the current COVID-19 pandemic—has deviated *La Junta* or the local government from their organized plan for the remaking of Puerto Rico's economy to suit the interests of private and foreign entities. In fact, to push their agenda through, they have cynically capitalized on disaster and the dramatic suffering and trauma of everyday Puerto Ricans.[47] Thus, the period from 2016 to the present has veritably turned Puerto Rico into an atrocious "austerity laboratory," as described by Puerto Rico's *Centro de Periodismo Investigativo* (CPI) and the *New York Magazine* in their April 2019 joint coverage, "The McKinsey Way to Save an Island." The report denounces the contract, paid with public funds in a bankrupt country, of the McKinsey firm as *La Junta*'s primary consultant:

> Among the many mind-blowing figures in the fiscal plan, one stands out: the $1.5 billion earmarked over the next six years for costs related to the restructuring process itself—more than a billion of which will go to lawyers, bankers, and consultants, McKinsey included. (The firm billed the board more than $72 million through January, and its ongoing contracts total about $3.3 million a month.) The projected overall fees are more than five times what Detroit spent on its $20 billion bankruptcy, previously the largest local-government default in U.S. history, and higher even than the bill for Lehman Brothers, the $613 billion corporate liquidation that nearly destroyed the world economy.[48]

As though all of the above was not enough, the succession of recent disasters has been met with an intensification of insularist ideology. Because the latter's dictum is that the lacks and limitations experimented on islands are the "natural" result of geography, insularist ideology necessarily concludes that "disaster is to be expected." But, beyond the issue of proportion, we must remember that insularity as a geographical formation is not inherently vulnerable to disaster.[49] As recounted in James Lewis's "An Island Characteristic" (2009), his and John Campbell's work, with examples from archipelagos in the Pacific and the Caribbean, demonstrates that island vulnerability to events such as typhoons, hurricanes, earthquakes, or volcanic eruptions is *produced* by what Lewis calls "disaster imperialism," which systematically erodes the forms of resilience that indigenous populations developed for millennia (2). Using the examples of Antigua, Tonga, and the Cook Islands, Lewis concludes that, after having been self-sufficient indigenous communities where "natural hazards had been a fact of life" (2), these islands became spaces subjected to "'disaster imperialism,' by which response to disaster was used to promote imperial power and beneficence" (2). The researcher insists that "disaster relief," a corollary of "disaster imperialism," has had a lasting "negative impact . . . upon self-reliance, a counter to vulnerability" (2). The insular communities' self-sufficiency constituted a crucial counterweight to vulnerability in the face of natural risks, so much so that "numerical comparison of deaths per thousand people resulting from natural hazards on insular and continental countries revealed '*no significant difference*'" (3, emphasis added).

In another register, Sir Hilary Beckles, contemporary leader of the Caribbean movement for reparations, also denounced insularist ideology's claims concerning "disaster" only days after Hurricanes Irma and María devastated the Caribbean:

> Hurricane Irma's fury preceded Maria's by a deadly Caribbean second. Together they constitute the familiar sound of death and destruction reminiscent of a colonial past that clings to the present and is determined to possess and own the Caribbean future. *The chain linked imperial legacy that still imprisons the islands, keeping them politically fragmented and economically divided, was exposed as both cause and effect of a fragile region still feeling the presence of an imperial ethos that assigns to them a reality of structural dependency.* Irma-Maria blew away the roof of the long and ongoing imperial cover up, and critically, was revelatory of the horrific history that dwells in the ruins of the present. ("Irma-Maria: A Reparations Requiem for Caribbean Poverty," 2017, emphasis added)[50]

La vitrina de la democracia ("democracy's shop window"), the phrase with which Luis Muñoz Marín celebrated the supposed "progress" in post–ELA Puerto Rico, was, then, a mere smokescreen, and is, today, "disaster's shop window." While the descendants of "the wretched of the earth" bleed out within our islands, feeling them as tombs from which it seems imperative to escape, the descendants of patriarchal White colonists, who travel in limousines, helicopters, and yachts, remake insularity as their paradise, not only of beaches, sun, and hypersexualized bodies but also of hideouts for their colossal war bounty: a mobile capital that evades all taxes, even all identification, and whose profit analyses revel in catastrophe.[51]

As we have seen, insularist ideology's premises that islanders are "naturally" inferior and inward-looking, and that islands are spaces of negation, privation, and lack by geographical "nature," are thoroughly false. With the complicity of neocolonial local masters, these ideas have been historically, materially, and imaginatively fabricated by power at its convenience. In Puerto Rico today, those who produce and benefit from the paradise of their smooth transportation in yachts and helicopters, their insular tax havens, their "cryptoutopias," and the issuance of debt while fully aware of the massive risks, cynically claim that "the crisis is an opportunity."[52] The exploitation of our islands as laboratories for experimenting with the politics of control, plunder, and extermination that ensure the dominant regime's development and expansion, with its booms, busts, and profit-seeking at all costs, can only result in death and all manner of misery for those of us who are born and want to remain—or return—*here*.[53]

THE ARCHIPELAGO AS LABORATORY OF/FOR LIBERATION

Puerto Rico's Affective Archive of Caribbean Relations

But that is History. In contrast, Puerto Rican "intimate histories" are overflowing with instances that, when approached from Glissant's and Aponte Alsina's conceptual, poetic, and methodological scaffolding, constitute an affective archive of Caribbean relations where our archipelagic lives and loves have been laboratories of experimentation of/for decolonization and liberation against power. The "files" in this archive, produced by Ferreira da Silva's "subjects of affectability," share a common passion for the archipelago—both Puerto Rican and Caribbean. They are brought together by the conviction that, as Brathwaite famously declared, our "unity is submarine," and that such maritime archipelagic consciousness must be continuously strengthened and materialized in Puerto Rico. This book engages and relates with some of these fulgurating "files," from the nineteenth century through the contemporary moment, as they pertain to traditionally conceived political figures and movements (part I), as much as to works and collectives of the imagination, the body, and our land- and seascapes (part II).

Thus, when *Affect, Archive, Archipelago* declares the materials it engages with—many of which are not "written" verbally and are, by design, chance, or force of conditions, ephemeral, "incomplete," and purely intuitive or "emotional"—as constituting an *archive*, it necessarily questions the hegemonic, architectural, imperial design of The Archive and the archiving praxis in the West.[54] Heeding Glissant's call to think with/from "the balls and chains gone green" and "the burning beach," Walcott's underwater history of the Caribbean,[55] and Aponte Alsina's "intimate histories" of our "liquid homeland" and "experimental islands," this book posits the fluctuating, and nevertheless unquestionable, existence of an archive brimming with "archivable" written materials *alongside* innumerable instances of what Achille Mbembe (2002) calls "the unarchivable."[56] To recognize such an affective archive, we must echolocate with Glissant's and Aponte Alsina's calls for a liberated "poetics," and with Ferreira da Silva's "intuition and imagination" (see below).

We must also think with/in the archipelago, what I call an archipelagic thought and practice, both at the local (Puerto Rican) and the regional (Caribbean) levels. Studying our affective archive of Caribbean relations requires deep-diving into literal and metaphorical, verbal and nonverbal, enduring and ephemeral, material and symbolic traces of Puerto Rico's commitment to decolonization and the defense of our multiple sovereignties.[57] By verbal, enduring instances, I am referring to written texts of various kinds (such as letters, manifestos, poems, essays, transcribed speeches and interviews, and screenplays), while by ephemeral, nonverbal interventions, I mean to conjure, among others, activist events interrupting business as usual,[58] performance pieces in any space, musical traditions,[59] political speeches, the practice of reading at tobacco factories, certain acts of walking or other bodily movements, spiritual lives, intuitions, relations, and friendships. We Antilleans, made against the backdrop of the plantation machine, of a forced cosmopolitanism through slavery and rape, violence and death, have always been engaged in liberating affections, in sharing common dreams, in shifting our subjected bodies through song, dance, and laughter, in fleeing the plantation, in becoming *others*.

Communitarian-Artistic-Bodily Sovereignties

Against the forces of power summarized above, the Puerto Rico of recent decades and, especially, post–2017 hurricane season, is reimagining, strengthening, and also creating new forms of participatory democracy—as opposed to those of traditional political parties and organizations. The labor, commitment, and imagination of everyday Puerto Ricans, working within and in between communities on the ground, lays claim to our multiple sovereignties.[60] Because it thrives on and multiplies relations of love, friendship, collaboration, and mutuality, and since it is characterized by decentralization, multifocality, and the small scale, this communitarian-artistic-bodily practice can be understood as archipelagic, in direct opposition to insularist ideology's immobilizing and exploitative definition of "island."

The collective name *communitarian-artistic-bodily sovereignties* designates a great variety of economic, social, political, cultural, and bodily practices performed in, by, and through individuals, collectives, and communities that are self-organized and autonomous, materializing through their daily actions and relations profound and diverse forms of sovereignty. Some of these initiatives—with an explicit Caribbeanist consciousness—are considered in chapters 4 and 5. In this sense, my understanding of sovereignty echolocates with Puerto Rican writers Aurora and Ricardo Levins Morales's *DeCLARAción/tion*, which opens with a claim to sovereignty as "the natural condition of all beings" and closes with the conviction that Puerto Rican liberation "won't be on a holiday, with speeches and parades. It won't be in the ceremony of signing treaties and taking oaths of office, nor at the moment when the last flag of the empire ceases to cast its shadow on our soil. It will be an ordinary Tuesday, in the middle of washing dishes perhaps."[61]

But these more recent sovereignty "files" in our archive are by no means unique, original, or separable from the deep, underwater, "intimate histories" this book is in relation with. As Ferreira da Silva's "Black feminist poethical" method of "imaging/reading" with "the Dead" (2020) invites us to, *Affect, Archive, Archipelago* aspires to "begin and stay with matter and the possibility of imaging the world as *corpus infinitium*" (42), that is, "an approach to reading, as a materialist practice, that includes imaging of what happens and has happened as well as what has existed, exists, and will exist otherwise—all at once" (43). This, she forcefully continues, "foregrounds the intuition and the imagination" (48). Reasoning will certainly be found in the following pages, but as an effect of intuiting and imagining. We forage for the echo and the trace.

Hence, this book lays claim to Puerto Rico's sovereign Caribbean lives as those that have "existed, [exist], and will exist otherwise—all at once" despite the "transparent," juridical, institutional negation of such conviction. Although in the terms of power we have not been, are not, and will not be sovereign and Caribbean, Puerto Ricans, have been, are, and will be sovereign and Caribbean.[62] The more recent instances approached in this book's part II and in our contemporary *living here* are only deepening forms in relation with this ancestral, submarine, underseen, intimate certitude.

But what do I mean when I say we lay claim to *sovereignties*? How are these different from the sovereignty that "defers genocide" for Native peoples (Andrea Smith 2020), that is, as Smith explains, from sovereignty as commodification of land? How are they *other* sovereignties from the nation-state kind, built by the "transparent" regime with cages and walls, blood and tears, whips and chains?[63] Puerto Rico's are—oh, yes, indeed—opaque sovereignties. That is, a myriad of economic, political, cultural, and bodily ways in which, submarinely, beyond the regime of intelligibility for institutions, political parties, the mainstream press, and empire, we—humans and nonhumans alike—claim, in wild flights of "intuition and imagination," our archipelagic "here," all at once, all together, the dead and the living, who are never altogether dead or alive.

While in Puerto Rico we continue struggling—and will do much more of it, as we must!—for Ferreira da Silva's illuminating definition of decolonization (see the Prelude), these multiple sovereignties must be honored, deepened, and "practiced as a religion," as they show the way. Nurtured by archipelagic historical traces and amplified through relational networks of material and affective solidarities, they "have been, are, and will be" woven daily on the margins of the local and federal governmental apparatuses, and of the multinational corporations and investment firms that have come to control the Puerto Rican colony's dependent economy. Likewise, communitarian-artistic-bodily sovereignties nurture solidarity, collaboration, and alliances not only within the Puerto Rican archipelago, but also with its significant diasporas and with the Caribbean region, as we will see especially in this book's part II. Finally, communitarian-artistic-bodily sovereignties foment crucial—even if most of the time "invisible"—processes of agency and political formation within and without the archipelago.

Some examples of communitarian-artistic-bodily sovereignties in contemporary Puerto Rico are the following:

1. the numerous ecological struggles contesting corporate-led contamination and irresponsible development in communities such as Isla Verde, Carolina (the rescue of several acres of beach from the Marriott Hotel's control, discussed in chapter 4); Tallaboa, Peñuelas (against the carbon incinerator AES); and Playuela, Aguadilla (against the construction of another mega resort), alongside a significant rise in agro-ecological projects, from Utuado to Vieques;
2. the growing support for clean solar energy, and its independence from private, or privatized, corporations, especially around the work of *Casa Pueblo* in Adjuntas and *IDEBAJO* in Salinas;
3. the significant opposition to the FOMB from multiple social justice organizations, such as *Se Acabaron las Promesas* and *Construyamos Otro Acuerdo*;

4. the essential struggle to resist and connect Puerto Rico's crisis to its violent racist, misogynist, and queerphobic dynamics, vigorously exemplified by the work of *Taller Salud, Colectivo Ilé, Matria, Colectiva Feminista en Construcción, Coalición 8M, La Sombrilla Cuir, Espicy Nipples,* and *CABE,* among others;
5. the mounting support for a citizen-led, transparent debt audit that would also bring the guilty parties to justice, exemplified by the *Frente Ciudadano por la Auditoría de la Deuda*;
6. the unyielding effort that culminated in the liberation of political prisoner Óscar López Rivera in 2017;
7. the continual struggle in defense of public and accessible education, both at the school and university levels, by organizations such as *Federación de Maestros y Maestras de Puerto Rico* (FMPR), various student movements, and UPR faculty collectives;
8. the fight to ensure a truly just recovery after the 2017 hurricanes for Puerto Rico's majorities, as unceasingly propelled by *Ayuda Legal Puerto Rico*;
9. *Kilómetro 0*'s citizen-led effort to investigate, denounce, and stop police brutality;
10. the proliferation of mutual aid brigades (*Brigada Solidaria del Oeste*, for instance) and communitarian centers (*Centros de Apoyo Mutuo*), and of transdisciplinary artistic-cultural spaces and projects (such as *Taller Libertá, Beta-Local, El Bastión, La Goyco, El Hangar, Editorial Casa Cuna,* and *Editora Educación Emergente*); and
11. the increasing reinvigoration of street and independent art, theater, and performance, with such long-standing or more recent collectives as *Taller de Otra Cosa, Agua, Sol y Sereno, Papel Machete, AgitArte, Vueltabajo Teatro, Bemba PR,* and *ACircPR*.

These collectives and movements, unsurprisingly, were some of the most vibrant, visible, and organized in leading the way during Puerto Rico's 2019 *Verano Boricua* and its enduring afterlives.

Affect, Archive, Archipelago is convinced that today's struggles in Puerto Rico against the savage intensification of neoliberal capitalism, racist colonial oppression, disaster pornography, misogyny, and queerphobia do not require inventing a new dream. Rather, this book witnesses, praises, and encourages the ways in which we already touch each other, with all our waters coming ashore. Let us gather the submarine forces of our volcanic islands. Let us encounter, study, sustain, and embody our archive of shared affections, brimming with relentless creativity and defiant joy. Let us remind ourselves of a future we have always been shaping.[64] Let us defy the dominant Western notion of linear time, insisting that every form of the Puerto Rican affective archive of Caribbean relations, no matter when artists, activists, and thinkers lived and died, is our contemporary. With "the humility of knowing that while we navigate the predictable there are phenomena old and ongoing that we've never even heard about, waiting for us to remember" (Gumbs 2020, 130), let us walk-swim-dive together into a deeper, archipelagic dimension of solidarity and love.

NOTES

1. "Underseeing" as a walking-cartographic practice, as opposed to "overseeing," shares its spirit with Annalee Davis's "innerseeing": "Opposing the practice of the plantation overseer, my own effort at disalienation inspired by walking, includes drawing inexact, uncertain and subjective cartographic expressions prompted by a practice of "innerseeing" this multivocal ground beneath my feet. Roaming, listening with another ear and seeing have become intimate acts of moving my aging body through these radically modified environments, provoking an interest in post-extractive ethics and prompting a sense of care for and relationships with human and non-human kin alike" ("Innerseeing versus Overseeing," 2021).

2. Elaine Stratford, Godfrey Baldacchino, Elizabeth McMahon, Carol Farbotko, and Andrew Harwood, "Envisioning the Archipelago," *Island Studies Journal* 6, no. 2 (2011), 114. Also of note in the same vein is Jonathan Pugh's "Island Movements: Thinking with the Archipelago" (2013), in which he argues for an archipelagic thought that "foregrounds how island movements are generative and inter-connective spaces of metamorphosis, of material practices, culture and politics" (10).

3. See, in particular, Martínez-San Miguel's recent pieces published in the online journal *80grados*, as well as the March 2020 co-edited—with Katerina González-Seligmann—collection of essays in *Small Axe* on the idea of confederation in the Caribbean. An important echo of my interest in this book in performative politics and political performances can be found in Lisa Fletcher's concept of "performative geography": "an approach to studying the island as a space of cultural production which privileges neither geography or literature (in their narrow senses) but insists on their interconnection" (quoted in Stratford et al. 2011, 118). Other scholars, such as Gillian Beer (1989, 2003), John R. Gillis (2004), Francisco J. Hernández-Adrián (2006, 2007), Lanny Thompson (2010), and Brian Russell Roberts and Michelle Stephens (2017), have also offered important historical, cultural, and artistic analyses with a focus on archipelagic relations. In the field of ecological humanities, as it pertains to the Caribbean and the Americas, I have been particularly informed by work included in the collection *Caribbean Literature and the Environment* (edited by Elizabeth M. DeLoughrey, Renée K. Gosson, and George B. Handley, 2005), as well as by Handley's book *New World Poetics* (2010).

4. Kamau Brathwaite's *tidalectics* has also been a potent methodological inspiration for this book. See my previous engagements with this concept in connection with Aponte Alsina and Glissant in the essays "'Armar una literatura de conexiones' en nuestra 'patria líquida'" (2016) and "I Believe in the Future of Small Countries" (2014). Antonio Benítez-Rojo's (2010) seminal, fractal reappraisal of the Caribbean region as composed of a "repeating" *pueblo del mar* (people of the sea) is, of course, a presence echolocating across this entire book. Puerto Rican writers Julia de Burgos (poetry, 2016), Luis Palés Matos (poetry, 2008, but most especially, his unfinished novel-autobiography *Litoral: Reseña de una vida inútil* [2013]), Ana Lydia Vega (stories in *Encancaranublado y otros cuentos de naufragio* [1982] and journalistic columns), and Vanessa Vilches Norat (stories in *Geografías de lo perdido* [2018] and several chronicles, most especially her 2016 "El mar de los pelícanos" and her 2020 "Mar de fondo") have also been fundamental in my thinking about maritime Puerto Rican and Caribbean relations. More recently, Puerto Rican poetry has also shown a renewed interest in our archipelagic geography, coastal seascapes, and relations with the sea. See, for instance, Amarilis Tavárez Vales's *Larga jornada en el trópico* (2015), Sabrina Ramos Rubén's *Mangle rojo* (2017), Cindy Jiménez-Vera's *Islandia* (2017), and Claudia Becerra's *Versión del viaje* (2018). Beyond the written word, in contemporary Puerto Rican visual arts, work by Sofía Gallisá Muriente—in particular, her 2020 film *Celaje*—and by NoSiri/Emilia Beatriz—notably, her piece *a forecast, a haunting, a crossing, a visitation* (2019)—is of signal importance. nibia pastrana santiago's transdisciplinary work in the 2019 series *not accidentally given: pesimismo tropical* is another important echo in this book. Multiple works included in the 2021 exhibition *El momento del yagrumo*, curated by Marina Reyes Franco at Puerto Rico's *Museo de Arte Contemporáneo* (MAC), and in Arnaldo Rodríguez Bagué's ongoing curatorial research platform Caribbean-yet-to-come, powerfully echolocate with this book, too. Puerto Rican live arts are also a constant reference in my thinking and living in our archipelago. They provide the performative lens through which I approach the historical-political figures in part I, and to them directly I devote significant portions of chapter 4 and the entirety of chapter 5. In addition to the artists discussed in this book, I must highlight the work of *Vueltabajo Teatro* in the west coast of the "main" island—and especially their street circus and recent *comparsas*, a couple of which had oceanic and coastal lives as their theme—as well as Helen Ceballos's performance work, particularly her pieces engaging the Hispanic Caribbean map, as well as the conditions (including the perilous maritime journey) of Dominican migrants in Puerto Rico. Beyond Puerto Rico, in the context of Hispaniola, and in collaboration with Haitian, Puerto Rican, and other Caribbean artists, Yina Jiménez Suriel has been lucidly engaging in archipelagic practices through her curatorial work (see, for instance, the 2020 exhibition *one month after being known in that island*, curated by Jiménez Suriel and Pablo Guardiola, as well as her interventions in the recent series with Puerto Rico's *Beta-Local*, entitled *otras montañas, las que andan sueltas bajo el agua*). The same can be said of María Elena Ortiz and Marsha Pierce's curated exhibition *The Other Side of Now: Foresight in Contemporary Caribbean Art* (2019) and of Bettina Pérez Martínez's 2021 curated virtual exhibition *Seascape Poetics*. More generally, Nadia Huggins's breathtaking photography from

St. Vincent and the Grenadines, and the visual arts work by Guadeloupean Minia Biabiany, Trinidadian and Tobagonian Wendy Nanan, and Barbadian Annalee Davis, including the latter's stunning 2019 book *On Being Committed to a Small Place*, are honeyed beehives for my archipelagic praxis. Finally, if interested in a comparative analysis of diverse artforms' engagement with insularity in contexts quite distant from the Caribbean (such as in the Canadian North Atlantic and the Great Southern Ocean), see Laurie Brinklow's work.

5. Note Relation's enduring conceptual-poetic-political potency in recent books not exclusively concerned with the archipelagic Caribbean region: *Otherwise Worlds* (referenced in the Prelude, 2020), and Yomaira Figueroa-Vásquez's *Decolonizing Diasporas* (2020), where the sea is also central.

6. The spiral as the preeminent, cosmic form of life and thus as that which ought to organize social and political life has been, and continues to be, known to many indigenous communities throughout the world. See, for instance, myths collected in Leeming (2013) and Leonard and McClure (2003). In the context of an essay connecting Glissant to biopolitics, Alessandro Corio convincingly discusses the spiral in Glissant's oeuvre as "the form of the living's inherent coming-into-being, as well as the form of language generated from this transition" (2013, 917).

7. With this phrase I summarize Western capitalism's hegemonic interpretation of the ocean. On this, see, for instance, Finamore (2004), Klein and Mackenthum (2004), Raban (1992), and Mancke (1999, 2004). Most especially, see Steinberg (2001). I return to "insularist ideology" in a later section of this introduction.

8. These choices should not distract from the fact that similar preoccupations were constant throughout Glissant's work until the end of his life, including in his poetry and novels. See, for instance, *Poetic Intention* ([1969] 2010); *Caribbean Discourse* (1989), *Treatise of the Tout-Monde* ([1990] 1997), *The Collected Poems* ([1994] 2005), and *The Fourth Century* ([1964] 2001). For further confirmation, see the recent and excellent collection of critical essays in the journal *Callaloo* (2013). The essays by Corio, Murdoch, Wiedorn, Britton, and Mardorossian are especially relevant. I situate my work along Forsdick's (2010) and the abovementioned writers' as an emphatic refutation of the argument put forward by some critics to the effect that Glissant became increasingly apolitical in his later work because of his more intense focus on poetics. As far as I am concerned, the whole of Glissant's work is an exemplification of the impossibility of separating the two realms—politics and poetics—and what is more, an unequivocal defense of the need for a freed poetics if a truly decolonial politics is to be achieved in the Caribbean.

9. The novel *The Fourth Century* ends with an equivalent clamor for the Caribbean mixed peoples' "open boat" ([1964] 2001, 292–94).

10. Glissant's conceptualization of *the trace* will be especially significant in chapter 5 of this book.

11. Both Corio (2013, 924) and Murdoch (2013, 884–89) provide compelling discussions of opacity that closely resemble, albeit in different contexts, my account of the concept.

12. In *Poetic Intention*, Glissant goes further: "Where histories meet, History comes to an end" ([1969] 2010, 199).

13. Gumbs's *Undrowned* (2020) mobilizes this historical fact to powerful political-ecological-poetic effect.

14. Cultural theory has also been a culprit of this. In a footnote on the urgency of a "semiological science," Barthes distinguishes between the sea and the beach in terms of signification: "Here I am, before the sea; it is true that it bears no message. But on the beach, what material for semiology! Flags, slogans, signals, sign-boards, clothes, suntan even, which are so many messages to me" ([1957] 1972, 112).

15. In *Caribbean Discourse*, Glissant develops what he understands as the mutually necessary concepts of *detour* and *retour* to refer to different strategies of resistance and creation (one of the most prominent of which is the creation of Creole languages) on the part of the enslaved and colonized (1989, 19–26).

16. J. Michael Dash, the critic and translator whose work has carefully followed Glissant's oeuvre, makes an analogous argument: "Consequently, Glissant visualizes the Caribbean as an unceasing struggle between the reductionist forces of homogenization, or sameness, and the capacity for resistance that is found in cultural opacity" (1998, 153).

17. "In the New World servitude to the muse of history has produced a literature of recrimination and despair, a literature of revenge written by the descendants of slaves or a literature of remorse written by the descendants of masters. Because this literature serves historical truth, it yellows into polemic or evaporates in pathos. The truly tough aesthetic of the New World neither explains nor forgives history. It refuses to recognize it as a creative or culpable force. This shame and awe of history possess poets of the Third World who think of language as enslavement and who, in a rage for identity, respect only incoherence or nostalgia" (*What the Twilight Says*, 1998, 37).

18. See Eco (2009) and Palenzuela (2006).

19. The titles translate, respectively, as follows: "Paths of Surprise," "Intimate Histories, Dispersed Stories: Words, Plots, and Identities," "The Liquid Homeland," "The Mother Metaphor," and "Mother of Fire: William Carlos Williams's Caribbean Identity." These essays were originally talks delivered at various events, or columns written for local digital magazines (in particular, *80grados*). Except for the last one listed, which was the talk delivered on the first Nilita Vientós Gastón Chair at the University of Puerto Rico–Río Piedras's *Programa de Género*, which the writer was bestowed with in April 2014, all these essays have been published in *Angélica furiosa*, Aponte Alsina's blog, between 2005 and 2014. Revised versions of several of these texts were also published as part of Aponte Alsina's collection *Somos islas*. I quote here from the essays' original versions available, without pagination, in the writer's blog or the *80grados* website.

20. See chapter 3 for a discussion of this issue.

21. In fact, beauty, closely connected with poetics, reemerges in a later essay by Glissant as that which we can only find in difference. In this context, Relation is invoked yet again as that which "links diversities and perceives and names differences and works persistently on our consciousnesses and provides movement and gives life to the endless and the unexpected" ("In Praise," 2013, 861). It is the collectivity of differences linked up by Relation that will have, according to Glissant, "the foresight to pursue the overall collective poetics that govern our general politics" (857).

22. See chapter 5 for another engagement with sargasso and the Sargasso Sea in Teresa Hernández's transdisciplinary art.

23. See also Palenzuela (2006) and Sánchez Robayna (2009).

24. In this, local elites feeding off colonial capitalism are to blame as much as foreign colonizers. In Puerto Rico's case, insularist ideology has a long and storied history, some of which I delve into below. To it, we must add a very recent—and quite obscene—instance of it: *#MeCagoEnLaIsla*. This hashtag was used in the *Telegram* chat involving Puerto Rico's ex-governor Ricardo (Ricky) Rosselló and his closest, corrupt "brothers"—as they referred to themselves—which ignited the 2019 *Verano Boricua*. Most often used by "communications expert" Rafael Cerame D'Acosta, the hashtag literally translates as "I take a shit on the island." Idiomatically, however, *#MeCagoEnLaIsla* denotes something more akin to "fuck the island." For an extended commentary on this, see my piece "The Maroons Are Deathless." For a comparative, global discussion on political institutions on islands as they relate—or not—to "small dimensions," see Anckar (2006).

25. Consult *Imagined Islands*' (2012) bibliography for a list of references on the uses and abuses of insularity included in this brief list, especially as they pertain to the Caribbean and the Pacific. On the latter archipelagos, see also *The Guardian*'s series "Pacific Plunder," an ongoing investigative journalism effort on the multiple forms of capitalist exploitation in the region (https://www.theguardian.com/world/series/pacific-plunder). If concerned specifically with the centrality of islands in the literary imagination, see recent work by Crane and Fletcher (2018); Patke (2018); and Kinane (2016) in Rowman & Littlefield's *Rethinking the Island* series.

26. Many have argued for considering the Caribbean the "origin of the modern world." See, for instance, the dossier *El Caribe: Origen del mundo moderno* (edited by Orovio, González-Ripoll Navarro, and Ruiz del Árbol Moro, 2020).

27. See also Eric Williams's *Capitalism and Slavery* ([1944] 1994), where he shows that slavery in the Caribbean and the Americas financed the so-called Industrial Revolution and the development of commercial banking.

28. For an ample and incisive historical panorama on racial-financial capitalism in the Anglophone Caribbean, which bears many connections with Puerto Rico's situation, see Peter James Hudson's *Bankers and Empire* (2017).

29. For a thorough discussion of this process, consult chapter 5 in my *Imagined Islands* (2012). Historical references for this process are included in a previous note.

30. See chapter 4 for an ample discussion of Puerto Rico's organization *Amigxs del MAR*, and its trajectory of struggle against this phenomenon. See also the valuable research and educational initiatives conducted and supported by the Sea Grant Program at the University of Puerto Rico-Mayagüez.

31. On racism in the Caribbean, Frantz Fanon's, C. L. R. James's, and Sylvia Wynter's lives and works remain the most fundamental and transformative references. Aaron Kamugisha has masterfully weaved their contributions in his outstanding book, *Beyond Coloniality* (2019). See also Shirley Anne Tate's and Ian Law's *Caribbean Racisms* (2015). Cedric Robinson's seminal work *Black Marxism* (2005), as well as histories of enslavement in the Caribbean and the Americas such as David Brion Davis's *Inhuman Bondage* (2008) and Gerald Horne's *The Apocalypse of Settler*

Colonialism (2018), are fundamental. Robert L. Paquette's and Mark M. Smith's edited collection *The Oxford Handbook of Slavery in the Americas* (2016) is also of the essence. Finally, consult Pedro Lebrón Ortiz's *Filosofía del cimarronaje* (2020).

32. On this topic, see the collection *Pan-Caribbean Integration Beyond CARICOM* (edited by Lewis, Gilbert-Roberts, and Byron, 2018), Anthony Payne's *The Political History of CARICOM* ([1980] 2008), Aarón Gamaliel Ramos's *Islas migajas* (2016), and Franklin W. Knight's *The Caribbean* ([1978] 2011).

33. Caribbean creative and critical texts have not failed to record this. In Puerto Rico, notorious examples include Antonio S. Pedreira's essay *Insularismo* (1934) and René Marqués's novel *La víspera del hombre* (1959) and story "En la popa hay un cuerpo reclinado" (1959). The Cuban Alberto Pedro's play *Mar nuestro/Manteca* ([1997] 2003) is a more recent example, although the fear of the sea in this case is directly related to the *balseros*' experience. Another Cuban, Virgilio Piñera, wrote "La isla en peso" ([1942] 1995), a remarkable poem representing the sea as an asphyxiating force. But "Isla," an often neglected poem on becoming an island as a liberating experience "from all restlessness," is also Piñera's.

34. From a strictly class-based analysis, Ángel Quintero Rivera's *Conflictos de clase y política en Puerto Rico* (1978) remains unsurpassed in examining the colonial power structures—and their attendant effects—that characterized Puerto Rican society under the Spanish empire, as well as the continuities and ruptures these underwent after the US invasion. For an ample, interdisciplinary panorama of Puerto Rican contemporary thought as it pertains to these processes, as well as to the multifarious forms of resistance to them, consult the *Antología del pensamiento crítico puertorriqueño contemporáneo* (edited by Santory Jorge and Quintero Rivera, 2019).

35. For a collection of interdisciplinary analyses of the 1898 war and its legacies in Puerto Rico and the wider Caribbean region, see *Cien años de sociedad: Los 98 del Gran Caribe* (edited by Gaztambide Géigel, González-Mendoza, and Cancel-Sepúlveda, 2000).

36. In fact, throughout the twentieth century and until the present, the law has functioned as the preferred neocolonial mechanism to enable Puerto Rico's most thorough spoilage. Beyond the results of the *Insular Cases* and the ELA (*Estado Libre Asociado*, or "Commonwealth") Constitution in 1952, both the use and imposition of the "colonial state of exception" (see Atiles-Osoria's *Apuntes*, 2016) to deflate, disorganize, and actively repress anticolonial opposition, and the design and approval of tax laws from the very moment of the invasion at the end of the nineteenth century (see Dick 2015), have been central in the efforts of the US to better exploit Puerto Rico.

37. See chapter 4 for a commentary on Puerto Rico's archipelagic condition as it pertains to Vieques and Culebra. For an ample panorama on US military installations in Puerto Rico, and studies on the US militarization of the Caribbean in general, see Humberto García Muñiz's seminal works. In "The myth of isolates" (2013), DeLoughrey, for her part, provides a powerful critique of the "island isolation" premise as it pertains to the Cold War–era militarization of the Pacific, under "President Truman's doctrine of oceanic colonialism" (169). To further contextualize the ongoing global reach and ineffably tragic ecological effects of the uses of islands

as laboratories for military development, training, and logistics, see the chapter "Thanatocene: Power and Ecocide" in Bonneuil and Fressoz's *The Shock of the Anthropocene* (2017).

38. In their analysis of this process, Rachell Sánchez-Rivera considers the representation and discussion of population control measures in three of the emergent Puerto Rican newspapers, from the mid-1940s through the mid-1970s. With brutal clarity, the following passage from a 1946 article in *El Mundo* quoted by Sánchez-Rivera reveals the unspeakable violence against women: "Concerning the population problem, Puerto Rico is called 'the world's population laboratory'" (2017, 102). See also Laura Briggs's *Reproducing Empire* (2003), a magisterial historical study of this phenomenon, in conjunction with the US empire's understandings of race as they were "applied" to Puerto Rico.

39. Concerning the insidious falsehood of the "overpopulation" discourse in Puerto Rico, see Luis A. Avilés' "El velorio de la sobrepoblación" in his book *Contra la tortura de los números* (2019).

40. This onslaught on women's bodies as fundamental to the US imperial project comes, boomerang-like, on the historical heels of Puerto Rico's first public feminist struggles, as well as of Luisa Capetillo's radical defense of women's sovereignty over their own bodies (see chapter 2). As I discuss in chapter 3, Pedro Albizu Campos's complex position on women and their reproductive capacities was also part of this ideological milieu, but from a politically radical, anticolonial angle, in contrast to Pedreira's neocolonial "go-between." Albizu Campos also held a more appreciative view of insularity. Both Pedreira and Albizu Campos, however, shared a deep nostalgia and admiration for the Spanish empire's legacy.

41. After Hurricane María, the amount of people forced to migrate because of the criminal negligence of the local and federal governments—which could be understood as indirect population control measures—is staggering. A study by Meléndez and Hinojosa at the Center for Puerto Rican Studies at Hunter College estimates that "between 114,000 and 213,000 Puerto Rico residents will leave the island annually in the aftermath of Hurricane María. From 2017 to 2019, we estimate that Puerto Rico may lose up to 14% of the population. In other words, Puerto Rico will lose the same population in a span of a couple of years after Hurricane María as the island lost during a prior decade of economic stagnation" (2017). On contemporary population displacement from the coast in several areas of the archipelago, including Vieques and Culebra, see chapter 4.

42. Contemporary avatars of this neocolonial form of exploitation are Puerto Rican Laws #20 and #22, approved in 2012. Creating, according to the *Partido Independentista Puertorriqueño*'s senator María de Lourdes Santiago, "a tax Apartheid," and in the words of the *Centro de Periodismo Investigativo* (CPI)'s Joel Cintrón Arbasetti, a "caste of intermediaries to obtain tax exemptions" for affluent foreigners, especially based in the United States, these laws "deepen the plantation economy," explains Rocío Zambrana, as well as processes of gentrification and population displacement (see, respectively, the reports by De Jesús Salamán [2021] and Cintrón Arbasetti [2021]). I return to this issue in chapter 4.

43. Diane Lourdes Dick explains: "Pursuant to the Tax Reform Act of 1976, Congress revised the U.S. Tax Code, purportedly to provide for a more efficient system of exempting possessions corporations from income taxation. In place of the exemption mechanism previously codified, Congress enacted a new provision (codified as section 936) enabling U.S. corporations to elect to receive a tax credit equal to the portion of U.S. tax liabilities attributable to taxable income from sources outside the United States that relate to the active conduct of a trade or business within a U.S. possession and from qualified possession-source investment income" (2015, 70).

44. For documentation on the historical processes summarized here, see Gibson (2014), Picó (1975), Díaz Quiñones (2000), Gaztambide Géigel (2006), and Ayala and Bernabe (2007). *PR 3 Aguirre* (2018), Marta Aponte Alsina's book on Puerto Rico's southwestern zone, where many of the aforementioned "experiments" have been imposed, explores these processes through a powerful combination of archival research, travel diary, and literary creation. About the southwestern coast of Puerto Rico as a "sacrifice zone," and the struggle in the area toward environmental justice, see de Onís, Lloréns, and Santiago (2020).

45. Consult Trigo's exhaustive analysis of the PROMESA law, *Los Estados Unidos y la PROMESA para Puerto Rico* (2018).

46. In discussing *La Junta*'s particularly perverse framing of Puerto Rico's present, Rebollo Gil explains how Puerto Ricans are made to believe that "the debt" is "the sum of our sovereignty":

> Moreover, when political pundits and the like offer a defense of *La Junta*, they speak not so much of governmental incompetence or negligence but of an unmet responsibility that transcends government, a responsibility that is somehow shared, socialized among the population. It is our debt in a way so few things are today. For while islanders, under PROMESA, can no longer speak of our government, or our democracy, or even of our way of life, the debt—insomuch as the USA offered no alternative recourse for its management—is the one thing we've got, the sum of our sovereignty. A sovereignty that can only be truly experienced by suffering through whatever terms *La Junta* deems fit for repayment. The debt is the one thing we can be certain will not be taken from us and for which we are, somehow, singularly responsible. (2018, 40)

Nevertheless, resistance "on the ground" is robust. See, for instance, Zambrana's introduction to "On Debt, Blame, and Responsibility: Feminist Resistance in the Colony of Puerto Rico" (2021), a recent dossier on the topic.

47. Among the massive documentation on these matters, I highlight the following: Stiglitz and Guzmán (2017); Cotto Quijano (2018); Caraballo Cueto (2018); Godreau-Aubert (2018); Klein (2018); Santory Jorge (2018); Bonilla (2020); and Brusi, Godreau, and Bonilla (2018). Consider, also, the *Centro de Periodismo Investigativo* (CPI)'s work on the deepening crisis after Hurricane María, the profuse materials included in the platform *Puerto Rico Syllabus*, and the special issue "Crisis" of the *Voces del Caribe* journal (edited by Atiles-Osoria, Herlihy-Mera, and Llenín-Figueroa, 2019).

48. Puerto Rico's CPI also assumed the responsibility—in the face of the local and federal government's incompetence and obstruction—of accounting for the

people who lost their lives for reasons directly or indirectly related to Hurricane María (consult their digital platform, *Los muertos de María*). For diverse responses, analyses, and contextual approaches concerning Hurricane María in Puerto Rico, see *Aftershocks of Disaster* (edited by Bonilla and LeBrón, 2019), *Eye of the Storm* (special issue of the *NACLA Report on the Americas*, 2018), and the Puerto Rican online magazine *Cruce*'s special edition on the hurricane (2018).

49. With "proportion," I am referring to the fact that, for instance, hurricanes of the magnitude of 2017's Irma and María will have greater impact over the majority, if not the entirety, of a population to the extent that the territory's extension is smaller. At the same time, however, it should be remembered that the climate emergency, for which smaller territories, such as islands, are not responsible, produces the increasing frequency, dimensions, and speed of such atmospheric phenomena.

50. More recently, Naomi Klein has also documented the crass capitalist profit-making from "disaster" in her book, *The Shock Doctrine* (2007). After her visit to Puerto Rico in January 2018, the investigative journalist published *The Battle for Paradise: Puerto Rico Takes on the Disaster Capitalists*, a brief recount of the deeper version of "disaster capitalism" in colonial, post-María, Puerto Rico. For more on "environmental injustice" in Puerto Rico as it manifests itself in the wake of Hurricane María, see Gustavo A. García-López's work. To learn about the deadly ecological effects of US disaster imperialism on the tropics more generally, consult Tucker (2007). Furthermore, even when the island-laboratory of Puerto Rico (as the rest of the Caribbean region) has felt most dramatically the horrors resulting from the experimentation power requires for its reproduction, the region has not received any legitimate reparations from imperial powers. I return to this in chapter 4, as well as in the Coda.

51. We owe what is known about who benefits from Puerto Rico's debt, amid an atmosphere of extreme secrecy, to the CPI, the journal *In These Times* (see the report by Cintrón Arbassetti, Minet, Hernández, and Stites, 2017) and the *Hedge Clippers* organization (see their reports "Vultures in Puerto Rico," n.d.). Concerning private profit after Hurricane María, consider the plethora of news, in both local and US media, about corrupt contracts, the privatization of Puerto Rico's Power Authority, and the dismantling of public education to foster the charter school system, among other factors.

52. The *Paradise Papers* (2017) investigation reveals the overwhelming use of Caribbean insularity in the mega-business of tax evasion and in the astronomical enrichment of a minuscule percentage of the planet's population. About the latter phenomenon, consult also Neate's reports for *The Guardian* (2017). Concerning "cryptoutopians," see Bowles (2018) and Brusi (2018).

53. In "Postdisaster Futures" (2020), Bonilla discusses "how Puerto Rico is currently undergoing an affective crisis that echoes the political disenchantment discernible within and outside the region." "Throughout the Caribbean and beyond," she continues,

> the twentieth-century project of postwar decolonization has resulted in debt economies, displaced diasporas, deep social cleavages, and shattered hopes for the future. I am in-

terested in thinking about the kinds of political life that can emerge in the wake of this postcolonial disaster. And, again, by disaster I mean not just "an event of unfortunate consequences" but also a failure—specifically, the failure of the modernist project of decolonization. (149–50)

I hope *Affect, Archive, Archipelago* can show us our affective exuberance—rather than its crisis—which has historically and continuously nurtured forms of archipelagic decolonization according to premises from *within* our region, rather than those of the failed "modernist project" Bonilla refers to.

54. For a discussion of this phenomenon and its limits, see Achille Mbembe: "[I]t seems clear that the archive is primarily the product of a judgement, the result of the exercise of a specific power and authority, which involves placing certain documents in an archive at the same time as others are discarded. The archive, therefore, is fundamentally a matter of discrimination and of selection, which, in the end, results in the granting of a privileged status to certain written documents, and the refusal of that same status to others, thereby judged 'unarchivable.' The archive is, therefore, not a piece of data, but a status" (2002, 20).

55. See his well-known poem "The Sea Is History" (2007).

56. Although not concerned with the Caribbean as such, also consider the Puerto Rican thinker Arcadio Díaz Quiñones's concept of *Arca-Archivo* (Ark-Archive). With it, Díaz Quiñones urges us to engage in a practice of *hacer memoria* (make memory) to account for the many *dones* (gifts) we have received from Puerto Rican artists and intellectuals of all areas and mediums. See his compelling and beautifully written essay, "El Arca de Noé," in *Sobre principios y finales (dos ensayos)* (2016).

57. For an anthropological study that conceptualizes and beautifully defends the importance of the *ephemeral* in present-day Puerto Rico, see Melissa Rosario's dissertation *Ephemeral Spaces, Undying Dreams*, where she analyzes the *Campamento Playas pa'l Pueblo* (see chapter 4 of this book) alongside the 2010 UPR student strike: "Ephemeral spaces and the unfixed possibilities they create, help participants to get past strict notions of rationality to push the limits of thought so much so that they can be shaken from expectations, and find the world anew" (2013, 79).

58. For a moving and compelling study of recent ephemeral activism in Puerto Rico deemed "irrational" or "insufficient" by many, see Rebollo Gil's *Writing Puerto Rico* (2018).

59. Although beyond my capacities, engagements with the musical affective archive of Caribbean relations in Puerto Rico—bomba, plena, salsa, merengue, reggaetón, calypso, and on and on—would be as fertile, if not more so, as the instances included in this book. The same can be said of our culinary knowledges, experiences, and creations.

60. After considering various angles of this recent process using the conceptual lens of "the Puerto Rican Left," Fernando Tormos-Aponte concludes that, "The Left's adoption of an inclusive and popular resistance organizing approach will help determine its ability to defeat the neoliberal attacks on its public services and institutions" (2018). For a participatory action research engagement with some of the most salient contemporary groups and initiatives noted in this section, see Aurora Santiago-Ortiz's

work (2020). For anthropological approaches to Puerto Rico's reframing of its future post–2017 and during the current crisis, see Adriana Garriga-López's scholarship (2018–2020).

61. Significantly, this text has been echoed in the previously referenced visual arts work of NoSiri/Emilia Beatriz and as part of the installation by *El Departamento de la Comida*, included in the *El momento del yagrumo* 2021 exhibition to which I referred above.

62. In this sense, *Affect, Archive, Archipelago* engages directly with questions posed by the recent collection *Sovereign Acts* (2017). Frances Negrón-Muntaner, its editor, explains: "What are the alternatives not only to colonial and settler-state sovereignty but also to the Western idea of sovereignty? . . . What (or when) is sovereignty? . . . Is it possible to engage in sovereign acts without "having" (or being indifferent to, or even rejecting) state sovereignty? Can sovereignty be thought of as less of a thing that one "has" and more as a tension between control and resistance, an argument over power? If so, under what conditions and through which practices do people and peoples affirm themselves as sovereign above other possibilities?" (5–6).

63. Gerard Prinsen and Séverine Blaise have recently proposed the concept "Islandian' sovereignty" to name a "unique approach to sovereignty" (2017, 58) characterizing "the relationship between non-self-governing islands and their metropoles" (77). "Islandian" sovereignty is underpinned, they continue, by five recurrent mechanisms, summarized as follows: "saying 'no' to Westphalian independence, negotiating continuously over ever-changing constitutional statuses, getting away with bending metropolitan regulations, complementing short-falls in domestic tax revenues by metropolitan transfers into the islands' public budgets, and signing agreements that are beneficial to the islands but may be uncomfortable to the metropole" (77). These, they argue, can be distilled from studying multiple formally non-sovereign islands across the globe, although their main case study is New Caledonia. In contrast with this book's argument, however, this analytical approach, while sensible to the geographic particularities of islands, is still governed by the notion of sovereignty as emanating from the nation-state. Moreover, from the standpoint of what I understand as archipelagic, decolonial, and sovereign thought and practice, Prinsen and Blaise's argument overestimates the "negotiating" capacity of islands within colonial constraints to achieve true emancipation.

64. In another register, this is what I understand Dominican scholar Silvio Torres-Saillant to be calling forth when he declares that "The necessity of knowing, valuing, and protecting ourselves mutually in the Caribbean still prevails. We also need to develop the strategy of affirming the good products of the Antillean intellect. We should contribute to the legitimation of the creativity, the imagination, the genius of this region's peoples" ("Conocimiento, legitimidad y el sueño de unidad caribeña," 2011, 38).

I

PERFORMATIVE POLITICS IN PUERTO RICO'S AFFECTIVE ARCHIVE OF CARIBBEAN RELATIONS

The three chapters comprising part I walk-swim with some of the nineteenth and early twentieth centuries' most salient political figures for Puerto Rico's emancipation and multiple sovereignties, relationally underseeing their lives and works, their "intimate histories," as indispensable instances of our affective archive of Caribbean relations. The chapters offer detailed commentary on the complex and nuanced ways in which both ostensibly well-known figures (Ramón Emeterio Betances in chapter 1 and Pedro Albizu Campos in chapter 3) and the lesser-known Luisa Capetillo (chapter 2) engaged with the main concerns of this book: Puerto Rico's Caribbean relations, the links between political imaginaries and experimentations and our archipelagic geography, and the question of sovereignties, both as they are embodied and aspired to. Echolocating with *Affect, Archive, Archipelago*'s driving impulse beyond the written word, the chapters pay special attention to the performative, bodily qualities of the three figures' political lives.

Chapter One

Feeling the Archipelagic Confederation

Ramón Emeterio Betances and *the* Confederación Antillana

[I]f "God is Spanish," as the colonial newspapers proclaim, one barely notices it in Puerto Rico, where epidemics continue wreaking havoc, bankruptcies are ever more frequent, insurrection proclamations circulate everywhere, and a cyclone full of electricity just devastated, burning them all, the fertile valleys of Cabo Rojo, town of beautiful eyes and courageous hearts.

— Ramón Emeterio Betances, "Escritos políticos: Periodismo militante," in *Ramon Emeterio Betances: Obras completas*, Vol. X, edited by Ojeda Reyes and Estrade ([1875] 2017), 256[1]

Chapter 1 walks-swims with the ostensibly well-known nineteenth-century Puerto Rican revolutionary, physician, diplomat, and writer Ramón Emeterio Betances, anticipating both similarities and contrasts with the later figures explored in chapters 2 and 3. In my effort to focus on underseen sands of his lifelong actions and ideas, the chapter wrestles Betances away from Puerto Rico's traditional leftist circles, which purport to "know" all about him and his struggles in overwhelmingly, and woefully narrow, patriarchal and nationalist terms. In contrast, I show that Betances's political commitments and ideological positions were enabled by a resolutely relational and affective archive, born out of his intensely maritime life. Bonded with archipelagic land- and seascapes in the Caribbean and beyond, as well as with lifelong friendships and collaborations, Betances's understanding of Puerto Rico's independence, and, further, of the very idea of "nation," hinged on emancipation-as-relation. The chapter pays special attention to the way Betances's archipelagic imaginary manifested itself in his unsurpassed—if limited—racial consciousness and centering of Haiti in Puerto Rico's, as well as the Caribbean's, becoming.

In an 1882 letter to his friend, the revolutionary poet Lola Rodríguez de Tió, Ramón Emeterio Betances sorrowfully recalls his 1861 flight from Puerto Rico with fellow abolitionist Segundo Ruiz Belvis:

> My wretched Cabo Rojo! My eyes swell as I think about it. Such a beautiful country and so miserable! I remember that when Segundo and I fled the darkness, the boat ran aground on a small beach of white sand, by Boquerón. I had a severe fever. We jumped and, crawling, I first got to an *uvero* [a sea grape tree], under which I rested; afterwards, climbing on all fours [on] a small hill that separated us from the rest of the island, I glimpsed and sent. . . a kiss for *Patria* [both the homeland and Lola's daughter, whose name was Patria]. (Rama 1971, 103)

Betances's body in pain, feverish, fleeing, trembling, climbing—what agony! And to think that at the top of that hill in Boquerón, Cabo Rojo—the town where I live—he could only see a land from which he must flee, to defend it. . . . Still, rather than claiming the island as his possession, à la Crusoe, the way patriarchy teaches men to do, Betances sends it instead something unknown to language—what else could the ellipsis in his letter mean but that it is impossible to make meaning out of that feeling?—and more akin to a kiss of love.

What did Betances think of the coastal seascape while on the boat with Segundo? What did the sands make him feel before they became the site of his involuntary escape? How did his relations with the coast and the sea change that night, when they were transformed into the perilous scene of his survival? Did he experience even a faint and fleeting desire to jump off the boat, to let himself die under the *uvero*'s shade? Did he find the comfort of a small form of liberation when he landed on another island's coast? Was that maritime journey, which became an entire diasporic trajectory, partly responsible for his *Antillas para los Antillanos*, his dream of an Antillean Confederation?

The political horizon of a *Confederación Antillana* (Antillean Confederation, AC) was shared by many of the most prominent nineteenth-century leaders of independence struggles in Puerto Rico, Cuba, and the Dominican Republic (DR).[2] Explicitly defining it as a *decolonial* project, in their introduction to the recent (2020) *Small Axe* special section on Caribbean confederations, Yolanda Martínez-San Miguel and Katerina González-Seligmann argue that "the *Confederación Antillana* fomented a decolonial imaginary of regional unity and sovereignty that was expected to culminate by the end of the nineteenth century in a diverse array of political projects linked to separatism, autonomy, and independence from Spain" (39). In one way or another, in fleeting references or in more sustained allocutions, uniting the Spanish-speaking islands in a common, political formation was a goal shared by Betances, Eugenio María de Hostos (Puerto Rico), José Martí (Cuba), Antonio Maceo (Cuba), Gregorio Luperón (DR), and Máximo Gómez (DR), among others.

Betances, however, was singular in his racial consciousness, in his vehement insistence on Haiti's inclusion—as well as Jamaica, St. Thomas, and, implicitly, all the Virgin Islands[3]—and in his recognition of Haiti as the historical antecedent and model, as well as the most radical historical force of liberation, in the Caribbean.[4] He was also remarkable in his own embodiment of the archipelagic, *confederacionista* dream, both because of his constant, maritime, inter-insular movement and experience, and because the dream itself shaped his thinking and actions.

Regarding the AC, Betances "did not leave us 'a unified plan harmoniously elaborated,'" but Félix Ojeda Reyes explains that the revolutionary leader "sees in the Antillean Confederation the possibility of forming a multinational state of 25 million inhabitants" (2000, 36; see also Betances's 1898 statements in an interview with Luis Bonafoux, included in Dilla and Godínez 1984, 367). Further—although there is no definitive expression of this in Betances's texts—"we can infer that Betances suggests the establishment of a Caribbean parliament with headquarters in America's primate city [Santo Domingo, DR]. Such an organism, freely and democratically elected, would be ruled by a constitution approved by the confederated peoples" (Ojeda Reyes 2000, 37). As we will see below, Betances offered his ideas and proposals in multiple texts of varying genres, all with significant oral, performative qualities: proclamations and manifestos, journalistic pieces, letters, essays, speeches, and translations.[5] Indeed, "the written word [but an overtly oral, performative, word, I would add] became a technology of advancement and resistance" (2013, 14), as Jossiana Arroyo points out concerning revolutionary Freemasons, Betances among them.

AN AFFECTIVE DREAM

Betances's texts explicitly concerned with, or including allusions to, the AC archipelagic political dream share the following premises, consistently sustained from the 1860s through the 1890s.

1. The Spanish empire is an absolute enemy, in all senses. Consistently and unequivocally, Betances crushes Spain, its "despotic" monarchy, its political elites (including the republicans), and its imperial and colonial history.

Indeed, the fact that "chance" put this hemisphere "in Columbus' path" was, according to the Puerto Rican, a "disgrace for humanity" (Godínez Sosa 1869, 52–53). In Betances's estimation, Spain's government in the Americas and the Caribbean is based exclusively on the most violent of extractions: "the gold and the slave." Its primary legacy, as a result, is blood and death. The historical "superiority" of the Spanish empire in subjugating lands and peoples has only one sordid explanation: "the rage to exterminate" (Ojeda Reyes and Estrade, Vol. X, [1876] 2017, 347). "Slavery," the Puerto Rican argues decades before Césaire and Fanon, "has debased the dominators. . . . Gold has corrupted them to the core" (Ojeda Reyes and Estrade, Vol. X, [1875] 2017, 266). Betances goes so far as to counter Spain's claim to the status of "civilization":

> We should . . . conspire because nothing should be expected from Spain or its government. They cannot give us what they do not have. They lack . . . all elements associated with a civilized people; they are over a century apart from the rest of the nations in sciences, arts, industry, navigation, commerce, etc., and even further behind in political sciences and administration. . . . They aspire to rule to distribute destinies and crosses among themselves. (Ojeda Reyes and Estrade, Vol. IV, [1867] 2017, 63)

Thus, it is fundamentally *against* what Spain stands for, in his view, that the Americas, and the eventual AC, must be built: "*being American*, in Puerto Rico as all over America, is precisely the contrary of *being Spanish*" ("Cuba y Borinquen," *Las dos Antillas*, 1875, 231), and "the more our countries move away from Spain, the more they will come closer to civilization" (Dilla and Godínez [1888] 1984, 246).[6]

2. Total independence from the Spanish empire—and from any empire whatsoever—and the absolute abolition of slavery are *collaborative* and immediate requirements for the Antilles' future. Considering Spain's retrograde recalcitrance, these goals must be conquered, if needed, through armed revolution, as was being waged in Betances's time throughout the continent, as well as in Cuba and the DR. This provides the necessary context to assess Betances's controversial defense of the right to bear arms (see his famous "Los diez mandamientos de los hombres libres," edited by Ojeda Reyes and Estrade, Vol. IV, [1867] 2017, 69–70), as much as his covert work in supplying weapons to Cuban, Dominican, and Puerto Rican revolutionaries. Indeed, with respect to the abolition of slavery in Puerto Rico (1873) and Cuba (1886), and despite its wretched limitations and the "indemnity" paid to former masters, Betances was adamant that the royal decrees resulted from mutual collaboration between Cuba and Puerto Rico, and from local, *criollo* pressure on Spain, rather than being

an initiative for which the Spanish monarchy deserved any recognition.[7] Total independence of each island/archipelago, however, must *not* be conceived as the ultimate political horizon for the Antilles.

3. The political and historical antecedent for achieving, and maintaining, independence from European empires, the abolition of slavery, and the collaboration with others in the same predicament, is Haiti, its 1791–1804 Revolution, the republican leadership of Alexandre Pétion, and the latter's collaboration with Simón Bolívar.

4. The ultimate political horizon, once independence is secured, is the AC, since Betances conceives the entire Antilles as a *Patria*, sharing all important aspects of a common identity (see, for instance, his "Carta al director de *El Americano*" in Ojeda Reyes and Estrade, Vol. X, [1874] 2017, 212). That is, although Betances does not mobilize the term "archipelago" politically, the Antilles are, in both his thinking and political praxis, an implicit archipelagic "homeland," as he does call it a *"maritime* nation" (Dilla and Godínez [1898] 1984, 367, emphasis added).

5. The principles upon which every independent island/archipelago, as well as the AC as an entity, must base their political constitution are republican, in the tradition of the Haitian and French Revolutions, and in economic terms, capitalist. Thus, civil rights and freedoms must be recognized, honored, and defended, while, economically, the Antilles must move toward that which Betances identifies with modernity: "every modern country is agricultural, industrial, and commercial; Spain is none of that" (Ojeda Reyes and Estrade, Vol. X, [1876] 2017, 359). In another piece, Betances intimates the significance of "revolution" for "an enslaved people" as "all that is great, all that is everlasting: Progress, Freedom, Justice and Civilization" (Ojeda Reyes and Estrade, Vol. X, [1877] 2017, 434). These, then, are the Enlightenment concepts, central to the Western liberal tradition, sustaining his Antillean metanarrative. More specifically, in his 1874 piece in defense of Haiti, "Miseria entre riquezas," published in *El Americano*, Betances provides the following definition of all the "civilizational goods" toward which Haiti—and, by implication, the future AC—aims: "definitive disappearance of paper money, roads, schools, colleges, commerce, special industries, wellbeing at the heart of the country, foreign respect, credit in Europe's and America's commercial zones, trust everywhere" (Ojeda Reyes and Estrade, Vol. X, [1874] 2017, 206).[8]

6. The diverse racial and ethnic composition of the Antilles must be safeguarded with constitutional political equality, rather than with the assumption of a transcendent racial unity that eclipses difference. However, as Khalila Chaar-Pérez makes clear in "Revolutionary Visions?" "he explicitly excludes racial difference as *a defining aspect* in his conception of

Caribbean affiliations" (2020, 51, emphasis added). Thus, "even though he writes about the plight of the region's people of color, Betances shied away from defining the Caribbean federation in racial terms" (49). But seeking not to define the AC as primarily a racial formation does not mean that Betances thought, as some of his contemporaries did, that racialized differences should be deemed nonexistent and therefore negligible for emancipatory struggles. As Jossiana Arroyo argues in *Writing Secrecy*, "while Hostos and Martí insisted on a raceless society that would consolidate a Creole elite that would negotiate with local metropolitan powers, Betances and leaders such as Firmin appealed to transnational mulatto/black solidarities in an effort to critique institutional racism" (2013, 71).[9]

7. The Antilles must, at all costs, remain united and *fraternal*. This premise is so overwhelmingly ubiquitous in Betances's writings that a twenty-first century reader concerned with understanding the Caribbean archipelagically cannot but recognize its implied premonition of the unremitting, deep struggles that the region would face to ascertain and sustain such unity.

8. The Antilles must also approach their struggle for independence in the context of a looming US empire during the closing decades of the nineteenth century, which Betances clearly foresaw as an unequivocal threat to both the Caribbean region and the nascent Latin American republics. Thus, independence and the subsequent AC was, for him, not only a proactive, liberatory political project, but also a defensive, historical necessity, because "every friend of independence is completely convinced that putting the Antilles in the hands of the US would amount to condemning our race to disappearance, either through destruction or exile," as he writes to the English consul in Port-au-Prince, Sir Spencer St. John, in an 1870 "Memorandum" (Ojeda Reyes and Estrade, Vol. IV, 2017, 211). In the same text, Betances also details the US's adverse and anti-independence trajectory with respect to Puerto Rico, adding that: "You can be sure to find in me, as in every soldier of absolute independence, Spain's irreconcilable enemy, the Americans' [referring to the US] fierce enemy, as long as they pretend to annex us" (Ojeda Reyes and Estrade, Vol. IV, [1870] 2017, 214).[10]

Still, how were Puerto Rico, Cuba, the DR, Haiti, Jamaica, and the Virgin Islands to concretely materialize the AC? Were the Francophone Caribbean and the Dutch Caribbean envisioned by Betances as part of the AC? Were the Caribbean countries in Central and South America? Even in the case of islands that were explicitly included in Betances's writings, such as Jamaica and St. Thomas, how were they, immersed in differing historical circumstances, to be integrated? Did Betances imagine a common constitution, as his idea of an Antillean *Patria* (homeland) and a "people of the Antilles" (Ojeda Reyes and Estrade, Vol. IV, [1867] 2017, 67) seems to suggest, and as Ojeda Reyes himself contends (see above)? Did he visualize something akin to his greatly admired French republic and its *départements*? How would archipelagic travel and collaboration be ensured and fomented? How would linguistic and other crucial differences between the countries of the Antilles be engaged with and negotiated? In light of the overwhelming historical and political exigencies to achieve point #2 and to avoid point #8 above, and of the fact that Betances considered himself a "quiet physician and diplomat and inveterate conspirator—three trades of confidentiality" (Ojeda Reyes and Estrade, Vol. IV, [1886] 2017, 129), who was devoted to the success and endurance of the DR's and Cuba's independence and to the pursuit of a Puerto Rican armed revolution, the answers to these questions remain largely unexplored in Betances's texts.

"ABSOLUTE INDEPENDENCE" AND THE QUESTION OF NATION-BUILDING

Reading Betances's personal letters, as well as his public declarations, manifestos, and profuse journalistic work, one gets the distinct impression that, from the 1860s through the 1890s, his daily life was all but consumed by pragmatic, immediate concerns to achieve what he conceived as the necessary first step: absolute independence from the Spanish empire and enduring independence from the impending US empire. Some of these concerns included the following:

1. the organization of the Puerto Rican revolution: the constant, yet repeatedly failed, lobby with Puerto Rican landowning and professional *criollo* men—for this was definitely a masculinist enterprise—to gather financial resources for the revolution; the acquisition and distribution of weapons; the constant organizing, agitation, and writing to influence public opinion both within the Puerto Rican archipelago and internationally; and the sorting of personal frictions between men involved in the struggle;
2. the struggle to maintain the DR's independence—preventing the sale of the Samaná Bay to the United States, for instance—and democratic institutions against right-wing local rulers, such as Báez and Heureux, who worked in tandem with US interests;
3. the relentless efforts to support and help finance the Cuban revolution for independence—first, the Ten Years' War of 1868–1878, then, the 1879–1880 war and, finally, the 1895–1898 war—as well as, through his

writing and diplomatic efforts, helping influence public opinion in the revolutionaries' favor.[11]

Betances was convinced of Cuba's ultimate triumph and of its ensuing help in launching a similar revolution in Puerto Rico, where Betances's 1868 uprising (*El Grito de Lares*), "whose only crime was haste" (Ojeda Reyes and Estrade, Vol. IV, [1868] 2017, 91), had been tragically suppressed. His devotion to these efforts was so steadfast that his personal finances had all but collapsed toward the end of his life, as he explains to his friend, Julio Henna, in an 1898 letter:

> Today I am like a pariah with whom those who want to continue on good terms with Spain want nothing; and there are those who, upon seeing me arrive, flee, fearful that I am going to ask them for help for Cuba's cause . . . Doctor Betances, as physician, has no clientele and has been forced, so as to live, to sell everything that had a price and could be easily sold. I am left with only one object of art, and precisely because it is [an art object], nobody wants to buy it. (Rama 1971, 241).

Indeed, in one of the pieces for his *Correo de las Antillas* series, published in the French newspaper *Le XIX Siècle*, Betances publicly writes about the degree of sacrifice revolutionaries are willing to make: "But us, insurrectionists and separatists . . . are thieves, thieves it's true, who have thrown their wealth to the fire; we are assassins who, all of us, are grieving brothers, sons, friends, who are dead for the homeland's sake; we are the lowlifes (*chusma*), and I take pride in that" (Ojeda Reyes and Estrade, Vol. X, [1875] 2017, 272). As with Luisa Capetillo and Pedro Albizu Campos (see chapters 2 and 3, respectively), Betances's lifelong work denotes a steadfast commitment to bodily sacrifice as a necessary requirement of the struggle for liberation. For example, in one of his multiple public texts calling for Puerto Rico's revolution for independence, Betances writes "that Spain cannot resist for long, since it is and will be increasingly starved of men, ships and money; that, in a word, patriotism is capable of everything, since he who knows how to die, always wins!" (Ojeda Reyes and Estrade, Vol. IV, [1867] 2017, 66). In appraising Alexandre Pétion's revolutionary legacy—a text I will return to below—Betances calls his the "sacrifice generation":

> Let us be the sacrifice generation, firm and constant in our purposes, for we should expect nothing else but the vile, tireless struggle, pain without pause, exile, martyrdom, death! But for our children, the fortunate fact of their indomitable independence—our legacy—the ineffable glory of not being the foreigners' possession, of being their own masters, which is the supreme happiness, bowed only to Justice's empire, and living under the sweetest sky of the Free

and Independent Homeland. (Ojeda Reyes and Estrade, Vol. IV, [1871] 2017, 237–38)

Later, in an evidently exasperated 1895 piece directed to Puerto Ricans, Betances writes: "Come on! Come on! What are you waiting for? I don't know. I must repeat this to everyone: saintly Freedom never fell from the sky like a virgin of peace; and it does demand of those who deserve her, to shed their blood in the homeland's name" (Ojeda Reyes and Estrade, Vol. IV, 2017, 113).

Moreover, in an 1874 letter to Eugenio María de Hostos, in which Betances tactfully chides his interlocutor for his egotistical ambitions, reminding him of the slow pace of historical change and the need, nevertheless, to plant "the seed," he asserts: "but, my friend, in a revolutionary life all the sacrifices are still just a few . . . A lot of patience, work, abnegation is required. There are those who find that Céspedes and Bolívar did not do enough. What, then, can we expect them to say about us?; but, always onwards!" (Rama 1971, 253). The degree to which Betances had assumed a life of revolutionary sacrifice (including the ingratitude of others), carefully avoiding the role of the singular leader and maintaining his collective allegiances intact, is movingly evident here, and even more so in a *postscriptum* to his testament: "I want my burial to be poor and lay, that no one is bothered with invitations, and, if it is not too painful for my wife, that they bury me in a common grave, next to the poor, who have always been my best friends."[12] Later in this chapter, I will return to the exigency of sacrifice in the "liquid homeland's" name.[13]

As we have seen, for Betances the AC was inconceivable without national independence as a precondition. This need has endured through the twentieth century's colonial liberation struggles—as can be corroborated in figures such as Pedro Albizu Campos (see chapter 3) and Frantz Fanon—and well into our present moment in many circles of the Puerto Rican left. Critics such as Carlos Pabón and Frances Negrón-Muntaner, however, have questioned the nation-state imperative, arguing that it shows an excessive commitment to exclusionary political categories, which they claim are anachronistic in the era of globalization, while Carole Boyce-Davies (2018), in a more generous tone, has written in defense of the "Caribbean Trans-Nation," a twenty-first century version of the AC. On her part, Katerina González-Seligmann, in discussing the West Indies Federation, rightfully insists on attending to what she calls "un-national" instances, in which "the conformation of federated subjectivities as 'structures of feeling' and desire [were] oriented to *sovereignty beyond the nation*" (2020, 77, emphasis added). These "un-national structures of feeling" are precisely what Puerto Rico's affective archive of Caribbean relations is made of, and they must mean something—something essential, urgent, generative—to the crafting of its decolonial future.

In contrast with the harshest critics of the nation-state imperative, I take the more nuanced perspective that Betances's commitment to the nation-building precondition responds to the historical context in which he was immersed and to the significant influence exerted by French republicanism on him and many other Caribbean and Latin American liberation thinkers.[14] Still, it remains true that the nation-state ideal has been a deeply contested concept in Puerto Rico and many other Caribbean islands, and that, ironically in terms of Betances's thinking, such an ideal has tended to work *against* an archipelagic political arrangement in the AC spirit. Particularly within nationalist circles of the Puerto Rican left, doubting the nation-state ideal tends to be read as immature political thinking on the part of the Puerto Rican majority, resulting from centuries of colonialism's psychological impact, and, more recently in the twentieth century, from the devastatingly violent repression of the Nationalist Party (*Partido Nacionalista*) and its leaders by the US Congress and US intelligence agencies (see chapter 3). The repression was aided and abetted by local Puerto Rican elites from both the pro–status quo Popular Democratic Party (*Partido Popular Democrático*), which was—and continues to be—interested in selling and consolidating the false sense of national sovereignty provided by the "Commonwealth agreement," and the pro-annexation New Progressive Party (*Partido Nuevo Progresista*), which was—and continues to be—invested in fabricating for the archipelago an "American" national identity to fit the nation-state (the United States) that Puerto Rico "already belongs to."[15]

Although the nationalist interpretation is supported by unquestionable historical evidence, it also tends to infantilize Puerto Rico's political capacities, avoiding a subtler, yet crucial, question. That is, whether the enduring ambiguity concerning "the nation" in Puerto Rico might reveal a pulsating, if unrecognized, awareness that the colonial subject should at least be able to hold the empire accountable for its crimes. In a scenario of colonial subjugation, in which reparatory justice *as such* has never been at the forefront of the nationalist struggle (nor was it in Betances's time, when the language was more of *patria* than *nación*), let alone in the political platforms of the hegemonic parties, how can the majorities possibly make such demands? To answer this question, we would have to turn to Glissant's traces and Aponte Alsina's intimate histories, to more immaterial manifestations of Puerto Rico's political awareness, akin to the affective archive of Caribbean relations this book explores: perhaps the empire is held somewhat accountable through Arcadio Díaz Quiñones's *el arte de bregar* ("the art of dealing with"), in all its opacity,[16] and through a latent, when not overt, desire to *cimarronear* (maroon), to break free from the imperial and partisan conceptual framework, which controls the terms of *both* the colony's subjugation and liberation.[17]

After the 2019 *Verano Boricua*—and despite the fact that we are still in the course of considering this historical event, as well as its effects, in all their complexity—one would be hard-pressed to deny that such immaterial political reserves have been nurtured for centuries.

Moreover, the Caribbean nationalist tradition—including Puerto Rico's, since Betances, through Albizu Campos, and to this day—has been characterized by a deep, even programmatic, commitment to the concept of sacrifice as an ideal. As a result, perhaps Puerto Rican independence movements have been willing to concede too much to imperial powers, be it Spain or the United States. The idea that forming a nation-state would automatically and unquestionably be better than the colonial condition has led the independent Caribbean to gain such juridical status without reparations for centuries of colonialism and slavery. In several cases, the former colonial masters even received "compensations for their losses" when slavery was abolished and independence achieved. In Haiti's case, these "compensations" are one of the reasons why the ostensibly independent nation-state was hampered with debt since its inception. This colonial-capitalist-racist calculus allowed neo-colonialism to take hold well into the future and is almost entirely elided by Betances in his writings about Haiti's history.[18] In fact, other instances of the Puerto Rican's writing show him willing to "indemnify" Spain in exchange for Cuban and Puerto Rican independence. In an 1895 letter to Henna, he explains: "You understand the importance of this decision [that Puerto Rico's name remains tied to Cuba's]—and this is confidential—if the Spanish leave Cuba, they would be demanded to leave Puerto Rico, too. I have published that they could be offered, at the opportune moment, an indemnity of 125 million dollars, of which 25 would be for Puerto Rico" (Rama 1971, 188–89).

The empires' absolute impunity, along with the complicity of "post-" or neocolonial elites, helps explain the continuous dynamics of class, gender, and race-based exploitation; economic dependency; and coerced migrations that the Caribbean archipelagos—even the independent countries—are forced to face. The lack of reparatory justice has also deepened the incommensurable difficulties that, precisely because of colonial subjugation, islands without their own capital accumulation, traditions of self-government, and production economies were burdened with while they attempted to start on a path *as if* they were "a nation-state among others" within a still imperialist, and thoroughly capitalist, world system.[19] In fact, in his constant engagement with Haiti and the DR, Betances had lifelong, direct experiences of their struggles to ensure and sustain a truly democratic and economically viable nation-state project. As it turns out, the nation-states of Western Europe and the United States were built by exploiting land, resources, and people for centuries. That *is* the nation-state. Thus, requiring our colonial territories to become truly independent nation-states without the imperial nation-states paying for their crimes is like requiring a tropical tree to grow in a desert.

In the context of this book, another limitation of the nation-state imperative has been the way it has precluded—rather than precipitated, as Betances thought—Caribbean unity. Or, perhaps, the most powerful form of Caribbean unity is its "un-nationality"? Eric D. Duke, in his otherwise extraordinary *Building a Nation*, attributes the lack of unity in part to "islandism" (2016, 153, 185, 256). However, far from a geographic natural destiny, such thinking seems more the result of, on the one hand, centuries of empire-led balkanization in the Caribbean region, and, on the other, the fact that liberatory struggles, without reparatory justice, were coerced to understand themselves in the empires' very terms, those of the nation-state.

AGAINST INSULARIST IDEOLOGY AND FOR AN ARCHIPELAGIC PROJECT

Despite all this, and as we have seen, although Betances did not explicitly mobilize the concepts of islands and archipelagos in a politically charged sense, his *confederacionista* dream was *implicitly* an archipelagic project. It was both shaped and exemplified by his diasporic routes and engagements with nineteenth-century Caribbean island life. Very early in his trajectory, Betances registered and opposed insularist ideology's (see the Introduction) argument that equates Puerto Rico's—and, by extension, the rest of the Caribbean's—"lack of resources" with its territorial smallness.[20] Already in 1867 he was making arguments in comparative insularity to debunk such determinist claims: "Crete, with far less resources than us, struggles against, and, in the end, will vanquish the Turks" (Ojeda Reyes and Estrade, Vol. IV, [1867] 2017, 65). A year later, in one of his multiple *proclamas* (proclamations) that would inspire the 1868 *Grito de Lares*, Betances made an insular claim to independence: "Our island's wealth, its dense and courageous population, its sons' education, its relations with both Americas, everything gives you the right to aspire to independence" (Ojeda Reyes and Estrade, Vol. IV, [1868] 2017, 85). In 1875, the Puerto Rican added the example of Margarita Island to his inter-insular thinking: "To those who are reluctant because of the Puerto Rican territory's (*territorio borinqueño*) small extension, they answer that courage and numbers make up for space, and that the inhabitants of Margarita Island—exactly one fourth of Puerto Rico's size—threw out to sea an army of twenty-thousand men" (Ojeda Reyes and Estrade, Vol. X, [1875] 2017, 231). Betances was still making explicitly archipelagic claims to embrace armed political resistance to obtain "absolute" independence in

1895, three years before the US invasion of Puerto Rico and his own death: "Puerto Rico is small? So what? Corsica is smaller, and it had a Paoli; Margarita is smaller . . . and it had an Arismendi, and even its women got rid of their jewels to wield weapons" (Ojeda Reyes and Estrade, Vol. IV, [1895] 2017, 113).

But in terms of its archipelagic thinking, it is his journalistic work, most of which he signed as *El Antillano*, that is truly remarkable, and, in the specific context of Puerto Rico, quite rare. Portraying every Antillean occurrence in relation, Betances constantly notes and compares developments in different Antilles (the Hispanophone Caribbean, St. Thomas, Jamaica, Curaçao) and in coastal Caribbean countries, including Venezuela. Indeed, Ojeda Reyes and Estrade, in their introduction to Volume X of Betances's *Obras completas*, write:

> The unequivocal rubric ["The Antillean," *El Antillano*] will always accompany him. The concept of *antillanidad* is so real, so vital, so urgent for him, that all our lands look like one, no matter what language they speak. . . . In such association, every nation in the Caribbean region—Curaçao, Haiti, the Dominican Republic, Saint Thomas, Jamaica, or Martinique—constitute a fraction of a whole. (2017, 12–13)[21]

Betances's archipelagic consciousness is perhaps most manifest in his journalistic writing situated *within*, and thought *from*, the standpoint of his exile in St. Thomas. Specifically, his 1875–1876 monthly *Correo de las Antillas* series, to which I referred above, constitutes a form of archipelagic archive itself, as well as a masterpiece of nineteenth-century comparative regional analysis. It is also a testament to the complex, and often fraught, ecological and bodily experience of tropical island life, as it makes constant references to earthquakes, volcanic eruptions, and hurricanes (see, for instance, Ojeda Reyes and Estrade, Vol. X, [1876] 2017, 391–92). In the same breath, Betances professes his love for the islands: "It is to this islet, constantly rocked by volcanoes, that I devote my preferences, having decided to remain standing, *impávidus*, on my trembling rock" (Ojeda Reyes and Estrade, Vol. X, [1875] 2017, 283). Betances seems to metaphorize St. Thomas's constant movement as his turbulent, never-still political life, within which, however, he is determined to sustain the principles that orient his work. For myself, I take the risk of fantasizing that the constant vibrations were also those of the Caribbean's echolocations, our "submarine unity" in affective relations.

In another moving passage revealing Betances's archipelagic understanding of his beloved *Patria*, he writes about Culebra, a Puerto Rican island municipality this book repeatedly returns to, along with Vieques: "The ship sailed towards Culebra, a pretty, small, desert island situated between Saint

Thomas and Puerto Rico, where, in my love for solitude, I would have gladly remained, if, like the English poet, I hadn't been looking in vain, ever since I am self-conscious, 'some island yet unclaimed by Spain'" (Ojeda Reyes and Estrade, Vol. X, [1876] 2017, 305). Rather than geographical-natural, the problem of/for Caribbean islands, and of/for Puerto Rico, especially, is explicitly understood as historical-political—that is, *made by* colonial rule and imperial expansion.

With the express intent of apprising the French audience, in the form of "chronicles" (Ojeda Reyes and Estrade, Vol. X, [1876] 2017, 345) of contemporary events in the non-Francophone Antilles, the *Correo de las Antillas* series also exemplifies Betances's continuous engagement with regional newspapers and events in islands and archipelagos he clearly understood as connected to the Caribbean, such as Crete and the Philippines. His constant reference to being *situated* in and from St. Thomas while writing the series denotes a significant insular consciousness, exposing the push and pull of its contradictions when subjected to imperial rule. Far from the familiar imperial trope of the isolated island, in Betances's writing the island's inherent maritime relations ensure ceaseless "echoes" of political ideas: "Not even the subterranean noises that make life in this islet nothing but a constant state of alarm, nor the winds that cross over our heads to produce storms in neighboring islands, run, fly and communicate as quickly as an idea; and that is how every political thought has, here, a sure echo" (Ojeda Reyes and Estrade, Vol. X, [1876] 2017, 340). Imperial design, however, can turn this inherent archipelagic connectivity, our relational echolocations, into "its ruin": "Saint Thomas, Danish colony, engages in commerce while depending, immediately and almost exclusively, on Puerto Rico, Spanish colony. That is its ruin. . . . This bare islet . . . had achieved a life with a light breath of freedom; but had, little by little, ceded to the influence of the Spanish governors, its neighbors, who see an enemy in every independent being" (Ojeda Reyes and Estrade, Vol. X, [1875] 2017, 243).

Betances's 1876 comparative analysis of St. Thomas and Puerto Rico, for its part, is even more revealing in terms of the historical *production*—rather than the ontological "nature"—of island miseries:

> Saint Thomas . . . has only fifteen or sixteen thousand inhabitants. It is one of the most trembling and arid rocks known in the Antilles. . . . it is thus in need of all its neighbors, Puerto Rico, Saint Croix, Saint John, etc. However, this island was for a long time the commercial center of the Antilles and even partly of Venezuela and Colombia. . . . What does this rock owe its prosperity to? To the relative freedom it has enjoyed. . . . and now that the other islands hold direct relations with Europe, what measure does the colonial council take [in Saint Thomas]? It establishes free, compulsory, and secular education, and a great

Institution of higher education. . . . The island [Puerto Rico] has close to seven hundred thousand inhabitants. The land there has an extraordinary fertility. . . . The consequence of all this is clear: the small, sterile rock of Saint Thomas is happier than the great, fecund island of Puerto Rico, due to the single fact that the former is not under Spanish dominion. (Ojeda Reyes and Estrade, Vol. X, [1876] 2017, 412–14)

In other words, a population might live on a very small, arid, and natural-disaster-prone island or archipelago, and still sustain what Betances considers a good life. The latter is for him resolutely the result of social, political, cultural, and economic decisions made by humans in response to such climatic and geographical conditions, rather than a preordained natural plan. Thus, Puerto Rico's plight, its poverty and its "backwardness," is entirely unjustified and cannot be attributed to its insularity. In fact, from the perspective of the exploiting empire, an archipelago like Puerto Rico is excessively bountiful, like a "plutogen," Betances declares:

Everyone knows this enchanting island. If you open America's map, and if you have good eyes, you will find, at the entrance to the Gulf of Mexico, a barely perceptible small stain (*manchita*), almost microscopic, in the form of a small rod cell or bacillus, as they say at the Pasteur Institute, a microbe; not a pathogenic microbe, like physicians say, but if I were a fan of barbarous neologisms . . . I would call it, indicating its wealth, a plutogenic microbe that every year delivers twenty million francs to the *madre patria* [Spain], a budget equivalent to that of Greece and greater than that of Java. (Ojeda Reyes and Estrade, Vol. IV, [1892] 2017, 151–52)

In Puerto Rican political and intellectual history, Betances might very well be the first political agent and thinker to notice, and openly denounce, the convenient use of insularity as ideological subterfuge to both mortally diminish islanders and endlessly enrich those in power.

THE BLACK REPUBLIC OF HAITI AS ANTECEDENT, MODEL, AND ASPIRATION

A more sustained discussion on Betances's understanding of Haiti, both in the context of the exigency of independence to achieve a future AC and of his own racial consciousness, is now in order.[22] A long-view approach to his work undoubtedly shows that Betances considered the Black Republic of Haiti, "the small but vigorous Haitian nationality" (Ojeda Reyes and Estrade, Vol. IV, [1871] 2017, 230), the most radical political project and aspiration in the Americas, as well as the historical model and antecedent of the independence struggles waged during the second half of the nineteenth century ("such are our precursors, oh Cubans! Can anyone believe that we are condemned to die as slaves?" [Ojeda Reyes and Estrade, Vol. IV, (1871) 2017, 233]). Haiti is where Betances's famous principle *Las Antillas para los Antillanos* (The Antilles for the Antilleans) was first materialized: "He [Pétion] . . . founded, democratizing the land, this democratic Republic of Haiti, which the yankee should respect, as much as it should the Dominican Republic and Cuba, if only he understood that his famous principle, 'America for the Americans' contains another, sacred, one: '*Las Antillas para los Antillanos*'" (Ojeda Reyes and Estrade, Vol. X, [1871] 2017, 167). Transpiring from this statement is also his prescient wariness concerning US imperial interests in the Caribbean region, to which I referred above.

A Masonic temple at Port-au-Prince, moreover, was the place where Betances delivered his most famous speech in defense of Antillean unification (Ojeda Reyes and Estrade, Vol. IV, [1870] 2017, 117–22).[23] In that speech, where Betances pleads, *¡Acerquémonos!* ("Let us come closer!"), he explicitly positions Haiti as the first "conqueror of civil and political rights." Thus, Haiti is for him the revolutionary tradition's most legitimate bearer. As such, to help them achieve their independence, L'Ouverture's land must work in solidarity with Cuba and Puerto Rico. For its part, the endurance of the DR's nation-state also hinged, according to Betances, on Haiti's collaboration. Understood by the Puerto Rican as the Antilles' "life itself," Haiti's interests were at stake:

> Who are the people, more than any other, with the right to assume the defense of the oppressed? Your hearts have already said it: Haiti, it is you. You are the ones . . . who first knew how to conquer for your own race all civil and political rights. . . . Brothers . . . we cannot afford to separate our present. I repeat: from one end to the other of the Greater Antilles, the same issue boils, it is the issue of the Antilles' future. . . . Because we are engaged in the same struggle [and] we combat due to the same cause, we should live the same life. You have triumphed, it is true, and have prevented a part of you from being delivered to the foreigner, but you are only the army's center, think carefully, the battle is still raging, and you are not out of danger. From both wings, the Dominican Republic and Cuba, you face the threat of engulfment. We must make a common front and bring our efforts everywhere; and after our total victory, we will start a new life, full of vigor because of the union of all our forces. . . . Let us come closer! (Ojeda Reyes and Estrade, Vol. IV, [1870] 2017, 119–21)

Within the historiographical tradition of "illustrious men," Betances avidly studied the "singular" history of Haiti (Ojeda Reyes and Estrade, Vol. IV, [1871] 2017, 221), taking it upon himself to help divulge it both through his labor as translator—understood as political work—most notably of the

US abolitionist Wendell Phillips's piece on Toussaint L'Ouverture and the Haitian Revolution, and his original writings, among which the extended biographical piece on Alexandre Pétion, whom he considered the epitome of Republican and democratic governance, stands out. In the specific context of Puerto Rico, Betances's engagement with Haiti is truly remarkable. No thinker or political activist since then has been as interested in learning Haitian history nor as invested in understanding Puerto Rican struggles as reverberations of Haiti's radicalism as Betances was. Moreover, as Chaar-Pérez explains in "Revolutionary Visions?":

> Betances' proposal [that "the Caribbean colonies should follow the path of Haiti's struggle against slavery and colonialism and proclaim political sovereignty as a moral principle"] clashed with the views of the great majority of the local elites in Cuba and Puerto Rico, who regarded Haiti as a negative reminder of the possibility of a black revolution in their homeland. Even revolutionary leaders such as Martí and Eugenio María de Hostos did not incorporate Haiti in their visions of Caribbean unity, including only the Hispanic Antilles. (2020, 48–49)[24]

Considering in more detail Betances's biographical work on Pétion, one immediately notices the importance he attributed to sharing the knowledge of a regionally conceived Antillean history: "the life of a man scarcely known among us [Cuban and Puerto Rican republicans]" (Ojeda Reyes and Estrade, Vol. IV, [1871] 2017, 215). After recognizing Pétion's "mulatto" mother, Úrsula, the writer denounces Pétion's White father as "the white man who died without having given his son anything else but signs of hatred and disdain," and, as a result, refuses to name him: "[he] does not deserve that posterity repeats his name" (216). Betances goes on to highlight the Haitian collaboration in the US War of Independence, to which Pétion wished to travel but could not (216), before extolling the Haitian leader's multiple attributes: "influence . . . genius . . . modesty . . . warring ability . . . generosity" (219); "his abnegation and patriotism, or his indefatigable ability and his consistency in giving the Revolution an organization capable of resisting France's attack" (225).

Pétion's eventual "unification and pacification" (234–35) government is greatly admired by Betances, who can only spot one limitation: "In only one aspect was Pétion unable to overcome his people's passion . . .: 'No white can be a property owner in Haiti.' In compensation, the proscribed races were invited by him to the banquet of a free life: 'The man of Indigenous or African race is, as a matter of right, Haitian'" (235). One should notice Betances's immediate racial qualification when explaining why Pétion was unsuccessful in overcoming the Haitians' entirely comprehensible and justifiable contempt toward Whites, and whiteness more generally. Not only did

Pétion's government become a radical force of antinationalist nationalism, in the sense that Haitian citizenship was afforded to "the proscribed races," but also, Betances explains, as Black Haitians "hated" the land—an explicitly antinationalist stance—for equivalent reasons, Pétion's most significant achievement was turning that hate into love:

> The land was fertile, the race vigorous, but the former reminded the latter of all his sorrows: the sweat in his forehead, the blood in his veins, shed to procure the white man's sensuality, without ever satiating it, pleasures never tasted by the African. Hatred, consequently, the man had sworn to feel for the land, and it was necessary to replace the hatred with love, for man to fecund the land and bless the union of the two elements, the People—the Homeland. (236)

Because, in Glissant's words, "the land-beyond" thus became "the land-in-itself," Pétion was, for Betances, the unequivocal "Father of the Haitian Homeland, the Haitian Republic" (236).[25]

Further, the essay on Pétion is one of the very few texts in which Betances, lifelong admirer of French republicanism, makes explicit indictments of the French empire: "Such was the atrocious trophy of cruelty and shame elevated to the love of gold, to the white man's greed" (220); "guided by the lonely star of freedom to break their brothers' chains and to expel from their land the race that . . . had desecrated at every instant and during the course of centuries, every law of human dignity" (221); "The assassinations committed by the French were perpetrated with a cruelty unworthy of that country" (225). Moreover, the Puerto Rican demonstrates his intimate geographical knowledge of Haiti's landscape when he recounts Pétion's revolutionary struggle, tracing in the process an insular Black hero's journey against the French empire:

> Sometimes traversing enemy lines, while others running in between equally fearsome friends; only here; over there; surrounded by enthusiastic patriots; always at the helm of those who fought against the oppressors; convincing the deceived, dragging the undecided; sieged by the French cavalry at the Pierroux estate; saved only because of his determination; hurling himself to a canal from which to arrive at the forests and find the army at La Coupe, which his mere presence incited to rise; waking, stirring at every step Rigaud's soldiers in the southern countryside, who were sleeping since Toussaint's triumph; rejected by Laore; suspected by Desrance; helping Lamarre against Rochambeau's secretary, the Polish Neterwood; crossing rivers; overcoming mountains; traversing the plains; always and everywhere equal to himself in his serenity and determination, prudence and courage, abnegation and humanity. (226)

The Puerto Rican revolutionary's centering of Haiti within Caribbean history was not only circumscribed to the written word, however. In his roles as diplomat, political organizer, and agent, throughout the first decades of his political activism Betances also worked vigorously with Haitian revolutionaries and political figures.[26] He visited Haiti on several occasions and lived for two years in Jacmel, where he was protected from Spanish persecution by Sylvaen Salnave's government.

BETANCES'S RACIAL CONSCIOUSNESS AND ITS LIMITS

Beyond his central and sustained relations with Haiti, Betances's racial consciousness is also manifested through two relevant aspects of his work.[27] First, there was his early abolitionist campaigning and the freeing of enslaved infants during baptism ceremonies in the Mayagüez, Puerto Rico, cathedral, actions he conducted with other abolitionists of the *Sociedad Secreta Abolicionista*, founded early in the 1860s along with Segundo Ruiz Belvis.[28] Indeed, two years before his death, in an 1896 speech that, to a certain extent, can be considered an appraisal of his lifelong commitment to revolution, Betances made the well-known claim that Antillean revolutions were not moved by "disdain" as "Lamartine said in 1848," nor by "desperation," as "Enrique José Varona, one of our great thinkers, said in Cuba in 1895." Rather, "despite the impious despotism that has fallen upon us over the course of four centuries . . . If I was allowed to reconcile two seemingly incompatible terms, I would say, instead, *revolución del amor* (revolution of love)." The first result that "corroborates" this revolution of love, Betances goes on immediately to declare, is "the free Black" (Ojeda Reyes and Estrade, Vol. IV, [1896] 2017, 167).

Second, Betances consistently recognizes the Antillean Indigenous populations as the "native race," as distinct from the enslaved and exploited "African race," which is, in turn, mixed with, and at the same time different from, the "*criollo* race" or the "Americans," by which he means those of European descent born on our side of the Atlantic. On these populations' backs, the European empires extracted their wealth (Glissant's "abyss"), and "America," in the ample sense, was built (Glissant's "womb"): "there are no traces left but those of the work of the Indians, the Africans, and the Americans" (Ojeda Reyes and Estrade, Vol. X, [1876] 2017, 359). It is this colossal pain— embodied, historically-experienced—that fraternally unites the Antillean populations beyond the practices of racialized distinctions that divide them:

> I have talked about our fraternity owing to the sorrows of the past. All of you have contemplated the scene, whose painful reality will seem in the future as

impossible as that of an apocalyptic description. It is a dreadful Jacob stair, where, from the bottom, you see nothing but irons, chains, slaves. On the first step, we see the African race chained and destroyed by the whip; in the middle, we see the *colono* (colonizer), whose pride is chained to work because of his soul's weakness and corruption; at the top, we see the despot—Spanish or French—in chains because of the vigilance that despotism imposes. These horrible scenes are repeated across the Antilles. Soon, four centuries will have passed, and they still endure. (Ojeda Reyes and Estrade, Vol. IV, [1896] 2017, 118)

Still, it is crucial to notice Betances's blatant lack of class consciousness here. Equating the work of "Indians, Africans, and Americans" eclipses the fact that the ranks of "Americans," of which he was certainly a part, were filled with *hacendados* and slave masters who led a very different life in the colonies.[29]

AN EMOTIONAL PATRIARCHY

One could claim that the distant possibility of materializing the AC, as well as the intense difficulties confronted to achieve what we have seen he and his comrades understood as its prerequisites, made Betances's commitment to an archipelagic political practice and horizon an intensely felt emotion and aspiration, manifested in deep bonds between his fellow comrades and collaborators. I thus agree with Arroyo and Chaar-Pérez when they observe that the AC was materialized primarily in and through homosocial relations between *prohombres* (great men) holding a deeply patriarchal view of leadership and liberation.[30] In "Revolutionary Visions?" Chaar-Pérez explains:

> [It was] a community [that of Betances and his fellow revolutionaries] in which the struggle against Spain was often articulated as a performance of fraternal masculinity. As Sylvia Molloy indicates in an analysis of José Martí's 1887 essay "El poeta Walt Whitman," this was "an all male affiliative model" in which the "revolutionary family of sons and fathers confounded in a continuum of natural masculine emotion." Not unlike Martí, Betances explicitly defined his vision for the Caribbean as a "revolution of love," a male-dominated project where affective affiliation and decolonization embrace together. (2020, 48)

Indeed, in 1896 Betances exasperatedly wrote to Henna that Puerto Rico was a *pueblo de mujeres* ("a people made up of women"), by which he clearly meant a cowardly and fragile people (Rama 1971, 227). This is even more evident in an 1888 address to Puerto Rican men who wanted to "save the country's dignity": "Do not advise . . . for the future so much docility and form [instead] '*corazones varoniles*' ('masculine hearts')" (Dilla and Godínez 1984, 246). The only pseudo-political role Betances seems to entertain for women—in sharp contrast with Capetillo (see chapter 2), but largely in agreement with Albizu Campos (see chapter 3)—is their status, not in any way their own, as a "sacred guide" to men, as he expounds in an 1886 letter to Lola Rodríguez de Tió.

Still, Betances's letters, as much as his public manifestos, proclamations, translations, political profiles, and journalistic work, show a rare, emotional patriarchy that does not shy away from open declarations of love between his "brothers" of ideas. Within such relations, as Chaar-Pérez explains in "'A Revolution of Love,'" (2013) the idea of the AC was made: "As he moved between territories, languages, and cultures in order to bring his project into fruition—the fulfillment of political sovereignty and a federation of states in the Caribbean—Betances articulated the idea of a revolutionary community, what he called, in reference to the Cuban Independence War, a 'revolution of love'" (14). Betances's "affective politics," as Arroyo (2013) describes them, his "intimate histories," must be underseen and mobilized while we stand today on our own precarious, bombarded boats, on our coasts of "exploding spray,"[31] echolocating Caribbean solidarity "as though it were a religion."

Betances, who was born in 1827 and devoted his lifetime to the revolutionary causes gripping the Atlantic/Caribbean world throughout the nineteenth century, died in 1898, the year of the US military invasion of Puerto Rico. In December 1897, the crumbling Spanish empire had promulgated the *Carta Autonómica* (Autonomic Charter) for Puerto Rico after a long, treacherous struggle led by Puerto Rican and Cuban *autonomistas* and *reformistas*, of whose ranks, as we have seen, Betances was *not* a member.[32] A few months later, in May 1898, the archipelago was besieged by US military forces. Now, a colonial population mired in misery and neglect had to endure the violent shift to a new master, for whom the *Carta Autonómica*'s provisos meant nothing, as Albizu Campos will repeatedly denounce a few decades later (see chapter 3). Puerto Rico was thus subjected to the ex-colony of Britain, now an imperial monster of deceit. In a flash, the archipelago was cursed by History once more.

Despite both Puerto Rico's failure to shed Spanish—and, eventually, US—rule through armed revolution, as Betances insisted, and the ongoing debate, in the archipelago and the diaspora, on the nation-state and the neglected need for reparatory justice, what remains true among Betances and his circum-Caribbean and circum-Atlantic comrades, as we have seen, are their affective relations, facilitated by a shared passion for a united Caribbean archipelago. These relations still hold a powerful potency for the struggle

Figure 1.1. *Betances in the Streets* at the Puerto Rican March for Black Lives, Harlem, New York, 2020   Courtesy of Molly Crabapple

toward a pluralized sovereignty, as Chaar-Pérez's "Revolutionary Visions?" convincingly concludes:

> In pluralizing and "unsettling" the concept of sovereignty from its Eurocentric practice, we can also widen the framework of decolonization beyond the developmental logic of national self-determination and postcolonial sovereignty.

We might therefore contemplate how the unfulfilled revolutionary dreams of Betances can still linger on as a potentiality to be illuminated again from the future and enlighten us on the path toward a truly radical project of unity, equality, and "freedom for all." (2020, 52)[33]

Against gigantic odds, the Caribbean union, then and now, is bodily felt and thought rather than juridically rationalized. Empire has been unable to destroy this affective archive continuum, whose traces still swim in the Caribbean Sea's depths and walk along our sandy coasts. I insist on reminding us that this is not a negligible feat.

Hunted Flesh

You will not believe this, dear Ramón! As though the preservation of your 1882 letter to Lola—and my encounter with it—was not improbable enough, right before sending this manuscript to the press, Marta Aponte Alsina, writer, friend, and inspiration, showed me your September 24, 1867 letter to your brother Adolfo. In it, you recount your experience at sea "all night and part of the [next] day," as well as your arrival at La Montalva, in the Dominican Republic. Answers to some of my questions after reading the letter to Lola can be intuited from your letter to Adolfo. Because the fever "devoured" you, you spent the entire voyage "crouching at the bottom of the boat, and somewhat wet." The "small form of liberation" was not felt precisely by where you landed, as it was "the most sterile place," full of "rocks covered by dried, little trees and populated by *caribe* mosquitoes." The heat was "suffocating," and yours and Segundo's "water was hot, crackers, stale, and cheese, rancid." You tried to rest, but the mosquitoes had other plans, so you resorted to leftover coffee. In that drink, with your friend, under almost intolerable conditions, you found respite, an ineffable moment: "The coffee was for me a nectar. 'This reminds me of my absent *Patria*,' I said to Ruiz, who smiled" (Carreras 1974, 39).

I live, love, walk, and write in Cabo Rojo, the small town where you, Ramón, were born, from which you treasured the image that "swelled" your eyes, and where your ashes remain. More than one hundred years after your letters, I walk on the Boquerón coast, thinking of you and Segundo, frantically gathering your traces in the form of broken seashells and the remains of corals, trying to imagine, to bear witness to, your pain, your rage, your trepidation. I let myself be overcome by your tragedy on that night of flight, but also by the remembrance of your "absent *Patria*," by your friendship with Segundo, and by the coffee—*that* coffee—in La Montalva.

You are still with us here, courageous Ramón, kissing your *Patria*, drinking that coffee. Your fever is gone, but your fervor rages on. We honor your memory and feel its potency.

NOTES

1. Ramón Emeterio Betances, in Ojeda Reyes and Estrade, eds., *Ramon Emeterio Betances: Obras completas*, Vol. X, "Escritos políticos: Periodismo militante" [1875] 2017, 256. To offer a sense of the trajectory of each figure's life and thought, parenthetical references on primary texts in chapters 1, 2, and 3 include the year of the primary text in question (when not provided in my framing of the quote), in addition to the name of the editor(s) responsible for the books where the texts are reproduced, and the corresponding page numbers.

2. See, among others, Rama (1971, 1980), Venegas Delgado (1994), Gaztambide Géigel (2010), García (2005), Arpini (2008, 2010, 2014), Arroyo (2013), Chaar-Pérez (2013, 2020), Buscaglia Salgado (2015), and Martínez-San Miguel and González-Seligmann (2020).

3. Betances's proposal for Jamaica's inclusion was explicitly manifested in a meeting he held in London with the British Prime Minister, William Ewart Gladstone, in 1882, as part of his efforts to free José Maceo, Cuban revolutionary and brother of Antonio Maceo (Rama 1971, xvii; Ojeda Reyes 2000, 36–37). Ojeda Reyes (36) explains that the proposal sought Great Britain's "guarantee," since the latter was interested in preventing the expansion of US influence in the Caribbean. Concerning St. Thomas, Betances writes: "perhaps later, after the necessary declarations of the islands' independent organization, Saint Thomas might be destined to be part of a confederated Republic of the Antilles" (Ojeda Reyes and Estrade, Vol. X, [1875] 2017, 234).

4. Despite Rama's assertion that "all Antillean peoples were conceived as part of the Antillean Confederation that he [Betances] thought of at least since 1867" (1971, viii), the AC's inclusion of—or relation with, for that matter—the rest of the Caribbean, including the Francophone islands and the "continental" Caribbean Republics of Central and South America, remains unclear.

5. Some of these texts have been compiled over the years by various scholars, primarily Andrés Ramos Mattei (1987), Carlos N. Carreras (1974), Carlos M. Rama (1971, 1980), Haroldo Dilla and Emilio Godínez (1984), and Mario R. Cancel-Sepúlveda (2018). More recently, Betances's writing has been further tracked down, compiled, and edited by Félix Ojeda Reyes and Paul Estrade, whose extraordinary efforts have resulted in the publication, in Spanish, of Betances's twelve-volume *Obras completas* (2017), along with two biographical volumes and one bibliographical tome. In this chapter, I quote from all these sources.

6. Among the overwhelming instances of what he calls "hatred of Spanish dominion, which is synonymous with love for freedom" (Ojeda Reyes and Estrade, Vol. X, [1869] 2017, 131), I add the following: "we are all, with the exception of a few dozens, victims of the Spanish colonial regimen, which, since Columbus, has been and will always be the negation of every right and every form of justice"; "Let Spain die forever in America!" (Ojeda Reyes and Estrade, Vol. IV, [1867] 2017, 61–62, 66); "Everything separates us from Spain! . . . More than the immensity of the oceans . . . the horrors in which it has bathed and continues to enjoy today, since the day it occupied the *borinqueña* lands and bled them to death with its ferocious claws" (Ojeda

Reyes and Estrade, Vol. IV, [1867] 2017, 67); "they pride themselves in a legacy of blood, blood, and blood; since at every corner of America where they set foot, we must fix a cross" (Ojeda Reyes and Estrade, Vol. X, [1869] 2017, 73).

7. "Cuba and Puerto Rico struggled for a long time to solve the problem of abolition, and since 1792, under the influence of the mother revolution, the period between [17]89 al [17]93, we find conspirators there who prepared the abolition of slavery. Since 1848, secret societies were formed on both islands, whose members simply risked their heads for the slaves' redemption" (Ojeda Reyes and Estrade, Vol. IV, [1896] 2017, 165–66).

8. It must be emphasized, however, that Betances repeatedly points to *the land* as the Antilles' most fundamental capital, and that he also uses this conviction to advocate for independence. For instance, in an 1874 letter to the director of *El Americano* newspaper, he writes: "The Antilles' wealth . . . is in the land. The experience of almost four centuries is worth nothing? The fact that all European peoples, Spanish, English, French, Dutch, Danish, etc., consented in taking Africans to our islands proves one thing: their absolute impotence to make work productive, with their own hands, in our lands. Thus, it seems natural that the lands are delivered definitively to the only forces capable of making them prosper, those of all sons of the country, and that 'THE ANTILLES ARE FOR THE ANTILLEANS'" (Ojeda Reyes and Estrade, Vol. X, [1874] 2017, 215–16). This understanding seems to run counter to his association of "progress" with "industrialization," which, of course, corresponds neatly with the increasing displacement of land as the fundamental base of industrial capitalism in the nineteenth century. On another level, Betances's centering of land is also at odds with his "maritime nation."

9. For a fascinating discussion of Alexander von Humboldt's racially defined Antillean federation, the *Confederación Africana de los Estados Libres Antillanos*, see Domínguez (2018), who convincingly argues for its radical nature, as it "entailed, on the one hand, a regional revolution and, on the other, reformulating the importance that Black populations would have in the region's postcolonial map" (59).

10. Remarkably, long before the 1890s, Betances was presciently aware that developments in the United States, which he called "the American minotaur," from which only Puerto Rican independence, "with the agreement of the rest of the Antilles, can save us" (Ojeda Reyes and Estrade, Vol. IV, [1868] 2017, 92), constituted a threat to both the Caribbean and the incipient Latin American republics. See, for instance, "Cubanos, erudimini" (Ojeda Reyes and Estrade, Vol. X, [1869] 2017, 131–33); "Miseria entre riquezas" (Ojeda Reyes and Estrade, Vol. X, [1874] 2017, 202–07); various personal letters, including several directed to his friend Julio Henna (reproduced in Rama); as well as his literary piece "Apariciones (Al emigrado)" (Ojeda Reyes and Estrade, Vol. III, 2017, 271–75), in which the author depicts the United States as Mephistopheles.

11. Indeed, in "La independencia de las Antillas," Rama asserts that "except for the Dominican Máximo Gómez, we believe . . . that no non-Cuban person did more [than Betances] for the freedom of José Martí's homeland" (1980, 135).

12. In addition to his abolitionist efforts, Betances devoted his work as a physician and surgeon, while living in Puerto Rico, to the impoverished and destitute populations (see Cintrón Ríos 2020).

13. Considering this lifelong trajectory, which left him in personal ruin, and the fact that his work as a revolutionary conspirator entailed a constant effort to raise funds to finance the Cuban Revolution, it is nearly impossible to understand Amado Martínez Lebrón's appraisal of Betances as, primarily, "an entrepreneur, a capitalist businessman, and a . . . bourgeois" (2015). Although I agree with his impassioned call to avoid hagiographic approaches, the fact that Betances's stance on economic matters was, indeed, capitalist, and that one might disagree with this position, must not cancel the evidence of a lifetime. Estrade's assessment in "El heraldo" of Betances's tactical flexibility is relevant here: "But his intransigence concerning the goal, was not so when it came to the means. . . . Betances is also the archetype of secret diplomacy, a man in the shadows, a cunning and creative conspirator who, upon facing any obstacle, immediately finds a way to overcome it. To turn him [exclusively] into the man of an idea is to mutilate him a hundred times" (2000, 8).

14. In "Revolutionary Visions?" Chaar-Pérez discusses the foundational importance for Betances of the 1848 French republican revolution (2020, 45).

15. See the Introduction for more on these two Puerto Rican political parties.

16. Translating the Puerto Rican concept "bregar" is particularly challenging. It is defined by Díaz Quiñones in multiple ways. In the context of this book, consider the following definitions: "another order of knowledge, a diffuse method without pomp to navigate daily life, where everything is extremely precarious, shifting or violent" (2000, 20); "putting in relation that which until then had seemed distant or antagonistic. It is a position from which one acts to dissolve without violence conflicts that are very polarized" (22); and, "the secret agent, or the double agent, of the Puerto Rican political culture" (26).

17. As far as I am aware, Bonilla's book *Non-Sovereign Futures* (2015), which studies the francophone Caribbean as deeply connected to the Puerto Rican experience, is the most thorough and careful exploration of this conundrum. As she explains in the introduction to her work:

> I argue that in both the independent and non-independent Caribbean, there is a common feeling of disenchantment with the modernist project of postcolonial sovereignty, even while there is also a lingering attachment to its normative ideals. For, although it might seem as if the project of postcolonial sovereignty has led to a political dead end, many populations still find meaning and power in the right to nation and state. National independence does not seem to guarantee sovereignty, but it is unclear whether societies without it can achieve what sovereignty—as a native category—has come to represent. Moreover, contemporary populations often lack the conceptual language with which to describe plausible (or even utopian) alternatives to the modernist projects of decolonization and national sovereignty. This is why Puerto Ricans routinely vote against political independence even while asserting a wish to see their island "free and sovereign" and why the Guadeloupean protagonists of this book repeatedly declare that they want sovereignty "even if it is under the French flag." (195–201)

On the enduring legacy of marronage, understood as a philosophical and political stance in contemporary Puerto Rico, see Lebrón Ortiz (2020).

18. See Laurent Dubois (2012, 97–104) for a discussion of the details concerning the "indemnity" agreement. See also Marlene Daut's recent column "When France Extorted Haiti" (2020), which forcefully makes the case for reparations to Haiti using this "colonial theft" as a primary argument. In one of his *Correo de las Antillas* pieces, Betances acknowledges Haiti's predicament, but makes no adverse comments concerning the French empire. Meanwhile, in the context of recommending that Cuba not emulate Haiti in that specific respect, he describes the extortion of Haiti as a *debt* with France (Ojeda Reyes and Estrade, Vol. X, [1875] 2017, 263). The topic receives the same matter-of-fact treatment in the "Ensayo sobre Alejandro Pétion" (Ojeda Reyes and Estrade, Vol. IV, 2017, 236). For a compelling discussion of the ways in which the nation-state also failed to protect Haiti from US imperialism, especially through the latter's occupation of the former in the twentieth century (1915–1934), see Dalleo (2020).

19. As Sir Hilary Beckles chillingly reminds us: "These ravished islands have done their best to clean up the colonial mess. They have spent beyond their means in the process of seeking to convert colonials into citizens. Left largely illiterate and riddled with ill health by colonialism they have built schools and hospitals that must be maintained. Social expenditure in the interest of building democracy exceeds financial income. This is the price they paid for participation in modernity. Now their public debt strangles their quest for economic growth. It is a debt that should be written off as an investment in democracy" (2017). I return to the urgent question of reparations, and of Puerto Rico's involvement, in both chapter 4 and the Coda.

20. Before the decades of archipelagic fleeing from and revolutionary organizing against the Spanish empire that characterize Betances's political efforts, he was engaged in clandestine archipelagic travel within Freemasonry. According to Arroyo, the full extent of Puerto Rico's archipelagic geography was used as the scenario for the secret and as the secret scenario: "The membership of "Unión Germana #8" consisted mostly of Dominican and French exiles coming from Hispaniola, with a mix of local Creoles. Symbolically, the lodge opened under the jurisdiction of the Great Orient of Santo Domingo (*Gran Oriente de Santo Domingo*). Their meetings were held in city houses or in small cays around the bays of Añasco and Mayagüez such as Caja de Muerto (Coffin Island) and Isla de Mona (Monkey Island). Their sessions were held at night and sometimes at great risk, since to reach these bays, a boat had to traverse the Mona Strait, one of the deepest and most dangerous sea basins in the Atlantic." (2013, 29)

21. However, and quite revealingly, Betances barely mentions the French colonies in the Caribbean. Perhaps doing so would blemish the French Republic that he held in such high esteem and for which he writes most of his journalistic work, making it unpublishable?

22. Beyond his writings, Betances's upbringing and early adulthood in Puerto Rico's west coast is relevant insofar as the latter was particularly crisscrossed by racial mixing and migration patterns from the DR and Saint Domingue/Haiti. For details, see Arroyo (2013, 73–74).

23. For more on Betances's Masonic life and its fundamental role in nineteenth-century Antillean revolutionary praxis and the articulation of the AC, see Dávila del Valle (1989) and Arroyo (2013). Significantly, the latter's transnational, comparative study concludes that, "more than being associated with forms of social power and middle-class status, Masonic affiliations for white Creoles and black Caribbean men were strongly linked with the legacies of slavery and colonialism. At the same time, they were connected to migration, memory, family, citizenship, spirituality, and politics" (4).

24. In an even broader context, Betances's centering of Haiti is even more significant, since, after the success of the Haitian Revolution, the imperial-*criollo*-racist "fear of Blacks" was intensely weaponized to demobilize revolutionary potentials in the wider Caribbean. See, for instance, Domínguez (2018) and Gaztambide Géigel (2010).

25. Due to Betances's ideological and methodological framework describing the Haitian Revolution, he certainly could not see the latter's even more radical implication *beyond* the nation-state and against White supremacy and anti-Black racism: "Scholars such as Sibylle Fischer and Jossianna Arroyo have shown how these movements [nineteenth-century liberation struggles] conceived race, internationalism, and regional identity in response to the lessons of the Haitian Revolution and the networks created by that event. Because, as Fischer puts it, 'the political unconscious of radical antislavery was not the nation-state,' recognizing the Revolution's legacy as a transnational project challenging white supremacy and anti-Black racism was incompatible with independence aimed strictly at the creation of liberal nations in the European mold." (Dalleo 2020, 61)

26. Consult Ramos Mattei (1987) for more details on this.

27. Although my interest here is to explore Betances's racial consciousness as part of his archipelagic imagination and politics, the nineteenth-century Puerto Rican context that ideologically informed the complexity of his understanding of himself and his family in terms of race should be kept in mind. To my knowledge, the most compelling and thorough discussion of this matter is María del Carmen Baerga's (1995). While elucidating Puerto Rico's nineteenth-century racialization dynamics, Baerga discusses Betances's "racial identity" through an analysis of primary sources concerning a process Betances's father pursued to ascertain the family's "whiteness", which was thrown into doubt as one of Betances's sisters was getting married. As Baerga explains, in nineteenth-century Puerto Rico, "the racial thought in vogue . . . did not reflect the influence of contemporary racialist theories from Europe—those that gave preference to biological differences (phenotypic and genotypic) in the process of assigning racial identities. Racial discourse among Puerto Ricans in the nineteenth century more closely resembled the ideas of the seventeenth and eighteenth centuries in colonial Hispanic America. Such concepts as quality, birth, and purity of blood were used to define a person's racial condition. This process of classifying bodies involved factors such as genealogy, the legitimacy or illegitimacy of a person's birth, the appropriate marital ties, the sexual behavior of men and women, and the private and public conduct of individuals and families" (110).

28. For thorough discussions of the Puerto Rican *criollos' reformista* brand of abolitionism, and its inherent class-based and racial limitations, see Domínguez (2018) and Flores Collazo (2011).

29. Concerning class hierarchies, Arroyo reminds us, however, that "as early as 1870, Betances understood that including black and mulattoes in the Cuban and Puerto Rican independence movements would challenge the established social hierarchies of race and class that colonial slavery had introduced in these societies" (2013, 93–94).

30. In "Revolutionary Visions?" while discussing Betances's piece on Pétion, Chaar-Pérez rightfully points out that "Betances' negative allusion to the 'passion of the people' signals that he ultimately believed in the power of a few 'great men' in solving the 'drama [of] liberty,' which for him entailed a confrontation not only with imperial violence but also with the excesses of the masses" (2020, 52).

31. This bombardment is not only metaphorical. As we saw in the Introduction, one of the main characteristics of the United States' use of its colonial territory has been the unilateral occupation of land for the establishment of multiple military bases throughout the Puerto Rican archipelago.

32. Indeed, in an 1889 letter to Lola Rodríguez de Tió, Betances writes: "but I say no more, my friend; as the pen overflows when I think of all the harm—which only I know—that the reformers, autonomists, and assimilationists have done to the country" (Ojeda Reyes and Estrade, Vol. IV, 2017, 248). The *Carta Autonómica* promulgated a limited form of self-government for Puerto Rico, composed of an "Insular Parliament" with two chambers and a Governor General who would have maximum authority in representation of the Spanish monarchy. For a thorough discussion of the process that led to the *Carta Autonómica* from the perspective of imperial politics in Spain, see Agustín Sánchez (2002).

33. Also consider Ángel López-Santiago's (2018) impassioned call for a form of AC to confront ecological catastrophe in the Caribbean, as well as *Small Axe*'s 2020 special section, *Con-Federating the Archipelago* (edited by Martínez-San Miguel and González Seligmann).

Chapter Two

Embodying Oceanic Sovereignties
Luisa Capetillo and the Tribuna on the Street

> I had a wonderful time, pleasant and enjoyable days, with my comrades of labor, struggles and ideals. Together, we strolled, ate, went to political sessions, and, like brothers, spent delightful and pleasurable hours.
>
> —Luisa Capetillo in Ramos, *Amor y anarquía* ([1909] 1992), 78

This chapter[1] discusses the lesser-known life and work of Puerto Rican anarchist, feminist, syndicalist, writer, journalist, and political performer Luisa Capetillo. Arguing for Capetillo's radically subversive and revolutionary ideological stances—notwithstanding some significant contradictions— toward our multiple sovereignties, this chapter emphasizes Capetillo's work as emerging from the sea: a constant relation between word and act, "rocks and sands," as she would have it. Such coastal situatedness enabled both her multiple kinds of performative writing, discussed in the first half of this chapter, and her profuse array of performative, bodily interventions as political work, with which I engage in the remainder of the chapter. Both in their distinctions and similarities with Betances and Albizu Campos, as well as in anticipation of the activist and artistic instances discussed in part II, I thus understand Capetillo's political bodily gestures and her prolific writing as essential sources of Puerto Rico's affective archive of Caribbean relations, resistance, and forms of lived, bodily sovereignty.

In her most intimate writing, which might not appear as important, enduring, or revolutionary as her more familiar position essays and didactic—even propagandist—dramas, Luisa Capetillo is *at sea*. Her most vital certainties are born, paradoxically, out of the liminal, littoral condition of her archipelagic geo- and biography. In passages where the writing subject explicitly situates her thought and practice on the coast and at sea, Capetillo allows herself a bodily, sensorial *destello* (gleam)—a word she likes to use—she scarcely does otherwise; indeed, she channels an oceanic sensibility in which poetry supersedes ideological exigencies. This pulsating sensibility ignites her entire oeuvre, characterized by multiple levels of liminality, connecting her thought with its constant performative embodiment.

As much as it did the revolutionary Betances fleeing from the Boquerón coast, it is the sea around her Puerto Rican islands that, in many ways, gave birth to Luisa Capetillo:

> I hear a murmur of a thousand voices penetrating through the window . . . I listen . . . It's the sea! The waves in their strange and eternal colloquiums, full of tenderness, sometimes, other times, of imprecations, as though they wanted to overflow their recipient because it is too small for their extension[.] Still other times, [the sea] moans as if it wanted to attract to its bosom something that would console it, lulling it sweetly, or gently moving its agitated waters with a boat's oars before, suddenly, becoming enraged and returning to its beaches, in a thousand pieces, the boats confided to its arms, wrapping in its white foam the remains that balance themselves on its irritated surface, *as if to caress that which it has destroyed. While I write in these sheets, I can listen to it still, and it seems to me as though I am seeing its waves crashing against each other to arrive at the shore and kiss the sand.* How beautiful and imposing is the sea! (Ramos [1911] 1992, 178, emphasis added)

Another passage, which comments on the sea's interactions with rocks and sand, reveals more explicitly Capetillo's sustained attention to the sea's contrasts as synecdoche of nature, her "sovereign life":

> Waves come and go without overflowing the ocean. . . . Waves bathe and knock the beaches' sand and rocks all the same. However, rocks fall from their base and roll on the sand, whereas the latter is always on the same spot; it does not fall. [Sand] plays with the waves, while rocks resist them, rebel against being moved according to the waters' rhythm, to their swaying. They are rocks, which is why they fall. They symbolize stubbornness, roughness. . . . On the sand, feet submerge as they do on water. Sand symbolizes softness, tolerance. It is the eternal enigma of nature . . . it seduces and dominates. It sings and cries. Moans and smiles. *The eternal contrast of sovereign life.* A contrast that is harmony, light and shadow, water and fire, love and oblivion, heaven and hell. . . . It is blue firefly and terrifying monster. Brilliant and sinister. . . . It is hyena and lamb; it kisses and bites and roars and sings. (Ramos [1911] 1992, 175–76, emphasis added)

Subsequently, Capetillo's oceanic reflections on the "sovereign life" of land, so to speak, focus on a specific life form. A coastal, "deformed" tree seems to stand in for her own condition, as much as that of all those crushed by power, who, nevertheless, continue to "rise" in search of the sun's radiance:

> It was a misshapen tree that vegetated on the shore; from the roots to the middle of the trunk it was bent, and from there onto the crown it wanted to be straight, to receive the solar caresses directly, rising despite its deformity.[2] Surely that tree suffered, as it could not show off its elegance or corpulence with natural freedom. . . . Every once in a while, a small bird landed on it, but everyone lamented the misery of the poor tree that offered no shade or fresh breeze, as it barely had branches or leaves. . . . what a desolate, ruinous condition on that splendid spot in front of the sea and the line of cars where travelers could contemplate the poor tree's solitude and orphanhood, deformed by human harshness. ([1913] 1992, 177)

The coastal *situatedness*, with its "contrast that is harmony," within which Capetillo invites us to approach her life's work, reverberates fractally, as this chapter will explore. In 1882, less than twenty years before Betances's death, Luisa Capetillo was born[3] in the coastal town of Arecibo. Her mother was a resolutely transgressive woman originally from France (Valle Ferrer 1990, 39), who had arrived as a "governess" in Puerto Rico, lived with Capetillo's father without marrying him, and pursued her own education and that of Capetillo through her avid reading and her participation at daily intellectual meetings (*tertulias*), even when she lost her work as a governess and had to become a laundress and presser for rich, *criollo* families in Arecibo (Valle Ferrer 1990, 43–45). Meanwhile, Capetillo's father was an equally unusual, politically left-leaning man originally from northern Spain, who had working experience in entertainment, but was forced to become in Puerto Rico a temporary worker in various trades, such as at ports, in construction, and in agriculture (Valle Ferrer 1990, 44). Capetillo nurtured her life force with self-taught anarchism, socialism, feminism, and *espiritismo* (spiritualism), within a context of enormous transformations in Puerto Rico after its imperial change of hands from Spain to the United States in 1898.[4] Over the course of her extraordinary life, cut short in 1922 by tuberculosis—and, surely, by every social-bacterial infection she struggled against—Capetillo openly embraced autonomous study *and* collective organization as revolutionary practices, which she understood as transcendent of the nation-state, of races, genders, and classes. Seeking to bridge the divides opened and deepened by all institutions—educational, religious, political, cultural—Capetillo systematically claimed the absolute necessity of word *and* act, of reading *and* organizing, of "private" writing *and* public expression through the performative appropriation of public space, a tactical diversity echolocating with that of Betances's strategies (see chapter 1). Teresa Peña Jordán rightly honors such multiplicity when describing Capetillo as a "transversal thinker." Unquestionably, as has been recognized by every Capetillo scholar, her life's work and struggles as a reader at tobacco factories—a performative work to which I will return below—as a sewing worker, anarchist, feminist, abolitionist, and *espiritista* (spiritualist) political organizer and agitator, and as a writer, journalist, dramatist, and performer, who partly sustained herself through the sale of her written work, distinguish Capetillo as exceptional in the context of Puerto Rico at the turn of the twentieth century.[5] Indeed, as Bird-Soto claims, Capetillo is "*the* public intellectual of her times" (2006, 182, emphasis added).

EMBODIED WRITING

Capetillo's written expression of her liminal, littoral position is convincingly analyzed as *escritura menor* (minor writing)—in Deleuze and Guattari's sense—by Julio Ramos in his 1992 influential introduction to the collection *Amor y anarquía*. According to Ramos, Capetillo's minor writing is characterized by the following attributes: (1) it claims "an alternate authority in experience and intuition" (18); (2) it gives "priority to a more immediate, spontaneous, experientially founded knowledge (*saber*)" (18); (3) it is fragmentary, conjunctural, hybrid, and open-ended (36); (4) its focus is on everyday life conflicts (36, 39); (5) it seamlessly includes others' writing, so much so that the "notion of the book as individual property" does not quite operate in her case (40); (6) its marginality is reflected in its syntax, diction, and orthography, which are deeply informed by orality (43); (7) it "radical[ly] reject[s] the literary institution's established norms" (49); and (8) it refuses "a monological concept of identity, a 'definition' of the 'essences' of Puerto Rican nationality, which authorized the positions taken by the Puerto Rican literary establishment" of her times (49).

Moreover, Capetillo's writing is always *performative* in at least two senses. First, emerging from her littoral situatedness, her writing attempts to move, like the sea, both rocks and sand through multiple public *embodiments*: "writing essays and propaganda for the union newspapers, writing correspondence to both her supporters and attackers, writing due to a creative spirit that almost compels her to do so, writing plays for the union halls and mutualist clubs, and so on" (Walker 2009, xvi). Second, the "experientially-founded *saber*" from where her writing gathers its legitimation is understood as an actively performed embodiment in and of itself:

> In most of her work, Luisa Capetillo projects her views into the future by addressing and instructing subsequent generations about an alternative lifestyle.

Most of her work is of a testimonial nature: not only her letters and diaries, but also her articles and books of essays or eclectic content, all *display herself and her life as a spectacle* from which to learn, either as an example to emulate or to learn from her mistakes. (Romero-Cesareo 1994, 775, emphasis added)

In a word, Capetillo's writing is to be actively performed rather than quietly read. Convinced that life cannot remain what exploitative human regimes make of it, Capetillo seeks to show us in her writing life's embodied artifice, so that we can bodily transform it toward freedom.

Of the essence in Capetillo's minor writing is her acute feminist awareness of women's exclusion from the institutions associated with reading and writing: widespread access to formal education and the resources and material conditions to foster a consistent practice of reading, writing, and nurturing a community of interlocutors.[6] While Betances's writings and proclamations, as we saw in the previous chapter, and Albizu Campos's, as we will see in chapter 3, are unquestionably performative, they are also matter of fact. Nothing prevents them from the certainty of their voice, that is, of being a subject with something to say, to denounce, to demand, and from commanding it freely.

In contrast, as an early twentieth-century woman confronting patriarchal social and political life, Capetillo is compelled, in a resolutely sovereign act, to *claim the possibility* of a voice, and to feel—and thus, register in writing—the need to legitimate its power and possibilities, a phenomenon aptly described by Romero-Cesareo as "a celebration of self-legitimization" (1994, 778).[7] Thus, Capetillo takes the revolutionary stance that her voice becomes embodied, *performed*, and, as such, must be heard on the basis of what *she has* ("a perfect comprehension of what I say, with a profound intuition that orients me" Ramos [1916] 1992, 74]), rather than what society prevents her from having ("I have not been able to study anything according to precepts from schools, academic lectures or higher education classrooms, since I was never sent to those" [74]). Her performative voice-body is publicly claimed even more explicitly when she presents herself as propagandist and journalist *before* she does as writer, and expounds on the fact that she stands only for her own self:

> Today I have presented myself as propagandist, journalist, and writer, with no more authorization than my own vocation and initiative, with no more recommendation than my own, nor any other assistance than my own effort, caring little about critiques from those who have been enrolled and able to complete their general studies to present their written observations, protests, or literary narrations. (Ramos [1916] 1992, 74)

A VOICE CLAIMED FOR A RADICALLY UNCONTAINABLE "UTOPIA"

As Rivera Berruz rightfully argues, Capetillo's public assertion of her own voice is ciphered on the recognition of her class and gender comrades and peers, rather than that of "a nation or an imperial power" (2018, 20).[8] As a result of her radical refusal to be contained within any institutional-patriarchal organization—including, of course, political parties and religious organizations—and because she clearly understood that her experience and embodiment *as a woman* was socially assumed a demerit and, thus, she ought to command a voice *of her own*, Capetillo stood for an openly embraced "utopia" (Ramos [1911] 1992, 73–74) with which both Betances's form of nineteenth-century anticolonialism and the eventual Puerto Rican nationalism of the *Partido Nacionalista* under Albizu Campos's leadership were irreconcilable. Thus, not only was Capetillo extraordinary because of her sustained, radical becoming as a political force against all patriarchal and capitalist odds, but also because she stood in open opposition to the primary "heavyweights" of the Puerto Rican left. Indeed, Capetillo was especially suspicious of the self-styled, egotistical "fathers of the homeland" (*padres de la patria*) of her time:

> All of those who judge an idea put in practice as utopian are obstacles, and obstacles must be pushed aside. They hinder great initiatives, good works. Despite that, they call themselves patriots and fathers of the homeland. What concept of homeland do they have? A selfish concept that starts with them and ends with them. They [think they] are everything. (Ramos [1911] 1992, 73–74)

Moreover, unlike both Betances and Albizu Campos, she presciently argued that "self-government" for Puerto Rico was insufficient, as it would not ensure authentic liberation if it did not come with a radical transformation of the Puerto Rican majority's real misery:

> but why is everyone not in agreement with self-government (*gobierno propio*)? Because they distrust their own brothers. And why do they distrust them . . . Because they have never fulfilled what they have offered, as it harms, in their eyes, capitalist interests, and because almost every principal supporter and leader of the 'Union' [in reference to the *Partido Unión*] is selfish, exploitative, and aristocratic. And since we do not accept privileges or distinctions, we represent a nuisance. They would like workers to continue taking off their hats and humiliating themselves in front of their masters. There is no slavery, but there are masters and slaves, and this is what we must abolish: the slavery of the miserable and paltry wage, which is unworthy of the free man who knows his rights.

Why don't they, supporters of freedom, destroy individual slavery and misery before demanding full freedom? (Ramos, [1907] 1992, 95)

Unlike Betances's gender, class, and racial status, which allowed him access to an institutional nineteenth-century education that brought him to France and enabled him to travel, support, and organize Antillean revolutionary processes (see chapter 1), and in contrast with Albizu Campos's gender status, which, through the *logia*'s scholarship and the legal recognition of his white, *criollo* father, allowed him access to Harvard Law School despite his racialized and impoverished upbringing (see chapter 3), Luisa Capetillo was born into falling social circumstances, and led a life of continuous and increasing material deprivations.[9] Thus, her capacity to overcome and bequeath us a written record of her political and personal aspirations outdoes all existing adjectives.

Capetillo's anarcho-feminist dream was the end of exploitation—that is, of class, race, and gender-based hierarchies.[10] For this, she openly embraces the need to connect Puerto Rico not only with the Caribbean, but also with the United States and all working peoples around the world. In her thought and action, what brought Puerto Ricans together was not so much their colonial subjugation, but their capitalist and patriarchal exploitation, and, as such, the majority of Puerto Ricans were, for her, part of a planetary common condition she describes as "wage (*salario*) slavery" (Ramos [1909] 1992, 76). Precisely because it is widely shared, "wage slavery" requires, according to Capetillo, "universal redemption" (77).

An early proponent of social constructivism, Capetillo envisioned freedom as that "of the planet" (Ramos [1911] 1992, 96), and her utopia was "nature" itself. Political struggles based on differences between humans, which were produced by human societies themselves, made no sense to her. In a letter to her daughter, Manuela Ledesma Capetillo, she explains: "liberate your mind from everything that might tarnish its natural simplicity . . . You must not forget that we are all susceptible to the environment in which we live, that if there is any difference between humans, in their character, manners, and figures, it is the result of their form of life, education, and customs" (97).

It stands to reason, then, that Capetillo would place education at the heart of all revolutionary struggles, trusting its capacity to make the oppressed conscious of the hierarchical structures of exploitation created by capitalist and patriarchal societies: "education was not just a descriptive endeavor, but rather a process by which people could un-learn the social norms that justified the exploitation of working people and working women" (Rivera Berruz 2018, 30). Indeed, Capetillo's defense of a radically open, accessible education (see Valle Ferrer's interview with Ramos, referenced above) contrasts dramatically with Albizu Campos's and the *Partido Nacionalista*'s later position on this topic (see chapter 3).

What is more, Capetillo openly defended the practices of reading and writing, as well as intellectual work, as *forms of production*, an especially revolutionary argument for her times. If not "products" per se, Capetillo argues, then the works of the intellect and imagination should be considered—in an especially poetic formulation—"gleaming sparkles, irradiations of light":

> You have told me that writers do not produce, that only those who work the land are producers. This is a mistaken concept of the phrase. . . . He who makes a house, makes something useful, but he does not create it, he builds it. Nature creates and produces; man uses its products. . . . A tree gives fruits, it is the natural product of the tree, whether it is cultivated or not; a man or a woman writes a book, and it is the product of their intelligence. You do not want to call it "product"? Well, we'll call it gleaming sparkles, irradiations of light. (Ramos [1916] 1992, 123–24)

And yet, alongside her deep commitment to the word was the act. Luisa Capetillo forged, too, an ephemeral nonwritten record of public performative politics that can be gleaned from the limited photographic documentation and, indirectly, through an examination of journalistic coverage at the time. To this, one of my central concerns and an insufficiently considered matter in the existing Capetillo scholarship, I now turn.

WOMEN'S BODIES-AS-PERFORMANCE AND PERFORMANCE-AS-STRUGGLE

To judge from the pro-Spanish *Boletín Mercantil de Puerto Rico*'s recurrent portrayal of Capetillo as a threatening force in her occupation of public space, one would be hard pressed in the contemporary moment—while we still struggle in Puerto Rico for women's and femme-identified bodies to be on the streets without fear of death—not to feel a deep bond of love and resistance with the unassailable revolutionary from Arecibo.[11] Inasmuch as the newspaper covered her "public scandals" on various dates in 1911 (April 13, April 19, August 9, and November 20), the *Boletín* seems to follow Capetillo around so as to record and condemn her transgressions. Especially significant is the column on Capetillo's performative intervention in De la Luna Street in Old San Juan on April 12, 1911.

The following morning, the *Boletín* chose to publish as its main piece a column under the header: "The culottes in our streets. Last night Luisa Capetillo made her first outing with the rare piece of clothing. De la Luna Street was a

battlefield. Police intervention. Public protests. AUTHORIZED OPINIONS."
The unnamed male writer opens his patriarchal "authorized opinion" on Capetillo's "queer" dress by announcing: "Last night was the dislocation. As the *Boletín Mercantil* had announced in its evening edition, the well-known agitator, Luisa Capetillo, wearing the now sadly famous culottes in this city's streets, was a sight to behold." In her taking the street, at night, with "non-feminine" clothing, Capetillo provokes an instant "dislocation." Things are ripped apart. A portal is opened. Capetillo's body, assumed as a sovereign, feminist scenario, flees from its prescribed position toward the crafting of its own figuration.

Inspired by scholar and artist Lauren Baccus's argument concerning the subversive use of textiles, clothing, and masquerade in the Anglophone and Francophone Caribbean contexts (see "A Pattern of Resistance," 2020), Capetillo's choice of dress should be understood within a continuum of Caribbean feminist forms of clothed resistance. With each one of Capetillo's performative public political transgressions, by virtue of an apparently inconsequential and ephemeral "change of dress," Puerto Rican women's lives are deeply, submarinely transfigured. I thus understand Capetillo's political bodily gestures, as well as her profuse writing, as essential sources of Puerto Rico's affective archive of resistance; Caribbean connections; and forms of lived, bodily sovereignty.

"Arrogant, audacious, without restraints," continues the *Boletín*'s journalist, Capetillo stepped out on the street having completed a "fregolistic transformation." Capetillo's resolute command of her own body in public space is thus immediately pathologized: her transformation can only be understood as a paranoid, Fregoli delusion.[12] Such rhetorical trashing, however, reveals a fundamental clue, which Capetillo clearly understood: different "disguises" can produce different people. Theatrical and performative gestures, bodily channeled through clothing, can become a political weapon, and, however ephemeral, can reverberate well into the future.

The journalist proceeds to characterize Capetillo's performative public gesture as "Troy." Those the column first describes as "curious onlookers" started following her in De la Luna Street, the group growing as Capetillo kept on walking and chastising them, to the point where even the hostile narrator portrays them as an "army of young men who did not let her breathe." Turned violent stalkers, the "army's" curiosity, the columnist continues, was "feline," becoming "unbearable." "Informal" patriarchy was about to extract from Capetillo's body the price of her freedom, once again. And it was then that, as with any public transgression in the colonial repressive model that survives to this day in Puerto Rico, "the police intervened": "The batons were brandished in the air and there was a general scattering, not before a rain of insults was directed at the police agents and at Luisa." The "formal," state-sanctioned patriarchy rubbed its hands together, satisfied with its apparent win.

And yet, let us remember, there was also another patriarchy attempting to cage Capetillo's memory: that of the written word for future imaginings of her subversive rebellion.[13] The columnist argues that "the public bears no responsibility" for police intervention having been rendered "necessary" that night. In fact, citing a violent attack on a woman wearing "men's" clothing in Madrid, the "army," he continues, could have acted much worse. The Puerto Rican journalist finally goes on to establish his definitive "authorized opinion "It seems that the wretched culottes is irremissibly condemned. After the unappealable public verdict, only the authorities' intervention was missing." As if his call for open state repression of women's bodies was not clear enough, he goes on to describe the dressing choice as "indecorous and inadmissible" and, significantly, only good for "caricature" and "some actresses of the *género chico* and other analogous people."[14] The macho point is driven home in closing the piece by reminding "serious women" that they "do not need to talk about this," since "it shall be enough that they show their opposition with their silence and indifference."

But, oh, did Capetillo talk! At least as much as she worked on the written word, she worked on an acted, embodied "writing"—what the artist Teresa Hernández would call "scenic writing" (see chapter 5)[15]—inscribing her political and feminist struggle through her body-as-project and potentiality. Romero Cesareo captures this beautifully when she writes:

> She [Capetillo] had a strong sense of her body as a signifying body; whether it was through her clothing, her expressions and poses in photographs, or her demeanor as she rode a horse through the crowds, she carried a banner that spelled out her contestatory stance. Her visualization of herself as the heroine of a spectacle—a spectacle for herself and for others—enabled her to pursue her political projects and, rather than merely theorize about them, to live them. She tried to be living proof of the fact that certain things can be achieved without waiting for conditions to be ideal. (1994, 775)

Contrasting the conservative journalistic coverage with Capetillo's own writing, one can immediately notice the irreconcilable opposition between patriarchal understandings of women's bodies and clothing and those of Capetillo's. The guns of no street "armies," police, or press have been able to contain the reverberations of Capetillo's political ripples. Like the waves she was so mesmerized by, these continue to expand up to the present feminist struggles in Puerto Rico. Perhaps they do so in many ways invisibly, but, like her "deformed" coastal tree, they rise nonetheless in accordance with

Capetillo's understanding of "sovereign life" as ultimately harmonious in its contradictions.

THE PERFORMATIVE POLITICS OF AN ARCHIPELAGIC WORKING-CLASS

If we are to understand the relevance of Capetillo's press-covered public interventions more fully, we should explore, albeit briefly, some aspects of the performative politics that the archipelagic working-class she was part of engaged in. During the first decades of the twentieth century, and within a milieu of escalating workers' political organization and *tribuna* (stand or platform) oral aesthetics, Capetillo understood more than most the body's power beyond its status as capitalism's exploited labor force: "Ah! you, honest propagandists who, in spite of not studying in fancy schools, nor ambitioning titles or distinctions, know how to tell the truth with more loyalty than those who have lucrative professions and more means and comfort to illustrate the people!" (Ramos [1909] 1992, 78). Thus, she nurtured her political commitments as bodily interventions in myriad ways.

Capetillo's creative production as a dramatist and theater director is of note, especially as it was predicated on the collective, working-class, and women's needs for a transformative education that would enable political action, and, at the same time, for rest, joy, and pleasure. As Ana M. Echevarría convincingly argues, Capetillo's plays reveal a great "audience awareness" by using parody, and literal and metaphorical cross-dressing, as political weapons:

> Critics like Julio Ramos and Ivette Romero have looked at Capetillo's literal cross-dressing as a metaphor to read her works, but little attention has been paid to the ways in which levels of cross-dressing were potentially performed in the staging of Capetillo's plays in working-class theaters. These literal and metaphoric levels of cross-dressing allowed Capetillo to reach a wider audience than would have been normally granted her, and they can best be exposed by looking at Capetillo's dramas not only as dramatic texts to be read but also as plays intended to be performed in front of a very specific audience. (2000, 27)

Questioning the habitual association of working-class theater with "backward" or "traditional" characteristics, Rayza Vidal Rodríguez (2016), on her part, insists on the "modern" quality of Capetillo's dramaturgy. Capetillo herself was very much invested in presenting her thought and practice—as well as that of anarchism and feminism—as "modern." Doing so also entailed mobilizing recognizable, "traditional" registers against themselves, as Lara Walker explains concerning melodrama:

> Capetillo sets up a melodrama with all the usual conventions, only to turn it on its head, making it appear as if it has finally turned right-side up. She subverts cultural, societal traditions and conventions of arranged marriages of convenience to create a new social harmony and sense of poetic justice. . . . Capetillo's subversion, always based on the collectivity of the working class, challenges the gender status quo within her class community while at the same time [confronting] that status quo in the dominant classes as well. Capetillo offers an alternate reality to her audience, a different mode of empowerment and happiness only found through the freedom from gender and class oppression. (2009, xxxi–xxxii)

Other instances of Capetillo's performative politics are her acute observations of the human body at work;[16] her job as reader at tobacco factories; and her archipelagic traveling, from Arecibo to Vieques, from Caguas to San Germán, from San Juan to Tampa, from New York to Havana, as political organizer, agitator, and propagandist in mobile *tribunas*. These daily experiences must have enabled Capetillo to study quite intimately the body's political power, as well as its collectivizing impulse. Indeed, on April 15, 1922, the newspaper *Unión Obrera* described her as

> That (*Aquella*) red spartan, when she left the city for the countryside, spent her days reading newspapers and books to peasants and giving speeches wherever she had the opportunity to do so . . . she spoke at the *tribuna* and led peasant strikes and walked long distances, at the head of manifestations, through roads and hills . . . She always had something to say and sustained herself through the sale of books and pamphlets, and newspapers and magazines. (quoted in Vidal Rodríguez 2016, 36–37)

And it should be remembered that the political manifestations mentioned by *Unión Obrera* were themselves profusely *theatrical*:

> In their manifestations, popular groups occupied the public space from which they had been historically excluded in a physical and *carnivalesque* manner. Pictures from working-class rallies and parades reveal the festive, rebellious character of groups of women, men, and children, who, with emblems and music—symbols and discourses—occupied public squares and main streets in towns and cities. (Ramos 1992, 33, emphasis added)[17]

Of all the performative "trainings" in Capetillo's revolutionary political life, I wish to offer a more sustained comment on that of reader at tobacco factories, for which a brief contextual word is of the essence. Drastic changes in the mode of production, from a mainly agrarian economy to an increasingly industrial one requiring a much larger labor force, were pushed through in Puerto Rico, in the interest of the US empire, during the first few decades of the twentieth century.[18] This process, which was accelerated by the 1917 passing of the Jones Act imposing US citizenship on Puerto Ricans, led to the integration of thousands of Puerto Rican women—who still retained all the responsibilities of the domestic sphere—into the labor force outside of their homes, particularly in the manual industries of hat-making, sewing, and needlework, but also as professional teachers and nurses.

The tobacco industry was, however, the site where the participation of women as tobacco strippers (*despalilladoras*) rose more quickly (Azize 1987, 20; Acosta-Belén 1986, 12–17).[19] As Suárez Findlay reports, "in 1910, women represented 27.8 percent of the tobacco industry's workforce, up from only 1.6 percent in 1899. By 1920, the percentage had increased to 52.9 percent" (1999, 144). However, while the tobacco industry was the "largest single employer of women, displacing domestic service, which had been women's primary source of employment in the late nineteenth century," the "tobacco-strippers' wages were even lower than those earned by their male counterparts; most women worked from ten to fourteen hours a day in the tobacco shops, earning forty cents or less for a full day's labor" (138). Thus, tobacco factories became the focus of a collective forging of class- and gender-based consciousness and struggle, which was central in the development, during the 1910s and 1920s, of "a multiracial, island wide labor movement and increased Afro-Puerto Rican political activism" (14). It comes as no surprise, then, that Capetillo, as much as Dominga de la Cruz, Genara Pagán, Juana Colón, and other early twentieth-century working-class women leaders, would find in the tobacco factories a fundamental site for collective self-education and political organizing. Indeed, as it pertains to the Puerto Rican feminist movement, rather than bourgeois suffragists, working-class women at tobacco factories were unquestionably the first protagonists in the early twentieth-century women's movement.[20]

Within this context, the figure of the reader at tobacco factories comes into sharper relief. First, one should note that the phenomenon itself was *archipelagic*, as Ramos's explanation reveals:[21]

> According to Fernando Ortiz . . . the institution of reading at tobacco factories originated in the galleys of imprisoned cigar makers at the *Arsenal* in Havana, Cuba. Around [the] mid-1860s, and facing resistance from factory owners, the reading practice was established as a custom among cigar makers, who thus claimed access to written culture and became familiar with the nineteenth century's most advanced ideological tendencies. Surely because of the continuous migratory flux of artisans, and through contacts between them enabled by the

emergent working-class press circulating in the various tobacco districts in the Caribbean and the US, by the end of the [nineteenth] century reading at factories was considered one of the defining institutions of the tobacco artisanal world, not only in Cuba, but also in Puerto Rico, Tampa, Ybor City, New York, Durham, and other centers of cigar production. (1992, 19, 21)

Second, readers were employed and paid by tobacco workers themselves, further deepening their bonds of solidarity and their understanding of study as revolutionary practice. Factory owners, of course, continually manifested their opposition to the reading practice (Ramos 1992, 21, 25), and banned it on multiple occasions, since "at the cigar makers' tables, reading was a political act" (27).

Third, the pieces that were read at tobacco factories—"a movable, clandestine library" (Romero-Cesareo 1994, 779)—were, for the most part, radically subversive: "Through the mediation of the reading institution, *avant garde*, European, literature enters Puerto Rico, which contributed to the configuration of the libertarian discourse of anarchist tendency that characterized early twentieth century trade union movements" (Ramos 1992, 27).[22] Crucially, Romero-Cesareo adds that the work of international radical women was also heard of in Puerto Rico through the reading practice at tobacco factories:

> Union and/or socialist newspapers (*Social Future, Democracy, Labor Union*, among others), which were also read aloud in the factories, published passages about or by outstanding women in the socialist and feminist struggles: names like Madame Roland, Clara Zetkin, and Rosa Luxembourg as well as other women from around the world were frequently mentioned. (1994, 778)

Fourth, although there is no available audiovisual documentation of the tobacco readers' ephemeral performances, one can imagine their performative-political force by considering especially, in addition to the contents of what was read and the fact that the practice was banned repeatedly by factory owners, the *performative form* it took. Readers stood atop raised platforms (*tribunas* in themselves), and must have projected their voices, for hours, across a wide expanse of factory space, reaching hundreds of ears at work and overcoming the challenge of significant noise.

That Capetillo would be employed by her fellow working-class comrades to do reading work must have afforded her an extraordinary opportunity for autodidactic education, as well as a significant position of power for a woman at the time, since even among tobacco workers, "the illiteracy rate was very high: in 1899 it reached 40% of that illustrated sector of the working class" (Ramos 1992, 32).[23] Thus, as Ramos argues, "the role of reader—and, later, journalist—situated Capetillo in a privileged locus of enunciation, but, at the same time, in a conflictive one between the system of cultural transmission of the dominant class and the oral culture of her own class" (32).

Still, young Capetillo's reading work must have also taught her the essential importance of a fully embodied voice, capable of traveling long distances convincingly, without audio systems, to be heard and understood by hundreds of people. It must have also prepared her for a persuasive command of space and time through and by means of her *body*, as that was all she ever had. In a word, it must have trained her to become a political performer.

CAPETILLO'S TRANSG/DRESSING

As I have tried to show, the connecting tissue between the diverse forms of Capetillo's steadfast political, intellectual, and cultural commitments was her understanding of the power of women's bodies-as-performative and of performance-as-struggle. Indeed, when reading both the *Boletín Mercantil* and venues of the US press such as the *Madison Daily*, which describes Capetillo as "Porto Rico's [sic] Joan of Arc," and the *Richmond Palladium*, which records, in its July 1, 1912 edition, a similar event of public performance on New York's Fifth Avenue that caused a congestion of "thousands of people and scores of automobiles and other vehicles,"[24] it becomes even clearer than from Capetillo's own writing that the well-remembered 1915 scene of her wearing "men's" clothing in Havana, Cuba, and being arrested for it, was far from singular in the revolutionary's life.[25]

Her commitment to social transformation, revolutionary struggle, and anarchist general striking was intimately combined with a consciousness of embodied dress that few observers have stressed, precisely as it seems secondary, trivial or, perhaps, too "feminine" a concern for serious political organizing.[26] Indeed, although it functions as an orienting image for his rich analysis of Capetillo's writing, Ramos ultimately deemphasizes the matter of dress: "*Although we are not very concerned with Capetillo's clothes*, that picture—emblematic—[referring to the 1915 Havana photo] orients our reading of her work" (1992, 12, emphasis added). However, beyond her written work, which has been the resolute focus of Ramos's analysis and that of the overwhelming majority of Capetillo scholars, my previous commentary on the journalistic coverage of Capetillo's public transgressions shows that her incisive performance of dress—as part of the continuum of performative political interventions discussed above—not only constituted a brilliant political tactic to draw attention—even sensationalist attention—to women's and the workers' plight, but also established that the suit in capitalist-patriarchal-colonial society might very well make the woman. She not only opposed hegemonic

Figure 2.1. *Luisa, café sobre hilo.* Courtesy of Editora Educación Emergente (EEE), Art by Zuleira Soto-Román for EEE's 2022 Commemorative Series on the Centenary of Luisa Capetillo's Death, Mixed Media, 2021

cultural and gender norms through the written embodiment of her voice—as we have seen, she also systematically did so through her embodied, clothed political performances in command of public spaces. Once again, the coastal imagery that ignites Capetillo's work "gleams" through: she is at sea, with its waves, constantly moving between water and land, rock and sand, word and act.

Indeed, if we turn to her writing, we find Capetillo making strong arguments concerning dress and women's bodies.[27] Clearly, her public, performative interventions were understood on a continuum with her written work, where she articulated the practical and health-related reasons to abandon traditional women's clothing, in addition to keeping a vegetarian diet and engaging in exercise routines. Her arguments, especially those concerning hygiene, were also consistent with her overall insistence on becoming "modern" according to "civilizatory" principles of science and "progress":

> Clothing, therefore, according to Capetillo is a strategic vehicle of masking and unmasking. Hygiene and its importance to modern-ness and civilization becomes the message of the essay. In fact she goes so far as to say, "in order to call oneself or believe oneself to be civilized, one must be clean" and "civilization, modern progress rests upon hygiene" (76). (Walker 2009, xxvi)

But I think there is more to Capetillo's argument here. Not only could women have better hygiene (and thus, health), and be more comfortable in their daily lives, depending on the clothes they wore. By implication, they could also relate much more intimately to their bodies as powerful weapons or vulnerable prey. That is, a change of clothes meant that women could exert a newly found agency over their own bodies. As we have seen, Capetillo certainly chose to do so, and early twentieth-century patriarchy's onslaught against her choice—indexed in the press coverage and her own writing in frustration at being "misunderstood"—is evidence enough of its potency.

Still, the early twentieth-century revolutionary from Arecibo held complex positions concerning women's bodies, desires, and roles. This chapter's last section turns to a fuller discussion of Capetillo's dense feminism as part of Puerto Rico's claim to bodily sovereignties.

A COMPLEX FEMINISM

Capetillo was not exempt from the significant complexities—and, at times, open contradictions—of early twentieth-century feminisms in Puerto Rico, which cut across class, race, and geographical allegiances.[28] Although, as Ramos argues, on the whole "Capetillo's discourse remains in continuous alert against essences. Her feminism never seeks to fixate the definition and project of The Woman. Rather, it proposes sites of encounter, conjunctural alliances between women from heterogeneous backgrounds" (1992, 53), her position concerning women's desires and sexual practices was quite essentialist. While she stood against the traditional trappings of marriage-as-institution, Capetillo systematically reproduced and defended heteronormativity. She considered same-sex desire unnatural (*contra natura*) and, thus, pathological, delinquent (Ramos [1911] 1992, 196), and "aberrant" (200).[29] Repeatedly, and despite her conviction that women's desires must be recognized and satisfied as much as men's, Capetillo argued that sexual practices should have procreation—not pleasure—as their exclusive objective:

> If the act of procreation was not mistaken for a pleasure instead of a necessity regimented by science and study and the dominion of the will, surely there would not be so many crazy, idiotic, hunchbacked, criminal, and lustful people. But most people have children casually, as the result of bestial passions, or while drunk, and in such conditions, what [kind of] generation can be produced if its genesis is a sewer of vices, abuses, and contaminations? Can we educate a generation that does not understand the exercise of its duties nor the ends for which it is created? (Ramos [1911] 1992, 86)

And, later: "Who has contributed to the fact that the most beautiful, sublime act made by two people who love each other has become a mere pastime of pleasure, without reproducing the human species?" (200).[30]

Moreover, the definition of womanhood as predicated upon motherhood is unequivocal in Capetillo's thought. Despite her own tragic biography in this respect, and her revolutionary defense of women's right to abandon an unsatisfactory marriage or partner and seek love and companionship with someone else, Capetillo does not question women's "essential" role as mothers, since, for her, it is imperative that women keep and raise children as primary caregivers. Ironically for Capetillo, who otherwise was extremely class-conscious, she seems to establish this mandate without consideration of the very different lived experiences and material conditions of women: "If you have children, then the father has the obligation of sustaining and attending to them until they are of age. The woman in this case must claim her rights and not allow anyone to use any pretext to take her children away from her" (Ramos [1911] 1992, 193).[31] In agreement with the position held by the Puerto Rican bourgeois feminist movement of her time—and the eventual argument found in Albizu Campos's nationalism (see chapter 3)—Capetillo's take on motherhood also links with her defense of women's education, since the mother is understood as the household's "first teacher":

The woman mother is the first one to educate, direct, the future monarch as much as the future minister and president, the useful worker and the intelligent educator. She forms, models carefully, but in a way that is sometimes mistaken for lack of an education, the future legislators and revolutionaries. If women were conveniently illustrated, educated, and emancipated from age-old formulas . . . politics would be different. (Ramos [1911] 1992, 194)

On the other hand, and as we have seen throughout this chapter, Capetillo's thought and political practice were a resolute defense of women's agency over their lives, bodies, and desires. Indeed, years before this became a central claim of materialist feminism, Capetillo was defining women's condition as that of a "slave because of her sex": "In the modern age, she has been given rights and privileges, but she is still a slave. A slave, not in intelligence or work, but because of her sex" (Ramos [1911] 1992, 189). Capetillo's work, resulting from the evidence of the "Encyclopedia of Private Life, as a codex [written] with letters of fire" (111), clearly sprung from a constant, devoted attention to women's conditions, experiences, and daily lives, directed toward an understanding of the ways in which patriarchal and capitalist society—not nature—produced subjugation's most adverse effects on women.

That which is traditionally understood as "private" must be brought to light as central in public discussions about liberation, an argument of which Capetillo was Puerto Rico's earliest and most ardent advocate. The following passages, as moving as they are incisive, on women's existential condition as that of *waiting*, society-induced *blindness*, and "incomprehensible" emotional mutations, movingly illustrate Capetillo's attention to that which has been proverbially kept behind the heteronormative household's closed doors:

[H]ow long are the hours of waiting, interminable nights waiting, always waiting . . . Oh! how unpleasant it is to wait . . . hours . . . and more hours . . . Days and more days . . . Those who have experienced these sorrows know their fatal consequences if one does not have the experience, does not know how to fight, alone, without friends . . . (Ramos [1911] 1992, 191)

How can women educate themselves truly if they do not see or observe things such as they are? For her, everything is hidden behind a mysterious veil that does not allow her to see in a real way; at a dance, at the theater, at home, everything and everyone deceives her, without her realizing it. She is the eternal blind, led, as a rule, by the libertine, who continually tells her: "do what I say and not what I do," and the woman keeps believing this traitor without realizing she is being fooled. And deceived she lives on, and with such constant tricks she is educated and perverted, without her noticing it. (194)

What I pay attention to is the fact that he does not look for a woman in equal condition to his, no, he must search for the virgin; and thus, in this inequality, he dares to speak of goodness. And the contemporary woman, who has equal rights, must deprive herself as a result of a supposed honesty, of being the property of her boyfriend, only to then martyr and sicken herself, annihilating her organism, atrophying her brain, getting old prematurely, suffering thousands of illnesses, dizzy spells, she gets hysterical, she laughs and cries without knowing why, all of this because she does not know her rights nor that which would truly make her happy. (200)

The same moral exigencies should be exacted from men and women, Capetillo contends. If they are not, society cannot in justice continue to make women pay the steepest price:

Who is guilty? Is it fair that men can be unfaithful, without anyone thinking he is guilty, and even so, believing he has the right to demand faithfulness? . . . If this woman is not willing, because of her temperament . . . to age prematurely, accepting a morality she does not understand, because it is against natural laws, and a virtue only of name, he has no right to accuse her. Is this true morality? And they dare demand it from women! If this woman does not understand why her lover or husband always leaves her on her own, why society orders her to be with him . . . and if a woman in these conditions is flattered by another man's charm . . . and finds in him more love, and following natural impulses . . . she does not maintain a faithfulness that an imposed morality and a violent and criminal virtue established by the tyrants of women who oppress her since Antiquity [demands] . . . Has he bought the woman as his slave, in a way in which she cannot decide over her own self? (Ramos [1911] 1992, 192–93)

Likewise, Capetillo's passionate defense of women's right to "make mistakes" and their duty to "improve ourselves" is nothing short of revolutionary, in light of patriarchy's constant exigency of female perfection. Only if not allowed to err and make changes in her life accordingly, Capetillo argues, would women be engaging in adultery:

[T]he woman who breaks these formulas and lives with the one she truly wants to is not an adulterer. But in this stupid society, the woman who joins a man, because of the rules of present-day institutions, is obliged to live, to like, and to love her husband. And it will be said, why did she marry him then? But isn't the heart susceptible to mistakes? If she married him when she liked him, but then she doesn't for many reasons that I cannot say in this book, because it would be called scandalous and immoral. But there is the "Encyclopedia of Private Life," as a codex with letters of fire, severely accusing those who, without fear of tears or resistance from women, want to turn her into a vile recipient of vices, and abuse her apparent fragility, or, better said, lack of instruction. Well, the woman who abstains from her freedom . . . and resigns herself to live against her own will with her husband, that is adultery. (Ramos [1911] 1992, 111)

Capetillo was also radically feminist in her open call for women to foster a political consciousness of their shared condition and to act upon it. As we have seen in the continuum of her performative politics, her public and private embodiment of political thought, as well as her claim of a voice of her own, were never individual gestures. She made this abundantly clear in her writing:

> Women from all positions, defend yourselves, as the enemy is formidable, but do not fear him, since his cowardice is of the same size! Those who believe woman's freedom has special limitations are mistaken. . . . We, women, must make this system change; we must transform these customs. No woman should accept a man that is not in her conditions; if men [*ellos*] do not want to abandon those customs, they will have to agree to concede them to us women as well. (Ramos [1911] 1992, 195–99)[32]

As we have seen, despite its contradictions, Capetillo's socialist, anarchist, spiritualist, and abolitionist feminism is unquestionably the earliest form of simultaneous women's struggle in word *and* action in Puerto Rican history. It is an indispensable part of our affective archive of Caribbean relations toward a decolonial future founded on communitarian-artistic-bodily sovereignties. Her oceanic sensibility bequeathed us the "rocks" of her profuse written record in the most adverse of circumstances, as well as the "sand," the trace, of her ephemeral, conjunctural, and equally important, performative interventions in public spaces. Capetillo's waves continue to crash on our contemporary littorals, destroying exploitative regimes in their rage and, at the same time, caressing our renovated struggles to rise to the sun, like the "deformed tree" that "gleams." Although her exhortations to be wary of reductive forms of nationalism did not find a particularly welcoming atmosphere in the immediate years after her death, we should realize, too, that the empire's grip squeezed ever more violently in the 1930s, as the following chapter discusses. But even within Puerto Rico's resolutely nationalist anticolonialism, under the aegis of Pedro Albizu Campos, both Betances's and Capetillo's forms of written and acted resistance continue nurturing submarine relations. So, too, do the deep bonds of immaterial affection relating them with friends and comrades, as this chapter's epigraph evidences. Indeed, they all reach our twenty-first-century present, when our embodied, archipelagic, decolonial struggles continue unabated.

Subversive Walk

My dearest Luisa, do you remember that dream we had where we just kept on walking with our skirt-pants, *faldapantalones*, from Luna Street in San Juan onto the coastal corridor that ends at the citadel, *El Morro*? A mob of accosting, angry men, was following us, shouting, whistling, hurling objects, attempting to grab us. I was trapped by them but loved by you.

At a distance, I had heard you so many times talking about "sovereign life," the end of social classes, the urgency of a radical transformation for women and the poor. But, Luisa, I needed to be near you, magnet of other worlds. And so that day, when you stepped out on Luna Street with your unabashed transg/dressing, I ran to you, disconcertingly overcoming my shyness. Dreams do whatever they want with us.

I couldn't tell how I got my *faldapantalón*. But as I walked beside you, I fantasized it was you who sewed it for me. You also had that skill! You had so many of them, with all odds against you!

As we walked together, I felt your squeezing, determined hand. In silence, you sensed my panic, and made me brave although I wasn't. Despite the noises of violence, I clearly heard your demand for me to use the newfound comfort of my clothes to walk more firmly, to take bigger leaps, to stay upright and to own it. Yes, to own the body, and to choreograph it according to your example.

With you holding me I felt a bird becoming. In the dream we arrived at the edge, the men still in pursuit, and flew over the imperial walls as though it was only natural. We took to the sea. Our *faldapantalones* became fluttering wings. The men were left stranded, their incapacity for love written on their limbs' aggressive postures. For all their shipwreck stories, men have no clue about the dissolving liberation of the sands. But coastal intimacy was yours, oh, Luisa, since the beginning in Arecibo.

And then there were the fish we became. We fell from the sky into the water, barely making a splash. The corals were waiting. We now seemed ready for a life in the depths . . .

As I wake, I drink sugar- and milkless coffee, and put on very short shorts to walk out with you, beloved Luisa, into the tropical heat.

NOTES

1. A fragment of this chapter, translated into Spanish by Eleonora Cróquer Pedrón with the title "Encarnando soberanías oceánicas: Luisa Capetillo y la tribuna en la calle," was included in the 2021 revised edition of *Amor y anarquía: Escritos de Luisa Capetillo* (see the following note for details on this new edition).

2. Capetillo's sensibility toward that which defies traditional forms is movingly registered elsewhere, too: "While reading and writing, on the paper I saw a brilliant little spot that gleamed, which made me stop the pen. I observed it. It was a small wrinkle, and I told myself: that which is misshapen, gleams. . . . and that stopped me, and made me think a lot, and analyze even more. Sometimes, the indescribable submerges in nothingness" ([1911] 1992, 175). Unless otherwise noted, Luisa Capetillo's quotes throughout this chapter are from texts collected in the 1992 edition of *Amor y anarquía: Los escritos de Luisa Capetillo* (edited by Julio Ramos). A revised edition of this book, which includes a new prologue by Ramos and a collection of critical essays on Capetillo's life and works, was published in 2021 by Editora Educación Emergente. In his new Prologue, Ramos anticipates reappraisals of Capetillo that are even closer to my arguments in this chapter:

> [Capetillo's] challenge to the labor/moral regime articulates a singular ethics that displaces and repositions the (exploited) laboring body in the display of an "art of existence" manifested in her practices, her stylization of life, and her critical reflection on apparently minimal details of everyday life. . . . It follows that, in the aftermath of the multitudinous protests in Puerto Rico in July 2019 and subsequently in other Latin American countries, Luisa Capetillo's radical thought provokes new readings and discussions. . . . Her antiauthoritarianism, her approximation to the work regime's disruption through the strike as an iconoclastic and festive instance of justice, acquire now a renovated meaning; as is also the case concerning her attention to the micropolitics of daily life, inseparable from the importance Luisa assigned to performativity in her analysis of social transformations.

On his part, in an essay included in Ramos's revised edition, Luis Othoniel Rosa, who describes Capetillo as "our witch grandmother in the Caribbean," provides a compelling commentary on the "gleam" quote above, arguing that "it is in contrast and plurality that Luisa finally finds the light." Rosa's emphasis on Capetillo's will and capacity to "create times and spaces with that which is already given, in the most adverse material conditions" is relevant in the context of this book's understanding of Puerto Rico's sovereignties, which can be thought of as our "ungovernability" in Rosa's sense: "if governing is the art of convincing others that they cannot govern themselves, Capetillo's intelligence is its ungovernability."

3. Teresa Peña Jordán's recent essay on Capetillo, included in the revised *Amor y anarquía* edition (2021), notes 1882 as the birthdate, as per a passport request by Capetillo that the researcher tracked down. Capetillo's biographer, Norma Valle Ferrer, noted 1879 in her 1990 biography.

4. Capetillo's understanding of socialist anarchism is clearly established in her writing:

> I am a socialist because my aspiration is that all advancements, discoveries, and established inventions belong to everyone; that their socialization be achieved without privileges. Some think that that [process] should happen with the State in place, so that it regulates it; I understand it can be done without government. I do not mean to say that I am opposed to the government regulating and controlling capital [*riquezas*], as it should, but I maintain my opinion as a resolute supporter of non-government Anarchist socialism. (Ramos [1911] 1992, 87)

Her conviction was that nature, in and of itself, is anarchist and, thus, the human species must conform to "natural laws" (Ramos [1911] 1992, 107). Crucially, Capetillo also supported—in both her essayistic and dramatic writing—the establishment of workers' coops, a matter I return to in the Coda, as the start of working-class control of the "modes of production," with the eventual result of the government's "annulment" (see, for instance, pp. 98, 127, and 158). For lucid historical discussions of early twentieth-century Puerto Rican anarchism, see Jorell Meléndez-Badillo's (2013, 2021), and Kirwin R. Shaffer's (2009, 2013) work. Regarding *espiritismo*, Capetillo was also emphatic about what she thought were its convincing claims ("plurality of existences, diverse habitable worlds, in a word, the peace and concord that should exist between enemies, through the embodiment between them, that is, universal harmony as a result of the plurality of existences" [Ramos (1911) 1992, 102]), and those that were not: "Spiritualists say private property should be respected, even if people are dying of hunger? Is the property of one or two individuals worthier than the life and health of thousands of people?" (101), and: "I do not understand the kind of spiritualism with residues of mysticisms or fanatisms from other so-called religious ideas. I do not accept the spiritualism that obeys criminal laws nor any kind of authoritarian regime. I do not comprehend the spiritualism that accepts customs, dogmas, and rites that come from obsolete, so-called religious institutions. Nor do I understand it if it accommodates the capitalist regime's exploitative practices" (103). For more on Capetillo's *espiritismo*, see Carmen Ana Romeu Toro's essay in Ramos's revised edition, referenced above.

5. See Bird-Soto (2006), Courtad (2016), Echevarría (2000), Martínez-San Miguel (1997), Peña Jordán (2021), Ramos (1992, 2021), Ramos Escobar (2003), Rivera Berruz (2018), Romero-Cesareo (1994), Rosa (2021), Suárez Findlay (1999), Valle Ferrer (1990), and Vidal Rodríguez (2016).

6. Still, Capetillo sustained complex and, at times, contradictory positions concerning women's struggles and roles in a truly "free" society. I will return to a discussion of Capetillo's feminism in a later section of this chapter.

7. Included in Ramos's revised edition of *Amor y anarquía* (2021) is an interview with Capetillo's biographer, Norma Valle Ferrer, in the context of which she provides an account of a significant moment at a rally in Ceiba, Puerto Rico, where Capetillo was performing one of her political allocutions from a balcony. As the police arrived to arrest her—making power's persecution of speeches in Puerto Rico historically much older than it has been presumed when discussing Pedro Albizu Campos's case (see chapter 3)—they demand her repeatedly to "Shut up!," which she adamantly refuses to do, as she recounts in a letter to Santiago Iglesias Pantín, while also mocking the police.

8. Martínez-San Miguel's essay on Capetillo, Roqué de Duprey, and the Puerto Rican *Generación del 30* also discusses Capetillo's preferred emphasis on the body over the nation (1997). Moreover, Bird-Soto contends that "with Luisa Capetillo the concept 'woman' sheds its patriarchal and nationalist burden, since the power of individual agency is highlighted. This agency is both of conviction and of action" (2006, 178).

9. See Valle Ferrer's biography, *Luisa Capetillo: Historia de una mujer proscrita* (1990) for details.

10. Concerning Capetillo's position on race, Suárez Findlay explains:

Capetillo never directly acknowledged racial differences in her writings, although she frequently spoke of women as slaves to both men and capitalism. Apparently, she considered gender and class to be the main axes of exploitation. For Capetillo, sexual autonomy was as key to women's emancipation as economic self-sufficiency, education, and class struggle. By 1910, when she founded a newspaper in San Juan for workingwomen, she had decided that her feminist campaign had to promote "women's freedom in all aspects of our lives." This included opening discussion on "the sexual question" (although not explicitly on race) and placing it at the center of politics. (1999, 160).

The critic also summarizes incisively Capetillo's ideological context in this respect:

Leading labor activists denounced racism among both the upper and working classes, while asserting that working-class unity in the struggle against "wage slavery" could overcome intraplebeian racial tensions. Female and male labor organizers began to formulate a newly self-conscious sexual politics based on popular sexual norms and practices. In the process, they rejected the fusion of immorality, blackness, and femaleness that for so long had permeated dominant social assumptions in Puerto Rico. (16)

11. As explained on the *Chronicling America* website (see https://chronicling-america.loc.gov/lccn/sn91099739/), "The Spanish colonial establishment had two basic means of communication: the government's *Gaceta* and the *Boletín Mercantil*, which was supported by and represented the prevailing Spanish commercial and land interests in Puerto Rico. The *Boletín* brought to the forefront, from a conservative standpoint, the daily life of the Spaniards and their descendants in Puerto Rico. It serves as an important resource to study the conservative pro-Spanish political currents in the colony."

12. As explained by Langdon, Connaughton, and Coltheart, the Fregoli delusion is "the mistaken belief that some person currently present in the deluded person's environment (typically a stranger) is a familiar person in disguise" (2014, 615).

13. As Walker reminds us, Capetillo was deeply aware of the constant onslaught she was subjected to: "As Capetillo tries to negotiate between her marginalization as female artist and activist and her desire to create real social change, she often becomes frustrated. She writes, 'in spite of all my frankness, I have not been understood, but instead, slandered, and misinterpreted' (66). This title she gives herself, 'una equivocada,' is representative of her writing and praxis, especially its use in the context of her essay, "I," and read in conjunction with daily activist 'performances'" (2009, xix).

14. *Género chico* (minor genre) refers to a subgenre, characterized by its brevity, of the Spanish *zarzuela*, a popular musical theater. In Luis Palés Matos's *Litoral* (2013), there is a fascinating firsthand account of the itinerant presentations of *género chico* companies throughout the Puerto Rican archipelago during the early twentieth century.

15. Indeed, I analyze one of Hernández's performances in Old San Juan as submarinely linked with Capetillo's public transg/dressing (see chapter 5).

16. A case in point appears in her writing while she was working as propagandist and journalist during the *Cruzada del Ideal*, an archipelagic "unionization campaign in which Capetillo participated as member and agitator between 1909 and 1911" (Ramos 1992, 35). Capetillo writes: "I left Arecibo for Isabela at 10 in the morning; the train departed and, on the way, in the fields . . . and plantations, on the land that had been prepared to receive the seeds, I saw a girl who, with one of her hands held her poor skirt, where she had the seeds, and with the other, spread the seeds on the open furrows. A beautiful and poetic figure! A beautiful symbol of the certainty of work that the implacable selfishness, the insatiable hydra of exploitation, asphyxiates in its monstrous arms, annihilating the beauty and health of that poor creature, leaving her squalid and miserable, without sustenance for her future and last days. And, after an entire existence of deprivations and painful misery, she must recur to handouts, or walk to the hospital, the only refuge for those who produce everything and enjoy nothing." (Ramos [1909] 1992, 75)

17. A genealogy of carnivalesque political struggle in the history of Puerto Rico has yet to be written, in the context of which the 2019 *Verano Boricua* should be linked to these early twentieth-century manifestations. Two additional details, which merit further investigation beyond the scope of this chapter, should be considered when approaching Capetillo's performative political engagement: her father's experience as an "[artistic] promoter of a funfair of sorts" (Valle Ferrer 1990, 44), and the frequent references to silent cinema in Capetillo's writing (Ramos 1992, 27).

18. See Suárez Findlay (1999), Ayala and Bernabe (2007), García and Quintero Rivera (1982), and Picó (2008). Specifically concerning these changes in the tobacco industry, Suárez Findlay explains: "Although tobacco farming remained in the hands of smallholders, US. companies focused their energies on taking over the processing and manufacturing stages of cigar production. Centered in Cayey, San Juan, Caguas, and Bayamón, with additional workshops and factories in Ponce and Arecibo, cigar production rapidly expanded in the early twentieth century and was soon reorganized on an industrial scale. Large factories, mainly owned by US corporations and employing hundreds of male cigar rollers and female stem-strippers, replaced the small artisanal shops of three or four male *tabaqueros* that had previously produced the bulk of Puerto Rico's cigars." (1999, 138)

19. For a historical account of one of the most significant tobacco factories in Puerto Rico and its community of workers in Puerta de Tierra, San Juan, see Bird Carmona's *Parejeros y desafiantes* (2008).

20. In her groundbreaking collection of essays, which traces the history of Puerto Rican feminism during the first three decades of the twentieth century, Yamila Azize writes:

The history books used in our schools indicate that feminist struggles in Puerto Rico began in 1917, when Ana Roqué de Duprey and the group of women associated with her begin their efforts to achieve women's vote. Thus, the "official history" in Puerto Rico has hidden the militancy of hundreds of women who were contemporaries of Ana Roqué, but representatives of another economic sector—the working class—and who also engaged in important struggles for the Puerto Rican woman. (1985, 9).

Women newly working outside their homes were oppressed not only as recent members of the working class, but also because they were paid less than their male peers and were, most certainly, subjected to constant forms of patriarchal assault. They also lacked any kind of representation in the unions and political structures. For its part, universal suffrage in Puerto Rico was not approved until 1936. Since women were initially rejected by some sectors of the organized workers' movements, female unions and groups started to organize both within and without male workers' unions. Although their agendas were similar to those of male labor movements' struggles for better working conditions, female unions also pushed for universal suffrage and achieved several directive positions in the FLT (*Federación Libre de Trabajadores*), the most influential working-class federation at the time. It was also due to their efforts that the writer and legislator Nemesio Canales presented in 1908 the first bill defending women's vote and the legal emancipation of Puerto Rican women (Azize 1987, 20). Thus, the first organized feminist movements in Puerto Rico *were those of proletarian women* (Azize 1985, 13). Ramos adds: "It is not a coincidence, in this sense, that feminism's first articulations in Puerto Rico manifested themselves at cigar factories and the working-class press well before the suffragist movement consolidated in the 1920s" (1992, 30). Romero-Cesareo expounds on this historical moment as follows:

> Many women, especially in the tobacco industry, saw the unions as vehicles through which changes can be achieved. Their struggle as workers developed into a feminist struggle and, among their claims and campaigns, the demands for the right to vote began to be heard in 1908. . . . With the establishment of new unions, women began to protest by the hundreds, striking, publishing essays or letters in newspapers, and delivering public speeches. . . . Many women, among others Luisa Capetillo, Juana Cofresí, Gregoria Molina, Paca Escabí de Peña, Isabel Gatell, Emilia Vázquez, Rafaela López Negrón, and Carmen Rosario, joined this new army of women becoming important leaders in the labor and/or feminist movement during these decades. (1994, 785)

21. See also Valle Ferrer (1990, 62).
22. For a discussion of Capetillo in the wider context of anarchist writers from the Spanish-speaking Caribbean, see Shaffer (2009, 2013). Importantly, he stresses that the performative manifestations of anarchist fiction could transcend the limitations of illiteracy among the working-class: "In addition, one did not need to be able to read to see plays staged at meetings or to hear poetry recited at fundraisers. Finally, because the tobacco trades were central locations of employment for Caribbean anarchists and sympathizers, and because anarchist at times were *lectores*—like Luisa Capetillo—we can surmise that some of this fiction (though we do not know which

fiction exactly) was read by the readers to tobacco leaf selectors, de-stemmers, and cigar rollers" (2009, 34).

23. In the general population, the numbers were even more staggering. As Ramos documents, "The 1899 Census, for instance, registers the illiteracy rate at 77% of the population. Among agricultural workers, who constituted the labor force's axis, illiteracy reached 87%" (1992, 14).

24. See, respectively, *The Madison Daily Leader* (July 5, 1912) and *The Richmond Palladium and Sun-Telegram* (July 1, 1912).

25. See Valle Ferrer's account of the incident (1990, 88).

26. Notable exceptions are Peña Jordán (in Ramos 2021), Romero-Cesareo (1994), and Walker (2009), who writes: "Capetillo then relates her strategic and manipulative processes of public image and use of the body, especially the female body, to 'speak' to her audiences in order to disrupt certain spaces and subvert power structures: 'Sometimes, in order that they don't forget that I possess an artist's soul, like most women, I dress up without ostentation. And if I were not such an anarchist, that is to say, such a "Christian," I would dress splendidly, with true art, and with exquisite taste; but, the unfortunate who lack all necessities? The hungry and the naked? ...What cruelty! What sarcasm!'" (66). (xix).

27. For instance: "This custom of pants adapts perfectly to the epoch of feminine progress. And [it] will result in the variation of fabrics, going from the thickest to the thinnest and most delicate, and we will end up using only a veil or muslin to cover ourselves. And in that future epoch, women in general will make sure they do not gain too much weight; she will prefer to be thin than thick. And it will be so natural and artistically beautiful that [I believe] such an epoch is upon us, arriving as quickly as sociological progress. . . . It is the sociological, communist, anarchist progress that imposes itself. We are founding societies and engaging in meetings without clerical benediction or authorization from the judge or mayor. Without realizing it, we have prescinded from ecclesiastical, civil, and political authorities we otherwise celebrated so much. And to this sociological development, women adapt admirably. From those ideas we expect our complete emancipation and all our rights and duties elucidated" (Ramos [1911] 1992, 184–85). Capetillo's gratuitous claim that women would prefer to be thin in the future is another instance of her contradictory positions concerning women's bodies.

28. See, especially, Azize (1985, 1987), Baerga (1995), Suárez Findlay (1999), Roy-Féquière (2004), and Briggs (2003).

29. For a moving encounter with this evidence from the perspective of a contemporary queer thinker and activist, see Lissette Rolón Collazo's letters to Capetillo in Ramos's revised edition of *Amor y anarquía* (2021).

30. Thus, although I agree with Rivera Berruz's claims that Capetillo understood class and gender emancipation as mutually interdependent, and that education as revolutionary praxis had to be at the center of the struggle for liberation, I question the critic's position that Capetillo's "advocacy of free love and the dissolvement of the institution of marriage" was "part of a radical sexual politics that placed sexuality at the centerfold of political life" (2018, 18). Her position on sex work ("prostitution")—an intensely debated and persecuted aspect of many women's lives in

Capetillo's early twentieth-century Puerto Rico (see Briggs's *Reproducing Empire*, 2003)—as the exclusive result of women's exploitation and a social ill that would be overcome with the advent of anarchism's true progress (96) is another instance in which "radical sexual politics" is not exactly what characterized her thinking. Still, one should note that the complexities of Capetillo's positions can also be registered on the topic of sexual practices, since, as Suárez Findlay rightfully reminds us: "While advocating the control of male sexuality, she also spoke boldly of women's capacity for sexual pleasure and their right to experience it. Women, she insisted, 'have strong sexual appetites, which, like in a man, are a great virtue.' Denying women the satisfaction of their desires, she argued, could even harm their health" (1999, 162). Moreover, as Bird-Soto explains, rather than reproducing a patriarchal norm, the heteronormative mandate in Capetillo's writing is the logical result of her commitment to what, at the time, she (and many others) understood, however mistakenly, as "natural law" (2006, 188).

31. Because she does not mention the possibilities for avoiding or interrupting pregnancies, it is also not clear what Capetillo thought of women who, by choice or physical circumstance, did not become mothers.

32. However, as I suggested above, one should keep in mind that Capetillo's strong exhortations, consistent with the tradition of *tribuna* imprecations that will also be replicated in Albizu Campos's political work (see chapter 3), were exceedingly difficult for many working-class and destitute women to follow. Suárez Findlay aptly explains the predicaments that prevented many women from following, even if they wanted to, Capetillo's suggestions: "It is entirely possible that Capetillo's assertion of both sexes' right to separation at any time was too frightening to working-class mothers. Plebeian women, especially those with children, faced deepening social and economic vulnerability with the increased mobility, fragmented communities, and shifting social relations of the early twentieth century. With no ability to count on state enforcement of child support outside of marital relationships, Capetillo's call for male economic responsibility was probably not nearly sufficient to counterbalance the fear of male desertion. . . . Capetillo's refusal to acknowledge the contradictions in women's lives may have limited her popular appeal as well. Her unrelenting scorn for all women, plebeian or wealthy, who depended on male income or feared to leave unsatisfactory relationships excluded great numbers of potential female allies" (1999, 164).

Chapter Three

Commanding the Islands' Liberation

Pedro Albizu Campos and the Partido Nacionalista

> North Americans have nothing to offer to the world for its improvement except the destruction of their empire.
>
> —Pedro Albizu Campos in Torres, *Pedro Albizu Campos: Obras escogidas 1923–1936 Tomo I* ([1927] 1975), 36

In the context of this book's main inquiries—namely, Puerto Rico's Caribbean relations, archipelagic thought and practice, and the kind of political project pursued to put an end to colonialism in Puerto Rico, especially as it pertains to bodily sovereignties—this chapter considers underseen aspects of the life and work of mid-twentieth-century Puerto Rican lawyer and nationalist Pedro Albizu Campos, as much as it reframes issues that his commentators have repeatedly addressed from contrasting angles. Exploring both similarities and differences with Betances and Capetillo, I delve into Albizu Campos's—and the Partido Nacionalista's under his leadership—radical gestures of refusal and love as they were expressed in primary texts of varying genres, and as they were embodied through a powerful performative politics consistent with the era's tribuna *aesthetic. The chapter offers a nuanced contextualization and discussion of Albizu Campos's ideological positions and struggles while living under the consolidation of US rule in Puerto Rico. Recognizing Puerto Rican nationalism as part of our affective archive of Caribbean relations toward a decolonial horizon, at the same time, this chapter considers its limits—especially as they concern its understanding of Puerto Rican history, as well as the question of the body, both in terms of gender and race—in conceptualizing a Puerto Rico beyond US colonialism.*

"The war after the war" is eminent historian Fernando Picó's description of the immediate aftermath of the 1898 war in Puerto Rico, with the ensuing US military occupation of the archipelago and the dramatic changes provoked as a consequence.[1] Before the labor and social transformations described in the previous chapter were underway, "negotiations" and instances of Puerto Rican opposition were aroused, the most notable of which were the raiding *partidas sediciosas* (seditious groups, see Picó 1987, chapter 3). But the latter were directed primarily at the defeated Spanish *hacendados* (landowners) and their *criollo* descendants, since the Puerto Rican majorities, as Betances ceaselessly denounced (see chapter 1), had been subjected to outright misery by this ruling class.[2]

Meanwhile, with very little knowledge of Puerto Rican life, US military forces were busy imposing a military government to consolidate the occupation (see Picó 1987, chapters 5 and 6). As Picó documents, against the hopes of many Puerto Ricans, the US military turned out to be an indisputable class ally of the White Spanish and *criollo* elites. When in 1899, scarcely a year after Betances's death and the US invasion of Puerto Rico, Hurricane San Ciriaco hit the archipelago, the cyclone was used by the US to further appease the destitute, racialized classes, which now found themselves in even more misery, and to secure control in their hands and those of their collaborators. As this book's Introduction elaborates, the ground was thus set for the complicity of local elites—whether they were loyal to Spain or not—with US interests, the ensuing flood of US capital primarily through absentee companies, the conversion of Puerto Rico into a tax haven, and the effective exploitation of the Puerto Rican working classes as cheap labor within a "new" colonial model. Once again, as Betances and Capetillo repeatedly lamented, most members of the local elite—that is, the class with more access to capital and resources to mount a vigorous opposition to colonialism—fell in line with the imperial masters. A few decades later, this would prove to be an insurmountable challenge for Puerto Rican nationalism. To this day, it continues to be one of the most obdurate barriers to the archipelago's sovereignties.[3]

The US Great Depression of the 1930s devastated Puerto Rico's economy further, deepening social fractures, contradicting at all levels the US promise of "progress" and "freedom," and intensifying the plight of the archipelago's most wretched. The "U.S. controlled sugar and tobacco plantation economy in Puerto Rico" was in frank "crisis and decline" (Acosta-Belén 1986, 10), while the needlework industry virtually disappeared (Azize 1987, 22). Coupled with the return of Puerto Rican male war survivors, the crisis implied "a downward trend in the rate of women's participation in the labor force" (Acosta-Belén 1986, 10), driving many "to work in home-based needlework or domestic service as a way of making a living" (10). The conditions that had, for a few years, enabled the emergence of proletarian feminism (see chapter 2) were now being reversed.⁴ Women were again forced into isolation from political organizations of every kind, and the everyday struggle to survive took its toll on the previous feminist fervor.

So much had changed in so little time since Betances's late-nineteenth-century archipelagic, anticolonial republicanism, and even since Capetillo's 1920s working-class, anarchist, and feminist mobilizations! Pedro Albizu Campos's 1930s–1940s Puerto Rico was being ever more deeply undone. As the time's writings and images did not fail to document, despair and death, loss and mourning, seemed to be the sum of Puerto Rican life.⁵ Within these intolerable conditions, alongside the international, anticolonial, nationalist struggles of his era—among which the Caribbean, via such figures as Aimé Césaire and Marcus Garvey, was central—Albizu Campos's thought and action emerged and necessarily responded to.⁶ This should help contextualize and better understand his politics of absolute repudiation of US domination,⁷ and the imponderable labor of Betances's "revolution of love" that Albizu Campos's defense of a Puerto Rican nationality, despite its limitations, entailed.⁸ The nationalist leader's simultaneous refusal and love, embodied, as in Capetillo, through a powerful performative politics consistent with the era's *tribuna* aesthetic (see chapter 2), garnered a contempt from the ruling classes—both in the archipelago and in the United States—as massive as the support it reaped from the Puerto Rican majorities. For that "crime," and because Albizu Campos refused to become a fugitive to preserve his life—as Betances did before him, and pro-independence leaders such as Filiberto Ojeda Ríos have done since—the US empire and its obedient Puerto Rican accomplices brought unspeakable horrors upon him and his supporters.⁹

Afro-Puerto Rican Pedro Albizu Campos was born in 1891 in an impoverished, working-class neighborhood of Ponce, Puerto Rico, to a *criollo* father who legally "recognized" his child only when Albizu Campos was a young adult—thus giving him a social class "ticket" that would eventually land him in Harvard Law School—and an Afro-Puerto Rican mother whose parents had been enslaved and who faced dire life conditions (Rosado [1992] 2009, 29–45).¹⁰ Upon returning to Puerto Rico as a lawyer in 1921, Albizu Campos committed himself to the struggle for Puerto Rico's liberation from colonialism, first institutionally through his immersion in party politics and, later, halfway out of institutions through his refashioning of the *Partido Nacionalista* (PN) as an organization closer to a liberation front than to a party in the traditional sense.

In what follows, I evaluate multiple primary texts of varying genres (political speeches and platforms, interviews, and several kinds of declarations from the 1920s up to 1950) as reflections of Albizu Campos's thought and the PN's platform under his leadership concerning this book's main inquiries, namely, Caribbean relations, archipelagic thought and practice, and the kind of political project pursued to put an end to colonialism in Puerto Rico, especially as it pertains to bodily sovereignties. In doing so, I wish to emphasize both Albizu Campos's and the PN's differences from and continuities with Betances's and Capetillo's ideological frameworks, on the one hand, and with turn-of-the-century Puerto Rican *criollismo*, on the other. Recognizing Puerto Rican nationalism as part of our affective archive of Caribbean relations toward a decolonial horizon, at the same time, this chapter considers its limits—especially in terms of how it understands Puerto Rican history, as well as the question of the body—in conceptualizing a Puerto Rico beyond US colonialism.

LA CAUSA CONTINENTAL

As with Betances and Capetillo, Albizu Campos's lifelong sacrificial devotion to the dream of liberation was, undoubtedly, a project of love: "Travel, see the world, and you will learn to love this [Puerto Rico] as one loves the mother of our children, with unconditional love, with a transcendental love that demands of us to give our lives and offer the ultimate thought of greatness and heroism and sacrifice" (Acosta Lespier [1949] 2000, 89). However, Albizu Campos confronted not the threat of US neocolonial violence and exploitation in Puerto Rico and the Caribbean, but its factuality and accelerating expansion, as well as the increasing complicity of Puerto Rico's ruling classes. Betances's trepidation that Puerto Rico would be doomed if it did not achieve independence at the same time as Cuba seemed to have been confirmed. Capetillo's internationalist, anarchist feminism, which sustained deep bonds with US-based efforts, was in many ways crushed by the global imperial power that the United States was becoming, a matter I return to toward the end of this chapter. In a word, Albizu Campos faced a world plagued by the violently competing interests and ideological agendas played out during, between, and after the two World Wars, with even more devastating effects for Puerto Rico.

As a result of this very different historical context and of Albizu Campos's ideological affiliations to *arielismo*—discussed below—neither he nor the PN—which he transformed to follow his vision starting in 1930, when he assumed its presidency[11]—dreamt of Puerto Rico's liberation as a Caribbean project. Despite the formal declaration that the PN's second objective, after the "reestablishment of the Puerto Rican Republic," was "the *Confederación*

Antillana, which includes the Republic of Haiti" (Albizu-Campos Meneses and Rodríguez León [1934] 2007, 28), the overwhelming evidence from Albizu Campos's and the PN's textual traces implies an understanding of Puerto Rico primarily as "Iberoamerican." Indeed, the PN's third objective, "Ibero-American unity," clearly states:

> The necessity of that unity is uncontestable. In the century and a half of our nationalities' independence, powers that are enemies of their existence have managed to snatch from us a precious part of our territorial racial patrimony (*patrimonio territorial racial*) because of our nations' division, which, when united, have always had and still have enough power to [oppose] themselves to all imperialisms. (Albizu-Campos Meneses and Rodríguez León [1934] 2007, 28–29)

When the party's platform refers to "the century and a half of our nationalities' independence," it foregrounds the Spanish empire's ex-colonies, which share, in this argument, a "territorial racial patrimony." This, as we will see, entails for Albizu Campos nothing short of a civilizational conflict, whereby a sanitized legacy of the Spanish empire takes center stage as a homogenizing force that supersedes all bodily, experiential, and geographical differences, and, in so doing, becomes capable of combating, and overcoming, the already-manifested new imperial enemy, the United States.[12] Albizu Campos's and the PN's outlook thus becomes quite hazy when attempting, if at all, to think of Puerto Rico as Antillean in Betances's sense.

Surely, Albizu Campos and the PN shared Betances's understanding of our archipelago in solidarity and connection with (primarily for the former) the Spanish-speaking Caribbean. But Albizu Campos considered Cuba and the DR more Iberoamerican republics than Caribbean archipelagos. Likewise, the scenario of profuse nonindependent peoples in the Caribbean region is glaringly overlooked by Albizu Campos in declarations such as the following, made quite later, in 1950: "The only captive flag in our America is Puerto Rico's" (Acosta Lespier 2000, 148). The necessary implication is that the Caribbean region, amply conceived, is thought of as not belonging to America.

Moreover, I have been unable to find any indication that the PN, or Albizu Campos personally, sought to establish connections with the West Indies Federation process, which intensified in the 1930s, precisely the time of Albizu Campos's rise to nationalist leadership.[13] Additionally, although he made a brief visit to Haiti during its occupation by the US (1915–1934), the evidence of such blatant intervention in a formally independent country did not call into question forcefully enough Albizu Campos's assessment that Puerto Rico's independence would withstand the US empire's onslaught (a matter I return to below). In contrast, as Raphael Dalleo makes abundantly clear, other Caribbean anticolonial leaders took Haiti's occupation into account in more complexly assessing the possibilities and limitations of traditional nationalism (2020, 63).[14]

Albizu Campos's 1920s maritime travels to gather support for the Puerto Rican independence cause merit a commentary of their own. While I agree with Albizu Campos's biographer, Marisa Rosado, that this was a "peregrination . . . fundamentally Caribbean and Antillean" ([1992] 2009, 143) in strictly geographical terms—although revolving primarily around the Spanish-speaking Caribbean—the fact remains that it was not conceived as a Caribbeanist project. As he prepared for his voyage, Albizu Campos made the following statements in an interview:

> Our painful situation under the US empire is the same that North America wants to impose *on all our brothers in the Continent. Our cause is the continental cause.* . . . Puerto Rico is America's most homogeneous people . . . with Hispanic culture and civilization. If [the US] empire triumphs in our midst it would be a terrible blow for the Iberoamerican race. . . . Puerto Rico and the other Antilles constitute the battlefield between yankee imperialism and Iberoamericanism. *The archipelago's solidarity* [is needed] *to reestablish continental equilibrium and ensure the independence of all Columbian nations.* Within that supreme necessity, our independence is indispensable. (Torres, *Tomo I*, [1927] 1975, 45, emphasis added)

This geopolitical framework clearly shows that Albizu Campos understands the "Antilles" as, exclusively, those that were formerly Spanish colonies, inasmuch as they are also "Iberoamerican." The waters around Cuba, the DR, and Puerto Rico were, for him, those of the conflict between US imperialism and Iberoamericanism. The greater Caribbean is, thus, absent from Albizu Campos's political thought. In stark contrast with Marta Aponte Alsina's defense of our "liquid homeland" (see the Introduction), Albizu Campos expressly states that the Puerto Rican nationalist cause, when considered beyond the immediate Puerto Rican geography, is *the continental cause.* Likewise, during his journey he was presented as "delegate of the Puerto Rican people in the Iberoamerican Republics and Europe," while his statements were summarized as "conferences on yankee imperialism and the need for *latin peoples of this hemisphere* to unite to stop the ferocious appetites of the Ogre from the North" (Torres, *Tomo I*, [1927] 1975, 56, emphasis added).

During his 1920s travels, the only explicit instance of an allegiance with Betances's Caribbeanist legacy is Albizu Campos's brief stop in Haiti (September 11–13, 1927) (Rosado [1992] 2009, 140), where he made declarations of solidarity and friendship with the American hemisphere's first free republic. But his assertions, which avoided a recognition of Haiti's extraordinary achievement as a Black triumph, were framed within Albizu Campos's overarching Iberoamerican concern:

> The end of Haiti's occupation is a necessity for all Iberoamerican countries, because, if we don't substantially, spontaneously, and unconditionally help the Haitians, the Haitian people will have to seek from our enemies the support we have neglected to offer them. It is a matter of high political interest that we win Haiti's sympathy through eloquent manifestations and the sentiments of friendship and justice that we feel for her. (Torres, *Tomo I*, [1927] 1975, 56)

The Puerto Rican's attempt at including Haiti within the wake of "Spanish civilization,"[15] *as though* Haiti had also been a colony of Spain, is rather bewildering: "our brother peoples in the race (*los pueblos hermanos nuestros en la raza*), Cuba, Haiti and the Dominican Republic" (Torres, *Tomo I*, [1924] 1975, 28). Insofar as the primary enemy was the United States, did Albizu Campos imagine for Haiti a possible integration into the Spanish-speaking Caribbean that would allow a common front against US interests? A speculation to that effect is possible when considering that the same journalistic report covering his visit to Haiti relates that the Puerto Rican leader "repeatedly pleaded with us to transmit this message to the Haitian public: 'Learn Spanish if you want to vanquish the yankee ogre'" (Torres, *Tomo I*, [1927] 1975, 55). This can be interpreted in at least two, not mutually exclusive senses: on the one hand, as a form of (limited) Caribbeanist consciousness, while, on the other, as a quite problematic use of Haiti for the advancement of purposes beyond it, since an equivalent exigency to learn Haitian Creole—or even French—was not made when visiting the DR.[16]

Meanwhile, Albizu Campos does not explicitly mobilize in his writing or speeches an insular or archipelagic consciousness concerning Puerto Rico or its decolonization. This was the case despite the facts that, first, insularity, as we saw in this book's Introduction, was very much discussed in Puerto Rico's *criollo* intellectual circles in the 1930s, and second, the Anglophone Caribbean was in the midst of its own efforts to create a federated archipelagic state at the time. In contrast to Betances's commitment, which, as we saw in chapter 1, was not programmatically designed, nor reflected as part of a formal party's platform, the PN offered a concrete agenda for the Republic of Puerto Rico, as documented in the 1922 "Declaración de Principios," as well as in the 1930 "Programa Político, Social y Económico del Partido Nacionalista de Puerto Rico" (both reproduced in Bothwell González 1979). In these political platforms there is no indication as to how the organization would pursue the *Confederación Antillana* (CA), which, as we saw, was identified as objective #2. Puerto Rico's sovereignty, moreover, is not envisioned as related to, or required by, the Caribbean region. For the nationalist anticolonial struggle in Puerto Rico, the CA thus became a distant, historical reference. It seemed to function more as a rhetorical gesture in claiming historical antecedents than as an actual political objective.

Albizu Campos's primary texts also reveal that his references to the greater Caribbean, overall, frame the archipelagic region *insomuch as it concerns the United States*, rather than as a political, cultural, or social zone on its own terms. The following passages exemplify this point.

> The Antillean Archipelago occupies a privileged position in world geography. It is essential to expel the US from its territories and to consolidate them in a confederation with enough naval power to resist any reprisals. (Torres, *Tomo I*, [1927] 1975, 36)

> The Caribbean Sea is the heart of the world. The tropical maritime currents that bring warmth and life to every continent on Earth depart and confluence from here. This will be the theater of the great war, which is eight or ten years ahead of us, to overthrow the US imperialist power. (Torres, *Tomo I*, [1930] 1975, 175)

> The Antillean people wished to bring that flag of unity to our brothers. During the viceroyship, the Antilles shouldered the weight of the Iberoamerican civilization's defense in the New World, and they still shoulder it. They will not renounce that privilege because we cannot allow the empire of barbarism to destroy our civilization. . . . In the struggle to preserve our civilization, Puerto Rico has revealed the strength of the Race (*la fortaleza de la Raza*). The North American intervention has not been able to damage our Hispanic American personality and our resolute march against the foreign imposition. (Torres, *Tomo III*, [1933] 1975, 32–34)[17]

To be sure, Albizu Campos makes occasional reference to Puerto Rico's insularity as a politically charged concept. He does so, however, to equate its "condition as an island" (note that Puerto Rico is not represented as a group of islands) as an "independence postulate because Nature has already made us free" (Torres, *Tomo I*, [1930] 1975, 73). This "natural freedom" allows Albizu Campos to make, then, a fleeting, but very significant, historical claim for Puerto Rico: "islands have always been the most indomitable territories in history" (Torres, *Tomo I*, [1930] 1975, 73). Unfortunately, such historicity finds no elaboration, since it comes on the heels of another instance of Albizu Campos's consistent argument that Puerto Rico is a "homogeneous" nationality: "Puerto Rico is the continent's most integrated nationality in the ethnic and cultural sense, we have America's most homogeneous, noble and intelligent mass" (Torres, *Tomo I*, [1930] 1975, 73). The PN's understanding of Puerto Rico itself, moreover, makes the party's geographic misjudgment painfully evident, as in the party's 1930 Program our "nationality" is said to be constituted by "Puerto Rico and its adjacent islands" (Bothwell González 1979, 461), thus making a stark distinction between an implicitly "main" territory and its "possession" of secondary islands.[18]

Still, writing about Vieques, which he visited in 1948 (Rosado [1992] 2009, 317–18), Albizu Campos suggests, albeit obliquely, an understanding of the US empire's use of islands as laboratories for wider applications of its various forms of exploitation and annihilation (see the Introduction). Here, the nationalist leader displays his acute understanding of the United States' strategic use of insularity by militarily overtaking piecemeal zones—a grotesque archipelagic practice—as well as by making inter-insular communication and travel nearly impossible for the majorities. According to Albizu Campos's prescient and enduringly relevant analysis, this practice enables the empire to expand its destruction of Puerto Rico:

> In Vieques the US government performs our nation's vivisection. The society of Vieques is dying, extinguishing itself under the cold, deliberate, and intentional attack of the US government. . . . At any moment that the US deems it necessary to exile the entire population of San Juan, Ponce, Mayagüez, or any other Puerto Rican city, or even all Puerto Ricans from our national Puerto Rican land, they believe they have the right to do so. And this is not a theoretical situation; rather, the military, naval, and air bases are already established throughout our national territory, from Mona Island to Vieques, and from San Juan to Ponce . . . Culebra, the Cabezas de Fajardo, Ensenada Honda and Vieques already constitute a closed circle for Puerto Ricans, under the direct occupation of the US Navy infantry . . . and everything as a terrible secret . . . it is in that secret that Puerto Rico's destruction lies. (Albizu-Campos Meneses y Rodríguez León [1948] 2007, 347–52)[19]

Evidently applicable to the rest of the Caribbean region since the disgraceful dawn of colonization, genocide, and enslavement, this understanding of imperial insular subjugation, however, does not lead Albizu Campos to a historical-political horizon of archipelagic connections, solidarity, and collaboration.[20] In order for that to happen, he would have had to face, and admit, Spain's brutal legacy of "blood and death," as Betances would have it, in tandem with that of the rest of Western Europe's empires. As we will discuss more amply below, such reckoning was, for Albizu Campos, unthinkable. It would have threatened the very foundation of the ideological edifice giving credence to his claim of a Puerto Rican, "homogeneous" nationality within a longstanding Hispanic tradition, which was impossible for the United States to own or destroy.

Even conceding such an impossibility in Albizu Campos's thinking, the potentialities of the Caribbean's shared historical condition were not mobilized by Puerto Rican nationalism against the Antillean "common enemy" of the United States, a situation Albizu Campos thought would turn, "inevitably," into a war in Caribbean waters: "The battlefield will be our waters next to Panama. Europe, Ibero America, and Asia will not tolerate seeing themselves reduced to the vassalage that the United States wants to impose on them, either by direct force against defenseless countries or through economic penetration" (Torres, *Tomo I*, [1927] 1975, 36). While mounting an anticolonial opposition to the United States was, of course, at the forefront of Albizu Campos's political thought and action, he reserved his appeal to unity as a defensive imperative to Cuba, the DR, the continental republics and, as we saw, to Haiti, insofar as Haitians "learned Spanish."

ARIEL FLYING OVER SPAIN

This brings us to a deeper examination of Albizu Campos's ideological orientation, marked, as Silvia Álvarez Curbelo has reminded us, by *arielismo* (1993, 87–88).[21] Taking its name from the Uruguayan José Enrique Rodó's well known 1900 book *Ariel*—itself a reference to Shakespeare's character in *The Tempest*—*arielismo* opposed the mounting US neocolonial aggression in Latin America by ideologically establishing a stark distinction between Spain's and Great Britain's ex-colonies in the Americas.[22] In the process, *arielismo* significantly whitewashed—literally and figuratively—the Spanish empire's history and legacies in our hemisphere. In contrast with both Betances's anti-Spanish republicanism and Capetillo's anti-class-system anarchism, *arielismo* approached the material conditions of early twentieth-century Latin America through the lens of a spiritual, civilizational clash. In Albizu Campos's and the PN's efforts to carve out a space to postulate a Puerto Rican *homogeneous* nation/ality (see Duchesne Winter 1993), the binary *arielista* logic between the "Latin" and "Anglo-Saxon" "races"/"civilizations"[23] necessarily resulted in overlooking, or outright denying, Puerto Rico's deep and expansive connections with the Caribbean region. This was especially true with regard to the legacy of slavery and, even more importantly, the many forms of resistance by Afro-Caribbean populations.

Indeed, perhaps the most salient of the continuous aspects of Albizu Campos's thought from the 1920s through 1950 is his loyalty to a "Spanish civilization" monolithically understood and significantly idealized. His devout adherence to Catholicism, his insistence on the fundamental superiority of the "civilization" that "discovered" our hemisphere and, therefore, "united the world," and his glossing over of the Spanish empire's sordid history, both internally in its dealing with racial and ethnic diversity, and externally, in the

Caribbean and Puerto Rico, are all manifestations of said allegiance.[24] This is explicitly displayed in the PN's first recorded "Declaración de principios" (1922), which already carries the deep imprint of Albizu Campos's thought:

> Castilian language should be the official language in the Nation of Puerto Rico, and the teaching of any other constitutes an attack on our Puerto Rican personality and a belittlement of our civilization. As the people of Puerto Rico constitute a nation with historical continuity, the teaching of Puerto Rico's and Spain's history should be a special object of study at public schools, with a deliberate emphasis on the feat (*obra*) of the discovery and colonization of America realized by the discovering nation, since this has been a target of persecution by current colonial politics . . . with the objective of justifying their supposed racial superiority (*superioridad de raza*). (Bothwell González 1979, 462)

Nothing distinguishes Albizu Campos's thought from Betances's more acutely than this. Therefore, it comes as no surprise that in Albizu Campos's frequent references to Betances as a father figure of Puerto Rican nationalism, the latter's fervent opposition to Spain, and his lifelong collaboration and engagement with Black revolutionary leaders and the legacy of the Haitian Revolution, are not mobilized. Because the basis of Albizu Campos's definition of nationality was the idea/spirit of a "homogeneous personality" created by God,[25] the Puerto Rican archipelago ought to be imagined as a fundamental part, heir, and participant of "the only civilization there is in the West," which effectively precluded Albizu Campos from imagining Puerto Rico within the centrifugal, archipelagic, and Afro-Caribbean context.

Although Albizu Campos was, in this respect, very much a mirror of the *arielista* sentiment running through Puerto Rico's *criollo Generación del 30* (see the Introduction), the fact is that other ideological orientations were circulating at the time, both regionally in the Caribbean and locally in Puerto Rico. Most notably, the *négritude* intellectual and artistic movement, championed by Aimé Césaire, among others, and including writers with similar concerns such as Nicolás Guillén in Cuba and Luis Palés Matos in Puerto Rico, was fostering an immanent recognition and celebration of the foundational African presence and heritage across the Caribbean, which entailed opposing enduring forms of White colonialism and achieving Afro-diasporic emancipation.[26] Likewise, given the Puerto Rican's steadfast rejection of the "Anglo-Saxon civilization," one must wonder what he made of its colonies in our region, and whether that prevented him from engaging, even if only as an inspirational reference, with the process, however limited and fraught, to form the West Indies Federation.

NATIONALITY AND RACE IN ALBIZU CAMPOS

A more thorough discussion of Albizu Campos's allegiance to Spain is in order, especially since it directly influences his understanding of Puerto Rico, the Caribbean region, and the category of race itself. When commenting on Albizu Campos's "hispanophilia," some critics argue that it responds to a historical, political, and discursive need to affirm Puerto Rico's existence and defend its dignity against the US imperial enemy (see, for instance, José J. Rodríguez Vázquez 2004), while others consider it an attempt to incorporate Puerto Rico into the metaphysical narrative strategies for the birthing of a modern nation (see Juan Duchesne Winter 1993). Whatever the motives, in the context of this book, Albizu Campos's adherence to an adulatory version of the Hispanic tradition helps to explain his version of nationalism's neglect of Puerto Rico's Caribbeanness, since the struggle against the US empire can only be framed as a step in Puerto Rico's path toward becoming another "Iberoamerican" republic proud of its "mother" Spain (*la madre patria, la Madre España*). Puerto Rico's eventual victory will thus contribute to the *continental* cause against US interests.[27]

Understood as differences that must be overcome within an overarching homogeneous whole,[28] and, thus, as variances transcended by the civilization that "united the world," the specific forms that racial oppression takes, as well as the ways in which it is deployed in conjunction with colonial and capitalist exploitation, will of ideological necessity go unheeded. As much as traditional socialism understands class distinctions as having precedence over all other forms of subjective embodiment, the Puerto Rican nationalist project will demand adhesion to its independence cause first and foremost as a recognition and defense of a "national personality," itself derived from a Spain primarily—though tacitly—conceived as White and masculinist. Indeed, Albizu Campos seems convinced that gender-based and racial-based oppressions experimented in Puerto Rico are the result of the United States' violent intrusion in our history. To be sure, the imprint of dominant US notions of race and gender in Puerto Rico are everywhere to be found, but racial and gender oppressions, while differently understood, were most certainly a defining feature of Spanish rule in Puerto Rico and across the Caribbean and the Americas.[29]

Insofar as Spain is never portrayed as an *empire* per se in Albizu Campos's work, but, rather, as direct inheritor of the West's "only civilization"—that of Greco-Roman origin (Torres, *Tomo I*, 1975, 35)—the nationalist leader only has celebratory claims to make concerning its "benevolence" and "glory." Spain did not annihilate Puerto Rico's indigenous population, nor did it colonize and enslave the archipelago; instead, it mothered it, for which Puerto Rico is "grateful":

> Tonight we celebrate the great epic of the race (*epopeya magna de la raza*) that discovered and civilized this continent. To Mother Spain we owe the immense gratitude of this *oeuvre* without parallel in human history. With Columbus' feat, the spheric form of the planet was definitively confirmed. (Torres, *Tomo I*, [1930] 1975, 174)

> If under Spain we suffered despotisms, they were nothing but a reflection of those suffered in the peninsula; the same men that governed there were sent to Puerto Rico. Under the present regime, in contrast, we endure functionaries of the lowest political level. (Torres, *Tomo I*, [1930] 1975, 182)

> That education was inspired by the Greco Latin sources, as transmuted by Spain's genius; thus, we are direct heirs of the only culture that exists in the West. Our revolutionary men aspired to build a republican state with a heterodox education, but in my estimation, in this regard they were mistaken, as every nationality should be founded upon the religious spirit animating their inhabitants. (Torres, *Tomo I*, [1931] 1975, 188)

Even while delivering a speech in Cabo Rojo in commemoration of Betances, who as we saw in chapter 1 was persecuted by the Spanish empire throughout his life, Albizu Campos claims that it was Spain, never the despot, which taught its "sons" *not* to submit to any power, including that wielded by Spanish authorities themselves:

> At the time of Betances, accepting a public post under the Spanish government was a dishonor. No man, no woman with patriotic honor pledged allegiance to the Spanish government. . . . The mother homeland did not inculcate despotism; the mother homeland Spain is the nation that, with the saber on the belt, imposed on the world a sense of honor and could not convert her sons into underlings. Nobody in Puerto Rico rose to pledge loyalty to the Spanish flag! (Acosta Lespier [1949] 2000, 71)

According to Albizu Campos, the nineteenth-century *padres de la patria*'s (fathers of the homeland's) struggle for independence from Spain was *not* motivated by economic needs, nor by slavery's impacts—although he recognizes the latter as intolerable. Rather, it ultimately responded to the fact that, since the *Grito de Lares* in 1868, Puerto Rican nationality had "matured" enough as to be distinguishable on its own:

> What economic motives led the fathers of the homeland to rebel against the government of the mother homeland Spain? Economic motives? No. . . . Slavery existed. That was a cause. Puerto Ricans had demanded, the masters of slaves in Puerto Rico had demanded, the abolition of slavery in Puerto Rico, with or without indemnity. . . . Yes, of course, the presence of one slave should

cause rebellion everywhere in the world. Where there is a slave, one single man, one single woman, the dignity of the entire human race is in danger. . . . Other nations, however, have never rebelled because of the civil status of slavery [notice the glaring overlook of Haiti here]. *An armed revolution responds to very profound motivations. What is the motivation? Puerto Rico is a nation.* Puerto Rico at Lares on September 23, 1868 felt the plenitude of its political personality; in the full consciousness of its nationality . . . And the only way of recognizing that right, was recognizing Puerto Rico's independence. (Acosta Lespier [1949] 2000, 81–82, emphasis added)

A few months earlier, in the Cabo Rojo speech honoring Betances quoted above, Albizu Campos had framed the latter's struggle as the "natural" movement of "children's emancipation" from their parents (Acosta Lespier 2000, 66). The nineteenth-century figure is exalted in heroic-religious terms that would have never coincided with Betances's own secular orientation (see chapter 1), while Cabo Rojo is described as a "sanctuary" and "holy land" (Acosta Lespier 2000, 66–67).

The Spanish empire, for its part, is figured as fundamentally benevolent and worthy of Puerto Rico's eternal gratitude.[30] In fact, Albizu Campos goes so far as to claim that, in 1898, the Puerto Rican archipelago was "the richest country in this hemisphere" (Acosta Lespier [1949] 2000, 89)![31] As Albizu Campos's crowning example of Spanish generosity, the 1897 *Carta Autonómica* plays the central role in the nationalist leader's legal claim to the illegitimacy of US rule in Puerto Rico:

And in '97 [Spain] consecrated Puerto Rico's independence in the first Treaty signed between the mother homeland and Puerto Rico, which in Puerto Rico's political history is called the *Carta Autonómica de Puerto Rico*. In international law, the mother homeland's public recognition of the intervened nation's juridical personality is an irrevocable recognition. (Acosta Lespier [1949] 2000, 83)

We had tariff freedom, we could celebrate commercial treatises, and we had our own postal service and currency. These liberal measures meant an incipient sovereignty, a personality recognized in the life of international relations. Spain could not sign any treaty that would compromise us if it was not sanctioned by our will. Thus, the Treaty of Paris does not rule over us because we were not consulted for that transfer. The American occupation of Puerto Rico, in other words, is a matter of fact but not of right. (Torres, *Tomo I*, [1930] 1975, 79)[32]

Albizu Campos's eclipsing of the Spanish empire's sordid trajectory of ethnic and racial "cleansing" and "unification" in the peninsula itself, as well as of native genocide, transatlantic slavery, extreme colonial exploitation, and violence at all levels of life—including the brutal imposition of cultural, religious, and linguistic attributes—in the Caribbean and the Americas, had a deep impact on the Puerto Rican's understanding of race. Spain's "Discovery of men by men" is, in Albizu Campos's view, the "greatest epic of contemporary times," a "conquest of human unity" implying, too, "racial unification." Since he defines race "culturally" as "perpetual virtues and instructions," Albizu Campos understands Iberoamerica's (and Puerto Rico's) "race"—that is, "blood" and "nationality" itself—as only one and the same ("homogeneous"), that which flows from his flawed interpretation of Spain's legacy:

> For us, race has nothing to do with biology. . . . Race is a perpetuity of characteristic virtues and instructions. We stand out because of our courage, our nobility, our catholic sense [coming] from the Aragón and Castilian kingdoms, and, once its independence was conquered with the expulsion of the Saracens, Spain, in its plenitude, launched itself to the epic of Discovery, the greatest epic of contemporary times. . . . The primacy of the Spanish race in Europe verified the benefit that an equilibrium of courage and sainthood can bring to the world. . . . Everyone has got from us their spiritual weapons because it was us who, by blood and fire, with the cross of the sword and the sword of the cross, gave old Europe and virgin America the tradition of virtue, courage, self-love (*pundonor*), sacrifice, disdain for death and material goods, that today make our race the world's only hope. (Cancel-Sepúlveda [1935] 2010, 118–119)[33]

Since "we stand out because of our courage, our nobility, our catholic sense," and not as a result of "biology"—which, it is implied, indicates bodily differences that power categorizes hierarchically and socially enforces accordingly, with its attendant nefarious effects—a White-masculinist-conservative Spanish heritage is indirectly privileged above any other, while, at the same time, its supremacy is hidden. Shared with such prominent figures of the Spanish-speaking Caribbean as Hostos and Martí, the hegemony of this form of racial thinking is still with us today. Described as the "myth of racial harmony," in Puerto Rico it continues to be ideologically used by many on the left as a bulwark against the United States, where, it is claimed, racism more clearly permeates social life as a result of "racial disunion."[34]

Albizu Campos himself establishes this distinction—for him, again, a spiritual, civilizational difference—quite forcefully. In fact, it is one of the very few contexts in which he makes a racial identification of himself as non-White, using the phrase *de color* (of color):

> [Ernesto] Ramos Antonini would not be able to stroll on the streets of Georgia. He would have to be called to order. He is a man of color, like I am. He is married to a white lady, like I am. Neither he nor I could walk on the streets of Georgia with our wives. We would be lynched immediately, and our wives would be sent to the insane asylum. They would believe them to be crazy. Every

person with one drop of African blood, which includes all Puerto Ricans, is not agreeable to the United States society. Socially, they are worthless. (Acosta Lespier [1950] 2000, 168–69)

There is more to be said and greater complexity to be examined here. As is clear from the previous passage, when Albizu Campos's interlocutor is the United States, his racial discourse—and consciousness—changes gears. If intent on stressing Puerto Rico's oppositional difference with respect to the United States, he explicitly names racial concerns *not* as a pan-cultural concept, but as categories that make, and socially enforce, hierarchical distinctions based on bodily characteristics. In doing so, Albizu Campos unmistakably seeks to bolster his negative critique of the US empire's society. Of particular importance is the fact that Albizu Campos explicitly self-identifies as a racial *other* when referring to blatant racism in the continental United States. In contrast, I have been unable to find another such instance of self-identification when discussing the Spanish empire in the Americas, the Iberoamerican republics, or his positioning of Puerto Rico within that genealogy. When the target is *not* US imperialism, Albizu Campos's concept of race is civilizational-spiritual, rather than bodily-social, which, as we have seen, means that it becomes divorced from the history and legacies of slavery and resistance in Puerto Rico and the Caribbean, and, thus, rendered inoperative in Puerto Rican society and for the nationalist struggle. But when the target is US imperialism, an important fissure opens where it becomes possible to nurture racial solidarities against power *beyond*—or, at least, alongside—the national question. I will return to this emancipatory opening in the chapter's last section.

The fact remains, however, that Albizu Campos's understanding of race within his affirmation and defense of Puerto Rican nationality concealed the dire racism structuring Puerto Rican society at the time, as built by the enslaving system erected by and inherited from the Spanish empire.[35] It also smooths over the significant ways in which anti-Black racism was at the heart of the dominant 1930s ideological stance—marked as well by Spanish nostalgia—concerning Puerto Rican "identity."[36] Finally, insomuch as it is only in the United States, per the passage quoted above, that women would be considered "crazy" while men would be physically attacked as a result of prevailing racism, Puerto Rican life under Spanish rule is characterized not only as race- but also as gender-harmonious. That is, a continuous, nonviolent, heterosexual reproduction across bodily difference is suggested as furthering the "unification" initiated by Spain when it "made the world a sphere." Surely, if told from the viewpoint of women, and most especially, Afro-Puerto Rican women, the story would be quite different. . . .

A MISSION TO SAVE AND THE POSITION OF WOMEN

This brings us to a discussion of Puerto Rican nationalism's views concerning gender sovereignty and the position of women, both in the struggle for decolonization and in the projected Puerto Rican nation-state. To broach it, we must start with Albizu Campos's religious—specifically, Catholic—framing of his mission, which has been consistently scripted as messianic, with Albizu Campos himself described by interviewers, biographers, and followers as its "Apostle," "Peregrine," and "Teacher."[37] Because "the ruling class in the United States is moved by Satan" (Acosta Lespier [1950] 2000, 157), achieving Puerto Rico's independence from the United States amounts to *honoring* its imagined past as a godly offspring, a mission for which Albizu Campos demanded of himself and all nationalists nothing short of martyrdom. This ideological-narrative thread, which is as "emplotted" in "Romance . . . drama of redemption" as many other anticolonial struggles have been (Scott 2004, 47), remains continuous throughout his life.

Just as unremitting is the way it manifests in the nationalist leader's understanding of party structure and people's allegiance and participation. Albizu Campos's written pieces and oral speeches are structurally built upon the concepts of *valor* (courage), *sacrificio* (sacrifice), *dignidad* (dignity), *orden* (order), and *disciplina* (discipline). This ideological cluster is, of course, deeply gendered. The desired attributes for the nationalist struggle are those of "real [implying cis, heterosexual] men," who must cultivate such ideals in the service and protection of the feminine *patria*, as much as of "their" women. Among the overwhelming evidence of this in primary texts, I highlight the following examples:

> To achieve immortality there is only one entrance: the door of courage that leads to sacrifice for a supreme cause. One must sacrifice oneself for the Homeland's independence. (Torres, *Tomo I*, [1936] 1975, 9)

> [referring to Luis Muñoz Marín] let him feel like a man, he should make at least one gesture of manhood . . . For a while it's been unclear whether [he's] male or female (*macho o hembra*). (Acosta Lespier [1948] 2000, 56)

> In the struggle for freedom, everything must be sacrificed. . . . Once conquered, freedom imposes a dynamic on us, a continuous exercise of will and a continuous sacrifice of blood . . . Think about one revolutionary movement without the sacrifice of blood; it is pointless. (Acosta Lespier [1950] 2000, 135)

> It is a sacred duty to defend and die for the cause of the homeland's independence even if personally we only have the glory of sacrifice, as this will ensure

the spiritual and material wellbeing of our nationality. (Torres, *Tomo I*, [1927] 1975, 46)[38]

Although, as we saw above, Albizu Campos does not mobilize a geographically determinist conceptual framework as explicitly as his contemporary Pedreira, the former's framing of the nationalist struggle necessarily replicates the latter's feminization of Puerto Rico (see the Introduction). Women—conceived of primarily as archetypical mothers—must be *as protected* as the homeland, and vice versa, since the latter's security, its life itself, depends on women's mothering:

> Woman is the source of life, and the homeland cannot render one single potential mother useless. . . . The lessons of war tell us that the nation can lose many men, which is why it can sacrifice them for her, but it cannot lose one single woman without great risk for its own security, and that is why it prohibits feminine participation in any action that puts life in danger. (Torres, *Tomo I*, [1933] 1975, 248–49)

Indeed, men must relate to women and the homeland with the same kind of all-consuming love: "The man who does not risk his life for the woman he loves, does not love her. The man who is not willing to risk his life for his homeland, does not love her. It is a matter of lack of love (*desamor*)" (Acosta Lespier [1949] 2000, 115).

Particularly striking, and in sharp contrast to Capetillo (see chapter 2), is the PN's opposition to gender-inclusive public school education. The matter was transcendent enough for the party to include it as the third principle in its 1930 Program: "The separation of sexes in Puerto Rico's public schools is one of the problems the country has to confront courageously, as the bisexual school is a North American import unadaptable to Puerto Rico's conditions, which tends to the easing of our customs and to the dissolution of the Puerto Rican home" (Bothwell González 1979, 462). As Díaz Quiñones argues, "Albizu's authority was charismatic, with all the implications of asceticism and initiation that the term carries. The only option was to eliminate any contamination, including the sexual one" (1997, 239). This position flew in the face of the working-class feminist struggle in Puerto Rico, led by Capetillo and others, which vigorously called for a generalized access to study and education as revolutionary and emancipatory practices for women, as discussed in the previous chapter.

However, Albizu Campos's and the PN's understanding of and relations with women, as well as with questions concerning gender in general, transformed—however subtly—with time, from the 1920s through 1950. Evidently aware of the struggle against patriarchy by Puerto Rican women—although, to judge by his pronouncements, his only female political interlocutors seem to have been bourgeois suffragists—Albizu Campos alternates between a more traditional understanding of women as politically passive objects of men's stewardship, and an appreciation of them as active political participants. The latter, as in Betances, tended to mean heteronormative, reproductive, and pedagogical roles, as well as women's capacity to "straighten up" weak men:

> As mother, the woman is the keeper of our existence . . . that honor cannot be tarnished in any way. Women must rise to their husband . . . so that they defend their homeland's honor. . . . When women realize that they are the homeland, that there is a case of honor, and a lame (*tullido*) man in the house who does not rise to defend that honor, she must put him out on the street until he solves said matter of honor. The power of a homeland's salvation lies in its women. If the woman is weak, we are all weak. (Acosta Lespier [1950] 2000, 130)

> Nations are as good as their women. The son is as good as his mother, and to compare a degenerate man with a woman, is not an insult to men, but rather to women. We must erase our idea that women represent physical or moral weakness. . . . And when women take the streets, dagger in hand, pistol in hand, and disdainfully look at men who run, there will no longer be any cowardly man in Ponce, Fajardo, Vieques, Mona Island, or any sacred corner of the homeland. (Acosta Lespier [1950] 2000, 143)[39]

The active participation of some women as PN members and supporters, the organization—however limited—of women groups in support of the nationalist cause, and their increasing recognition as political agents to be convinced and publicly challenged to become nationalists, also reflected significant changes in Albizu Campos's acknowledgement of women's political capacities and importance.[40] By 1950, Albizu Campos more explicitly recognized women as political figures who could, as much as any courageous man, represent the religious virtues that were central to his understanding of nationalism and of the struggle for Puerto Rico's independence:

> The feeblest woman can tear down an empire if she has courage. Let them grip their rosaries, be inspired by the eternal. And our women will then push our men to become the glorious men they were born to be. . . . One is not worthy of a woman's entrails in Puerto Rico, if one does not defend with one's life the homeland's honor. Here, in Cabo Rojo, the resurgence must take place . . . here, the greatest patrician of nineteenth century Puerto Rico [Betances] was born. His ashes are here. (Acosta Lespier [1950] 2000, 151)

Although Albizu Campos and the PN leadership remained thoroughly patriarchal in their party structure and political outlook, failing to fruitfully engage with and integrate the gender-conscious political work advanced by Puerto Rican feminists, the changes in Albizu Campos's thought suggest that feminist politics were making their way to the forefront as a *requirement*—rather than a secondary addendum—for the archipelago's liberation. Partly to counter this fundamental, inherent limitation of Puerto Rico's nationalist tradition to imagine a truly *sovereign* archipelago, feminist struggles have increasingly insisted since then that *la revolución será (trans)feminista o no será* ("the revolution will be [trans]feminist, or it will not be"). They have also become leading protagonists of the archipelago's movements toward decolonization and true liberation, as chapter 4 documents.

Indeed, if racism, misogyny, queerphobia, and all forms of discrimination are not recognized as structural to colonial oppression, a political project of liberation that would overcome them becomes impossible to imagine. These forms of exploitation will not simply fade away with juridical-political sovereignty. Our decolonial struggle must be conceived regionally *and* as a struggle to ensure our communitarian-artistic-bodily sovereignties.

BEYOND THE TEXT AND INTO THE BODY

While the arguments offered throughout this chapter are amply substantiated by evidence from Albizu Campos's and the PN's available primary texts, it is also true that, when moving beyond them, as well as beyond the immediate context of the Puerto Rican archipelago, one can encounter unexpected submarine relations and much more nuance. This last section briefly considers two further instances of Puerto Rico's archive of Caribbean relations as they pertain to Albizu Campos, but these are of a more bodily and ephemeral quality, in contrast with the texts examined so far. The first concerns some biographical considerations, while the second relates to the Puerto Rican's performative embodiment of his political struggle. Both matters bring Albizu Campos closer to Betances and Capetillo, as well as to the artists and activist collectives explored in part II of this book.

Primarily as a result of Cristina Pérez Jiménez's (2019) and Gerald J. Meyer's (2011) research from the standpoint of the Puerto Rican, Hispanic, and wider Caribbean diasporic nodes in the continental United States, and especially in New York, Puerto Rican nationalism becomes a much more complex phenomenon.[41] Meyer discusses the allegiances and collaborations—both in the archipelago and in the continental US—between American Labor Party Congressman Vito Marcantonio, Albizu Campos, and Gilberto Concepción de Gracia, the founder, in 1946, of the *Partido Independentista Puertorriqueño*.[42] On her part, Pérez Jiménez studies the 1943–1944 weekly newspaper *Pueblos Hispanos*, financed by the American Communist Party for the advancement of Puerto Rican independence, where such prominent nationalists as Juan Antonio Corretjer—the main figure discussed in Pérez Jiménez's essay—and Julia de Burgos regularly published. Pérez Jiménez argues that "*Pueblos Hispanos* reminds us that the Nationalist Party was never a homogeneous bloc, but rather was fractured into groups, including a socialist-leaning wing of the party that came to thrive in the barrios of New York, for whom nationalist and Communist ideological standpoints were not incongruent" (2019, 57).[43]

A regionalized perspective on Puerto Rican nationalism thus becomes noticeable if approached from an expanded archipelagic consciousness that includes our diasporas. As we saw above, gathering nationalism's relations with the Caribbean region from an exclusive consideration of nationalist texts, and of Albizu Campos's interviews, texts, and speeches, is an exercise requiring the greatest of subtleties and results in a limited reading. As was the case for Betances in the nineteenth century and for Capetillo in the early twentieth century, in New York and other such metropolitan, imperial cities, ironically, it was—and perhaps continues to be—significantly easier and more accessible to meet, collaborate, and dream with fellow Caribbean peoples.[44]

The second instance in Albizu Campos's affective archive bringing him closer to every other figure and collective in this book is the performative quality of his politics, or, in other words, its embodiment. Although an extensive commentary on this is beyond the scope of this chapter, at the very least it must be said that the available visual archive suggests that Albizu Campos (as well as the PN's *Cadetes de la República*) was as committed to a politics of dress as Capetillo, although, of course, not subversively in terms of societal gender expectations. When making public appearances, Albizu Campos was meticulous in his sober, ascetic elegance, typically wearing a light or dark grey three-piece vested suit with white shirt and bowtie. Images from nationalist meetings and rallies clearly show his command of the stage and the audience's attention, which was the result not only of the contents of his speeches—amply considered in this chapter—but also, and simultaneously, of his performative embodiment of the liberation ideal: bodily performance, voice, dress, *mise en scène*.[45] Images and available documentation also reveal that the PN was meticulous in its staging and symbolic use of rites/ceremonies of allegiance (Rosado [1992] 2009, 185), commemoration, and memorial services, as well as images and objects, prominent among which were the flags of Puerto Rico and Lares, and the machete (Dávila Marichal 2015–2016, 43–45).[46]

Figure 3.1. Pedro Albizu Campos at the Partido Nacionalista *Tribuna* Courtesy of the Ruth M. Reynolds Papers 1915-1989 at the Archives of the Puerto Rican Diaspora, Center for Puerto Rican Studies, Hunter College, City University of New York

Moreover, the aural documentation—ironically made as part of the local and federal persecution of the nationalist leader for "the crime of being an effective rhetor" (Víctor Villanueva 2009, 632)—has been amply discussed as a demonstration of Albizu Campos's unquestionable command of the voice as political weapon and of the crafting of a public persona with the most intense magnetism. Incontestably, as Mara Negrón has argued, the *tribuna* aesthetics and performance cultivated at the beginning of twentieth-century Puerto Rico (see chapter 2) finds in Albizu Campos its epitome, which continues echolocating until the present and beyond:

> Albizu's speeches were performative, they *said and did* something. Of course, not what he would have wanted them to. But his speech has done something in Puerto Rico's oral history . . . His figure blinds and reappears. It is a specter, in the Derridean sense, with which we continue speaking, consciously or unconsciously. The nation has related itself and has made itself through speech, which gives his words a powerfully theatrical character. It has been insisted upon quite a bit that a tale is crafted to create the illusion of something. But perhaps we

should not forget that the act of the performative word ends up producing an event. (2009, 955)

It thus comes as no surprise that the most complete and celebrated theatrical adaptation of Albizu Campos's political life—Nelson Rivera's 2005 *El Maestro*, one of the cultural productions analyzed in Negrón's essay—revolves around his recorded speeches, highlighting throughout the command of the voice and its power by Puerto Rican actor Teófilo Torres.[47]

Afro-Puerto Rican Pedro Albizu Campos devoted his extraordinary life to a heroism in many ways conscripted by its historical context, but, nevertheless, characterized by an unparalleled determination toward Puerto Rico's liberation. Perhaps his most astonishing achievement is to have drawn very different conclusions from his Spanish-nostalgic, Catholic, *arielista* ideological stance than those of the ruling White *criollo* political-intellectual class in his immediate Puerto Rican atmosphere. His would not become a project of obedience, accommodation, and financial calculus, as he repeatedly denounced had been the case with the *Partido Unión*, in which he was once a member, and which would become the precursor of the *Partido Popular Democrático*'s neocolonial apotheosis under Luis Muñoz Marín's leadership.[48] Albizu Campos stands to this day as perhaps Puerto Rico's most uncompromising symbol of dignity in the midst of the most humiliating and disgraceful material and immaterial conditions. His clairvoyance concerning the harms of US imperialism—unabashedly declared since the 1920s—was nothing short of prophetic.[49] Despite its limitations, his was an enduring project of resolute love for these, our assailed islands.

Resounding Voice

Before you became Albizu, you were Pedro and I waited for you next to the boat at the San Juan port. I was already an enthralled, if slightly intimidated, admirer. Of course, you had your world-making voice. The bloody grains of persecution and torture had not yet coarsened it.

When you arrived, with your effortless elegance, I heard you talking to the press, representing your upcoming maritime journey as a mission. Since Homer, and probably before, it seems nearly impossible for narrations of such voyages in our hemisphere to avoid that kind of grand, heroic language. But I think I understand the ways in which you needed the lofty tone, dear Pedro, to summon us all. The unabashed denouncement of our subjugation that you were willing to make netted me. You spoke truth to power, oh yes, indeed! You taught us language can forge the real. But you also reminded us that language is never enough.

I wish I had had the courage to jump clandestinely on the boat and travel with you to the Dominican Republic, Haiti, Cuba. I don't know if we could have become friends in an intimate sense, but I would have certainly loved to walk with you from *tribuna* to *tribuna* wearing one of your gray three-piece suits. I'm sure you wouldn't have liked my choice of dress, but maybe you could have found it in you to excuse me for it once you witnessed my skills at being a nerdy assistant against empire.

I continue naming my desires, as you did: I wish I could have spoken with you hours on end about the sea and the islands. I know deeply that you loved this place, in spite of History, as Walcott would say. But I wonder what you felt about the sands. About the beach? About studying our common, insular outlines on the horizon?

I wish I could have cried with you, for a long, long time, and I wish I could have held you.

Did you have time, dearest fighter, for the oceanic wind to beat your skin, for the mouth of rivers to flow into your anguished eyes? What bodily sensations overcame you when you felt, intensely, every day, the need for freedom?

Did you like to swim? Where?

Did you ever feel like you were living underwater? Is the suffocation absolute?

Despite the evidence of the systematic attempt to asphyxiate you, my dearest Pedro, you grew gills. For you and for all of us. Your anticolonial spirit, fierce animal, roused fires nobody could extinguish. They are still burning today. They are indeed.

NOTES

1. See his 1987 book, *1898: La guerra después de la guerra*.
2. In response to a long quote from Pedro Albizu Campos in which he displays an idealized representation of Puerto Rico's conditions under Spanish rule—a matter I discuss extensively in this chapter—Picó summarizes the realities uncovered by twentieth-century Puerto Rican historians as follows:

> [I]t is obvious that by 1898, life and work conditions for a great number of Puerto Ricans had been substantially modified by means of processes such as the concentration of land in sugar estates (*latifundios cañeros*), the mechanization of the sugar production's manufacturing phase, the expansion of cigar and cigarette factories, and the control of the harvest, selection, and shipment of coffee grains. The prevailing economic and political structures at the time tended to privilege the aspirations and interests of some sectors, especially businessmen and traders. The generalized discontent with these structures and the virulence of social conflicts induced the state's representatives to display mechanisms of repression and intimidation that, however, never managed to extinguish resistance. (1987, 22–23)

In the following pages, Picó (1987, chapter 1) goes on to detail the extreme inequality and destitution that the Puerto Rican rural majorities were experiencing at the end of the nineteenth century, which helps us understand why, initially, the US intervention would not be vigorously opposed.

3. In *Beyond Coloniality* (2019), Aaron Kamugisha amply documents a similar phenomenon across the Anglophone Caribbean region.
4. During this time, furthermore, thousands of Puerto Rican workers moved to the island's capital—San Juan—and emigrated to the United States under the auspices of an economic scheme designed to encourage emigration. Originally published in 1976 as *Puerto Rico y Estados Unidos: Emigración y colonialismo*, Manuel Maldonado Denis's *The Emigration Dialectic: Puerto Rico and the USA* (1980) studies the colonial motivations behind the exodus that has greatly determined Puerto Rican history ever since.
5. See, for instance, Mario R. Cancel-Sepúlveda's and José Anazagasty's *Porto Rico: Hecho en EEUU* (2011) and Lanny Thompson's *Imperial Archipelago* (2010).
6. See Franklin W. Knight's "The Caribbean in the 1930s" (2003) for an illuminating panorama of the regional political transformations at the time. See also Margarita A. Vargas Canales's essay "La revuelta también vino de la caña" (2010), where she provides an illuminating discussion of the significant bonds between Puerto Rican cane workers—especially active in class struggles and strikes in 1930s Puerto Rico—Albizu Campos, and the nationalist cause. For a comparison between Albizu Campos's and Garvey's nationalisms, as well as their respective understandings of the categories of "race" and "nation," see Juan Manuel Carrión's "Two Variants" (2015). In so historicizing Albizu Campos's anticolonial stance—as much as this book does with every other figure and collective it engages—I am deeply mindful of David Scott's caution: "These ['postcolonial'] critics have sometimes assumed that the questions to which the anticolonial nationalists addressed themselves—questions about their presents and their connection to their pasts and their hoped-for futures—were

the same as the ones that organize their own contemporary concerns and preoccupations. . . . In my view, an adequate interrogation of the present (postcolonial or otherwise) depends upon identifying the *difference* between the questions that animated former presents and those that animate our own" (2004, 3).

7. As Rebollo Gil has written: "And perhaps the only terms acceptable when facing a seemingly impossible situation is the will to say no. To not be defined from above or outside" (2018, 61).

8. It also helps to understand the eventual popular appeal of Albizu Campos's political enemy, Luis Muñoz Marín.

9. Marisa Rosado's biography of Pedro Albizu Campos, *Las llamas de la aurora* ([1992] 2009), is the most thorough account available. It documents Albizu Campos's popular appeal, as well as the extreme violence of the persecution he was subjected to. Over the course of his life, the nationalist leader was arrested and imprisoned on three occasions, both in Puerto Rico and in the United States, and subjected to torture that included sleep deprivation and solitary confinement. Albizu Campos also declared that, during his second imprisonment, his body was the object of irradiation experiments, which effectively burned him alive, with long-lasting health effects (Rosado [1992] 2009, 374–87). Nationalist leaders and supporters, as well as their families and loved ones, were repressed, and even massacred, multiple times, the most notorious of which were the massacres in Río Piedras (1935) and Ponce (1937). Upon returning to Puerto Rico from prison in the late 1940s, Albizu Campos was subsequently submitted to constant surveillance and persecution, under the auspices of the neocolonial government's 1948–1957 Law 53, popularly known as *Ley de la Mordaza* (Gag Law), explicitly approved to contain Puerto Rican nationalism, and with the overt complicity of the first elected (in 1952) Puerto Rican governor, Luis Muñoz Marín, who had previously been a nationalist sympathizer. Although this chapter only covers Albizu Campos's trajectory until 1950, it should be noted that the violent repression of Puerto Rican nationalism performed by the local police force under the direction of the US government, and with the notorious support of right-wing Cuban exiles after the 1959 triumph of the Cuban Revolution, persisted and intensified during the 1950s and beyond. After the 1950 Jayuya uprising led by Blanca Canales, who declared Puerto Rico a free republic and raised its flag, the attack on the US president's Blair House the same year, and the 1954 attack on the US Congress led by Lolita Lebrón, the local government launched a massive persecution campaign popularly known as *carpeteo*, in reference to the voluminous binder files that the Puerto Rican police, under the FBI's COINTELPRO program, amassed. Among pro-independence, socialist leaders actively persecuted and violently harassed well into the 1970s, Juan Mari Brás and Carlos Gallisá stand out. Likewise, the federal government continued arresting nationalists and pro-independence fighters—both women and men—through the 1980s. The last political prisoner whose sentence was commuted was Óscar López Rivera in 2017, a case I return to in chapter 4. The 1976 assassination of Mari Brás's son, Santiago Mari Pesquera; the 1978 police assassination, under orders from the then-governor of Puerto Rico, Carlos Romero Barceló, of Carlos Enrique Soto Arriví and Arnaldo Darío Rosado Torres at *Cerro Maravilla*; and the FBI-led assassination of pro-independence leader Filiberto Ojeda Ríos in 2005, are the most recent

instances of outright assassination on the part of the US and Puerto Rican governments. Beyond Rosado's biography, for more on the history of political repression in Puerto Rico against anticolonial movements and leaders, see Atiles-Osoria's *Jugando con el derecho* (2018), José "Ché" Paralitici's *Sentencia impuesta* (2004) and *La represión contra el independentismo puertorriqueño* (2011), Luis Nieves Falcón's *Un siglo de represión política en Puerto Rico* (2009), and Jacqueline N. Font-Guzmán's *Experiencing Puerto Rican Citizenship and Cultural Nationalism* (2015). Specifically on Puerto Rico's political prisoners, see Jan Susler (2006).

10. For a fascinating account of Albizu Campos's experience at Harvard, see Anthony De Jesús (2011).

11. By mid-1930s, after the Río Piedras Massacre, Albizu Campos announced the PN would no longer participate in electoral politics, since elections—and most dramatically as the eventual *Estado Libre Asociado* (ELA) "pact" drew nearer—worked purely as instruments to establish a "colony by consent" (Rosado [1992] 2009, 321).

12. For the United States, as well as for the Puerto Rican neocolonial agents, Albizu Campos reserved his harshest language, just as Betances did concerning Spain and Puerto Rican *autonomistas*. A few examples serve as an index of a consistent rhetorical treatment that, within a colonial context increasingly servile to an idealized US government toward the mid-twentieth century, undoubtedly constituted a crucial political statement: "[the United States] confused the word democracy with assassination . . . We are fattening them up; they are feeding themselves with our blood; sucking us every day . . . they come to suck the blood of our nationality" (Acosta Lespier [1949] 2000, 53); "they want to strangle us, drown us, assassinate us" (Acosta Lespier, 84); [referring to Luis Muñoz Marín:] "the great puppet" (Acosta Lespier [1950] 2000, 163); concerning Muñoz Marín's and the Partido Popular Democrático's (PPD's) 1952 ELA Constitution, "The master never trusts its slaves. He trusts a free enemy. But a slave offers his signature, and it is worthless" (Acosta Lespier, 180); "That oath by Muñoz Marín that you heard on the radio: 'I swear, . . . that I will defend the constitution and the laws of the United States.' That is what he swore, and he mocked you. And today, well, you have him at the governor's mansion. For what? To govern? He can't govern here. If Muñoz Marín or the legislators believe that . . . they're crazy" (Acosta Lespier [1949] 2000, 58); "The governor's mansion has become a hotel, a great hotel, and you pay that hotel's expenses . . . and when a puppet comes from over there [*allá*, the United States] he must be served a banquet and Muñoz is the head waiter" (Acosta Lespier, 59–60).

13. "[T]he 1932 West Indian Conference at Roseau, Dominica, which called for federation through self-government, and . . . the widespread labor uprisings in the British Caribbean colonies that escalated the movement for federation" (Martínez-San Miguel and González Seligmann 2020, 41).

14. Dalleo offers an illuminating and compelling pan-Caribbean analysis of the aftermath of the US occupation of Haiti. His analysis leads him to posit the need for a non-nationalist alternative. Although Dalleo focuses on the West Indies Federation, "we can also think of Aimé Césaire's advocacy of departmentalization or the development of the Associated Free State status in Puerto Rico as reflecting a regional uncertainty about the nation-state that Haiti's occupation highlighted" (2020, 63).

Concerning the relations between Haiti and the Spanish-speaking Caribbean, see also Vanessa K. Valdés (2020).

15. Referring to "civilization" and its heritage, Albizu Campos also used, rather interchangeably and in tandem with senses prevalent in the Latin America of his time, the terms "blood" and "race."

16. Valdés provides another relational instance between Albizu Campos and Haiti through her analysis of the 1936 lectures delivered by Dantès Bellegarde, Haitian ambassador to Washington from 1930 to 1933, at UPR–Río Piedras, the site of the Río Piedras Massacre the year before. Valdés argues that, in presenting a panorama of his sovereign archipelago for a Puerto Rican audience, Bellegarde's four lectures, published as *Haiti and Her Problems*, offer a significant critique of the United States and multiple commentaries on the strategically unmentioned nationalist struggle in Puerto Rico. Indeed, the critic finds that "Bellegarde's message resonates with that of Pedro Albizu Campos" (2020, 65).

17. See also Torres, *Tomo I*, [1930] 1975, 98.

18. Albizu Campos uses the same vocabulary himself: "All the adjacent islands, Vieques, Culebra, La Mona, El Desecheo, Caja de Muerto, are directly considered property of the US government. There is no reason not to declare the coasts in front of those islands as US property, too" (Acosta Lespier [1949] 2000, 105).

19. I return more amply to Vieques and Culebra—and the ongoing *destierro* (exile, banishment)—in chapters 4 and 5.

20. If committed to a very subtle analysis, this statement can be complicated by ephemeral details emerging from Rosado's biography, such as the fact that, during the 1936 trial that resulted in Albizu Campos's first imprisonment, "letters from residents of Saint Thomas sent to addresses of nationalists were read" (2009, 258). Much further research is required to assess the quality and extent of these possible archipelagic collaborations.

21. To be sure, Álvarez Curbelo argues that Albizu Campos's thought shows a confluence of *arielismo*, "the right of nationalities to self-determination," and "economic nationalism" (1993, 88).

22. For a thorough discussion of the afterlives of Shakespeare's *The Tempest* across the Americas and the Caribbean, see Peter Hulme (2002). It should be noted that *arielismo* was countered by the Cuban Roberto Fernández-Retamar through his focalization of the enslaved, openly combative Caliban as a more apt symbol for the American hemisphere's resistance.

23. "In Albizu there is no possible bridge between both empires: the drama is moral, binary. His heroes are the nineteenth century separatists, whom he 'Spanishes' (*españoliza*) as part of his exaltation of the Hispanic symbolic universe. The year 1898 was a dividing line signaling a clear moral rupture" (Díaz Quiñones 1997, 238).

24. "It was part of the providential order of things that our people's ancestors would give light to the world. In the logical order, it couldn't have been otherwise, as the Greco Latin civilization is the only one in the west. . . . they consecrated themselves to [human unity] and with the indigenous race and the African race, they reunited humanity, integrating it in the Race (*la Raza*) we are part of, unique, because of its constitution, steadfast in its mission of being the interpreter of life and the ends

of existence. The Anglo Saxons followed our fathers' trace and established themselves in similar latitudes to those they already inhabited. But they have not learned the human significance of the discovery, which is the discovery of humanity by itself, and they have experimented with the indigenous race, and remain separated from the African race, imported to exploit the conquered territory, within a providential racial purism (*purismo de raza providencial*), and what they call a problem of race is more fundamental, it is a problem of civilization" (Torres, *Tomo I*, [1923] 1975, 16–17).

25. "God is the creator and protector of nationalities and men are impotent at destroying its divine oeuvre" (Torres, *Tomo I*, [1933] 1975, 248).

26. *Négritude* appears, of course, in the wider context of Pan-Africanism, which was becoming a significant ideological and political force across the Atlantic at the time. Concerning the Puerto Rican context, in "'Isla de quimeras'" (1997), Arcadio Díaz Quiñones provides a particularly illuminating comparative analysis of contemporaries Antonio S. Pedreira (see this book's Introduction), whom he calls "the intellectual"; Luis Palés Matos, "the poet"; and Pedro Albizu Campos, "the prophet" (230). Specifically on Palés Matos, a writer whose significance I signaled in the Introduction and whose poetic echo returns in chapter 5, Díaz Quiñones provides essential clues that help us understand why his thought would have been irreconcilable with Albizu Campos's—and Pedreira's—positions: "Palés the poet is perhaps the most complex: he says, openly or metaphorically, what Pedreira or Albizu avoided or were incapable of seeing about the relations between culture and sexuality, and culture and race. In his verses, something very modern persists that was impossible to insert in Pedreira's or Albizu's discourses: the link between sexuality and subjectivity, the incommensurability of the body's desires" (239).

27. In commemoration of the *Grito de Lares*, Albizu Campos proclaims: "Lares is the bolivarian repercussion of Ayacucho in the Antilles. In that heroic deed, the american homelands, most especially Venezuela, the birthplace of the *Libertador* [Simón Bolívar], represented themselves by their blood. Those illustrious men knew this archipelago's greatness, which served as the basis for the expansion of the Christian civilization in America and is today the fortress of resistance against the barbarism coming at us from the North" (Torres, *Tomo I*, [1933] 1975, 273).

28. See Carrión's essay (2015) for a thorough discussion of this understanding in Albizu Campos.

29. For a general panorama on this issue, see Buscaglia-Salgado's "Race and the Constitutive Inequality" (2016). Specifically in the Puerto Rican context, see Baerga's *Negociaciones de sangre* (2015) and Rodríguez-Silva's *Silencing Race* (2012).

30. Because of this, reparations from Spain were surely unthinkable for Albizu Campos or the PN. This idea, as a political exigency and requisite for independence and, indeed, nation-building, is entirely absent from the primary documents examined. However, in one of Albizu Campos's speeches he notes in passing that reparations from the United States are in order "for thirty-three years of military occupation" (Torres, *Tomo I*, [1931] 1975, 211).

31. This idealization of Puerto Rico's condition at the turn of the twentieth century has been amply discredited by Puerto Rican historians, as we saw at the beginning of this chapter.

32. See also Acosta Lespier [1949] 2000, 122.

33. The argument of "racial unification" as a Spanish accomplishment that Puerto Rico shares with the Iberoamerican republics is also evident in Albizu Campos's commentary on the Mexican thinker José Vasconcelos's visit to Puerto Rico (Torres, *Tomo I*, [1927] 1975, 46).

34. Contrasting interpretations of Albizu Campos's concept of race, which consider it a radical, liberatory stance, can be found in Carrión (2010), Mariani Ríos (2016), and Santiago-Valles (2007). The latter, in particular, offers a very different take on Albizu Campos's allegiance to the Hispanic tradition:

> [F]or him [Albizu Campos], Hispanization involved the unequivocal transformation of "the [entire Hispanic/Latin] Race" which, logically and by implication, could no longer be white insofar as it now included "illustrious families of pure blooded Africans" who were no less Spaniard, nor any less Ibero-American (Albizu Campos 1972:203). This counter-civilizational perspective, of a plebeian black/mulatto transfiguration of Iberian bodies and Hispanic Culture, is once again strikingly similar to the contentions of several Afro-diasporic organic intellectuals in the U.S. (122).

However, even if we concede that Albizu Campos's position on race radically transformed "Hispanic" and "Ibero-American" to make them *no longer (only) white*, in his thought, Puerto Rico is still, resolutely *not* Afro-Antillean and, therefore, its struggle and eventual independence from the United States is not understood in allegiance with the Caribbean archipelagic region. For a contemporary discussion on the "myth of racial harmony" in Puerto Rico, listen to NPR's April 2020 "Puerto Rico, Island of Racial Harmony?"

35. This is still ongoing today, as denounced by multiple political organizations and collectives, some of which are discussed in chapter 4. See also the work of *Colectivo Ilé* and its radio program *Negras*, broadcast from the University of Puerto Rico's radio station, as well as *Revista étnica*.

36. For a thorough discussion of both race and gender issues as they were reflected and discussed in the work of male and female intellectuals and writers of Puerto Rico's early twentieth century, see Roy-Féquière (2004).

37. I provide just one example: "The visionary patriot, the man of mythical-religious temperament, of traditional, acid-proof, morals, the politician loyal to his ideas, the apostle of the Puerto Rican cause, as his fanatics call him, has emerged" (Torres, *Tomo I*, [1931] 1975, 197). For an ample discussion of the religious discourse assumed by and associated with Albizu Campos, see Rodríguez Vázquez's *El sueño que no cesa* (2004), in which he traces the significance of the nationalist leader's turning of "political struggle into metaphysical mission" (261). Although this discussion is beyond *Affect, Archive, Archipelago*'s scope, the religious-political thrust exhibited by *albizuista* nationalism should not be discarded out of hand as a revolutionary force, considering its invaluable importance for African-American and Afro-Caribbean liberation struggles, as well as for Latin American social movements associated with *teología de la liberación* (liberation theology).

38. See also Torres, *Tomo I*, [1931] 1975, 209, and Acosta Lespier [1949] 2000, 77.

39. See also Acosta Lespier [1950] 2000, 149.

40. Among the most notable women nationalists are Dominga de la Cruz Becerril, Trina Padilla de Sanz, Blanca Canales, Ruth Mary Reynolds, and Lolita Lebrón. The extraordinary, archipelagic life of Afro–Puerto Rican *tabaquera*, political agent, singer, and theatrical performer de la Cruz Becerril, who was born in 1909 into abject poverty in Ponce, merits a study in and of itself, to which I am committed in the future. In the meantime, see Margaret Randall's *El pueblo no sólo es testigo: La historia de Dominga* (1979), as well as essays by Ivette Romero-Cesareo (1994) and Margaret Power (2018). Gladys M. Jiménez-Muñoz (2018), for her part, comparatively discusses de la Cruz Becerril and Padilla de Sanz in terms of their contrasting class and racial status. For a general overview of women's active participation in and support of the PN, see Margaret Power's (2018) and José Manuel Dávila Marichal's (2014) essays. Power writes: "The most prominent women members were and understood themselves to be important participants in the Nationalist Party. They dedicated their life to it and to the independence fight, despite the risks this meant for their wellbeing. By participating in the Puerto Rican independence struggle, they transgressed prescribed gender roles, but as *independentistas* and Nationalists, not as feminists. Neither publicly nor, possibly, even consciously, did they challenge established ideas regarding womanhood, but they certainly did in practice" (2018, 131).

41. Significantly, Dalleo's work points to the same diasporic circuit as crucial in fostering a twentieth-century version of the *confederacionista* dream: "Major thinkers of federation and decolonization, particularly Richard B. Moore and George Padmore, developed their political perspectives through engagement with the [US] occupation [of Haiti]. New York was the site of a pan-regional community for the Barbadian Moore and Trinidadian Padmore, who at various times worked closely with Nevis-born Cyril Briggs, Jamaican W. A. Domingo, Surinamese Otto Huiswoud, and Puerto Rican-born Arturo Schomburg . . . The diasporan location of so many supporters of federation, echoing the emergence in New York and Florida of much support for the *Confederación Antillana* in the nineteenth century, usually leads to a focus on how this context made it easier for these activists to think regionally because of their dialogue with Caribbean people from neighboring islands" (2020, 62–63).

42. A necessary analysis beyond the scope of this book concerns the Caribbean relations pursued—or ignored—by later, formal parties appearing in the wake of the *Partido Nacionalista*, which include the enduring *Partido Independentista Puertorriqueño*, the *Partido Socialista Puertorriqueño*, and the more recent *Partido del Pueblo Trabajador* and *Movimiento Victoria Ciudadana*.

43. Rosado's biography also covers Albizu Campos' networks of relations and support from communists in the US, both while imprisoned and during his period of convalescence in a New York hospital in the early 1940s. Still, as Rosado documents ([1992] 2009, 302-04), the interwar struggles to advance an internationalist-as-communist agenda sustained a difficult, strained relationship with the enduring exigency of as-yet-existing colonies in the traditional sense. Two main positions vied for predominance: that national independence was a prerequisite for communist internationalism, and that communist internationalism, if victorious, would bring an end to colonialism. This debate is reflected in the relations between Puerto Rico's PN and the

American Communist Party, as well as in the relations sustained by leaders from both political formations. In contrast with Capetillo's "socialist anarchism" and the socialist and communist allegiances of contemporary nationalists such as Corretjer, but in tandem with Betances, Albizu Campos never propounded socialist or communist economic views. His main and constant struggle was for Puerto Rican independence. Thus, for him, "the cause of Puerto Rico's independence could not be postponed or submitted to the Allies' interests" during World War II (Rosado [1992] 2009, 304).

44. This has been a repeatedly experienced phenomenon by intellectuals, artists, and political agents from across the Caribbean. See Kamugisha's *Beyond Coloniality* (2019) and Torres-Saillant's *An Intellectual History of the Caribbean* (2006).

45. See multiple examples of this in the selections of photographs from the Ruth M. Reynolds archives held at the Center for Puerto Rican Studies. Among many others related to the PN and the nationalist struggle in Puerto Rico, this archive also includes images of the dramatic physical harm experienced by Albizu Campos while in prison. As Luis A. Avilés reminds us, using the examples of Albizu Campos, Lolita Lebrón, and Filiberto Ojeda Ríos, this politics of elegant dress, which does not preclude its "exchange for persecution and jail clothing, which are clothes of humiliation and torture," has been shared by multiple nationalists and pro-independence fighters in Puerto Rico's tradition (2019, 177–78). Moreover, an oblique confirmation of the enduring validity of this point can be found in recent news reports that Albizu Campos's "costume," worn by actor "Moncho" Conde in his representation of the nationalist leader for the theatrical piece *La víspera del grito*, staged as part of the 2018 commemoration of the *Grito de Lares*, was stolen in what the actor denounced as a politically motivated theft (see Quiñones Maldonado 2018).

46. Áurea María Sotomayor has analyzed Albizu Campos' and the PN's reliance on these ritual and theatrical elements in terms of Eric Hobsbawm's "invented traditions," with the purpose of "creat[ing] the national cohesion" and "a consciousness about *lo puertorriqueño* (Puerto Ricanness)" (252), as well as "constitut[ing] the [revolutionary] subject through its interpellation" (256).

47. Significantly in the context of this book, Negrón offers a comparative analysis of Rivera's *El Maestro* alongside the movie *Babel* and Teresa Hernández's piece, *Nada que ver: Composiciones escénicas sobre el yo* (2006–2007), an artist to whose work I turn to in chapter 5.

48. See the interview entitled "Pedro Albizu Campos" (Torres, *Tomo I*, 1975, 43), and various other statements on Puerto Rico's political parties also included in Torres's compilations.

49. Mónica Jiménez has recently argued that Albizu Campos's "warn[ing] . . . not to be lulled into believing that the US could offer the island something other than colonialism" might be even more relevant in today's Puerto Rico than it was in Albizu Campos's time (2019, 269).

II

POLITICAL PERFORMANCES IN PUERTO RICO'S AFFECTIVE ARCHIVE OF CARIBBEAN RELATIONS

The two chapters comprising part II walk-swim with late twentieth- and early twenty-first-century activists and artists in Puerto Rico, both in the form of collectives (*Agua, Sol y Sereno*; *Amigxs del MAR*; *Comuna Caribe*; *Mujeres que Abrazan la Mar*; and *Coalición 8M* in chapter 4) and as solo artists (Teresa Hernández in chapter 5). Their works, within the continuum of our affective archive of Caribbean relations, stand as vital contributions to Puerto Rico's communitarian-artistic-bodily sovereignties. The chapters offer detailed commentary on the politically charged, embodied, performative practices that these activists and artists nurture in relation with our archipelagic region, our coastal and maritime realms, and our "liquid homeland." Echolocating on the other side—and in the wake—of the performative politics that the figures explored in part I engaged in, the following chapters on political performances defend the desirability of collective, horizontal, underseeing organization toward Puerto Rico's emancipation in connection with the Caribbean, which necessarily entails reparations and all forms of bodily sovereignty (see especially chapter 4). The chapters also argue for the political importance of imaginative, intuitive, speculative works, as well as for the material and affective solidarities that such fulgurations enable and amplify in the region (see particularly chapter 5).

Chapter Four

Tidal Relations of Art, Struggle, and Liberation

Agua, Sol y Sereno, Amigxs del MAR, Comuna Caribe, Mujeres que Abrazan la Mar, *and* Coalición 8M

> My utopia is for that great Confederation where Puerto Ricans could contribute our strengths to all Caribbean peoples and vice versa . . . Building that dream is nothing new; we had it before the European conquest. I do not think it is impossible to achieve.
>
> —Hilda Guerrero, interview with the author, April 2021

The end of the twentieth century in Puerto Rico was characterized by a disenchantment with the traditional nationalist project—a significant measure of which was deliberately enforced by power—and a simultaneous explosion of the colonial, neoliberal model, which functioned as a phantasmagoria of progress while, in fact, precipitating the present's deep crises. Situated on Glissant's and Capetillo's relational sands—between art and activism, Puerto Rico and the Caribbean, our immediate shores and those of our region—the collectives explored in this chapter emerged precisely then, in the 1990s. Ever since, the theater collective Agua, Sol y Sereno, as well as the activist groups and individuals comprising Amigxs del MAR, Comuna Caribe, Mujeres que Abrazan la Mar, and Coalición 8M, have been engaging and furthering—often in collaboration with each other—underseen forms of Puerto Rican communitarian-artistic-bodily sovereignties. This chapter walks-swims with some of their myriad productions, interventions, and positions, particularly as they pertain to our Caribbean affective imaginary and relations, the coasts and the sea, Puerto Rico's island municipalities, the struggle for reparations and debt cancellation, and the defense of all forms of life.

When asked about the use of the feminine *la mar*, Hilda Guerrero answers unequivocally:

We use it intentionally because we perceive *la mar* as our mother and feminine. We sustain a very intimate relation with Yemayá. We make many offerings to *la mar*, when we celebrate the solstices and equinoxes, among other ceremonies we perform there [referring to the *Pocita de Piñones*].[1] We always finish our sessions with an offering of flowers and chants to *la mar*. There is always a relation, and we name her, also, as Yemayá, the goddess of *la mar*'s waters. But also, the relation, not only with the sea, but also with water as our first mother, because when we are in our mother's womb, we are surrounded by water. So, water is the first element with which living beings, including plants, are in relation, and without which we would not be able to survive.[2]

Indeed, our "liquid homeland," *la mar*, brings into Glissantian relation all the artistic-activist-artivist groups this chapter engages with: *Agua, Sol y Sereno* (Water, Sun, and Night Breeze, ASYS), *Amigxs del MAR* (Friends of MAR, AMAR), *Comuna Caribe* (Caribbean Commune, CC), *Mujeres que Abrazan la Mar* (Women Who Embrace the Sea, MAM) and *Coalición 8M* (8M Coalition, C8M), the majority of which—with the exception of C8M—were founded in the 1990s and have remained active ever since.[3] The continuing governmental and capitalist colonial abuse, as well as the dogged resistance and survival of Vieques and Culebra, Puerto Rican island municipalities regularly described as "colonies within the colony," also traverse these pages as a fundamental embodiment of the archipelagic decolonial project this book aspires to.

In what follows, I discuss the archipelagic ways in which all these collectives and struggles, working in and through political performance and performative politics, have engaged in a practice of mutual collaboration in diverse efforts and initiatives, as well as in connection with other Caribbean activist and artivist groups beyond Puerto Rico. This chapter also considers the groups' common relation with *la mar* as the natural-material-imaginative scenario and context of Puerto Rican and regional healing and emancipation.[4] Finally, I consider the collectives' insistence on intersectional creation and struggle, where demands for debt cancellation and reparations are propelled on a par with urgent ecological concerns and an equally imperative opposition to colonial-, gender-, race- and class-based exploitation.

A TIDAL THEATER

The experimental, transdisciplinary, and community-driven theater collective *Agua, sol y sereno* (ASYS) was founded in 1993 in Puerto Rico by Pedro Adorno and Cathy Vigo, and was officially incorporated with Rosabel Otón as part of the team. Artists Miguel Zayas and Rudek Pérez joined ASYS soon after, while others, such as Ronald Rosario, Kisha Tikina Burgos, Julio Ramos, Israel Lugo, Taina Rosario, Jessica Rodríguez, and Cristina Vives, have been (or still are) members of the group in different moments of its trajectory. The collective's name, as Adorno recounted in our interview, comes from a popular saying in Puerto Rico: *Eso aguanta agua, sol y sereno*. The saying translates literally as "That resists water, sun, and the night breeze," which means that if something (in ASYS's case, the theater collective itself) can endure all three natural elements, then it can withstand anything. Having "learned by doing" (Geirola 2013, 166) with theater masters such as *Los teatreros ambulantes* (Rosa Luisa Márquez and Antonio "Toño" Martorell), *Teatro Pregones*, Bread and Puppet Theatre, Peter Schumann, Augusto Boal, and several independent theater collectives from various Latin American countries, such as *Yuyachkani*, *Malayerba*, and *La Candelaria*, the collective's work is directly related to the bodily, affective archive of the Caribbean: "(The collective's) scenic proposals are tied to the development of the so-called 'dramaturgy of the body'" (*Agua, sol y sereno* n.d.). Moreover, ASYS's foundational impulse is deeply imprinted by political struggles for liberation, as much as by a steadfast ecological and Caribbean consciousness, which Adorno has described as an "ethical and ecological translation and the act of perceiving the space of the homeland not from a specific place, but from a broader Caribbean" (*Agua, sol y sereno* n.d.).

ASYS is further sustained by an unwavering commitment to vulnerable populations and communities where, "usually, theater in Puerto Rico does not reach" (*Agua, sol y sereno* n.d.). This affective bond "has had a vital repercussion in the very development of the creative process in the country's arts" (Quintero 2012, 31), resulting in a theater that transcends "traditional theater spaces" (Irizarry 2005, 42). ASYS's work has been extraordinarily diverse in terms of content, form, and *mise-en-scène*, including "costumed groups and parades, processions, passacaglias, dramatic and theatrical pieces" (*Agua, sol y sereno* n.d.). They also regularly participate in popular festivals and celebrations—most notably, in the *Fiestas de la Calle San Sebastián*, which take place every January and constitute the traditional end to Puerto Rican Christmas—with vibrant, rhythmic *comparsas* (costumed groups and parades) that include their signature *zancudos* (stilt-walking) and *cabezudos* (big-headed puppets). The latter usually embody important figures of contemporary struggles and triumphs in Puerto Rico, such as celebrated athletes—ping pong star Adriana Díaz, for instance—and activists—for example, Alexis Massol and the recently deceased Faustina "Tinti" Deyá, from *Casa Pueblo*, with its long trajectory of leading ecological and sovereignty struggles. *Cabezudos* also include significant historical figures, such as Betances. Moreover, ASYS organizes a continual program of community workshops and has been involved in multiple social justice struggles in the country.

In what follows, I explore ASYS's piece *Marea alta, marea baja* (*High Tide, Low Tide*) (hereafter *Marea*), which was staged in 2002 at the Escambrón beach in San Juan. As explained by Adorno in our dialogue, this setting provided an extraordinary seating space—the littoral at sunset—for an audience of between one thousand and two thousand people every night, including hundreds of kids from public housing projects, in a massive theater experience very rarely achieved in Puerto Rico. As is customary in ASYS's trajectory, the collective piece included dialogue in conjunction with dance, puppets, live music, and improvisation, elements that were characterized at the time by the *El Vocero* journalist Jorge Rodríguez as "a masked language and . . . amazing props" (2002, 9). Conceptualized by a group of ASYS members and collaborators (Pedro Adorno, Cathy Vigo, Mareia Quintero, Santiago Benet, María Soledad Agosto, and Natalia Oliveras), *Marea* boasted the work of forty actors ("acrobats of sand," as Adorno described them to me), musicians William Cepeda and Choco Orta, and the inclusion of multiple members of the surrounding communities.[5]

Roberto Irizarry, the only other critic who, to my knowledge, has written about *Marea*, summarizes the plot as follows:

> *Marea* dramatizes a combat through several historical periods between local rebels called *Prójimos* (Neighbors) and external presences called *Grises* (Grays).[6] At the same time, the struggle is fed by the phantasmagorical return of historical and mythical figures, such as the Spanish conqueror Diego Salcedo, whose fame is the result of having been killed by indigenous Taínos in 1644, thus demonstrating the Spaniards' mortality, and Mackandal, the Haitian Revolution's hero fictionalized by Alejo Carpentier in *The Kingdom of this World* (1949). In the midst of the struggle, the private guard David Sanes, who was killed in real life during artillery practice by the USA Navy in the Puerto Rican island of Vieques, dies, as well as Encarnación, the archetypal representation of Dominican immigrants to Puerto Rico. In the end, both (Sanes and Encarnación) are initiated as ancestors in a funerary ritual led by Salcedo and Mackandal. (2005, 49–50)

About the decision to do theater at the beach, Adorno has explained that "it was not staging, but rather the main character" (Geirola 2013, 168), while Irizarry has written: "*the beach is the dividing line* between the interior and the exterior, between the local population, the invaders, and the rebels who land on the island in solidarity, *between Puerto Rico and the rest of the Caribbean*, and between the soundness of land and the ambiguity of the Atlantic Ocean's water" (Irizarry 2005, 50, emphasis added). However, I believe there is much more to this decision when considering the piece's contents.

Figure 4.1. *Agua, Sol y Sereno*'s *Marea alta, marea baja* (promotional material). Courtesy of Pedro Adorno

Marea deliberately intermingles historical events and figures with mythic elements that make it "cosmic," an adjective used by Adorno in our interview. Some significant examples of "the cosmic" in *Marea* are the "sea turtle's egg, principle of life" encountered by the blind man at the piece's onset (*Agua, sol y sereno* 2002, Script 1), the arrival of a turtle that has come to lay her cosmic eggs and die on the coast (an implicit reference to the Native American myth of the cosmic turtle), and Mackandal's transformative search for the "Tanze," the "ancestral fish," as the Narrator recounts:

> After escaping from the fire in neighboring Haiti, Mackandal submerged into the ocean. With grouper, shark, octopus, and manta ray skin, Mackandal follows the trace of Tanze, the ancestral fish.... His drum song crosses the Atlantic. Through the coral kingdoms where his brothers who did not reach the coast live. Through the oil-stained kingdoms that whales have led him to discover. Mackandal owned the fire, and, among dolphins, he breathed peace. But today he reaches the sand because he knows that in the sea's immensity his song becomes foam, while on the coast, his voice reached the kingdom of this world [notice the direct reference to Alejo Carpentier's 1949 novel]. (*Agua, sol y sereno* 2002, Script 4)

For their part, the cosmic eggs,

> were fish tanks with a floating candle inside. The first egg would come out and one of our children would come in running and take it. The kids collected the sacred turtle's eggs.... Then, the actors with trees on [their] backs entered, which were gigantic sculptures ... that were like three turtles with trees, and they would plant themselves. Then, the children would climb on top of the turtle with its eggs ... and, as the night set in, they would be carrying these eggs with candles. The island's future. (Adorno interview with the author 2019)

A poetic chant accompanied this moment, which Adorno shared with me in our interview: "Every person who dies, evaporates, and, since we are seventy percent water, if somewhere on Earth the sky exists, it is in the sea. So, every time you see the salty sea, you are touching something of your grandparents, your great-grandparents, and your great-great-grandparents" (2019). Can one find a more indelible, bodily manifestation of our "submarine unity" across time and space than this performative, ephemeral moment?

Contrary to Irizarry's (2005) interpretation of the beach as a "dividing line," I perceive the beach and its constant tidal movements (*mareas*) as the piece's "main character," as Adorno pointed out. The beach and its tides contain the fundamental cosmic origins *and* the recurrent submarine archipelagic connections—emerging from the ineffable violence of transatlantic slavery and ongoing patters of "clandestine" migration, *as well as* from liberatory flight and volcanic seabed union—that the piece insists upon. This is exemplified well in the following instances: "The sea sweeps, baptizes, drowns, cleanses, carries and brings, returns" (*Agua, sol y sereno* 2002, Script 1), and "With her eyes wide open and her submarine sense of smell, Encarnación has traversed day and night the foundations of *that bridge of islands that is the Caribbean. Always awake. Watching them come and go. . . . Trying to help some of her brothers. . . . pointing the way of favorable currents*" (*Agua, sol y sereno* 2002, Script 7, emphasis added).

Marea potently reminds us that imperialism's legacy of Caribbean balkanization has never been able to erase the relations that have always been—and remain—in the ocean's depths. This is also made abundantly clear in ASYS's description of *Marea* in its 2002 promotional materials:

> Uniting the lands of the many coasts lapped by the Caribbean Sea, *Marea alta, marea baja* tells stories of voyages and shipwrecks that seem *to have always been there, hidden in the depths of the sea*. This creative piece is part of *our contact with that other world, its mythologies and its relation with our everyday lives*. . . . Internal experimentation and exploration have been the starting point to *achieve a connection and integration* with that which surrounds us. This piece represents an *appropriation of a space so intimate for us as the sea*; it constitutes a new look at that great mirror that we call the Caribbean Sea and an opportunity to see ourselves reflected [in] it and, consequently, to *recognize ourselves as what we are, an island*. Thus, this ode to the Caribbean Sea . . . that *blood of the great body that we call the Antillean Archipelago*. (*Agua, sol y sereno* 2002, emphasis added)

Later in Irizarry's essay, he makes claims that contradict the "dividing line" interpretation and, as a result, more closely relate to the arguments presented here: "the space of the beach, perpetually borderline and connected to an ocean in eternal movement, becomes an echo of the unresolved opening of Puerto Rican society" (2005, 51). Indeed, I agree with the critic when he finds in *Marea* an impulse to go *beyond* the national, which is at the heart of the archipelagic and bodily understanding of sovereignty this book is concerned with: "the funeral reunion [of Mackandal, Salcedo, Encarnación, David Sanes, and other historical figures] celebrated in *Marea* underlines the importance of communities greater than the national one, and the constant necessity to revise the elements that constitute local membership" (52–53). Irizarry also registers the archipelagic, Caribbean claim underlying the piece through the inclusion of Mackandal as an "inspiring ancestor to the *Prójimos*" and Encarnación, whose "fatal voyage in *yola* to the island is staged through a dance in the sand suggestively accompanied by the *Prójimos*' leader" (53). As with the activist collectives discussed below, with the work of transdisciplinary artist Teresa Hernández in chapter 5 and, more or less obliquely, with the three figures comprising part I, the stage for the continuous encounters with our Caribbean fellows-in-relation is, precisely, the coastline, the liminal sand, where we rehearse in art and struggle the regional, communitarian, and bodily sovereignties we need.

When asked in 2009 with which piece in ASYS's trajectory he was most unsatisfied, Adorno chose *Marea*:

> It is one of the most attended shows by our public . . . A visually stunning set . . . but I think that, in dramaturgical terms, it remained more like an *auto sacramental* where one did not know very well what was being proposed. . . . It's a piece that I will return to, and I want to do more pieces like that throughout the Caribbean, more pieces in front of the sea. (Geirola 2013, 169)[7]

I take this to mean that the piece failed to communicate a more familiar dramaturgical composition, in the tradition of Aristotle's conflict-driven drama. But perhaps that is precisely *Marea*'s greatest strength: its capacity to encompass conflict within, in Capetillo's spirit, an overarching reflection on relation and unity. The history of the Caribbean and Puerto Rico has been so overdetermined by conflict and violence that a theater collective with a mission to "heal" (Geirola 2013, 187) is a welcome and desirable accomplishment. All those whom this book honors, having fought for the Caribbean archipelagos' union and nurtured their affective bonds through such struggle, are cosmically applauding, in the depths of the Caribbean Sea, ASYS's tidal theater. They, as much as us, will be delighted to see *Marea* again "throughout the Caribbean," as Adorno promises.

KAYAKS FOR RELATION AND LIBERATION

In the fourth scene of ASYS's *Marea*, and as part of the conflict between the *Prójimos* and the *Grises*, the former set up camp on the west side of the beach while the latter build a golf course on the east. Soon we learn that the camp is, at the same time, a historical *rescate de tierra* (land rescue) and the site of a working-class family's Sunday beach trip.[8] Then, both the camp and the golf course acquire another incarnation—and the most historically immediate. In the Puerto Rican island of Vieques, the camp becomes a civil disobedience exercise to prevent the US Navy from further military practice, the perimeter of which is the golf course-turned-bombing zone. The dead man carried to the aquatic stage in the ninth scene turns out to be David Sanes, who was killed by Navy personnel, in a tragic "mistake," in Vieques in 1999.[9] Sanes's death sparked the massive movement *Paz para Vieques* (Peace for Vieques), which achieved the US Navy's exit from Vieques in 2001—though the clean-up of radioactive materials is still unfinished. The movement's most distinctive tactic was the establishment of civil disobedience camps.[10]

However, before the camps were set up, people put their bare bodies in the bombing zone to prevent the Navy from continuing their "practices." One of the first activists to sit down in the Vieques bombing zone was Alberto De Jesús Mercado, who goes by the name Tito Kayak and has been a lifelong direct-action political activist–performer in a myriad of struggles.[11] "Facing the lack of a movement that combined environmental education and consciousness-raising with direct social actions in order to elevate our demands to the public sphere," Kayak was also the co-founder, in 1995, of *Amigxs del MAR* (AMAR), which was instrumental in Vieques's struggle against the US Navy. "MAR" stands for *Movimiento Ambiental Revolucionario* (Revolutionary Environmental Movement), but *mar* in Spanish also means "sea." The activist organization is therefore named after the affective bond of friendship (*amigxs* means "friends") linking Puerto Ricans, at once, to the sea and to revolution.

As discussed with its current president, Vanessa Uriarte Centeno, the organization's ideological and material commitments, which ultimately respond to the objective of Puerto Rico's decolonization, are captured by the suggestive concept *manatiburón*.[12] A combination of the words in Spanish for manatee and shark, AMAR defines *manatiburón* as "the conjunction of the manatee's passiveness through our daily educational work and the shark's sagacity through our direct political manifestations." Deepening this relation between manatee and shark, Alexis Pauline Gumbs's celebration of both is relevant here:

> The West Indian manatee has teeth that move, a migrating set of molars in her mouth that she replaces after use. The West Indian manatee has nails, so do her West African cousins. The West Indian manatee, like all manatees, knows how to move between salt and fresh water in search of warmth, hydration, and vegetation. . . . Could we communicate more like manatees, who stay in communication in all kinds of emergencies, place their bodies in a way that protects children, touch each other to remember and know? (2020, 159–61)

> I love each of you [sharks] for stretching your cartilage and opening your gills. Thank you for remembering the ancient rule of cycles that [you] are still protecting. And what a celebration when we realize that our survival need not make us into monsters. . . . When we evolve in our assignment of brave guardian vulnerability. (2020, 26–27)

Feeling deeply and practicing constantly how to care for each other, how to traverse the waters, salt and fresh, while, at the same time, stretching and opening the breath, surviving without becoming the enemy, and being vulnerable in our bravery: all of this sounds exactly like AMAR!

Significantly, Uriarte Centeno continues, the organization uses participatory democracy's "horizontal models of equitable and inclusive participation," while their ideological and political orientation is "ecosocialism," which they define as "a contemporary branch of socialism that is much more inclusive and opposed to exploitation not only of humans by other humans, but also of nature by humans and by our economic system. At the same time, ecosocialism considers gender and race intersections as essential to the struggle for social equality" (personal interviews with author, 2019 and 2021). Struggling against the life-and-death effects that ecologically exploitative real estate, development, and corporate tourist firms—which have been traditionally supported by the local, colonial government—have on racialized, impoverished, and marginalized Puerto Ricans is at the heart of AMAR's political trajectory.

As part of their defense of Puerto Rico's ecologies, AMAR has focused especially on the protection and restoration of bodies of water and their surrounding environments, as well as on the struggle to prevent the privatization of beaches by developers.[13] In this, they are the most visible activist collective laying claim to our coastal "here" over the past thirty years. But it should be remembered that AMAR comes on the heels of a longer archive of struggles against power's devouring of our littorals. A 2016 *Primera Hora* news report, entitled "Medio siglo de lucha por el mar" ("Half a century of struggle for the sea"), notes that, at least since 1970, there are recorded instances of Puerto Ricans fighting against the tourist industry's privatization and destruction of our archipelagic coastlines.

As noted by Uriarte Centeno, "fomenting in Puerto Ricans the sense of us being Caribbean peoples and of the sea as an intrinsic part of our very being, are recurrent themes in our [AMAR's] discourse and actions" (personal interviews with author, 2019 and 2021). Indeed, to AMAR we owe in Puerto Rico the constant insistence, turned rallying call, that *las playas son del pueblo* (beaches are the people's) and *las playas son nuestras* (beaches are ours). As recently as May and June 2021, demonstrations led by this call—and violent police repression against them—were developing in the already intensely gentrified and foreign-controlled western town of Rincón, where private developers intend to build a pool for an apartment complex on the shoreline (see Hernández Pérez 2021).

AMAR's conceptual and political struggle is for both environmental and racial justice, since, as Uriarte Centeno explains:

When we talk about our ancestors here [in Puerto Rico], we talk about the mountain *jíbaro* [peasant], who works the land, but the reality is that most of the population has lived all their lives on the coasts. It is a site of mobility, where our ports are located, where the sugarcane industry was set up, where enslaved, Black peoples lived and worked, and they constitute the basis for population growth in the country. To eclipse our blackness, we erase the coast. And we only see it when talking about foreign tourism, oh! What beautiful beaches we have! . . . And the Puerto Rican people who live along our littorals [oceanic or riverine] are Black Puerto Ricans or Afro-descendants. They are also the people who are worst off economically. . . . To this, which is already a pressure valve, you must add changing climatic conditions, sea level rise, coastal erosions. (personal interviews with author 2021)

Along one such marginalized coastline, and in the wake of a successful mid-twentieth-century struggle led by Enrique Laguerre[14] against the construction of three hotels in "the long beach that extends from Violeta Street [Isla Verde] to Piñones [Loíza]" (Costa 2011) and for the creation of the public *Balneario de Carolina*, AMAR performed one of its most extraordinary and long-lasting actions. In 2005, the collective occupied five acres of beachfront public land in Isla Verde, San Juan, right next to the *Balneario de Carolina* and the primarily Afro-Puerto Rican communities who live in Carolina and Loíza, to prevent the expansion of the Marriott Hotel in the area. As Uriarte Centeno explained, *Coalición Playas pa'l Pueblo* (Beaches for the People Coalition) emerged after AMAR's initial direct action and, together, they established a civil disobedience camp to protect the area. After ten years of continuous occupation, with a fraught and complex history of resistance, creation, popular education, and reforestation initiatives, on March 16, 2015, AMAR posted the following text on their Facebook page, which recounts the camp's history and its motives:

> On March 15, 2005, *Amigos del MAR*[15] occupied a coastal area under legal dispute, making real what the State's policy should be: "the most efficacious conservation of its natural resources will be public policy of the Commonwealth [of Puerto Rico]," according to the Constitution. Ten years ago, because of the decision to preserve our coasts at all costs from developers' hands, who are only interested in accumulation and the multiplication of their own capital, we founded the *Playas pa'l Pueblo* Coalition. This group has unwaveringly defended the only portion of coast that has not been impacted by edifications in the northern littoral, from the San Juan area through to the Carolina Bay. This achievement is not only a cause for celebration. Although as Puerto Ricans we claim this as a victory, ten years of struggle for five acres of land constitutes a call for the unification of a country in defense of its resources, which are threatened by our own State . . . It is amply demonstrated that only by being united and conscious of the importance of our natural environments, can a people stop the government and developers from destroying our resources. The beaches are of the people. They are not for sale.[16]

Figure 4.2. *Amigxs del MAR, Coalición Playas Pa'l Pueblo,* and *Agua, Sol y Sereno* Celebrate Their Triumph in Carolina, 2019   Courtesy of Luis López

AMAR and the *Playas pa'l Pueblo* Coalition, which brought together multiple groups, organizations, and individuals committed to the defense of public access and ecologically conscious enjoyment of Puerto Rican beaches, maintained the camp for fourteen uninterrupted years, due to the lengthy process to determine the legal standing of the ninety-nine-year rental of the disputed land to the Marriott corporation on the part of Puerto Rico's government.[17] The coalitional movement was victorious in 2019, when the Marriott corporation withdrew and the municipal government of Carolina assumed jurisdiction over the land so as to keep it in public hands. In a further submarine relation, popular celebrations of the camp's success on the now-protected beach included a parade of ASYS's *zancudos* and *cabezudos* (Betances was one of them), against the setting sun in *la mar*'s horizon.[18]

Another of AMAR's astonishing gestures as part of the Puerto Rican affective archive of Caribbean relations was Tito Kayak's 2012 *Kayakeando por el Caribe por la libertad de Óscar López Rivera*. The effort, which contributed immensely to the international campaign that eventually led to the Puerto Rican political prisoner's liberation in 2017,[19] was characterized by a simultaneous flashback to the Arawak past of constant inter-insular travelling by sea, as well as a foreshadowing of a Caribbean integration to come. Kayak travelled over one thousand nautical miles in a glass fiber kayak (the *Cetáceo*), built for this purpose in Venezuela, from where he started his journey north. Stopping at most of the islands on his way back to Puerto Rico, the activist made connections with Caribbean peoples, while bringing regional and international attention to López Rivera's case. Along the way, he received all kinds of assistance from an array of Caribbean peoples, in a show of support resembling a synthesis of Caribbean history: freemasons (recall that Betances and most of his Confederation comrades were masons), Rasta families, fishermen and women, diplomats, owners of small-scale hotels, owners of ferry businesses, and political figures.[20] For three months, Kayak became, in a word, Puerto Rico's own Odysseus, without the violence, arrogance, or power wielded at home. Is it surprising, therefore, that Lowell Fiet, longtime theater historian and critic, would describe Kayak as an "environmental and political '*performer*'" (2011, 248, emphasis added), and his deeds as "virtuoso acts of ecological and political protest" (249)?[21]

Kayakeando explicitly envisioned the liberation of López Rivera, the longest-held political prisoner in the United States, as a project of Caribbean integration. AMAR's initial call for artistic support attests to this, while emphasizing the integration of bodily and cultural practices through music, dance, and rhythm, which we also saw in *Marea*:

> One of our pending tasks is to weave a network of Caribbean collaboration toward environmental integrity and the strengthening of our capacity to unite as Caribbean peoples in achieving our common goals of solidarity and mutual aid and support. Our objective is to inspire musicians of all Caribbean musical genres to use their productions and musical videos as forms of support for [Tito Kayak's] voyage to achieve the immediate liberation of Óscar López Rivera. . . . the desired effect [is] to create a tsunami of support for the immediate liberation of Óscar López Rivera, and for a Caribbean free from aggression and from projects averse to animal life and the viability of preserving our Caribbean cultures and the unity of Caribbean peoples.[22]

This last aspect of Kayak's feat was particularly emphasized by Uriarte Centeno in our dialogues:

> I think . . . the idea was to recreate our ancestors' movements from island to island, and the ways we related, to claim publicly, not only that Óscar was imprisoned and [that for his liberation] Caribbean solidarity [was necessary], but also how to establish those bonds with the rest of the Antilles and how to show that our realities are the same . . . *Kayakeando* was extremely challenging. It was such a difficult thing to do! But the sentiment was there. (personal interviews with author 2021)

Moreover, Uriarte Centeno highlighted that AMAR is primarily interested in contextualizing Puerto Rico within the Caribbean region, rather than continuing the dominant trend in the archipelago's public opinion of thinking within the US framework. She shared with me ideas about food, water, and energy sovereignty as achievable if pursued collaboratively in the region, while adding:

> Since we [referring to Puerto Ricans, in general] do not think of ourselves as part of [the Caribbean], it is always easier to look at ourselves in comparison with [the US]. It blows my mind that we can compare ourselves so much with the US, Europe, or the rest of Latin America when we . . . are much more like the people of Guadeloupe, and we confront and share the same geographical realities and the same environmental challenges. Colonial control continues [there as much as here] in a much more latent and, perhaps, violent way. We are Black, we are something different. (personal interviews with author 2021)

She also rightfully insists on the contemporary urgency of regional relations while confronting the climate emergency:

> As an environmental organization, we are Caribbeanists because it is imperative. What happens on any island of the Antillean ark will evidently affect us all, and in a situation of vulnerability due to climate change, we see this as a totality. Not as something isolated. We are the most vulnerable region, in addition to the Mediterranean, precisely as the islands that we are. Our communities continue surviving situations in common but, due to the different colonialisms, we find ourselves separated. . . . The Caribbean could really set the terms for the world's economy since everything travels through here.

Kayakeando was, however, far from Tito Kayak's first incursion into a creative-activist event in favor of Puerto Rico's liberation as part of a Caribbean integration project.[23] Michael Niblett and Kerstin Oloff (2009) recount some of Kayak's previous actions at sea:

> On 24th July 2006, the Puerto Rican environmentalist activist . . . "Tito Kayak" arrived in the Dominican Republic . . . after venturing for the third time on a long and dangerous crossing of the shark-infested Mona channel in a small kayak. Tito Kayak, a modern day popular Caribbean hero, forms part of the group *Amigos del MAR*. . . . As a member of this group, he has often emphasized that the Caribbean Sea should belong to the Caribbean peoples rather than being defined as international waters open to international traffic. His journey, undertaken in the name of a united Caribbean, a free Puerto Rico, and in the hope of establishing more harmonious relations between humankind and the environment, highlights a number of the defining features, forces and problems

shaping the region, most notably perhaps that of migration and the continuous movements between the islands that have existed since pre-Columbian times, when settlers crossed from one island to the next in canoes. (9)

As such, they conclude, "Tito Kayak's actions can be seen in the context of a longstanding history of popular resistance in which individual or national attempts to secure liberty have looked out to the surrounding territories for their fulfillment" (9–10).

Tito Kayak's recurrent mobilization of the kayak, even using it as his chosen name, merits a word. As a contemporary version of the ancestral Arawak *yola* that united the Caribbean archipelagos and of the contemporary, precarious *yolas* of fishermen and women, as well as Caribbean migrants at sea, the kayak is perhaps the most potent symbol of exploited Puerto Rican and Caribbean peoples' struggles against the forces of power. Propelled exclusively by the precarious human body, the kayak's movement is necessarily slow, gentle, and noiseless, a walk-swim in our "liquid homeland." Thus, it is the most ecologically sound, though the riskiest, mode of transportation at sea, situating the human in communion with *la mar* and its living species, while reminding us of our deep fragility.

The potency of the kayak as a symbol and the politization of its historical echoes are often present in struggles for justice in our archipelago. In addition to the notorious participation of people in kayaks surrounding the governor's mansion in Old San Juan during the 2019 *Verano Boricua*, as recently as March 2021 a group of women activists performed an effective blockade in Vieques using kayaks. Bringing attention to the dire transportation issues faced by both Vieques and Culebra residents, this action denounced the colonial Puerto Rican government's grossly preferential treatment—through outright design or indifferent abandonment—of tourists and affluent foreigners over our archipelago's residents. For islands with extraordinarily high rates of cancer and other potentially lethal conditions related to long-term effects of military contamination, and that lack basic services guaranteed by the state, including functioning public hospitals, the constant failures, delays, and cancellations of the now-privatized ferry system between the so-called "main" island and Vieques and Culebra have, quite literally, deadly effects.[24] In light of this, the kayak blockade also became a platform from which to amplify the residents' demands and proposals for a sensible and immediate solution to the transportation crisis.

At the same time, however, Vieques and Culebra are also the sites of some of the oldest forms of historical relation, affirmation, and exchange between the Puerto Rican archipelago and other islands in the Caribbean, what Carlo Cubero would call "transinsularism" (2017). In many ways, they constitute the most potent embodiment of our archipelagic condition, of our affective archive of Caribbean relations.[25] Although this is scarcely known and taught in Puerto Rico, various waves of bidirectional migration bond Vieques and Culebra to the US Virgin Islands since the US "bought" them from the Danish government in 1917, not coincidentally the same year the US Congress approved the Jones Act for Puerto Rico (see the Introduction).

Furthering the revolutionary, submarine memory of Betances's *confederacionista* dream—which, as we saw in chapter 1, was very much situated in St. Thomas while he lived there as a result of Spanish persecution—in Vieques's case this history has been researched and documented primarily by Robert Rabin, a notable activist and historian who was imprisoned for his role in the struggle against the US Navy in Vieques, by Johanna Bermúdez-Ruiz in her documentary *Sugar Pathways* (2015) (www.vimeo.com/ondemand/sugarpathways), and by Nadjah Ríos Villarini (2016), who has argued that Puerto Rico should be thought of as "bridge islands" rather than its usual representation as a "frontier" between the "Lesser" and "Greater" Antilles.[26] For its part, Culebra's deep history of "transinsularity" is the subject of Cubero's book *Caribbean Island Movements: Culebra's Transinsularities* (2017), in which he argues:

> [T]he Culebra island experience is shaped and expressed through a double condition of being simultaneously isolated and connected, mobile and insular. It is a condition that acknowledges the peculiarity of island narratives, understands that they are shaped in movement, in contact with otherness, and relies on these multiple references and travel to constitute an insular world view. I call this double condition transinsular. . . . Transinsularism also acknowledges the ways in which islands retain and develop their specificity in relation to other sites, rather than assimilate, collapse, or otherwise fold into a single entity with its relational locations. Transinsularism is an attempt *to make a positive case for the creative potential of Caribbean island experiences on their own terms*. (3–4, emphasis added)

Moreover, both Cubero and Ríos Villarini have documented a potent history of cultural, bodily, and performative "transinsularity" and creolization in Culebra and Vieques, respectively, through the "liquid homeland" that *la mar* brings together: the vigorous tradition on both islands of calypso music results from relations with the US Virgin Islands and the generalized adoption of steel drums through embodied, sensory, and performative relations with Dominica and Trinidad and Tobago. The music, dance, and rhythm so important to AMAR and ASYS is thus echoed in our historical archive of Caribbean relations across Puerto Rico's eastern littorals.

Performative politics at/with *la mar* have characterized, as we saw above, AMAR's extraordinary trajectory, which continues evolving to this day. Indeed, as Uriarte Centeno discussed with me, AMAR has fruitfully transformed over recent years to deepen its understanding of intersectional—specifically, race, gender, and environmental—and regional struggles. In its trajectory, moreover, AMAR has sustained multiple collaborations with *Comuna Caribe* (a collective to which I turn in the following section):

> Our collaboration started when *Comuna Caribe* was traveling regularly to the Dominican Republic to work with Haitian-Dominican communities at the border . . . we collaborated with the organization of numerous events, with fundraising and media support. Tito Kayak also has a personal relationship with them. . . . We have also participated in multiple manifestations in solidarity with Haiti and the Dominican Republic, and some of them were organized and celebrated at the *Playas pa'l Pueblo* camp. . . . Several actions have also been developed . . . to publicly advance the argument of our Caribbeanness. (personal interviews with author 2021)[27]

As this book goes to print, AMAR is furthering a Puerto Rico–wide campaign to gather volunteers who will document, map, and publicize abandoned and destroyed edifications unlawfully made along our coasts on the *zona marítimo-terrestre* (maritime land zone), as well as to identify potential sites where new constructions are advertised or identifiable. This participatory, citizen-led effort seeks to better understand the actual conditions of our "coastal crisis" to more robustly pressure the Puerto Rican legislature to approve the *Ley de la Zona Costanera de Puerto Rico* (Coastal Zone of Puerto Rico Law) and the *Ley de Moratoria de Construcción en la Zona Costanera* (Law for a Moratorium on Construction in the Coastal Zone), both presented in January 2021 by senator María de Lourdes Santiago.[28]

Additionally, deploying the *manatiburón* approach of both popular education and direct political action, AMAR and others will use the campaign's resulting information to lead communitarian initiatives—and demand state support and funding, both at the local and federal levels—to guarantee environmental protections, mitigation, and, crucially, physical reparations for Puerto Rico's ecosystems using native vegetation, and mangrove and dune recovery projects. In post–Hurricane María Puerto Rico, Uriarte Centeno explained, AMAR understands these efforts as part of contemporary struggles for the archipelago's *recuperación justa* (just recovery) in the context of environmental justice, as part of initiatives in collaboration with other organizations such as *Ayuda Legal Puerto Rico* and *AgitArte*. Specifically, AMAR is currently working alongside two ecologically dissimilar coastal communities in the municipalities of Loíza and Vega Alta, with the purpose of empowering residents to create their own recovery and reparation plan and to execute it with the recovery funds that are currently being sought for their use.[29]

AMAR's continuing struggle, as Uriarte Centeno movingly told me, ultimately defends everyone's—humans' and nonhumans'—*derecho a permanecer* (right to remain) and *derecho a regresar* (right to return) to their archipelagic habitats. The systematic—albeit often indirect—displacement of coastal populations has been a characteristic feature of capitalist colonial exploitation in the Caribbean, including Puerto Rico, as Uriarte Centeno knows intimately. Citing Vieques's historic and contemporary plight as a paradigmatic example, she explained in our interviews: "if there are less and less people participating in political processes, it is easier for power to exert its violence, taking us away from where and what we are" (personal interviews with author 2021)[30]

LA MAR'S HEALING EMBRACE

Against power's onslaught, Hilda Guerrero, longtime activist and biographical embodiment of Caribbean archipelagic relations, has resolutely been "from where and what we are" (personal interviews with author 2021). In the 1990s, while neoliberalism inaugurated its far-reaching grip on colonial Puerto Rico, and the Caribbean and Latin American regions more broadly witnessed new forms of capitalist exploitation via Clinton-era trade agreements, Guerrero was coming into contact with the myriad organizations, collectives, and individuals involved in the 1991 celebration of the hemispheric campaign *500 años de resistencia indígena y popular*, which organized hemispheric gatherings, events, and interventions.[31] In its joint efforts, the campaign denounced the official, government-sponsored commemorations across the region of the five-hundred years since the so-called "encounter" between the "Old" and "New" worlds. The campaign *500 años de resistencia* also sought to accurately represent 1492 as the inauguration of "a genocide, an extermination, which installed a colonial system that is still with us today" (Rodríguez 1991, 81). The campaign argued for celebrating the unwavering resistance of Caribbean and American Indigenous and Black civilizations, at all levels of social life, from 1492 until the present. Significantly, one of the campaign's key demands in the early 1990s was "the struggle against our countries' external debt" (Rodríguez 1991, 82).

The Caribbean region was included in the campaign, albeit limited to Cuba (as coordinator), the Dominican Republic, Haiti, and Puerto Rico. Specifically in the Puerto Rican 1990s context, seeking to participate in such a campaign was quite revolutionary, as the official, dominant discourse—greatly propelled by Pedro Rosselló's larger-than-life, neoliberal administration—was that of an unequivocal celebration of the "civilizational legacy," the "progress" and "development" enabled by European "discovery," and the racist fantasy of Puerto Rico as intermediary between the "Latin/Hispanic" and "Anglophone/American" worlds.[32] Going against all this is precisely what Guerrero set out to do. Never a partisan of apathy or cynicism, Guerrero travelled from Puerto Rico to Guatemala for the campaign's 1991 *Encuentro* and presented Puerto Rico's case—and that of the Caribbean more generally—as fundamental for regional integration. As she recounted the experience to me, she intimated how deeply liberatory it was, insomuch as the unprecedented, multitudinous, and diverse gathering of *los de abajo* (those from below) demonstrated a collective will for an *other* world.[33]

A few years later, in 1999, Guerrero also participated in the *Grito de los Excluidos* (Scream of the Excluded), "a popular manifestation born in Brazil in 1995, with the impulse of the Social Pastoral areas of the National Conference of Bishops, and in response to the increasing situation of social exclusion in that country resulting from the application of neoliberal adjustment cuts" (León 1999). In 1999, the *Grito* was expanded to the entire Latin American region, becoming instrumental in the development of *Jubileo Sur Américas* (South Americas Jubilee), a social movements network that, to this day and as we will see below, constitutes the leading voice against capitalist debt and for reparations in Latin America and the Caribbean.[34]

These late twentieth-century experiences were Guerrero's primary inspiration, both ideologically and affectively, to found in 2003 the *Comité Pro-Niñez Dominico Haitiana* (Committee Pro Dominican-Haitian Childhood), which changed its name to *Comuna Caribe* (Caribbean Commune, CC) in 2011. Since its inception, CC, which includes in its logo the motto *En la ruta de Betances, hermanando a las Antillas* ("On Betances's route, uniting the Antilles"), is an active member of *Jubileo Sur Américas*, as well as of the *Asamblea de los Pueblos del Caribe* (Assembly of Caribbean Peoples), where Guerrero and CC's collaborators have historically demanded the recognition of Puerto Rico's colonial plight and its active participation in regional discussions and decisions, especially in the face of the US government's prohibition of Puerto Rico's active membership in CARICOM (the Caribbean Community). Conceived as a "space of solidarity and critical reflection" (rather than an organization), CC's first and second struggle commitments, as listed on its Facebook page, are "against capitalism, colonialism, white supremacy, and patriarchy" and "for human rights and equality for all, but especially, for women, children, migrants, and marginalized communities, particularly in the Caribbean."[35]

Figure 4.3. *Comuna Caribe* Logo Courtesy of Hilda Guerrero

Figure 4.4. *Comuna Caribe* and *Mujeres que Abrazan la Mar* Handwoven Solidarity Banner Courtesy of Hilda Guerrero

As far as I am aware, CC is the contemporary space with the longest uninterrupted trajectory of political, educational, and cultural actions; campaigns; and collaborations explicitly concerned with linking Puerto Rico with other Caribbean archipelagos, and most especially, with the Dominican Republic and Haiti.[36] Among others, some of its actions, initiatives, and collaborations have included the following:

1. collaborations—including summer camps and other educational and cultural initiatives—with the *Movimiento de mujeres dominico-haitianas* (MUDHA, Dominican-Haitian Women's Movement) in support of impoverished and marginalized women in Haitian communities (*bateyes*) in the Dominican Republic[37]
2. collaborations with the Haitian feminist organization SOFA (*Solidarite Fanm Ayisyèn*, Solidarity Haitian Women), including support for the feminist camp established after the 2010 earthquake in Haiti[38]
3. collaborations, brigades, and humanitarian and medical aid provided jointly with *Le Group d'Appui aux Repatriés et Réfugiés* (GARR, Support Group for Refugees and the Repatriated), among which CC's support for the post-earthquake construction of the cooperative community *Village Solidarité* in the Laskawobas area in Haiti stands out[39]
4. fundraising for the establishment of a water transportation system coop run by women in the Mapou community in Haiti after the 2004 flooding emergency in the area[40]
5. support and solidarity with feminist movements in the Dominican Republic, which include the current struggle for the defense of sexual reproduction rights.[41]

More recently, CC has been directly involved, along with *Frente Ciudadano por la Auditoría de la Deuda* (Citizen Front for Debt Audit) and other Puerto Rican organizations—among which the *Colectiva feminista en construcción* (Feminist Collective under Construction, better known as *La Cole*) stands out—in crafting a regional campaign for debt cancellation and reparations in collaboration with *Jubileo Sur Américas*' regional leadership. Debt as a capitalist colonial form of control and exploitation is staggeringly rapacious in the Caribbean, with many countries having debts amounting to well over a 100 percent of their gross domestic product (GDP). Indeed, a 2021 report indicates that "several countries in the region have been among the most indebted in the world (measured in terms of the public-debt-to-GDP ratio) since gaining independence beginning in the 1960s."[42] Alongside Puerto Rico's *Centro de Periodismo Investigativo* (Center for Investigative Journalism), *Frente Ciudadano* has been instrumental in gathering most of the information available on the secretive, unconstitutional, illegal, and odious nature of Puerto Rico's $74.8 billion debt.[43] On its part, *La Cole* has been Puerto Rico's leading voice in direct political actions linking the debt crisis with gender and race exploitation in the archipelago.[44]

In 2019, these organizations, led by CC as part of *Jubileo Sur Américas*, launched the campaign *Haití y Puerto Rico: Deuda y Reparaciones* (Haiti and Puerto Rico: Debt and Reparations). Concerning Puerto Rico, the campaign had the following objectives: (1) Expose and raise consciousness concerning the harms caused by colonialism and the processes associated with Puerto Rico's debt; (2) join efforts stemming from the multiple, international expressions of resistance and struggle toward achieving Puerto Rico's independence and self-determination; and (3) demand reparations for the harms caused by the processes associated with Puerto Rico's debt.[45] As Guerrero explained in our dialogues, the campaign was scheduled to be launched first in Port-au-Prince, Haiti, but when that became unviable due to an uprising that made traveling to Haiti increasingly difficult, the campaign was instead presented in Trinidad and Tobago, in the context of an Assembly of Caribbean Peoples' meeting. Meanwhile, in Puerto Rico, the campaign was first launched on September 19, 2019, in Vieques.[46] Since then, it went on to be publicized on several occasions in 2019 and is still ongoing, although the 2020 pandemic year has adversely impacted its development.

In the context of this campaign, as much as in CC's work more generally, reparations are understood multidimensionally, in terms of historical, social, and ecological debts. Beyond the most immediate debt crisis, Guerrero highlights the demand for reparations for harms such as, among others (1) the use of Puerto Ricans as military cannon fodder for wars led by the United States, as well as the militarization of Puerto Rico itself through the establishment of military bases and the ensuing ecological and social effects; (2) the use of women's bodies as territories for experimentation; (3) the use of Puerto Rican lands for toxic experimentations, such as Agent Orange in the *El Yunque* rainforest and the ongoing harms of Monsanto and other corporations; (4) the multiple programs for population control and displacement; (5) the measures taken for rich foreigners to control lands and property and deepen gentrification processes; and (6) the misery and death resulting from governmental negligence and abandonment post–Hurricane María.[47]

Despite significant challenges—not least of which is the traditional Puerto Rican left's refusal to open itself up to true Caribbean, archipelagic collaborations (see chapter 3)—this campaign, and the possibility of linking it with wider Caribbean efforts for reparations currently underway (see the Introduction), are of the absolute essence. Moreover, CC's intersectional insistence on the defense and affirmation of multiple sovereignties (race, gender, class, migratory status) as integral to its decolonial struggle is a living example of a contemporary *confederacionista*, a truly liberatory and participatory political project for Puerto Rico and the Caribbean region. Guerrero herself gifted me the most moving articulation of her archipelagic dreams, with which *Affect, Archive, Archipelago* wholeheartedly agrees:

> My utopia would be that Betances's dream becomes concrete . . . that what was, in a sense, initiated by Chávez's ALBA [*Alianza Bolivariana para los Pueblos de Nuestra América*, Bolivarian Alliance for the Peoples of Our America] concerning mutual exchanges of products, becomes generalized. . . . my utopia is for that great confederation where Puerto Ricans could contribute our strengths to all Caribbean peoples and vice versa, a process whereby we would all strengthen each other. As [José] Martí said: "We are united by the mountain range below the sea." . . . [I dream for us to sustain] the wave of support and collaboration witnessed after the 2010 earthquake in Haiti . . . and for bringing down all borders. I wish for a universal citizenship . . . which first requires the struggle for regional citizenships. In our case, a Caribbean regional citizenship . . . which would allow us to travel freely between our islands, like our ancestors did. Building that dream is nothing new; we had it before the European conquest. I do not think it is impossible to achieve. (personal interviews with author 2021)

As Guerrero repeatedly reminded me in our dialogues, CC is also a home for multiple other projects that respond to its intersectional ideological and political position. Especially relevant in the context of this book is *Mujeres que Abrazan la Mar* (MAM), founded in 2017 in the Piñones area of the Afro-Puerto Rican coastal municipality of Loíza. As recounted to me by Guerrero, MAM originally responded to an invitation by longtime activist and community organizer Tati Fridman to create a women's aquarobics group in the area. At that time, Piñones was engaged in a struggle, which was ultimately successful, against a real estate developer's plan to build the *Costa Serena* megahotel in the area with the support of the Puerto Rican government. The construction would have had dire ecological consequences and would have displaced human and nonhuman communities. Significantly, and in connection with AMAR's work against beach privatizations discussed above, the battle in Piñones had the following as its primary slogan: *La playa es el patio de tu casa, defiéndela* ("The beach is your backyard, defend it").[48]

As a result, Guerrero did not want MAM to be solely about aquarobics. She thought the will to care collectively and collaboratively for women's health and bodies must be understood politically, historically, and ecologically. Thus, to this day MAM also considers itself a defender of our beaches and coastal communities.

Figure 4.5. *Mujeres que Abrazan la Mar* 2014 Calendar for Haiti   Courtesy of Yvette Pérez Álvarez

Figure 4.6. *Mujeres que Abrazan la Mar* 2016 Calendar for Ivania Zayas Ortiz   Courtesy of Ernesto Robles

Primarily women and nonbinary folks come to the *Pocita de Piñones* at least twice a week to heal and nurture their bodies at *la mar*, while also embodying spiritual and political work. The *Pocita de Piñones*, as Natalia Ramos Malavé (2019) poetically describes it, is a "beach in calm, sheltered by a reef that separates it from the swelling waves of the open sea."[49] On MAM's encounters and actions, Guerrero explains:

> We are convinced that *la mar* heals in many ways, not only physically, but also emotionally and spiritually. There is a very intimate connection between most of us and *la mar*. We go there not only to exercise, but also to perform ceremonies, rituals, [such as] the welcoming of solstices, equinoxes . . . and the *bendición de camino* (path blessing) for pregnant folks. We organize events to reflect on and heal our historical traumas from the Spanish conquest and enslavement . . . to support important political work in Puerto Rico, such as the defense of bail rights [in reference to the 2012 attempt by the Luis Fortuño government to limit them] . . . and to organize communitarian solidarities, such as we did after Hurricane María in 2017 and the earthquake sequence in 2020, as well as through CC's multiple initiatives in solidarity with Haiti. We have also made nude calendars in support of multiple causes, including raising funds for medical supplies for Haitian women, honoring the memory of singer and songwriter Ivania Zayas Ortiz,[50] and as a form of affirmation of our right over our own bodies and against the capitalist and Eurocentric dominant aesthetic of thin, tall, White, and straight-haired bodies imposed on us. (personal interviews with author 2021)

In the context of this book's argument, I wish to highlight two of MAM's most recent political embodiments of our relational, liquid homeland. The first was its participation, alongside AMAR and some members of C8M and other groups, in a call for the Puerto Rican government to lift restrictions on public access to the archipelago's beaches during the 2020 pandemic lockdown. On May 16, 2020, the groups gathered at the Ocean Park Beach in San Juan to demand a responsible reopening of public access to *la mar*'s healing capacities. On that occasion, Guerrero told the press that "sea water has properties that constitute excellent healing resources . . . due to their antitumoral, antibacterial, anti-inflammatory, and antiviral qualities" (*Noticel* 2020). Meanwhile, Uriarte Centeno declared:

> The sea is part of our lives. It is one of the spaces where we encounter our environment, where we can appreciate and share [a space] with other living beings that inhabit the earth. If this pandemic and our experience with hurricanes have taught us anything, it's the urgency of knowing, coexisting, and protecting our first home, planet Earth. The return to the sea should be made carefully, not only preventing contagion, but also respecting the rest of the flora and fauna that inhabit the sea. We need to return to *la mar*.[51]

Figure 4.7. *Amigxs del MAR, Mujeres que Abrazan la Mar*, and Members of *Coalición 8M* Demand Public Access to Beaches at the Ocean Park Beach, San Juan, 2020   Courtesy of Vanesa Contreras Capó

In connection with Uriarte Centeno's observation above concerning the silencing of Puerto Rico's Black heritage as the cause of the archipelago's generalized lack of attention to its coasts, Guerrero noted in our interviews that Afro-Puerto Rican coastal communities themselves have a fraught relationship with *la mar* precisely because of the historical trauma of enslavement, the Middle Passage, and genocide. Thus, MAM does not conceive of the urgent, and ongoing, healing practice it is engaged in as an individual, depoliticized process. Quite the contrary, it is understood as a collective, political need for Black and Afro-Puerto Rican coastal communities to nurture an affirmative relation with *la mar* and, through it, with the Caribbean region as a whole:

> It is a trauma, which is still very relevant, cutting deep in our flesh, in our collective unconscious, because, although we are islands, a lot of people, including myself, do not know how to swim or are scarcely skilled at it despite being Caribbean. . . . this fear of *la mar* . . . we talk about it a lot, and about what the Middle Passage was like, and that is why when we make offerings to *la mar*, we say that we are making offerings to our ancestors, who arrived precisely by

la mar. But also, that *la mar* carries the trauma of millions of bodies, of lives that were lost there.... I am also attentive to the fact that many people from this same community [Piñones, Loíza] do not come to the beach very often. (personal interviews with author 2021)

The second event I would like to emphasize is *Junto a la mar: Vivas y en resistencia* (Next to *la mar*: Alive [in feminine form] and in Resistance), held on October 12, 2020, as part of the *Grito de los Excluidos y las Excluidas*'s practice of denouncing "discovery" celebrations and as Puerto Rico's way of joining the Global Week of Action for Debt Cancellation.[52] On that day, CC, MAM, and C8M organized a moving ceremonial gathering at the Piñones *Pocita*. Streamed live, held on the sand around a *mística* (ritual offering), and accompanied throughout by the drumming and singing of Afro-Puerto Rican musician Choco Orta, the action first included an educational section on the true motivations and effects of European and North American colonization, genocide, and enslavement.[53] Then, it featured several creative interventions to recognize, honor, and celebrate Indigenous, Afro-Puerto Rican, and Afro-Caribbean heritage as the foundation of Puerto Rican society. Finally, the participants—most of whom were Black and Afro-Puerto Rican women and nonbinary folks—took flowers from the *mística* and, while chanting in honor of Yemayá, engaged in a collective ritual offering to the Caribbean orisha of the waters in honor of our common ancestors who, despite everything, survived and continue thriving.

BEYOND THE *PATRIA* AND BEYOND THE HUMAN

The last collective relationally considered in this chapter is *Coalición 8M* (C8M), an umbrella organization founded in 2009 with the specific aim of coordinating a common, intersectional front for political organization in and around International Women's Day on March 8 every year. In Puerto Rico, C8M brings together over twenty-five organizations working toward gender, race, class, and ecological sovereignty through different emphases: services related to health, reproductive, and gender violence; direct political actions, campaigns, and interventions; pedagogical and cultural initiatives; legal aid; queer collectives and organizations; women's commissions within socialist and pro-independence political movements and parties; and healing and sustenance collectives, among others. Over the years, however, C8M has worked in collaboration with its members and others for actions and interventions beyond March 8, as we saw, for instance, in the previous sections of this chapter through C8M's alliances with AMAR, CC, and MAM.

This section is nurtured by my dialogues with activist and professor Vanesa Contreras Capó, co-founder of, and active participant in, C8M.[54] In addition to C8M's archipelagic, sea-bound commitments in collaboration with the groups previously discussed, Contreras Capó notes that her and C8M's Caribbeanist allegiances were already evident through her work as part of *La Cole*, since the latter organization was interested, much like Capetillo (see chapter 2), "in going beyond the *patria* and embodying a Caribbean sentiment" (personal interview with author 2021).[55] Significantly, Contreras Capó added that, while active in *La Cole*, and after listening to Yarimar Bonilla discuss the 2009 strikes in the neighboring islands,

> I researched and worked on the idea of Martinique and Guadeloupe as referents of struggle [for Puerto Rico]. People on the left would always talk about the Cuban revolution, the Zapatistas, or US-centric struggles, but let us go again to the Caribbean, to the contemporary Caribbean . . . with very similar demands and in a colonial situation like us. For me, the project was to take refuge in our space. For me, Caribbean identity is a political identity. . . . It is from here that we must think and see ourselves. (personal interview with author 2021)

In what follows, I briefly comment on other areas of C8M's activist engagements that point us toward the sovereignties and forms of participatory democracy that *Affect, Archive, Archipelago* suggests should be the cornerstones of Puerto Rican decolonization. First, in terms of the ways in which C8M organizes its activism, it is itself an embodiment of coalitional, participatory democracy, with difficulties, tensions, and fluctuations in terms of its level of activity, as Contreras Capó explained to me in our dialogues, but inspired by the principle that "it is a *junte* (gathering) for people to come and go whenever they want," and "for all of us to learn from each other" (personal interview with author 2021).

Moreover, the 2020 *Alacena Feminista* (Feminist Pantry) initiative in San Juan—which has already been replicated in other municipalities outside the capital city, such as Mayagüez and Luquillo, and which was materially supported by many groups, including MAM—is a concrete example of a food-sovereignty effort inspired by a cooperative model of mutual aid that echolocates with Capetillo's anarcho-feminism. The *Alacena* seeks to confront the grave food crisis in Puerto Rico, as well as its differential effects on women and marginalized populations. Describing this initiative as an effort to amplify the conversation on the need for "collective care," Contreras Capó continued:

> People would tell us, "You have to put these supplies in closed containers, and you have to organize to distribute them yourselves because people are just going

to take them all at once." But we always reply that we do not believe in policing. This is about *dona lo que puedas, llévate lo que necesites* (donate what you can, take what you need). This motto must be put into practice.... We must break with individualism, but to do so, we must practice against it. (personal interview with author 2021)

The commitment to the creation of coops, another key characteristic of participatory democracy within the robust legacy of anarchism, is also evident in C8M's work in tandem with union movements in the archipelago. As Contreras Capó explained, contributions by C8M feminist organizers and activists as part of the multisectoral convergence of working-class groups at the May Day 2021 demonstrations were essential in achieving the adoption of two fundamental demands toward a truly emancipatory sovereignty in the archipelago: replicating the coop model as widely as possible, and transforming the zoo in Mayagüez, Puerto Rico—a longtime site of contention due to multiple reports of animal abuse—into an ecological park.

This last demand corresponds to Contreras Capó's insistence that intersectional, ecological, decolonial, feminist, and antiracist struggles, as exemplified by the Puerto Rican collectives considered in this chapter, need to also highlight animal rights and the radical transformation of the human animal's relations with other animals. As she currently propels this discussion within C8M, Contreras Capó clarified that it has been a concern of hers since *La Cole*'s founding years. Indeed, the latter's first *Manifiesta* (Manifest [in feminine form]) discusses "the exploitation of all bodies, which must be eradicated." Adding that this expansive conception of feminist struggles comes from "Black feminism, especially for me, from the work of Alice Walker and Angela Davis," (personal interview with author 2021) Contreras Capó and C8M seek to deepen and amplify our Caribbean liquid homeland to a relational practice among all living beings, beyond the precedence of the human. Alexis Pauline Gumbs, who is ancestrally linked to the Caribbean via Anguilla, shares the same affection, turning it into a breathtakingly beautiful call in *Undrowned* (2020):

> My hope, my grand poetic intervention here is to move from identification, also known as that process through which we say what is what ... to *identification*, that process through which we expand our empathy and the boundaries of who we are become more fluid, because we *identify with* the experience of someone different, maybe someone of a whole different so-called species.... In other words, this is not a book in which I am trying to garner sympathy for marine mammals because they are so much like us (though we do have things in common). Instead, the intimacy, the intentional ambiguity about who is who, speaking to whom and when is about undoing a definition of the human, which

is so tangled in separation and domination that it is consistently making our lives incompatible with the planet. (8–9)

Traversing common littorals—Escambrón Beach, Ocean Park Beach, the five acres in Isla Verde, the Piñones *Pocita*—embodying common struggles and dreams for communitarian-artistic-bodily sovereignties; voyaging in common kayaks and *yolas* in our shared *la mar*; walking on joint stilts with common *cabezudos*; and going deep beyond the human, the artistic, activist, and artivist collectives and spaces of encounter woven together in this chapter constitute essential instances of our affective archive of Caribbean relations toward a truly emancipatory, sovereign, decolonial future. These collectives call upon all of us to join them, furthering and expanding their work, demanding in unison our due reparations, finding ways to nurture ever more relations with Caribbean archipelagos over the horizon and under *la mar*'s surface. With them, let us walk-swim. Let us become others and ever more our maritime selves.

Embracing Coast

"This has saved me," one of the *Pocita de Piñones*'s *Mujeres que Abrazan la Mar* says, before adding, "and I think it has saved us all."
By "this" I think she means all of it: the regular Thursday and Saturday morning meetings on the water; the fact that the group reclaimed the practice on May 2020, even while in COVID-19 lockdown; this strip of calm sea between Loíza and Isla Verde, sheltered by a coral reef beyond which Walcott's "spray [our only power] explodes"; the being together of a thirty-plus collective of women and nonbinary folks; the ceremonies and rituals and celebrations they hold together every week.
"We are all so different, in all kinds of ways, and always together," she continues. I ask whether she thinks water has anything to do with this ineffable harmony-in-difference. "Oh, it has everything to do with it!" she says.
Hilda starts directing the two-hour aquarobics class with a stunning blend of serenity and command, intimacy, and gravitas. A new friend next to me tells me jokingly, this is Hilda's bootcamp and we love it! People around me spontaneously help me to better follow Hilda's instructions, to move in ways that help me avoid lesions, to go deeper, to gently orient my body toward better balance and coordination.
I am undergoing a transformative workout at all levels: physical, spiritual, cosmic. My breaths become expansive, as the oceanic wind beats my skin with disarming gentleness. Everything within feels liquid-becoming. I sense us all floating at the edge of the water's surface. A love current moves, unmistakable yet invisible, underwater. It is an *other* country. With each movement that our legs, arms, and torsos make, I feel we say here goes and here comes our archipelagic water, it is for you, and me, and all of us. I find myself amid a sequence of the most beautiful, life-changing choreography. We move on our own and in unison, at once. The different exercises have names of love:

el Alicia Alonso, la sirenita, el péndulo, el sapito. Some collective sequences are called forth by *vámonos pa Loíza*—we all move to the left—and *vámonos pa Isla Verde*—to the right.

A circle of intentions closes each session. Today, people talk about the tragedy of schoolchildren this year, with the vast school closures during the Ricky Rosselló era, the early 2020 earthquake sequence, and the ensuing pandemic year; about the LUMA company overtaking the Puerto Rican public energy corporation; about the attack on workers' pensions by the *Junta*-imposed austerity measures; about a sister who's very ill; about the demand for a hospital in Vieques. No judgement or opinion is made about each person's intention or the language they use to represent it. Hilda is adamant with that instruction, which we all respect resolutely.

Three other women and I came today for the first time. Once intentions are collectively sent forth with an *así sea, así será*, us novices are summoned to the center of the circle. It's time for the *bendiciones del agua* (water blessings). A collective chant repeats blessings for you, you, and you, and for me, me, me, and for all of us, while we splash each other with these, our waters. Us newcomers are hugging and turning and smiling and feeling buoyed by this embracing, oceanic love.

As the *Mujeres que Abrazan la Mar* are now in the sand putting together a feast in a flash to celebrate a birthday, I float out of the *Pocita* just in time to meet Vanessa at the rescued littoral in Isla Verde where *Amigxs del MAR* and the *Campamento Playas Pa'l Pueblo* planted what is now a veritable coastal forest, and preserved for the Puerto Rican people public access to the beach. Greeting me with her three-year-old nephew, Gael, she points to all the native trees around us and explains the supreme importance of this forest—which includes many of Betances's *uveros* and some of Capetillo's "deformed trees"—and the rolling dunes to prevent erosion and preserve the coastal ecology's necessary harmony and diversity.

I am especially drawn to the *ceibas*. One of them is taller and wider than the rest. "That was the first one we planted," Vanessa explains. "A beautiful, big tree like that is more difficult to cut down. It is only fifteen years old, but look at it! I think some of its amazing growth has to do with the fact that we planted it on the spot from which we were trying to stop the Marriott Hotel's advancement," Vanessa continues.

"Yes," I answer, "I can totally see that. That *ceiba* is a guardian. ¡No pasarán! [They shall not pass!]"

Vanessa nods. I sense us both swelling.

I ask her how she feels being here this morning. She says it's been a year since she last came.

"We really did it. We saved this for the people. This is truly *la playa del pueblo*. And everything in this strip feels different than the rest of the *Balneario de Carolina* [Carolina Public Beach]. People seem to be much more conscious now, Beatriz, but there is so, so much to do. This takes everything out of you. And we can't be everywhere at once. We need more people to put their bodies in this constant fight for our collective lives, for the ecology of this place, for our survival."

I nod. I sense us both swelling.

Gael desperately wants to go in the water. I suggest Vanessa take him while I walk on my own below the trees. I approach each *ceiba* and, gathering my most heartfelt emotions, make a small ceremony of gratitude to them, which I had just learned from an extraordinary ethnobotanist the week before. Suddenly, rain starts pouring. I barely get wet as I shelter below a profuse group of coconut palm trees, thanking the waters "touching each other."

When I get back to Vanessa and Gael, he is playing with sand, giddily throwing it up in the air. I feel like he knows something that we don't about Glissant's trace. Vanessa and I lock eyes upon witnessing his joy.

"Let's see how *este futuro* turns out," she says, referring at once to Gael and to *the future*. "We're doing the best we can," she adds.

I know, and I recognize and honor and thank you for it, Vanessa.

I take out my box of Cabo Rojo coastal offerings, in memory of Betances and his dream, and provide a ridiculously clumsy explanation of what I am trying to do with these ceremonies. I'm overcome and nervous. The small exercise with tiny objects and moving quotes, which was meant to be solemn, now feels like the most inadequate idea in the face of a woman who has been willing to give her life to the struggle for this place. Vanessa asks why I keep undercutting the moment, *si es bello* (if it is beautiful). Even then, she keeps teaching me.

I manage to tell her that I am convinced she is in Betances's *confederacionista* wake.

Incredulous, she accepts the compliment, which for me is an indisputable truth, and we agree that, from now on, we have each other.

NOTES

1. *Pocita* is the diminutive of the feminine noun in Spanish, *poza*, which translates as "puddle." But in the Puerto Rican context, a coastal *pocita* means a shallow, calm beach. *Piñones* is the name of a neighborhood in the northern coastal town of Loíza, to which I return throughout this chapter and in chapter 5.

2. Hilda Guerrero is an Afro-Caribbean woman, as well as an activist against patriarchy, White supremacy, and colonialism. (The brief biographies of the activists included in this chapter were provided to the author.)

3. The temporal conjunction of these groups' foundation is significant, responding to the neoliberal rule of Pedro Rosselló in Puerto Rico (see chapter 5 for an elaboration of this historical moment). ASYS was founded in 1993 and AMAR in 1995. As we will see below, CC's direct antecedents were the 1991 hemispheric campaign *500 años de resistencia indígena y popular* (*500 Years of Indigenous and Popular Resistance*) and the 1999 *El Grito de los Excluidos* (*The Scream of the Excluded*). C8M, although founded officially in 2009, is composed of multiple groups and organizations with longer trajectories in gender and feminist struggles in Puerto Rico. For its part, and although it is beyond the scope of this chapter, *Colectivo Ilé*, referred to in the Introduction, is another fundamental organization founded in 1992 and with an explicit emphasis on racial justice and grassroots community organizing.

4. Indeed, the recent *Ley de la Zona Costanera de Puerto Rico* (Coastal Zone of Puerto Rico Law) informs us that "Puerto Rico's coasts have an approximate extension of 799 lineal miles, distributed throughout 43 municipalities, in which 56% of our population resides" (1).

5. Choco Orta is also part of MAM (see below) and has performed in several of the group's coastal actions. Unfortunately, there is no audiovisual documentation of *Marea* available now, but from Mareia Quintero I was able to personally recuperate a version of the script, which was a collective creation. For this reason, some of the lines I quote here might have not been delivered exactly the same in the actual performances, but I am assured that the fundamental elements of the piece's verbal components are there.

6. I prefer to translate *Prójimos* as Fellows rather than Neighbors.

7. The *auto sacramental* is a sixteenth and seventeenth centuries form of Spanish drama concerned with representing Christian sacraments allegorically.

8. *Rescate de tierra* (land rescue) is the affirmative name given in Puerto Rico to dispossessed people's occupation of abandoned lands. See Liliana Cotto Morales's *Desalambrar* (2006) for a history and analysis of Puerto Rican *rescates*.

9. Although beyond the scope of this book, another notable live-arts "file" in our affective archive of Caribbean relations concerning our archipelago's struggle against US (military) occupation and exploitation is choreographer and dancer Viveca Vázquez's filmed piece *Las playas son nuestras* ([1989] 2018), available on YouTube.

10. Likewise, the island municipality of Culebra has endured a long history of US military occupation and tourist exploitation, with all its attendant economic, social, ecological, and public health effects. Culebra residents also engaged in a popular

struggle that led to the US Navy exit from the island in 1975. I will return to Vieques and Culebra in the following section, while discussing AMAR's trajectory.

11. These have been primarily related to environmental struggles against capitalist-colonial exploitation and destruction (for instance, construction of gas pipelines; deposits of toxic waste; and coastal "developments," pollution, and erosion), but they have also been concerned with Puerto Rican independence, the plight of the working class, and the 2019 *Verano Boricua*, among other factors. For a list of only those direct actions for which the police have arrested Kayak, see *Noticel*'s 2017 news report "Los arrestos de Tito Kayak."

12. Vanessa Uriarte Centeno was born in Loíza to a mother from Santurce and a father from Ponce. She holds an interdisciplinary BA in Social Sciences with emphasis on Latin American and Caribbean Studies, and an MA in Cultural Management and Administration from the UPR-Río Piedras campus. She has worked for over a decade in multiple social projects and non-profit organizations as artist or coordinator. In particular, she has been involved with environmental movements, popular education on human rights, and the rescuing of urban spaces through sociocultural initiatives. She is currently pursuing a Juris Doctor degree at the Interamerican University of Puerto Rico and is AMAR's president, an organization she has been active in for the past nine years.

13. See the organization's Facebook page (www.facebook.com/amigxsdelmarpr/) and *Travesía Libre*'s "Antecedentes" section (www.travesialibre.wordpress.com/antecedentes/).

14. Enrique Laguerre was a canonical Puerto Rican writer whose literature is traditionally conceived as *de la tierra* (of the land) in the same vein as Abelardo Díaz Alfaro's, Manuel Méndez Ballester's and René Marqués's. His coastal commitments, however, should cause literary scholars to pause. On Laguerre's struggle, see Marithelma Costa's "¿De qué color es la utopía?" (2011).

15. The organization recently adopted the more gender inclusive "Amigxs."

16. The post also includes an aerial picture showing the extent of reforestation achieved by the *Playas pa'l Pueblo* camp during those ten years.

17. In her subtle anthropological study of the camp and the 2010 University of Puerto Rico student strike, Rosario explains that the contract was: "awarded to the Marriott by a defunct branch of the Government in 1996, [and that] HR properties—the developer—start[ed] to clear the land without holding public hearings or submitting the needed impact reports . . . When I spoke to my interlocutors early on, they were keen on highlighting the contract's secrecy and its duration as evidence of the Government's interest in facilitating a *de facto* privatization of public lands" (2013, xv–xvi). Moreover, this extraordinary episode in Puerto Rican history is a further submarine connection between ASYS's *Marea* and AMAR. At the end of the theatrical piece's eighth scene, and right before the dead body of Sanes is brought on stage, the conflict between the *Prójimos* and the *Grises* comes to a head: "The *Grises* invade the *Prójimos*' territory. The *Prójimos* establish a perimeter of defense. The *Grises* run around the perimeter. They hand the *Prójimos* an eviction notice. The *Grises* destroy. Each *Prójimo* takes a little piece of their home with them. The *Grises*

build the hotel [this is the last incarnation of the golf course, turned bombing zone, turned hotel]" (2002, 6).

18. ASYS also often participated in cultural and artistic programming organized by the *Playas pa'l Pueblo* camp over the course of its duration.

19. Chapter 3 provides an overview of the US-led repression, which includes multiple political imprisonments of anticolonial, nationalist, and independence movement members and sympathizers in Puerto Rico during the twentieth century and up to the present.

20. See Marithelma Costa's chronicles—published in *80grados* from June 29 through September 14, 2012—for more details on Kayak's trip, including the multiple dramatic moments when his life was in danger and the *Cetáceo* gave way. See also the event's website, *Travesía Libre* (www.travesialibre.wordpress.com).

21. Coincidentally, it should be noted that Fiet's comparative argument in this essay, whose overarching theoretical scaffolding is based on Benítez Rojo's work (1996, 2010), includes, in addition to some of Tito Kayak's interventions, and among other performative works, two theatrical productions based on Pedro Albizu Campos's life and work (see chapter 3).

22. See "Convocatoria Artistas" at the *Travesía Libre* website (www.travesialibre.wordpress.com/about/).

23. See "Biografía" at the *Travesía Libre* website (www.travesialibre.wordpress.com/oscar-lopez/) for a full list of Kayak's Caribbean Sea voyages as activist initiatives.

24. The most recent case was the death of thirteen-year-old Jaideliz Moreno Ventura, whose story is documented in a recent episode of the *La Brega* podcast (https://www.wnycstudios.org/podcasts/la-brega/articles/vieques-and-promise-build-back-better). Significantly, residents of Vieques and Culebra are currently engaged in discussions on the possibility of managing the transportation system through a transportation coop. Moreover, working-class and social justice organizations in Puerto Rico included "safe and reliable maritime transportation for Vieques and Culebra" and "hospital construction in Vieques" as two of their May Day 2021 demands (see the Bibliography for the location of the full document). A recent episode of the *Puntos de partida* radio program provides an overview of the current panorama of struggles (www.ivoox.com/puntos-partida-20-abril-de-audios-mp3_rf_68792944_1.html). Finally, consider Marie Cruz Soto's recent essay "The Making of Viequenses" (2020), in which she makes a convincing case to reconsider the *viequense* struggle to evict the US Navy as "fundamentally shaped by the concerns and actions of women who placed reproductive rights at the center of the struggle" (360).

25. We will notice this again in the work of transdisciplinary artist Teresa Hernández (see chapter 5).

26. For biographical information on Rabin's activism and leadership in cultural projects in Vieques, as well as his current work and struggle with cancer, consider Mari Mari Narváez's (2021) and Benjamín Torres Gotay's (2021) recent interviews with him. Concerning Ríos Villarini's work, see her essay "Ritmos que unen islas" (2016) and *Vieques, ¡manos arriba!* (2020, https://www.youtube.com/watch?v=_Nl2Xn1rn2w), a short documentary based on her research in Vieques. Ríos Villarini's

2014 radio interview with the Puerto Rican theater artist Rosa Luisa Márquez is also illuminating on the extent of Puerto Rico's eastbound archipelagic connections.

27. Uriarte Centeno also highlighted the 2015 collaborations between AMAR and environmental groups opposing mining projects by a Canadian transnational in Loma Miranda, Dominican Republic.

28. For thorough journalistic investigations on the state of Puerto Rico's beaches and coastlines—including forms of privatization, lack of public access, pollution, and erosion—as well as the grave effects of the climate emergency on the archipelago, see the CPI's series "Isla ¿sin playas?" (Alvarado León 2017), "Islands Adrift" (2018), and "Erosión de costa elevada amenaza a comunidades e infraestructura en Puerto Rico" (Díaz Torres 2021). See also the ongoing scientific analysis (2021), led by Maritza Barreto, on the state of Puerto Rico's beaches post–Hurricane María. In chapter 5, I amply return to coastal erosion from an instance of Puerto Rico's artistic sovereignty, Teresa Hernández's ongoing *Bravatas* artistic platform.

29. Also of note is AMAR's collaboration with community organizations currently struggling to protect Jauca Bay (located in the southern municipality of Santa Isabel) from privatization in the form of a luxury hotel. See the *Salvemos Jauca* Facebook page (www.facebook.com/playajauca/) for more information.

30. On the increasingly alarming phenomenon of "population displacement" in Puerto Rico, anticipated by Albizu Campos (see chapter 3) and decried consistently in Vieques and Culebra, as well as around coastal municipalities such as San Juan, Dorado, Rincón, Aguadilla, and Cabo Rojo, see recent pieces by Mariah Espada (2021) and Frances Solá-Santiago (2021). This process has been dramatically accelerated by the substantial tax breaks offered to affluent foreigners through Laws 20 and 22 in Puerto Rico (see the Introduction).

31. See Martha Rodríguez's (1991) informative bulletin on the campaign.

32. The recent piece "Puerto Rico, atrapado en el tiempo" (2021), by Puerto Rican journalist and writer Ana Teresa Toro, affectively captures the Puerto Rican "think-big" 1990s *zeitgeist* under Pedro Rosselló's governorship (see also chapter 5): "I was eight years old when over 250 ships arrived in San Juan for the commemoration of the *Gran Regatta Colón* [Columbus's Great Regatta] in 1992. I remember walking on the docks, listening to people speak in different languages, feeling myself so much a part of the world. During those years in Puerto Rico, we dreamt big. A committee was preparing our nomination for the 2004 Games. We imagined and designed futures; we did the things countries do. During those same years, scientists from all over the world wanted to visit the Arecibo Observatory to use the radio telescope, the biggest in the world at that point, and a global epicenter for astronomy. From Puerto Rico, it was not only possible to be part of the world, but we could even see outer space. We had an expanded, large, dignified outlook. We even felt universal."

33. Fast-forward to 2019, when the "think-big" fantasy has violently exploded in a Puerto Rico that barely survives amid generalized ruins, and find *Comuna Caribe* replicating, at a small scale, this seed concerning the need to transform our narratives of the past. As part of a campaign for debt cancellation and reparations for Haiti and Puerto Rico discussed below, CC engaged in a direct action at the Columbus Square in Old San Juan. The action involved turning the Columbus statue into a public

statement of our refusal to pay and our demand for debt cancellation and reparations, making it strikingly evident that the colonized and enslaved by imperial powers are, in fact, the legitimate creditors of a monumental debt that is, in many ways, and as David Scott (2018) reminds us, irreparable. This same Columbus Square had been overtaken by artist Teresa Hernández in her 2014 performance piece *(a)parecer* (see chapter 5). The submarine, ephemeral connection between these activist and artistic interventions is fundamental here, as both actively and powerfully re-signify Columbus's figure and legacy.

34. Visit the *Jubileo Sur Américas*' website (www.jubileosuramericas.net) for more information.

35. See CC's Facebook page, www.facebook.com/pages/category/Community/Comuna-Caribe-393502544171381/.

36. This is evident in CC's struggle commitments #6 and #7, which are "We denounce the invisibility and exclusion that the Dominican-Haitian community and the Haitian community living in the sister Dominican Republic are facing, as well as the anti-Dominican prejudice prevalent in Puerto Rico, and wherever racism and xenophobia manifest themselves," and "We repudiate all foreign military interventions in our hemisphere, and particularly in Haiti, and we demand the cancellation of all our external debts. We join the international outcry against illegitimate and immoral debts, and we declare that our peoples are the legitimate creditors of historical, ecological, and social debts."

37. More information is available at the *Comité Pro Niñez Dominico Haitiana* blog (www.comiteproninezdominicohaitiana.blogspot.com). Concerning Haitian *bateyes* in the Dominican Republic, listen to *Radio Ambulante*'s "Bateyes: la frontera del conflicto" (2015) episode, at www.radioambulante.org/extras/bateyes-la-frontera-del-conflicto.

38. For more on SOFA and Haitian feminist movements in general, see Sabine Lamour (2020).

39. Jones's 2015 news report covers the construction of this community.

40. Information and documentation are available at CC's Facebook page (www.facebook.com/pages/category/Community/Comuna-Caribe-393502544171381/).

41. Information and documentation are available at CC's Facebook page.

42. See Mooney, Prats, Rosenblatt, and Christie (2021). See also the 2020 virtual dialogue "La vida antes de la deuda" ("Life before Debt"), organized by *Jubileo Sur Américas*' *Articulación Caribe*, on Caribbean struggles against debt and for reparations (https://www.youtube.com/watch?v=nygnTtTIdY0).

43. Excellent resources to study compiled materials on Puerto Rico's debt crisis can be found at the *Puerto Rico Syllabus* (puertoricosyllabus.wordpress.com/verano-boricua-rickyrenunica/), *Centro de Periodismo Investigativo* (www.periodismoinvestigativo.com), and *LittleSis* (www.littlesis.org/search?q=puerto+rico) websites. See also *Frente Ciudadano por la Auditoría de la Deuda*'s Facebook page (www.facebook.com/FrenteCiudadanoAuditoriaDeLaDeuda/).

44. See the July 2015 bulletin "¡No la debemos, no la pagamos!" ("We Don't Owe It, We Don't Pay It!"), where *La Cole*, founded in 2014, pronounces itself in unison with *los pueblos del sur* (the peoples of the South), in support of *Jubileo Sur*

Américas' campaign for debt cancellation, and for the premise that the overwhelming creditors of the "illegal, illegitimate, and unsustainable debt" are women and racialized and marginalized populations, including migrants in Puerto Rico. Also consider *La Cole*'s multiple 2019 initiatives with the leitmotif *Nosotras contra la deuda* (Us [in the pronoun's feminine form] against the Debt), a commitment inspired, as Vanesa Contreras Capó explained to me, by none other than Hilda Guerrero and her work as liaison with *Jubileo Sur Américas* and Puerto Rican feminist struggles. On the structural-patriarchal ties between the debt economy and women more generally, see Luci Cavallero's and Verónica Gago's *Una lectura feminista de la deuda* (2019). A more comprehensive analysis of *La Cole*'s activism around the debt crisis can be found in Rocío Zambrana's recent *Colonial Debts* (2021). On the exigency of putting people before debt, Rebollo Gil makes the following illuminating claim: "'The people before debt' and 'we don't owe, we won't pay' are incomprehensible demands, for what have the Puerto Rican people been made to be, in this particular historical juncture, other than those who owe. Or more precisely, those that have been called to pay with their health, their homes, their education, and their jobs. *To demand that people come before the debt is therefore to beckon and attempt to constitute another people*: those who do not see themselves beholden to whatever political relationship might exist between the USA and Puerto Rico and who, therefore, do not have to own up to whatever is owed by the latter under the rule of the former. The people before the debt are the people with the will to say no to reason inasmuch as reason in a colonial context can only serve to extend the colonial project" (2018, 59–60, emphasis added).

45. The information concerning this campaign comes from a working document generously shared with me by Hilda Guerrero. Although there is no exact, corresponding word in English, I should note that the word used in the Spanish original is *endeudamiento* (indebtedness), rather than *deuda* (debt), which captures the deliberate process/series of actions for turning Puerto Rico into an indebted country.

46. Listen to Guerrero's account of this process in a recording of a December 2019 event with fellow organization *Comuna Antilla* (Commune Antille), at www.facebook.com/comunaantilla/videos/1013996852286862.

47. For commentary on all these issues, see the Introduction.

48. This recent case is part of a long trajectory of capitalist and racist exploitation of Piñones, where descendants of nineteenth-century Maroon communities live on rescued land. Fridman, in fact, is one of the co-organizers of the *Jornadas Adolfina Villanueva* in honor of Villanueva, a Black woman from Loíza who was assassinated by the Puerto Rican police in 1980 while protecting her home and family from a forced eviction. See Cotto Morales's *Desalambrar* (2006) for more on Villanueva. Bárbara I. Abadía-Rexach's recent piece "Adolfina Villanueva Osorio, *Presente*" (2021) is also essential reading, forcefully demonstrating the inherent link between anti-Black racism and police brutality in Puerto Rico. Within the archipelago's live arts, consider the following: (1) Viveca Vázquez's 1980 choreographic piece *Bailo por Adolfina*; and (2) the 1989 theatrical piece *La pasión y muerte de Adolfina Villanueva*, a collaboration between Puerto Rico's *Teatreros Ambulantes* and Bread and Puppet Theater, both groups with deep ties, as we saw previously, to ASYS.

180　　　　　　　　　　　　*Chapter Four*

49. The potent image of the swelling sea, at once threatening and liberatory, constitutes a central feature of the following chapter.

50. Ivania Zayas Ortiz, who was 39 years old at the time, was killed the night of February 8, 2015, by an inebriated driver who fled the scene. The case became a central focus of Puerto Rico's feminist movements around the phrase *andando la calle sola* (walking the streets alone), as the police officer in charge of the investigation made immediate comments upon Zayas Ortiz's death questioning the victim for walking alone on the streets at night.

51. See *Noticel*'s "Protestan en Ocean Park para exigir apertura de playas" (2020).

52. More information on this global effort can be found at the *Global Action for Debt Cancellation* website, www.debtgwa.net.

53. The event's recording can be found on CC's Facebook page, at www.facebook.com/watch/live/?v=351682209384864&ref=watch_permalink.

54. Vanesa Contreras Capó was also a co-founder of *La Cole*, in which she was active during its first years. She describes herself as activist, animalist, feminist, and syndicalist. Contreras Capó also teaches in the Modern Languages Department at the Interamerican University of Puerto Rico, where she is a member of the Interdisciplinary Center for Gender Research and Study (CIIEG) and of the Center for Environmental Education, Conservation, and Interpretation (CECIA). Her political and academic interests are the intersections of forms of oppression related to race, class, gender, place of origin, and species.

55. See chapters 1 and 3 to fully appreciate, within emancipatory and anticolonial struggles in Puerto Rican history, the radical implications of this impulse to transcend the homeland and embody the Caribbean.

Chapter Five

Sea, Salt, Survive

Teresa Hernández's Multitudinously Small Art

> Creating paths, bridges, tunnels . . . We [Puerto Rican artists] know very well that there is not a single route, and that the main one will not make way for us.
>
> —Teresa Hernández, interview with the author, July 2019

In the context of part II's emphasis on political performances, this chapter moves between, first, a long-view engagement with solo transdisciplinary artist Teresa Hernández's trajectory, and second, a sustained focus on some of her pieces and productions. The chapter's first half includes a commentary on the historical and aesthetic contexts of Hernández's emergence as a resolutely independent, experimental artist in turn of the twentieth-first century Puerto Rico. Then, the chapter engages with Hernández's 2014 performance piece (a)parecer *in connection with Luisa Capetillo's political transg/dressing, as well as with several productions within her ongoing artistic research platform,* Bravatas: Sal, sargazo y cansancio *(Swelling Seas: Salt, Sargasso, and Exhaustion). Throughout, I walk-swim with Hernández's underseen work in relation to most of* Affect, Archive, Archipelago's *concerns: the embodied affirmation of our sovereign, small, archipelagic condition and imagination; our marine and coastal bodies, experiences, objects, materialities, and traces; the indispensable political impetus of imaginative, intuitive, speculative works; the exploration of human and nonhuman life at the edge of colonial-capitalist-climate-crisis survival; and the material, bodily, and affective solidarities that such fulgurations enable and amplify between Puerto Rico and the Caribbean region.*

At dusk, having shed the kitchen knife with which, as *la mujer del cuchillo* (the knife woman), she had stabbed—always with jabs from below—the Fort Conde de Mirasol's walls in Vieques's historically overburdened territory (see the previous chapters), as well as the thick, dark-blue cotton dress evocative of "a working-class woman lost in time,"[1] and the conch with which she had become *la mujer de la concha* (the seashell woman), the woman looks out at the ocean, above the Spanish colonial walls and their cannons.[2] She stops walking. For an instant, her eyes soften, and she smiles, a minuscule, potent, smile. The contents of the noticeably heavy burden she is pushing in a cart in front of her—as though reversed luggage from someone who, rather than lightly and briskly moving at the airport while pulling their life in a bag to leave, is laboriously and methodically pushing it in front to remain—are only suggested to the public by the sign *Empresas Padilla, sal de mar* (Padilla Enterprises, sea salt). Because she could have easily chosen to carry a smaller quantity of salt, or to have divided it in several portions, this woman clearly wants to (or *must*) carry it all at once.

The horizon at dusk, with its accompanying breeze, seems to comfort the woman pushing—somewhat à la *Mother Courage*—the voluptuous weight in her cart, so much so that it appears to convince her to set up house right there and then. Standing in front of the same ocean where this woman decides to stay, and having witnessed the trail of sargasso the artist arrived at the scene with, we intuit that the sea might be the protagonist of this piece, *Bravata: El comienzo de un comienzo* (*Swelling Sea: The Beginning of a Beginning*) (2019).[3] The ground where the woman stops is bare, painfully dry. Colonial ruins are all around her. She is out in the open. Exposed to the elements. And yet, she stops. *To stay.*[4]

With the smile still visible on the same mouth that, first, bit and licked the kitchen knife and then, sucked the conch, she stops the cart and starts pulling out its contents. Emptying the first sack on the ground, we realize that, indeed, it is sea salt. Two huge sacks from a climate-emergency-induced dwindling enterprise in Betances's hometown of Cabo Rojo, Puerto Rico, the historical sea salt industry's site of both extraordinary labor exploitation and enduring class struggle. Each sack weighs one hundred pounds, the same "unit of measurement"—equivalent to one *carretilla* (handbarrow, the artist's version of it being a present-day hand truck)—traditionally used in Cabo Rojo's sea salt industry.[5]

La mujer del cuchillo, turned *la mujer de la concha*, is now *la mujer de la sal* (the salt woman). Her land—her body, her class, her material context—has been overcome by the sea, which has evaporated her back to us as a body of salt, both corrosive and preservative. Or, perhaps, we are faced with another transformation. Before becoming *la mujer de la concha*, she

Figure 5.1. *La mujer del cuchillo* Climbs the Colonial Wall, *bravata: el comienzo de un comienzo*, Fortín Conde Mirasol, Vieques, 2019   Courtesy of Rafael Orejuela

had asked us, while signaling the now-absent knife with her arm across her mouth, whether we did not think the time had come for us to say *¡basta ya!* (Enough!). Was it, then, that her body, by becoming-the-sea (*la mujer de la concha*), had overcome the land controlled by *ellos*? *Ellos* were responsible for the constant failure of volunteers from the public to properly "build" an edification with the fort's fallen bricks. As soon as each volunteer started putting down bricks following the woman's instructions, she reprimanded them. "Not there! But here!" "No, not here, but over there!" As though to console the volunteers' understandable impatience, she had explained with exasperation: "It's not my fault. *Son ellos*." *Them*, an explicitly masculine them, the masters, constantly force us to try and build with ruins and according to undecipherable, unsatisfiable instructions. *Bravata: El comienzo de un comienzo* in Vieques was, indeed, prophetic: the piece was performed in May 2019. In July of the same year, the Puerto Rican people ousted the governor with a massive uprising against *ellos*.

It is this *¡basta ya!* that compelled *la mujer del cuchillo* to shed her dress in a strenuous gesture over the botched attempt at edification. She undresses atop the colonial bricks—from which, clearly, nothing can be built—revealing another blue dress below. But this one is a light, satin baby doll. Slowly, she becomes *la mujer de la concha*. As she did with the knife on her mouth, she rolls with the conch in a movement evocative of the tides. But it's clear now that she is in/within the sea. She has become it. Her movements are no longer solid, ravenous, desperate, as they were when she knifed the walls, ran with the knife in her mouth, took it out of her mouth and manipulated it as though cutting sugar cane or tall grass; as though stabbing the enemy; as though getting ready for a war with invisible, yet monumental, forces. Her movements are now those of a body in water, fluid, flapping, swimming, flooded, orgasmic. Is her body, then, not the land but the sea roaring, too, *¡basta ya!* with its swelling, with its *bravata*?

And then, she drops the conch. Walks toward the salt cart. And starts pushing the monumental weight of Caribbean history, exploitation, enslavement, survival, exhaustion, corrosive erosions . . . At the same time, her action evokes salt's preservation of life. From the sharp, glistening lines of the knife, through the curvy, voluptuous contours of the conch, the woman has now become the unassimilable materiality of salt, the sea's and our liquid homeland's trace (see the Introduction). First, she makes a meticulous mound, as though preparing for some unknown ritual, and echoing the sea salt workers' task. Then, she spreads the salt with her bare hands, forming small, subtle ridges that look like the mountains of our Caribbean islands and, at the same time, like the islands themselves when seen from the horizon. She has, indeed, built a salt archipelago.[6] But salt, unlike the knife, unlike the conch, has no lines unless she defines them with her hands, her legs, her mouth, her pelvis. So, she throws her body against it, falls onto it. The falling is sometimes violent, other times extenuated, yet others sensuous. She rubs her skin with the salt, the salt with her skin. She licks and tastes it. She submerges in it. She seems to relate to it, as the artist has said she relates to her country, at once "as a rival and a lover" (Hernández 2016, 67). And yet, the lines made with salt are, necessarily, lines erased, and remade. The fragility of what salt can build is laid bare. Capitalist coloniality and its attendant ecological disaster submits us to oblivion. Nothing remains. Everything must be invented. At all times. We must, then, go out to sea.[7]

A DEFINITION-DEFYING ARTIST . . .

Teresa Hernández, a transdisciplinary artist whose embodied trajectory traverses the languages of theater, dance, performance, film, and video, began her career in the early 1990s. In a spatial practice one can aptly describe as archipelagic, overflowing with "unarchivable," underseen, ephemeral actions-movements, she has occupied, invented, and transformed conventional and unconventional stages in Puerto Rico. The traditional, fourth-wall theater stages she has engaged with have become something *other*, as much as she has turned open spaces, the street, public squares, buildings, bridges, statues, balconies, floors, and ruins into stages.[8] A definition-defying artist, Hernández describes the (her) body-in-action as the generative force propelling her work in multiple directions: movement, images, objects, "scenic writing." Preferring suggestion and evocation—that is, in this book's terms, poetics, intuition, imagination, and the relational underseen—over representation, Hernández's work systematically delves into the fraught yet infinitely fertile conjunction of "the personal" and "the collective." As she has explained in personal communications and as is documented in her unpublished MA dissertation (2016), Hernández's scenic imagination tends to ignite from what seem at first individual concerns, dreams, desires, fears, or from autobiographical events and encounters, and, in the process, are revealed as spilling over, imbricating, echolocating with collective impulses. Thus, hers is always a multitudinous art—even if, paradoxically, in most works her body is the only one on stage.[9] Hernández's entire artistic trajectory and, most especially, the pieces and interventions discussed in this chapter, constitute fundamental instances—as potent as they are small, as beautiful as they are sharp—of our affective archive of Caribbean relations and artistic-bodily sovereignty.

When taken together, Hernández's works reveal a dogged refusal of containment, both in the external sense of institutional or "official" capture,[10] as much as in the internal sense of the art itself: her *personas*, images, objects, texts, and *animals* move freely, archipelagically, from one piece or intervention to another. In contrast with more recent pieces featuring what the artist calls "silhouettes" or "scenic presences," her earlier work included characters with "proper names"—for instance, la Teniente Cortés and others in *Acceso controlado* (1995); the sisters Perdóname, Perpetua, and Pragma in *La nostalgia del quinqué . . . una huida* (1999); Rubí in *Nada que ver (composiciones escénicas sobre el yo)* (2006–2007)—but even then, these characters were not understood in terms of the conventional dramatic tradition. They did not "pertain" to a dramatic conflict and an established, closed plot. Rather, they—as much as objects (wigs, costumes, furniture pieces), situations, themes, and the more recent "presences"—travel, relate, are developed or flattened, in/for different pieces and interventions, to such an extent that they, too, are multitudinous. Brimming with Aponte Alsina's "intimate histories," this endless process has been described by the artist as "post-inventions" and "post-productions" (Hernández 2016, 20).[11] Hernández's art, thus, assumes flesh not only in and through the artist's body, but is itself a body, since bodies are held together precisely because of their being *on the move*.

Shed are the Aristotelian dictum of conflict as the neuralgic center of drama, as well as the post-Shakespearean emphasis on individual character and its "interior psychology." In an archipelago excessively laden with conflict and character, drama is already everywhere. Hernández—as much as other transdisciplinary and experimental artists of her generation—is thus interested, and asks us to accompany her in, in the direction of a thornier exigency: What and how can a resolutely nonincorporated, lowercase, small art say and do within and about a place where it has no place?[12] As with the walking man at *Le Diamant* beach in Glissant's *Poetics of Relation* (see the Introduction), at least part of the answer seems to be a body in increasing precariousness, uncertainty, and ruin, but, nevertheless, moving.

Hernández, who often talks about her work as an aesthetic of *el casi* ("the almost"), and of *hacer mucho con poco* ("[doing] much with little"), or *todo con nada* ("everything with nothing"), powerfully echoes Glissant's and Aponte Alsina's affirmation of, and faith in, smallness (see the Introduction). Indeed, as a 1999 artist declaration clearly reveals, smallness has been a fundamental horizon of her work since its inception:

> I like smallness because it gives me space to make mistakes. It is small because it does not pertain to "established or official" ambits. The question is how to make something of reach out of that. But the small is chosen as an homage to the intimate, and because it allows *el hacer* (the doing), the tireless question, the delight of the imagination, and the control of concessions. The bigger it is, the more concessions you are forced to make. Such an equation does not satisfy me. . . .

Moreover, and without question, my work helps me to live my country. Sometimes it pains me, but I enjoy my small artistry, trying to be realistic, without losing my humor or my ideology. Vindicating smallness is my new discovery. We have been led to believe that what is small is insufficient, incomplete. Recognizing the strength of that "incompleteness," valorizing it, has allowed me to situate myself more firmly on what I think is our essence: we almost are, but . . .
For all these reasons, I am a local and small artist.[13]

To recognize the extraordinary—and enduring—importance of this late 1990s statement requires some historical contextualization, to which I turn below.

. . .IN AN ARCHIPELAGO DEFINED BY EXPLOITATION

A panoply of Puerto Rican artists and collectives from the late 1960s through the 1980s took theater—and all live arts—to the streets, partly in response to the rise of the US neocolonial and neoliberal regime and its deleterious effects on Puerto Rico and the wider Latin American region, and partly to explore and denounce the multifarious oppressions that marginalized populations in Puerto Rico increasingly faced.[14] Constituting instances of Puerto Rico's communitarian-artistic-bodily sovereignties, the multiple pieces and interventions created, produced, and staged during those decades honored local and regional forms of popular, collective, and street art, such as carnival, puppetry, and *vejigantes* (traditional carnival characters). Of immense importance is the work of *El tajo del alacrán*, *Anamú*, *Teatro del Sesenta*, *Nuevo Teatro Pobre de América* and its founder Pedro (Pedrito) Santaliz,[15] *Los teatreros ambulantes* and their founders Rosa Luisa Márquez and Antonio "Toño" Martorell, and Tere Marichal, among many others. *Vueltabajo* and *Papel Machete*, referenced in this book's Introduction, as well as *Agua, Sol y Sereno*, discussed in the previous chapter, are heirs of this outpouring of theatrical, collective practices onto the streets.[16]

Since the late 1970s, in both collaboration and contrast with the groups mentioned above, other artists more inclined to radical and transdisciplinary formal experimentation were furthering their own sovereign claims to an antiestablishment and emancipatory spirit in dialogue with international experimental artists.[17] In particular, the *Pisotón* dance collective, self-described as an "Antillean modern dance group," constitutes, according to Arnaldo Rodríguez Bagué ("Archipelagic Performance," n.d.),

> the foundation of an experimental turn in dance and theater practices on the island (or at least in San Juan) . . . *Pisotón*'s Antillean modern dance is not necessarily grounded on postmodern aesthetics but in the Caribbean contemporary

aesthetics of the 60's and 70's in Puerto Rico, the Caribbean, and Latin America. The "Antillean" in *Pisotón*'s Antillean modern dance is not only a reaction but a delinking from Puerto Rican 1950's and 1960's colonial dance aesthetics. . . . [This] can be read as a "decontinentalization" of Western dance by an opening up of the group's dance practice to experimentation with the island's colonial, historical, political, geographical, and environmental reality from the standpoint of the contemporary aesthetics and politics of their Caribbean island time-space.[18]

Composed by "ballet dancer and choreographer Petra Bravo, dancer and painter Awilda Sterling, dancer and choreographer Viveca Vázquez, theater artist Maritza Pérez, improvisational dancer Gloria Llompart, dancer and musician Jorge Arce, and dancer Pepín Lugo" (Rodríguez Bagué n.d.), *Pisotón*'s "decontinentalizing" legacy—note the Glissantian echo here (see the Introduction)—and its resolute situatedness within Puerto Rico's geography and condition is directly linked with the primary concerns and proposals in Hernández's work, as discussed above. But the affective connections in this archive go deeper, as Hernández became Petra Bravo's, Maritza Pérez's, and Viveca Vázquez's student, and, eventually, Vázquez's lifelong friend and collaborator. In 1991, Vázquez founded *Taller de Otra Cosa*, an experimental artist and cultural organization and administrative umbrella in the context of which Hernández and others have created and produced work since then, and at whose helm Hernández has been for the past twenty years.[19]

Taking more evocative forms than those associated with the 1960s theater groups, the 1990s experimental, transdisciplinary work—whose intensification historically coincided with the emergence of the activist groups and collectives discussed in chapter 4—was very much politically charged against the most explicitly violent, racist, and sexist form of local governance Puerto Rico had experienced until then. The last decade of the twentieth century was characterized by the rule of the *Partido Nuevo Progresista*'s Pedro Rosselló, father of the recently ousted Ricardo Rosselló. The pediatrician-turned-politician transformed the ELA's collapsing fantasy into a shamelessly militarized, securitized, and extremely violent rule that sought to reposition Puerto Rico as newly important for the US imperial power by claiming it as a model for the racist and classist "cleansing" of crime—especially drug-related—as a cover for neoliberal privatization and public defunding.[20] Rosselló's *mano dura contra el crimen* (strong hand against crime) effectively reconfigured urban space; enclosed and besieged, military-style, public housing complexes; fomented the proliferation of controlled-access urbanizations and the rise of the security industry; and left a still unaccounted for trail of blood and suffering among Puerto Rico's most impoverished and racially marginalized populations.

At the same time, the *rossellato* was characterized by a careful crafting of a larger-than-life celebrity persona of the *macho* Rosselló himself—an antecedent, indeed, of Donald Trump. Both discursively, in his interventions and publicly funded publicity campaigns, and through a massive network of corruption schemes and an unprecedented intensification of public debt,[21] the Rosselló administration relentlessly bombarded the Puerto Rican population with a demand to *pensar en grande* (think big) and to support *obra que se ve* (work you can see). Massive construction projects were undertaken to promote an illusion of limitless "progress," public goods and corporations were privatized at an alarming rate, and an aggressive tourist campaign with the sloganss "Discover the Continent of Puerto Rico" and "Puerto Rico Does It Better" was launched.[22] The 1990s material, affective, ideological, and sensuous atmosphere was, indeed, a lethal mixture of moral panic, fabricated economic "bubbles," the most extreme forms of prejudice and violence, a generalized disdain toward everyday Puerto Ricans, and the negation of Puerto Rico's geography itself, a matter that runs deep in Puerto Rico's White *criollo* elites, as we saw in the Introduction with #MeCagoEnLaIsla. Indeed, Rosselló's regime demanded Puerto Ricans to engage in a sweeping psychosis and to be thankful for it.

That Hernández would choose to become an independent, nonincorporated, noninstitutionalized, small woman artist right there and then, who is also determined to *remain* in Puerto Rico, was, thus, quite revolutionary, and no less perilous. Of course, her work through the 1990s and early 2000s forcefully responds to these personal and sociopolitical circumstances, as can be corroborated in pieces such as *Acceso controlado, La nostalgia del quinqué . . . una huida, Salve la Reina*,[23] and *Coraje I* and *II*, all concerned with the violent and, indeed, mortal effects of neoliberal colonialism and militarization, Rosselló-style. Moreover, since then and throughout her trajectory up to the present, Hernández has created, produced, and directed work in constant exploration of her condition as a woman, colonial subject, political actor, and cultural worker. In so doing, she has managed to capture the "PRUSA"—her "body country" (Hernández 2016, 65)—condition itself.[24]

BECOMING ARCHIPELAGIC: BODY, OBJECTS, MATERIALITIES

Taking on more recent "body country" work, the remainder of this chapter engages Hernández's performance piece *(a)parecer* (2014) and her ongoing *Bravatas: Sal, sargazo y cansancio* (*Swelling Seas: Salt, Sargasso, and Exhaustion*), an artistic research platform (2018) of which the Vieques site-specific piece explored in this chapter's opening is the second production. As part of the transformations both the artist and her work have undergone from the nineties to the present, during the second decade of the twenty-first century Hernández's scenic presences seem to be increasingly echolocating with and emerging from the depths of the sea, of history, of memory. The contours of her work's scenic presences seem determined not so much by who or what they might be, but by that which they hold and are held by; move, or are moved by. The object-material-trace-echo is thus more alive than ever.

But it's not exactly that. Or, rather, to say that is not enough. The body-object relation has taken precedence. It is no longer possible to say that an object is worn, as one could have said of Perdóname's wig, for instance, or of Teniente Cortés's uniform. Now, the object on stage has become its own body, convening and being convened by the human body. Indeed, in the wake of a personal experience of deep abandonment and loss, as well as within the context of Puerto Rico's increasing colonial-capitalist exploitation and eventual fiscal and political collapse, it was an object—*el sillón* (the rocking chair)—that accompanied the artist's survival and activated, so to speak, a fuller transition from characters to presences:[25]

> Swaying in *el sillón* presents itself to me as an aesthetic task to act upon uncertainty, sadness, exhaustion, or simply, upon being stuck in this apparent transition of country-person. Swaying as a possibility to overcome the waiting.[26] And it is with this action that I am creatively moving in my longing to sustain and further explore my artistic practice. *meciéndome en la transición* (swaying in the transition), as I have called it, is my most recent performative investigation, which conceptually flows over my being person-country. (Hernández 2016, 81)

El sillón, a domestic object evocative, at once, of lullabies for babies and of Puerto Rico's long-standing cultural tradition of having balcony conversations while on rocking chairs, moves back and forth between the private and the public, the known and the unknown, indecision and conviction, fear and determination. It is also a powerful image of movement-in-stasis, and of the sea's tidal, relational dynamics. The artist's rocking chair, however, is not the traditional, artisanal, wicker *sillón*. Rather, it is a metal rocking chair made for the outside, covered in rust, an evident victim of time and the elements, of the sea's salty trace, of our collective and personal unshelteredness. Thus, as much as the artist-country, the rocking chair *transitions-in-relation*.

La mujer del sillón, who first appeared around 2013 with *meciéndome en la transición* and who, almost spectrally, continues emerging to this day as part of the *Bravatas* platform, is directly tied, both temporally and conceptually, to the *(a)parecer* piece I will discuss below. After pursuing an MA in cultural management and administration (*Gestión Cultural*) at the University of Puerto Rico–Río Piedras Campus, Hernández decided to turn her dissertation defense into an artistic exploration that would help her redraw her personal and artistic lives. Taking the public to a bridge, the artist *swayed in the transition* in defense of her dissertation. Since then, *la mujer del sillón* has appeared in multiple actions and pieces, including her intervention in the 2016 cultural event *Mezcolanza PR*, where the rocking chair and Hernández commanded the Río Piedras *Plaza de la Convalecencia* while the artist counted every single year since 1898 to the present while structurally improvising movements, images, and actions between body and *sillón*.[27] The result was a powerful meditation on and critique of what seems like an endless subjugation to the same colonial exploitation, as well as to the two main political parties' alternation in power (see the Introduction).

As recently as October 2020, Hernández participated in a video series in which movement artists occupied abandoned spaces as a commentary on the increasing neglect evidenced by the rotting corpses of the ELA and the colonial-capitalist infrastructure of debt and exploitation. With *la mujer del sillón*, Hernández took to the Luchetti school in San Juan, one of the hundreds of schools closed by decree of Julia Keleher, the corrupt Secretary of Education appointed by Ricardo Rosselló. Wearing a shirt emblazoned with the *Frente Ciudadano por la Auditoría de la Deuda*'s campaign to audit Puerto Rico's odious debt (see the Introduction), *la mujer del sillón* moves through our abandoned education with increasing desperation, raising and flapping her arms as target of a constant, unrelenting assault. *La mujer del sillón* is also a recurrent action-image in the artist's ongoing platform *Bravatas*, as we will see below.

Over the past decade, other body-object relations have appeared and traversed Hernández's work alongside *la mujer del sillón*. Through a commentary on the 2014 piece *(a)parecer*—understood here as a historical echo of Luisa Capetillo's political performances with dress as discussed in chapter 2—and the multiple, and ongoing, pieces and interventions associated with the artistic research platform *Bravatas*, I now turn to a dialogue with *la enjaulada* (the caged woman), *la mujer de la cola* (the tail woman), *la mujer del corazón* (the heart woman), *la mujer del cuchillo* (the knife woman), *la mujer de la concha* (the seashell woman), *la mujer de la sal* (the salt woman), and *la erizada* (the sea urchin woman) as they embody, question, and elucidate this book's primary concerns.

THE *COLA'S* ECHO

On the night of September 5, 2014, only a couple of blocks away from De la Luna Street in Old San Juan where Luisa Capetillo's transg/dressing was performed (see chapter 2), Hernández floored the public gathered at the *Plaza Colón* for her site-specific performance piece *(a)parecer*, as part of the series *Plaza Tomada*. Wearing a thick, black "Cinderella" gown, with a long, heavy, draped tail, the artist became *la mujer de la cola* (the tail woman).[28] For a moment, it seemed the woman's body had returned, performatively, to the time before Capetillo's culottes, when only dresses and skirts were imaginable for women. But, crucially, the conventional image of the bride was, through Hernández's embodiment, that of a woman in a botched wedding, a wedding-in-mourning. Her head, *la enjaulada*, was caged in white, "the coloniality of power and of being . . . in our-my heads" (Hernández 2016, 118).[29] She held—alternately in her extended arm, in her chest, and, when conscious of a male spectator's gaze, in her face—a wooden heart pierced with twenty-three nails, evoking *la mujer del corazón* (the heart woman). And oh, did she shed the tail, the nails, the cage!

In Puerto Rico, having *cola* (tail) metaphorically means carrying much more weight, baggage, and dimensions than what might appear in the first place. *La mujer de la cola* appears publicly appearing to be something she is not, or at least, not only. Thus, the wordplay in the piece's title: "to appear" (*aparecer*), "to look like" (*parecer*), and "apparently" (*al parecer*). The woman in *(a)parecer* was not only the singular non-bride-in-mourning; in "crossing through the walls of the house" (Hernández 2016, 118), she both united with and brought with her the *cola* of all other women, as the performance's voice-over—the artist's own voice—declares: "The woman with the body of a heart nailed by 23 nails, takes the plaza. Alone. While doing so, her mourning transcends the personal; it moves to other frontiers, undergoing longer suffering, more violent [suffering]. Now her mourning is transatlantic. Oh, how many small screams! What horrifying silence!" (Hernández 2016, 114).

As Hernández has recounted to me in personal communications and has also described it in her MA dissertation, *(a)parecer* partly responded to the artist's intimate life being *taken away* from her, a shared history with a male partner erased. But the artist knew very well that such intimate stories are refractions of the transatlantic, collective story of women, many of whom have historically taken to public squares to politicize their mourning, to turn that most "private" of emotions publicly against the perpetrators. Thus, the contemporary, personal man was to the historical, impersonal colonizer as a grain of sand is to the sandpile. The Columbus statue at the plaza's center *had,*

Figure 5.2. *La mujer de la cola* with the Heart Pierced by 23 Nails, *(a)parecer*, Plaza Colón, San Juan   Courtesy of Antonio Ramírez Aponte

thus, to be overtaken. This was, as Capetillo's a century before, an *acto vivo*, a live act, "thought but not rehearsed" (Hernández 2016, 117). The impossibility of overtaking the statue by the exclusive means of her body—"that is all I have," as the artist told me—was, precisely, the point: "My objective as a performer was not to climb the statue successfully, but rather to attempt it: this auto-direction distanced me from the fear of not making it or of falling. The woman-I ends her enunciation climbing the statue of the colonizing power, that which imposed the erasure of memory and installs an apparently new history that dis-locates us" (Hernández 2016, 118).

The piece *(a)parecer* was a deliberately prepared performative intervention announced in advance for a public to gather. In contrast, as we saw in chapter 2, Capetillo's performative gestures of taking the streets with "nonfeminine" or "masculine" clothes did not necessarily involve any theatrical technical elements and, clearly, were not divulged in advance, provoking a spontaneous—and much riskier for Capetillo herself—crowd to gather. The latter difference, concerning the accosting or accompanying public, is fundamental in valorizing what Capetillo's struggle has, indeed, *achieved* over the past century. While the improvised "public" for Capetillo's performance was characterized by violent attack, Hernández felt her performance ignited the possibility of an "ephemeral community" that shared the responsibility for/of women's suffering: "The temerity of attempting to climb the statue made the spectator-other assume responsibility. Then, it was not just me who was involved, but rather, we were all participants. In becoming implicated in the act of the social-woman's body . . . a momentum of ephemeral community was created" (Hernández 2016, 119). This is itself another potent, ephemeral, affective "file" in the archive that *Affect, Archive, Archipelago* is concerned with.

Capetillo and Hernández, in their taking over the open sky, the street, the plaza, the colonizer, and the patriarchal institutions by means of their bodily gestures, actions, and clothing are deeply, yet "invisibly," connected. The underseen relations are evident even in the smallest of instances, which are very much central to the "conceptual clothing," as Hernández would have it, of this book and of her entire artistic trajectory. For instance, as we saw in my discussion of Capetillo's public intervention, the *Boletín Mercantil*'s journalist denounces the "dislocation" she provoked (1911). Meanwhile, in *(a)parecer*'s text, Hernández writes: "Her body is dislocated. The woman of the heart with 23 nails is dislocated." A trace echolocates between Capetillo performing and, thus, claiming her freedom and that of all women, in De la Luna Street, and Hernández radicalizing the act a couple of blocks away and a century later.

The power of the image in both instances—Capetillo in 1911 and Hernández in 2014—is extraordinary precisely because, as Hernández herself writes:

"The visual or textual poetic image bursts through like a force, like an origin of consciousness; it arises from an emergence that runs above and beyond signifying language. To determine the being of an image, one would have to experiment its resonance" (Hernández 2016, 115). The "consciousness origin" that is the image of Capetillo's "dislocation" of the woman's body carries its resonance, its echolocation, beyond verbal language, through the vitality of all revolutionary Puerto Rican, Caribbean women. Capetillo's gestures, as much as contemporary performance pieces, might seem small as political weapons, but, as Hernández explains, "the tireless question that valorizes that which is small but overwhelming" (Hernández 2016, 113) is what impels her artistic trajectory and, I might add, Capetillo's anarcho-feminist struggle and the struggle of all Caribbean, archipelagic seekers of liberation.

AN ARTISTIC PLATFORM OF/FOR THE ARCHIPELAGO'S SURVIVAL

I need more regional investigations to make the connections. I want *Bravatas* to travel the entire Caribbean. . . . it is our experience. It is not continental at all. It is pure island.

—Teresa Hernández, personal interview with author, July 2019

In the days of swelling seas (*marejadas*), the valley trembles with its spongy, heavy voice, producing the sensation of a great silence. When listening to it, in the dozing of cold dawns, I feel a frightening and somber pleasure. Tomorrow the coast will be full of fresh algae, of blue jellyfishes, of seashells, sponges, starfishes, of everything that the monster, revolving within itself, has teared off from its entrails as though it had opened its guts with an olympic harakiri! And that smell of beast in heat that fills the air . . .!

—Luis Palés Matos, *Litoral: Reseña de una vida inútil*, 2013

Since 2018, Hernández has been working with/from the artistic research platform *Bravatas: Sal, sargazo y cansancio*. The concept *bravata* allows her to explore the "thematic spaces" of uncertainty and survival in contemporary Puerto Rico by using "tragedy as anchorage," that is, as the artist herself told me, "history, how do I make way for myself here, from a totally impossible place because, how does one fight?" (personal interview with author 2019). This premise-question comes across very clearly in the Vieques action of stabbing the immense, colonial brick wall with a bare kitchen knife. The tragic, exhausted experience-sensation amid constant catastrophe and the onslaught of colossal enemies is metaphorized by Hernández through the sea and its materials. *Bravatas* is resolutely situated within our condition as archipelagic land- and seascapes, making the sea the main trope of exploration and creation. Since tragedy's ancient Greek tradition is, indeed, geographically developed in a seafaring culture, the resonances are as multifarious as they are potent.

In interviews with the artist, she has traced the genesis of *Bravatas* as a conceptual platform to the early months after Hurricane María's 2017 devastation:

> I heard the concept *bravata* for the first time in 2017, when I went to Puerto Rico's northwestern coast, and a significant event of swelling seas had just taken with it great portions of coastline . . . in [the municipality of] Camuy, I heard someone say, "if only you had seen when the *bravata* came; that took all of this with it." "What is *bravata*?" I asked. "Swelling sea!" they answered.

Apparently, the concept is used with that meaning specifically in the northwestern littorals of Puerto Rico's main island, but not throughout the archipelago. The coastal-dwelling Puerto Ricans from whom Hernández learned the concept characterized it as both a highly dangerous and a potently beautiful phenomenon. In contrast with the spectacularly destructive forces of tropical storms, the *bravata* is more akin to geological time's slow rhythm, a movement imperceptible to the inattentive. The dual character of the *bravata* as a cyclical force of life and as a slow death grip powerfully evokes Puerto Ricans' constant battle with the "slow death" and ceaseless erosion produced by "the crisis," at once sociopolitical, economic, and ecological, as well as our capacity to overcome through autonomous systems of collaborative and creative action. With *Bravatas*, Hernández invites us to question whether we have been forced to survive rather than to live, and whether becoming-*bravatas* might be a political horizon in our effort to abandon power's death regime.

Indeed, for Hernández, *Bravatas* primarily concerns "labor survival, colonial exploitation, unearthly poverty, and the tragic" (*Beta-Local* 2019). In one of our interviews, the artist explained that *Bravatas* is also conceptually moved by a reflection on her own condition as a "mature" woman and cultural worker struggling to survive in the constant uncertainty of a decrepit, bankrupt colonial regime, a situation that connects her with all Puerto Rican women workers, regardless of the kind of labor they perform:

> What is it that conceptually moves *Bravatas* more than anything? Labor as a euphemism for exploitation. My cultural worker connects with women workers in any other area. [It is about] the precariousness that so many of us are living

through, and which has a face and a body. These are, primarily, those of women. That is the reason behind the knife on the mouth, the image of the knife woman; this image provokes what is to come. It is a way to condense the image of labor, exploitation, and our colonial experience, which are not separate things. (personal interview with author 2019)

Since 2018, the *Bravatas* platform has produced seven artistic pieces, interventions, and research work sequences, including the Vieques site-specific piece this chapter opens with. As documented by the *Bravatagrama*—the platform's diagram shared with me by the artist—these seven iterations have been distributed in three phases and a transitional one toward upcoming works.[30] Phase 1 included (1) *Bravata: El comienzo de un comienzo* (installation and site-specific performance in the Diagonal Gallery in Santurce in September 2018, marking the one-year anniversary of Hurricane María's landfall); (2) a series of research workshops entitled *Re-Conocer-Nos* in Aguada, Arecibo, Vieques, and Culebra (March–May 2019); and (3) *Bravata: El comienzo de un comienzo* (site-specific performance in Fort Conde Mirasol in Vieques in May 2019). Phase 2 encompassed *Bravata: Versión escénica* (performance and video at the Julia de Burgos Performance and Arts Center in New York in October 2019) and *la mujer del cuchillo* (site-specific performance as part of the political manifestation *La marcha de las Lolitas* in November 2019).[31] For its part, the video-performance piece *inciertas: espectáculo erosionado*—the focus of this chapter's closing section—constituted phase 3 and was presented as an official selection of the *Instituto de Cultura Puertorriqueña*'s Virtual Theater Festival in November 2020.

Between July and September 2020, the artist also initiated work on *bravata: encuesta a domicilio*, an itinerant investigative performance project with residents of coastal communities who "have historically survived, struggled against, and been dramatically eroded by ecological, colonial, and racist plunder." Thus, these interventions explicitly contextualize the entire *Bravatas* platform as an embodied, coastal, ecological engagement with "the multidimensional catastrophes Puerto Rico confronts, recently intensified with the PROMESA law's imposition (2016) and a succession of natural-human disasters (2017–present)." As part of this transition phase toward the eventual creation of a performance video-documentary piece of the same title (phase 5), Hernández staged encounters with residents of Aguada, Arecibo, Loíza, Carolina, and Vieques using "a socio-poetic survey as a detonator [to] reveal the *bravatas* (of sea and people, ecology and history, past and present) as beauty, mystery, exhaustion, courage." As the "performer-woman pollster," and in contrast with the typical academic stance, Hernández "puts her body, survival, and exhaustion at stake as much as her interlocutors do."

She also produces images and performs actions—as versions of *la mujer del cuchillo*—with salt, sargasso, and the rocking chair, both at residents' homes and in their surrounding eroded seascapes.

Because Hernández conceives of her artistic work as "study spaces," where "I educate myself through *el hacer* (the doing)," it had become increasingly clear that she wanted to move beyond San Juan to establish relations that would enable her "to talk with others [outside of the metropolitan area] about what is happening to us in Puerto Rico" (personal interview with author 2019). Beyond the evident littoral geographies thematized in general by the *Bravatas* platform and in particular by the *bravata: encuesta a domicilio* in-progress project, I read the artist's efforts to produce work elsewhere than the capital's art circuits, as well as her insistence on making a site-specific piece in Vieques, with its historical and ecological resonance of subjugation and resistance to Puerto Rican neocolonialism and US imperialism (see chapter 4), as a desire to become more archipelagic. The difficulties in doing so, of course, are themselves the provocation for *Bravatas*: with increasingly fewer possibilities of justly remunerated artistic production, and even less outside San Juan, the lives of independent artists, and especially those of women and other marginalized subjectivities, are ever more precarious. Her November 2021 participation, as part of *Bravata*'s phase 4, in *Mar de islas: Encuentro de performance del Caribe* in Aguadilla, is another archipelagic move in the direction of connecting her work with the rest of the Caribbean region.

As the artist has explained, *Bravatas* "investigates the relations between the sea and its events, and daily and historical survival in an increasingly besieged archipelago" (personal interview with author 2019). Indeed, the sea and its connective, archipelagic forces, at once material and imaginative, historical and poetic, are embodied throughout the platform's works. The embodiment is twofold: on the one hand, bodily movements/actions (in particular, rolling, walking, and swaying) turn bodies into seas. A consideration of this kind of embodiment is the focus of the *inciertas* discussion below. On the other hand, *Bravatas* has engaged consistently, and in varying ways, with two marine materialities: sea salt and sargasso. Signaling yet another shift in Hernández's creative trajectory, these are not properly objects; rather, like her body itself, salt and sargasso are organic, live-dead substances and, at the same time, traces-echoes of our liquid homelands, of archipelagic bonds on multiple levels: imaginative-mythic, socioeconomic, political, and ecological. A word on these marine materialities is of the essence before we turn to this chapter's closing section.

SEA SALT AND SARGASSO

Described as "the other white gold," sea salt has understandably not received as much attention as sugar has in the history of the Caribbean region. Concurrently with its powerful symbolic meanings concerning the Caribbean's history of colonization and enslavement as maritime phenomena, Cynthia M. Kennedy's work on present-day Turks and Caicos and British colonialism is pivotal in starting to account for the centrality of sea salt's material commodification in the development of transatlantic Western capitalism through colonial and enslaved exploitation. As she elaborates:

> Until the twentieth century, when modern geology revealed that nearly all places on this planet have salt, trade routes were established to transport it, governments taxed it, alliances and empires were built upon it, revolutions were precipitated over it, social classes were partly distinguished by it, and people were enslaved to secure it. Salt also served as one link among the continents of Europe, North America, and Africa, as well as between the Atlantic and Caribbean worlds. During the seventeenth and eighteenth centuries, virtually all European countries engaged in the contentious enterprise of appropriating islands in the West Indies to plant sugarcane. The English and Dutch in particular also set out to grab "salt islands" or to steal salt from islands already claimed by rival European powers. The Dutch procured salt from their own colony of Bonaire in the Antilles, but they also sailed to the nearby northeastern shore of the South American coast and pilfered salt from the beach of a Spanish-held area, Araya, now Venezuela. Nearby, the British also gathered salt illegally at "Salt Tortuga," also called Isla la Tortuga, a small island off the north coast of Venezuela. But the English also produced salt in Anguilla, an island in the northern part of the Lesser Antilles that they would claim for the British crown. (2007, 218)

In addition to the Caribbean-wide colonial exploitation of sea salt, Kennedy's study forcefully reminds us of the "insidious trade pattern" that resulted in Caribbean sea salt being primarily shipped to eastern US ports, from where it came back as salted fish to feed enslaved populations, themselves the producers not only of salt, but also of sugar:

> The result of this trafficking in solar-evaporated salt, a practice that was well established by the last quarter of the seventeenth century, is that salt soon outranked sugar, molasses, and rum as the leading cargo, as measured in tonnage shipped, carried from the West Indies to North America. Heading in the other direction, the ships carried salt cod, a commodity used to feed slaves on the infamous sugar islands and the leading cargo from North America to the Caribbean. An insidiously efficient trade pattern had been forged: slaves facilitated the harvesting and shipment of salt, which the cod fisheries along the northeastern

coast of North America used to produce "slave food," which they, in turn, sent southward to islands in the West Indies. (2007, 219)

Thus, to an important extent, sea salt made possible the all-encompassing sugar plantations in the Caribbean region.

Turning to Puerto Rico, we notice a similar neglect in the historical discussion of sea salt-as-commodity. A notable exception is Luis A. Ramírez Padilla's *Sal, sangre y sudor: Memorias históricas de las salinas de Cabo Rojo* (2012). The book traces the origins of sea salt production in the Cabo Rojo area to an official 1511 Spanish imperial document in which the governor, Juan Cerón, was entrusted with the oversight of the Cabo Rojo *salinas* and Puerto Rico's gold mines (2012, 9). Although sea salt was produced under Spanish rule over the next few centuries, it never attained the degree of formal organization noticeable in the Caribbean "salt islands" (see Kennedy 2007). Only in the second half of the nineteenth century did Puerto Rican sea salt start circulating toward the US markets, which, as we saw, had been previously nourished primarily by the British "salt islands." However, Cabo Rojo's sea salt was a main commodity in the feverish contraband trade with multiple European powers—especially the Dutch—during the seventeenth and eighteenth centuries (Ramírez Padilla 2012, 16), connecting the Puerto Rican archipelago to the Caribbean region as far as the "ABC" islands controlled by the Dutch, a phenomenon that further contextualizes Betances's archipelagic travelling discussed in chapter 1.

Akin to that of the enslaved workers in the salt ponds in Turks and Caicos documented by Kennedy (2007), extreme labor exploitation characterized nineteenth-century life for Cabo Rojo's *salineros* (sea salt workers), who were routinely described as "lazy," "criminal," and "immoral" by the *criollo*, bourgeois families controlling the sea salt industry and their bodies (Ramírez Padilla 2012, 30).[32] Describing the area as a "penal colony," Ramírez Padilla explains:

> Just as it had been since the beginning of the nineteenth century, during the administration of the Ramírez de Arellano and Pabón Dávila [families], hundreds of workers continued working the *salinas* in a state of semi-slavery and living in infrahuman conditions. . . . This was achieved through a system of labor organization known as *libreta de jornaleros* (day workers' notebook), which guaranteed the owners a constant provision of laborers. This system limited the workers' mobility, forcing them to establish themselves in the area where they worked. (2012, 31)[33]

Toward the end of the nineteenth century, the *salineros* became a cohesive political force. Both the intolerable paradox of working in such enslaving circumstances while slavery had been formally "abolished" through the

Abolition Act of 1873, and the spread in the area, with Betances's leadership, of a strong anticolonial, republican stance against Spanish rule (see chapter 1), enabled the *salineros'* increasing politization. Eventually, during the 1920s and 1930s—the heyday of Puerto Rican nationalism under Albizu Campos's *Partido Nacionalista* (see chapter 3)—*salineros* led, in tandem with sugarcane workers, the Puerto Rican workers' struggles.[34] Indeed, the *Unión Independiente de los Trabajadores de la Sal* is one of the oldest Puerto Rican workers' unions in existence (Ramírez Padilla 2012, 112). Although the *salineros* were violently suppressed (104–05), their 1938 strike managed to achieve a rise in their salary and the distribution to workers, in 1940–1941, of the second *parcelas* (parcels of land for workers to live on) in Puerto Rico, known until today as Pole Ojea (107). Their struggle was also amply supported by civil society in Cabo Rojo, according to Ramírez Padilla's historical study (108).

These regional and local antecedents provide a historical, material, and socioeconomic frame in which to better understand and appreciate the centrality of sea salt—specifically, sea salt from *Empresas Padilla* in Cabo Rojo, which controls the much-decayed sea salt industry since 1998 (Ramírez Padilla 2012, 132)—throughout Hernández's *Bravatas* platform. Fundamental in the artist's work because of its qualities (texture, color, taste), its extraordinary importance in preserving food for the reproduction of human life, and its metaphorical associations, sea salt is also immensely potent in its materialization of an essential, yet underseen and scarcely discussed, story of unspeakable exploitation and dogged resistance and survival in Puerto Rico and the wider Caribbean region:

> Studying our sea salt industry, evoking its workers (*salineros*), the flesh of exploitation . . . one of our first massive worker strikes as Puerto Ricans was led by the *salineros* in the Cabo Rojo area [referring to the 1938 strike]. Indeed, everything started in Cabo Rojo, in the summer of 2018 . . . when I went to the *salinas* (salt ponds) in Cabo Rojo as a tourist, I realized that this is a materiality. The object is as fundamental as the thought with and from the body. . . . Also fundamental are the materials that accompany me so that I can create the concepts or themes I wish to deal with. And when I encountered the sea salt, which is so beautiful, and I started investigating, I realized how much poetics, how many meanings, can emerge from it. Salt is a ritual space; it's work, island, marine ontology, preservation agent; the word *salario* (salary) comes from "salt," and we had that great industry. (Hernández, personal interview with author 2019)

Finally, the exploration of the Puerto Rican archipelago's multiple forms of erosion in the completed and upcoming *Bravatas* pieces and interventions is also intimately related to sea salt, as the *salinas* area in Cabo Rojo—a rich biodiversity site and temporary home to multiple migratory bird species—is under severe ecological stress. The possibility of it disappearing as the ocean rises both in level and temperature is now at its most acute.[35] As the *Bravatas* platform links the sea, its materials, and events with survival, it is not only that of Puerto Rican workers, cultural and otherwise, but also that of our very own insular geographies.

The same material-poetic fecundity, coupled with ecological disaster, characterizes sargasso, the other sea materiality making suggestive appearances throughout *Bravatas*'s productions. Sargasso covers the performer's car as she arrives at the first two site-specific pieces (Santurce and Vieques); it is spread on the floor both in the Diagonal gallery and in the Arriví theater; it closes *inciertas* in an extreme close-up. Composed of two species of algae called "pelagic"—that is, adrift, due to their natural buoyancy—sargasso's reproduction is asexual, meaning that the algae multiply every time they are fragmented (Cabrejas Quintana 2020, 141). In contrast with sea salt's preservation-corrosion of life, once dead, foul-smelling, and accumulated on the coastline, which is the predominant image in *Bravatas*, sargasso evokes a memory of the future, that of its free-flowing vestiges.

In the Caribbean, as Aponte Alsina has reminded us (see the Introduction), the notorious Sargasso Sea, which is, significantly, "the saltiest part of the Atlantic" (Carson 1950), has had a significant imaginative hold since the first Spanish colonizers arrived in the area and reported on it. Indeed, the oceanic phenomenon was turned into an enduring metaphor for the Caribbean region, its conditions, and its intersectional conflicts of class, gender, and race, in Jean Rhys's *Wide Sargasso Sea*. More recently, sargasso has become a notorious and hazardous excess of the ocean's traces on Caribbean coasts, both insular and continental, "affecting over twenty countries so far" since 2016 (Cabrejas Quintana 2020, 144), the year of PROMESA's imposition in Puerto Rico. Sargasso's dramatic acceleration is an effect of the climate catastrophe—especially warmer oceanic temperatures—that the *Bravatas* platform in part responds to, as well as of chemical pesticides and fertilizers that flow into the ocean from deforestation and other industrial agricultural practices, and of the massive destruction of mangroves across our regional coasts.[36] So vertiginously are the algae reproducing that the traditional Sargasso Sea has expanded, "prompting some to talk about a new one," that covers "an ample region from Africa to Central and South America," and thus has become "a phenomenon at a global scale" (Cabrejas Quintana 2020, 142).

All these imaginative, historical, and ecological associations are activated throughout *Bravatas*'s productions. As a result of humanity's own folly, the swelling, salty seas discharge on our coasts ever more sargasso, which, as we have seen, has increasingly become a potent symbol of ecological emergency, the most extreme form of deadly survival. In other words, the ever-increasing sargasso signals the ways in which being forced, by humanity's very own regimes of exploitation, to live in a constant knife-on-mouth struggle for survival becomes its own catastrophe, an impossible tragedy commensurate to knifing colonial walls and climbing colonizer's statues. Hernández knows full well these are failed exercises, but she invites us to join her in the tenacious attempt of insisting.

UNCERTAINLY BECOMING OTHER, OCEANIC

> This is our entire history:
> salt, aridity, exhaustion,
> a vague, undefinable, sorrow,
> an immobile fixity like a swamp,
> and a scream over there, [over here,] in the depths,
> as a terrible and obstinate fungus,
> settling on the flabby fleshes
> of useless, muffled, desires.

—Luis Palés Matos, fragment of "Topografía," in *la erizada*'s voice, 2008[37]

The most recent *Bravatas* production, *inciertas-eroded spectacle*, is a video performance piece originally streamed online as an official selection of Puerto Rico's *Instituto de Cultura Puertorriqueña* Virtual Theater Festival on November 28, 2020.[38] The piece dives more profoundly onto the myriad forms and effects of erosion, at once that of theater itself as a live, present art in pandemic times, as well as that of all our ecosystems, biological and otherwise, and our lives in Puerto Rico's increasingly precarious conditions. *Inciertas* is a resolutely insular, Puerto Rican/Caribbean, piece, brimming with salt and sargasso. As *la erizada* (the sea urchin woman)—one of the piece's women "presences"—tells us, *inciertas*'s "plot is the *bravata*" in the sense that the word is used, as explained above, on Puerto Rico's northwestern coast. On stage, Hernández and guest artist Miosoti Alvarado Burgos are two uncertain, eroded Puerto Rican women who seem to embody legions of other women. In little over thirty-five minutes, *inciertas-eroded spectacle* tells the story not only of theater, of Puerto Rico and the Caribbean, of our region's women, and of our literal and metaphorical erosions, but also of the human species itself, in backwards action. From a city in ruins to the womb of water, from *güiro*[39] to sargasso, from knife to seashell, from cement to salt.

At first, each woman appears on her own moving in the outskirts of a ruinous city/archipelago: the demolition of a building in Río Piedras; the closed ferry terminal from the town of Fajardo (on Puerto Rico's east coast) to the island municipalities of Vieques and Culebra; Hernández—*la mujer del cuchillo*—attacking the US Customs House with jabs of her knife from below; and Alvarado Burgos—*la mujer del güiro* (the güiro woman)—using her *güiro* as a sonic onslaught on the main offices of Puerto Rico's Department of Labor. In a word, their movements-actions are in and around the ruins of Puerto Rico's bankrupt ELA and its exploitative, colonial, debt-addicted "arrangement" with the United States, as well as in and around the ruins of the bipartisan, patriarchal, neoliberal regime. In the voice of *la mujer del cuchillo*, a powerful text resonates alongside their bodies and the *güiro* sounds. In its ritual repetition, the words are as much a rallying call as they are an elemental cry:

> Uncertainty is not unfamiliar.
> Over here they flood and flush us.
> Extraction is sinister.
> The winds are not random.
>
> A hyperreality smears everything.
> The prolonged present is a threat.
>
> We are more and more, we are more,
> the women who earn less.
>
> The guilty should beware,
> for the insular *bravatas*
> can reach their hideouts.

Knife and *güiro* meet, resolved, in front of the Arriví theater in Santurce. Before entering together, stepping on sargasso, the women walk below a random banner of Manuel Natal's candidacy for San Juan's mayoralty—which was so closely contested that significant doubts remain as to the legitimacy of the eventual winner's victory—under the newly formed *Movimiento Victoria Ciudadana*, a multisector coalition that managed to win four legislative posts. The image reminds us of *inciertas*'s immediate Puerto Rican context: the lead-up to the November 2020 elections, when a significant dent was finally made on the bipartisan ruling edifice of the pro–US statehood *Partido Nuevo Progresista* and the pro–status quo *Partido Popular Democrático*.

Upon entering the theater building, Hernández's and Alvarado Burgos's temperatures are taken—this is a pandemic piece, as well—before they start walking through corridors and going up and down stairs in a seemingly endless effort to arrive on stage. The survival of theater and its artists is increasingly more arduous. While walking, the artists encounter a history of dramatic theater told in posters hanging on the walls of the Arriví. Visually highlighted by Gabriel Coss Ríos's camerawork are two that illustrate patriarchal female archetypes: on the one hand, Molière's satire, *The Wise Women*, which mocks the educational aspirations of women, and, on the other, *The Passion according to Antígona* Pérez, Luis Rafael Sánchez's rewriting of *Antigone*, in which the woman protagonist is a political subject, but must pay for it with her life.

Traversing with these women the interiors of a theater that, as a live audience, we would not have been able to see, we feel a potent, if invisible, undercurrent: two historical rewritings are traveling in tandem. The first is that of theater itself. The Arriví is not yet a ruin, but it might well be on its way to becoming one, as has been the fate of so many other theaters in Puerto Rico. Explored by Hernández herself in previous works, the ruination is compounded today by the pandemic world's "hyperreality," a recurrent concept in *inciertas*. At the same time, however, the conventional theater's ruin-erosion opens the possibility of *other*, underseen theaters in its interior, of which *inciertas* is an offering. The second historical rewriting is that of the women that dramatic, patriarchal theater has named: their ruin-erosion is welcome. We, the *inciertas*'s audience, are positioned to prefer the knife's and *güiro*'s impetus and potency. We feel called upon by them. We come. Ready. Avid.

When we finally reach the theater's stage with the two women, we discover that it is the sea, with Puerto Rico's "big island" silhouette made of sargasso on the floor. Vieques and Culebra, in contrast, are made of salt, and their topography is complete, solid. They are lovingly placed on a coffee table, their salt illuminated, radiant. These Puerto Rican islands are highlighted in a way they never are in the archipelago's political discourse. Considering the rest of the objects brought on stage—two rocking chairs, one sea salt sack from *Empresas Padilla* in Cabo Rojo, a blue tarp, a stool with casters, and a lectern—the table with Vieques and Culebra stands out as an altar of sorts around which we could mobilize our most sensible archipelagic wills to live differently, honoring our scale and our land- and seascapes.

My observation above that *inciertas-eroded spectacle* is the human species' history told backwards is not the same as saying that the piece returns to an idealized past of intimate knowledge concerning the liquid origins of life. Rather, it *bursts into—bravata—*the intolerable present of a Puerto Rico/Caribbean that is almost, but not yet, terminally collapsed. Whether such an eruption is "a gift or an invasion" is asked very early in the piece by *la erizada*. Upon their arrival on stage, in the interior of Puerto Rico's map, the women—who were knife and *güiro* before—become rolling bodies, swells,

Figure 5.3. Vieques and Culebra Made of Salt, *inciertas-espectáculo erosionado*, Arriví Theater, Santurce, 2020   Courtesy of Teresa Hernández

uncertain tides between littorals, seaweed dancing to the water's rhythm, just like the seaweed that accompanies the piece's title when projected on screen. They are *las mujeres marejadas* (the swell women).

Over the course of *inciertas*, we feel the bursting *bravata* with increasing potency. The next scene features *la mujer del cuchillo*, now without the knife, swaying in *meciéndome en la transición*'s *sillón* with a violence that ranges from subtle to overt. The woman and the *sillón* are in the ruins of a cultural center in Loíza—a municipality on Puerto Rico's northeastern coast considered a bastion of Black, Afro-Puerto Rican, and working-class heritage and struggle (see chapter 4)—confronted by an imposing swelling sea. Meanwhile, *la mujer del güiro*, now without it, sways, with the same alternating motions, in another *sillón* inside the theater. She is surrounded by empty seats and projections on the theater's walls of the agitated sea and a military boot on a ferry. As in *inciertas* the *sillón*, which in Puerto Rico tends to be situated within the same nationalist liturgy of the *güiro*, is the same rusty, outdoor *sillón* Hernández has been working with since 2013, its echolocation, its trace through sea salt's residue on the object's metal, becomes ever more evident. Precisely because political complaints—proverbially shared in *boricua* rocking chairs—have come out into the open, in *inciertas* the rocking chairs have been turned into *tribunas* (see chapters 2 and 3), political platforms from which to demand, and achieve, a justice that we are still in the course of naming. There is a thunderous whisper of Puerto Rico's 2019 *Verano Boricua* in the rocking chairs with which Hernández and Alvarado Burgos maneuver in sways that become leaps.

Figure 5.4. *La mujer del sillón* in an Abandoned Cultural Center in Loíza, *inciertas-espectáculo erosionado,* 2020   Courtesy of María del Mar Rosario

The next scene features Hernández as *la mujer marejada* counting wooden clothespins at the lectern. She talks to us while pinching her face, ears, head, thus becoming *la erizada* (the sea urchin woman). She worries about us ("I wonder how you are"), and because "even if I don't see you, I always imagine you," she begins a solitary conversation. With the tone of a measured professor, she gives the official dictionary—"threat proffered with arrogance in order to intimidate someone"—as well as the Puerto Rican—referenced above—definitions of *bravata*. She poses unsettling, half-poetic, half-sociological, questions, such as, "Are you a *bravata*?," "Are the *bravatas* only those of the sea?," "Do you step out of your house with salt?," "Is a life with lots of salt necessarily a *salaera*, an unfortunate life? If not, what kind of life is it?," "Is surviving today, in Puerto Rico, a *bravata*? How so?," "Are there other tempestuous things that come onto land? Do they provoke fear or pleasure in you?," "What or who is responsible for the erosion?"[40] Referring ostensibly to the *inciertas* piece itself, she declares that "there's no drama" in this "something" (*algo*), and that "the narrating voice is not yet defined," but her irony's embodiment disarms her words. With *la erizada*, Palés Matos's "history" becomes "hysteria," the "literal" becomes the "littoral." The drama intensifies, bringing the myth's trace—its irruption—increasingly closer to the present. That trace may well be a *bravata*, "another tempestuous thing that comes onto land."

After asking us, "Don't you have the sensation that the crises wear down the body just as the erosion wears away the coast?," *la erizada* falls between empty seats to the following scene, where she has become an *other*, once again. She looks like *la mujer marejada* but is no longer swelling. Now in the theater's basement, and in the space of a low-lying square, she executes

Figure 5.5. La erizada, the Sea and the Theater's Empty Seats, *inciertas-espectáculo erosionado*, Arriví Theater, Santurce, 2020   Courtesy of Teresa Hernández

a long sequence of arrested, mechanical, compressed movements. We have the palpitating sensation that, at any moment, she could be crushed, attacked, restrained, turned into dust. Her circumstance—that of the multitude of uncertain women "who earn less"—reveals an unsayable anguish, a no-exit, a confinement, a merciless hammering over the head, an I've-tried-everything, a disturbing drama, an absolute exhaustion. One of her hands-eyes reaches for the camera, for us, for something underseen, for all that we are owed.

Then, the stool with casters bursts into the basement. It is a small *bravata*, capable of rescuing this woman, returning her, now on wheels rather than on her feet, to the theater's main floor as *la erizada*. While she rolls across the aisles, there is a gestural echo of the piece's initial rolls on the map. The sea projections on the theater's walls are not the only indexes that continue telling us that we are *at sea*. In an instance of the masterful resignification act that theater can perform, the stool with casters is the sea, within which *la erizada* searches "over here, over here, over here" for the liquid homeland's trace of salt and sargasso, the track of the origin we have forgotten, in turn ruining ourselves.

As we saw, earlier in the piece, *la erizada* had posed perhaps the most important political question for our present island lives: "Are *you* a *bravata*?" Thus, it comes as no surprise, although it hurts all the same, when she now reminds us that, having turned our islands into "the zone of transition and transaction," "they want our habit of misery."[41] Still, she declares assuredly, "Over here, in the country taken by investment banking, *we are alive*!" Precisely at this point, *la erizada* proceeds to remove the pins of her-our pain. The sound of the *güiro* accompanies the liberatory gesture, which feels antithetical to the basement's confinement. Her skin, hung out to dry in the merciless sun of colonial, capitalist, and patriarchal pillage, is left marked, wounded. Showing us the evidence of her harm with an astonishing sense of calm, *la erizada* leaves us with her last question: "Could this be the moment to take our eyes out in order to see?"

The reference to classical Greek tragedy is evident, but I think this question, considered in the context of the entire piece, becomes something more. Because sight has been the overwhelmingly privileged human sense in the artistic and ideological traditions of Western modernity, "to take out our eyes in order to see" necessarily entails becoming *nonhuman*.[42] Only if we are willing to roll in the salt and sargasso that the *bravata* leaves in its wake, which means, as we have seen, rolling in our shared, archipelagic, affective history and memory, "will we see" that the horizons are common in our uncertain, Caribbean islands. If our species, with its capitalist, colonial, racist, patriarchal violence, has unleashed a colossal erosion—in every sense of the word—*inciertas-eroded spectacle* seems to tell us that such is the result of disregarding, abandoning, humiliating the foundational vitality of water and its traces of connections and becomings. *That* is our tragedy.

La mujer del güiro—who, since the beginning of *inciertas*, has turned the instrument, a "national, traditional symbol," into a defying weapon—had already taken her eyes out to see, insomuch as she breakdances onto the undercover exit of the empty, elegant theater. None of the piece's women had exited the theater on their own feet until now. But *la mujer del güiro*, with her *bravata*, goes up a very long stairwell toward the theater's rooftop, from where she furiously activates her weapon. Her forceful scratching seems to produce a rain of the sea salt that shelters the last, which is also the first, becoming of Hernández: *la mujer de la concha*. In *inciertas*, the mutation of this woman-presence from her initial appearances in the Santurce and Vieques site-specific pieces has intensified climactically.

What in the initial scene was a blue tarp—activating all its devastating associations with Hurricane María (2017), state abandonment, FEMA's criminal neglect, and generalized misery and death in Puerto Rico's recent history—is now the salty sea. In it, a body's naked flesh and loose hair toss. This body becomes, all at once, insular promontories, gelatinous creatures from the ocean's depths, and the closest to the bare human-woman-artist that we have seen in *inciertas*. This body's movement, characterized by carefully studied and at the same time spontaneous, even primitive, fluidity and slothfulness, dramatically contrasts with that of the rest of the women in *inciertas*. The amalgam of flesh agitating in the depths carries a seashell in its mouth. From knife to seashell there is a long stretch, of course. But faced with the most mythic, atavistic, feminist scene in the piece, I feel—and I repeat myself—that there is no return. There is only irruption. Without the seashell, there is no knife. Without salt, no life. Without the sea, no land.

The women in/of *inciertas-eroded spectacle* have become *so* human that they are not anymore. They have taken their eyes out to see with such passion, that it is only when *la mujer de la concha* looks *through* the shell, with her *nonhuman*, oceanic eyes, that she can stand on her own two feet. Now, she has seen. Powerfully echoing *(a)parecer*'s *la mujer de la cola, la mujer de la concha* walks, dragging her salty seas—those of historically exploited and enslaved women, workers, *salineros*, and nonhuman lifeforms—while, at the same time, leaving us with their trace-echo of salt on stage. Having also taken the Puerto Rican archipelago with her, she finds the exit. She returns their plenitude to the waters, as she does not have, nor will she make, a habit of misery. Staring directly at us with new eyes of defiance and conviction, she disappears through the elevator, leaving her resonance and that of the exploited multitude's salt and survival—but not the map—on the floor of a theater that, if we were also to take our eyes out, we would see is always an *other* theater, capable of reviving us.

Hernández's relational sea of smallness and movement, her archipelagic, ephemeral scenic practice, her echolocations with other Puerto Rican women's transgressions, her experimentation with embodied, material, land- and seascapes' lives, in a word, her transdisciplinary, multitudinously small art, are all gleaming, sometimes "unarchivable," iterations of our affective archive of Caribbean relations. They stand as examples of Glissant's trace on the sands, as much as of Aponte Alsina's liquid homeland. Along with the rest of the oral and written texts, as well as the performative, embodied, ephemeral interventions, actions, productions, and friendships *Affect, Archive, Archipelago* is in relation with, Hernández's art is a claim on our sovereignties, igniting ever more imaginative possibilities for our islands to truly see and touch each other, imperial walls overcome by our shared horizons.

Overflowing Sea

I insisted we take Carla. I always insist when it comes to dogs (and cats, and horses, and turtles, and birds, and any living, nonhuman creature). But Carlita doesn't like water, Teresa explained. That's okay, we'll manage, I pleaded. Persuading her while rubbing Carlita's tummy was easy. And so that morning, Carlita came to Loíza for our walk-ceremony.

There had been a possibility we would go to Ocean Park, which Teresa often visits as her most readily accessible, urban beach. The sea there is always overflowing, just like us, she had said a few weeks before. But the artist discarded that idea in favor of Loíza, as she wanted to show me various seascapes where she had been—and continues to be—moved for/in/with her *Bravatas* project. Vacía Talega Beach, with which she holds a cherished relation since childhood, is also located in Loíza.

As we drove through several Loíza neighborhoods beyond the better-known Piñones (see chapter 4), Teresa brought my attention to the warm knowledge about this littoral that *Bravatas*—in other words, art—has gifted her. She knew people chatting under the shade of mango trees. She celebrated balconies and sandy patios with flowers. She is especially intimate with the many chairs lining the façades of most houses. "Isn't that beautiful," she exclaimed. *¡Bello!*

Upon arriving at *Paseo del Atlántico*, we found the sand full of diggers. Boulders are being piled to hold the sea-level-rising *bravatas* from furthering even more the dramatic erosion that has already eaten away most of the coastline. A few feet away, boulders placed some years ago have already been taken by the sea. But heavy machinery is putting them up again, anyway. Nobody in charge seems to think of trees.

On top of the half-made rock wall sits what is left of a community center where *la mujer del cuchillo* performed with the *sillón*. The dilapidation is almost absolute, if not for the fact that all around us *loiceños* are playing on the beach and riding their bicycles and chatting and living and loving.

Teresa likes danger, she says, as my maternal *abuela* used to demand us not to. And so, as part of her performance work, she has walked—and wanted to today—on the eroded remains of a sidewalk, platforms of cement perilously hanging sideways, this way and that, our bodies in balancing acts, falling, almost, but no. Carlita's four legs are her blessing.

While witnessing Teresa hanging on, it occurs to me that this action-movement literalizes what it feels like for a body to survive here, within our everyday tragedy unfolding in an oceanic scenario of breathless beauty.

A man whose name I soon learn breezes past us on his bike. Teresa stops him.

"Do you remember me from our interview last year?"

"Oh yes, it's you, *Doña Sal*, Lady Salt."

There was no parody in his tone—this is his name of love for Teresa. I am instantly at home.

"I see you continue making your *artesanías*." She points to the vegetable materials from coconut palms he is holding in his hands while maneuvering the bike.

"Oh, yeah!"

Can I come back to see you again?" Teresa asks.

"Of course! After 7 am and before 9 pm. If you see this bike around here, or that black *guagua*, I'm home! Here, I just got these mangoes from the neighbor's tree. Do you like mangoes?"

"Yes!"

"Then take these." We thank him profusely and carry on with our pink mangoes and his smiling arrow of charm.

As soon as we start walking on the remaining beach sand corridor, a big, luminous stray dog appears. He jumps all over the place, clearly overjoyed with Carla's presence. Carla is not as happy, though, since she now must sort, at once, the water she dislikes and the intensity of a love she did not bargain for. Neither Teresa nor I can bring ourselves to outright reject Bello, the name I've given him since his image on the beach has become an evocation. We talk to him in all kinds of ways. But he persists, all morning, hanging onto our legs and making us—well, me—fall over. We then decide we must carry twenty-five-pound Carlita in our arms to better handle Bello's onslaught of enthusiasm. I ask to do it, since she's here because of my insistence. I secretly think Carlita has thus become my *Bravatas*'s sack of salt.

The silent, seated ceremony I had imagined for relating Betances's littoral with this one in Loíza and with Teresa's art was thus made impossible. I decide not to mention it. I'll give Teresa the vestiges of Betances's flight, his confederation dream from Cabo Rojo, once we get back to her house on Independencia Street.

We stop to get a beer at a place owned by an Afro-Puerto Rican woman who had once been a singer and who, as we learned that morning, had recorded with Donna Summer and Prince. Her place is next to the mouth of Julia de Burgos's *Río Grande de Loíza*. Standing on the sand, we talk for some time about Teresa's art, about difficulty and endurance and love, about horses and about this book, and I tell her that she should get in touch with a scientist to clarify some questions she has about the sea.

Teresa's every word is punctuated by a turn. As a movement artist, she is always on the move, uncontainable. And so Carlita and I are forced to move, too. In one of our twists, we are unexpectedly met with a group of children playing, splashing, giggling, on the spot where river meets sea. We watch, in awe.

"All waters touching each other."

A light mist starts falling.

The ceremony had taken place. My little box with seashells and coral remains, and the paper with quotes from Betances, Glissant, and Aponte Alsina are insignificant symbols, after all.

With the light rain, Carlita has more water to deal with, and so now, she really wants to go. Teresa also has a workshop to teach.

As we drive back to Hato Rey, we alternate silences with the rapid succession of palm trees and the memory—our eyes glistening with brewing tears—of Fernando Picó. The Puerto Rican government said nothing, nothing at all, when he passed a few years ago.

So much affective remembering to do here, in this small place "forsaken by History." So much archiving-honoring we owe. Our true debt. One we can never repay. But try we must.

NOTES

1. All unattributed quotes in this chapter are from Teresa Hernández in personal communication or interviews with the author.

2. The enduring image of *la mujer del cuchillo* is her gripping it with her mouth (*con el cuchillo en la boca*). Although Hernández's *apparition*—a concept I will discuss below—is, indeed, biting the knife's handle and otherwise manipulating it, the idiomatic expression *con el cuchillo en la boca* evokes in Puerto Rico someone who is engaged in a daily struggle for sheer survival.

3. A fragment of this piece is available in the artist's *Vimeo* page, at www.vimeo.com/355940804.

4. Frank Lestringant's "Pensar por islas," a philosophical-literary approach to insular topography, is a fulgurating echo here, considering Hernández's strong commitment to the languages of space and site-specific performance: "space, and more concretely, topography, is a form of thought. From which the following paradox emerges: the problem is not to think space, it is space that thinks. Instead of fixing space, one must allow it to move and breathe" (2009, 9–10).

5. "Each *carretilla* carried one *quintal* or 100 pounds. This was the unit of measurement. Each worker earned . . . one cent and a quarter per *carretilla*. Workers raked the sea salt, making straight lines inside the crystallizer. Then, they shoveled the salt to fill the *carretillas*. The same workers had to carry the *carretillas* to the storage area, where salt was accumulated in mounds similar to pyramids. . . . all this work, including the raking and the carrying, was paid at one and a quarter cent per *carretilla*. The youngest and strongest workers worked from 1:30 am until 6 pm, that is, a total of 17 hours. These workers carried between 180 and 210 *carretillas* and were paid $1.75 and $2.00 respectively. Most workers, however, earned between 75 and 80 cents per day. That is, they carried between 40 and 50 *carretillas*" (Ramírez Padilla 2012, 119).

6. In the first site-specific piece (in the *Diagonal* gallery in Santurce) within the *Bravatas* platform, the artist asked the public to make the silhouettes of the Puerto Rican islands with the salt she carried.

7. Stimulating commentaries on this piece are also those of Kairiana Núñez Santaliz (2019) and Arnaldo Rodríguez Bagué (2020).

8. Recordings of some of the artist's pieces (in their entirety or as samples) are available at the Hemispheric Institute's digital archives (see https://hemisphericinstitute.org/en/hidvl-collections/itemlist/category/343-thernandez-works.html) and at the artist's *Vimeo* page (see www.vimeo.com/teresanoinc).

9. For another synthetic account of Teresa Hernández's work, see Martínez Tabares (2007).

10. She has made a point of calling her work as producer of her own pieces *producciones teresa, no inc.* (teresa productions, non-incorporated). Notice the deliberate use of lowercase letters as part of her commitment to smallness, a matter I will return to.

11. A recent case in point, relevant in the context of this chapter, is the appearance of *la mujer del cuchillo* in José Ciénaga's music video "Materna," directed by Sofía

Gallisá Muriente (see www.youtube.com/watch?v=pEuYm8BWNEw). Although unrelated to the artist's *Bravatas* conceptual platform (discussed below), this production is very much informed by Cabo Rojo's coastal seascapes. In this video's different context, which uncannily explores motherhood, the "mature, working-class" *mujer del cuchillo* unsettles with her weapon and her moves the hegemonic, patriarchal associations of women "naturally" and "saintly" performing motherhood.

12. "How do I deal with the country from within it? How do I deal with my scenic proposal in a country, in a city (San Juan), characterized by its harshness, its segregation, its scarce interest in a work that does not adjust to languages or aesthetics of readily accessible comprehension?" (Hernández 2016, 66) Also recall here the discussion in the Introduction concerning the hegemonic Western representation of the island as a "no-place."

13. Hernández has further elaborated on this as follows:

[S]mallness presented itself to me as a place for personal and artistic vindication, as a way of combatting the invisibility and exclusion that hegemonic discourses impose. The experience of living in a *no lugar* ("no-place"), an invisible country in the cartography of those who make History (to paraphrase Eduardo Lalo), led me to understand that which is small, contingent, intrinsically precarious, fragmented, as a space where my perspective on theater is formulated and reformulated. In other words, the concept of smallness connects me with the possibility of. . . . (Hernández 2016, 55).

The centrality of smallness has continued unabated in Hernández's reflections on her practice, as can be corroborated in a 2020 artist statement: "I assume that which is small as a place of confidence, encouragement, and resistance."

14. The taking of theater out of its traditional architectural spaces in Puerto Rico had already been initiated by the extraordinary work of the University of Puerto Rico's *Teatro Rodante* in the 1950s, which staged classic and contemporary dramatic pieces throughout the country in a *carromato* (cart-turned-stage).

15. In the context of this book's concern with affective archives and "the unarchivable" (see the Introduction), a recent trace-echo merits mention here. The 2021 live arts piece *Archivo Santaliz*, by Kairiana Núñez Santaliz, Pedrito Santaliz's niece, movingly explores the luminous and arduous, even impossible, task of encountering, honoring, and preserving written and visual traces of an artist's (Pedrito's) trajectory in an archipelago besieged by institutional oblivion toward its independent artists. Núñez Santaliz, engulfed on stage by plastic bowls and lids, transgresses the dramatic distinction between character and actor, inserting her own archival traces—and Puerto Rico's present of debt crisis—into her uncle's dogged commitment to creation despite increasing poverty, and vice versa. In the process, we are reminded that our affects have the potency of turning any fulgurating moment, however tragic, into a sustaining relation.

16. The fullest available account of and commentary on this genealogy is Lowell Fiet's *El teatro puertorriqueño reimaginado* (2004).

17. As Hernández herself has explained, "their transdisciplinary questioning of artistic conventions has shown me that rigor is preferable to rules, processes to fixed results, risks to complacency" (personal interview with author 2019).

18. An important 1970s dance school in San Juan, which held collaborative ties with the live arts collectives mentioned in this chapter, was the *Escuela de Baile Alma Concepción* (see Concepción 2021).

19. Hernández's MA dissertation (2016) further discusses the central importance of *Taller de Otra Cosa* for her work's development and sustenance. Viveca Vázquez's lifelong trajectory, including the organization of several editions of the *Rompeforma* live and visual arts marathon in Puerto Rico over the course of the 1990s, merits a study of its own. A recent dialogue between Hernández and Vázquez—as part of *Teatro Público*'s and *Instituto de Cultura Puertorriqueña*'s 2021 series on women in Puerto Rican theater—also sheds light on *Taller de Otra Cosa*'s historical and aesthetic significance (see www.facebook.com/267199020049032/videos/1326690814360925/?__so__=watchlist&__rv__=video_home_www_playlist_video_list).

20. For more on Pedro Rosselló's police state, see Marisol LeBrón's *Policing Life and Death* (2019).

21. For more on these corruption schemes, see Atiles-Osoria's *Profanaciones* (2020).

22. See the Coda for a reflection on a contemporary avatar of the Puerto Rican tourist industry's phobia against the archipelago.

23. Dolores Aponte (2010) offers a commentary on *Salve la Reina* as a piece confronting the question of Puerto Rico's "regional belonging" in the Caribbean.

24. "When I participated in the *Segundo Encuentro Hemisférico de Performance y Política*, in Monterey, México, in 2001, which was one of the first occasions in which I presented work outside of Puerto Rico, the ID they gave me as an event participant had my name and my country of origin listed as: PR-USA. . . . It was not the first time I had to confront such play of acronyms, so I underwent an improvisation trance and invented a new place of origin, PRUSA. I saw myself in an experience of frontiers between territories, but in contrast with other geographical frontiers, mine was not literal nor visible" (Hernández 2016, 74). See also Negrón's (2009) compelling commentary on Hernández's *Nada que ver (composiciones escénicas sobre el yo)* and its *gemido* (moan) and *jadeo* (panting) beyond the word. *Nada que ver* is a 2006–2007 piece in which, among other appearances and becomings, including a female dog, the character Rubí, "a prusana artist," is central.

25. Hernández reflected on this moment and the importance of *el sillón* very recently (January 2021) in an interview with experimental Puerto Rican artist José "Pepe" Álvarez, as part of PEPOSA, his ongoing research project on Puerto Rican improvisational live arts from the 1970s to the present.

26. Notice the potent connection here with Luisa Capetillo's emphasis on women's experience of waiting (see chapter 2).

27. Recall that in 2016 the US Congress imposed the PROMESA law and the Financial Oversight and Management Board (FOMB) on Puerto Rico, while 1898 was the year of the US invasion of the archipelago (see the Introduction).

28. This presence had first appeared in Hernández's *Nada que ver* (referenced above), and has travelled to political protests in the street, such as the 2010 student strike at the University of Puerto Rical and a 2015 collective action, which included

an intervention from *Agua, sol y sereno* (see chapter 4), in front of Puerto Rico's *Capitolio* against the government's dramatic funding cuts to nonprofit organizations.

29. *La enjaulada*—as well as scenic work with the cage as an object per se—is another of Hernández's presences that has traversed multiple pieces and interventions, most notably the 2017 multimedia piece *Privada*.

30. These future works are themselves distributed in phases 4–6, and include more site-specific performances, installations, and exhibitions.

31. In the context of this book, the latter action also acquires relational relevance. Calling themselves *Las Lolitas*, a group of numerous women organized the choreographed action in Old San Juan, within which Hernández performed, to commemorate the centenary of Lolita Lebrón's birthdate in 1919. Theatrically minded, *Las Lolitas* were dressed as Lolita Lebrón was on the day she led the nationalist attack on the US Congress (see chapter 3), while also maneuvering fake guns with red carnations in their muzzles. A video of the action's closing sequence, including Hernández's intervention, is available on YouTube (see https://www.youtube.com/watch?v=Glo1XnPymw0).

32. Kennedy offers one of the few extant testimonies of enslaved women as synecdochal evidence: "Bermuda-born Mary Prince reported that 'my master sent me away to Turk's Island. I was not permitted to see my mother or father, or poor sisters and brothers, to say good bye, though going away to a strange land, [where I] might never see them again.' This unnamed slave owner had sold Prince to one of the holders of the salt ponds on present-day Grand Turk. Prince described long hours and grueling labor involved in salt raking. 'I was given a half barrel and a shovel, and had to stand up to my knees in the water, from four o'clock in the morning till nine.' After a rushed break to gulp down a bit of corn, she and her fellow laborers 'worked through the heat of the day; the sun flaming upon our heads like fire, and raising salt blisters. . . . Our feet and legs, from standing in the salt water for so many hours, soon became full of dreadful boils, which eat down in some cases to the very bone, afflicting . . . great torment.' Continuing her brief description of labor in the salt works, she recounted that 'we then shovelled [*sic*] up the salt in large heaps' and 'sometimes we had to work all night, measuring salt to load a vessel; or turning a machine to draw water out of the sea for the salt-making.' When allotted time to sleep, they 'were so full of the salt boils that [they] could get no rest lying upon the bare boards' serving as poor substitutes for beds. In desperation, they 'went into the bush and cut the long soft grass' to make 'trusses for [their] legs and feet'" (215).

33. As Rodríguez-Silva explains in *Silencing Race* (2012), the *Reglamento de la Libreta* (Notebook Regulation), decreed by the Spanish Governor, General Juan de la Pezuela, in 1849, "required each *jornalero* [dayworker] to carry a notebook (*libreta*) in which his name, physical characteristics, occupation, and employment history was noted" (32).

34. Ramírez Padilla characterizes the intense ideological atmosphere in Cabo Rojo, which marked the *salineros*' political consciousness and struggle, as a mixture of nineteenth- and early twentieth-century republicanism, socialism, and anarchism (2012, 96).

35. See news reports by Alvarado León (2019) and Martorell (2021).

36. For a discussion of excessive sargasso's dangerous ecological, economic, and public health effects, see Cabrejas Quintana (2020). Moreover, coastal erosion—a central concern of *inciertas-eroded spectacle*—is accelerated by efforts in many countries to "clear" the accumulated sargasso with industrial machinery.

37. *Acá* (over here), an adverb of special importance in *inciertas*, was an addition by Hernández to Palés Matos's verse.

38. For additional commentaries on *inciertas*, see Fiet (2020) and Platón (2020).

39. A *guiro* is a traditional Puerto Rican musical instrument, a hollowed-out, notched gourd that is played by running a wooden sticklike object across it.

40. In turn, these and other similar questions constitute the socio-poetic survey in the ongoing *bravata: encuesta a domicilio* project referenced above.

41. *La erizada* does not specify who exactly "they" are. But it is clear from its context that she means the *ellos* of the Vieques's piece in this chapter's opening, the rulers, both in Puerto Rico and the United States: bankers, corporate CEOs, politicians, investors, patriarchs, and all those who benefit from the exploitation of the majorities.

42. There is a strong echo here from Hernández's previous *Nada que ver*, where the artist, among other *yoes* ("I"s) who have *nada que ver* (a phrase that, in Puerto Rico, means both that there is nothing to see and that things hold no common relation), becomes *la perra* (the female dog). Important commentaries on this piece are Negrón's (2009) and Vilches Norat's (2006), who highlights *Nada que ver's* decentering of vision and emphasis on the legs—and, indeed, on the entire body—as the artist's means to reflect on the self.

Coda

The Liquid Homeland of Our Reparative and Sovereign Relations, or, For the Love of Us

> I think often about the consequences of colonialism within a threatened group. The cost of losing almost everything. The impact of military normalcy. The multiple violences we endure. . . . What is the solidarity, evolutionary sistering, ancestral imperative called for in this moment where US colonial territories are in active refusal? . . . What life would spring up, what recovery is possible if the colonial force actually shuts down?
>
> —Alexis Pauline Gumbs, *Undrowned*, 2020 115

At the beginning of June 2021, Puerto Rico's Tourism Office launched a promotional campaign to foster "local tourism" over the summer, estimating an "8-million-dollar injection" to the economy. In the same 1990s' "thinking big" vein I remarked on in chapter 5, the initiative is bombastically—and improperly—entitled, "One Island, 78 Destinations." On the campaign, Manuel Cidre, current secretary of the Department of Economic Development and Commerce, declared: "first we have to know ourselves before we can sell ourselves to the world."[1]

It is nothing short of astounding, even if predictable, that the Puerto Rican ruling *criollo* classes, which control the government's floundering institutions, continue exemplifying today such levels of paternalism, mediocrity, and willful ignorance as when Betances, Capetillo, and Albizu Campos confronted their ancestors. In stark contrast to every figure, collective, and creation archived in *Affect, Archive, Archipelago*, they certainly do not "know" us. We are not "one island," nor have we been anything else but sold by them for over five centuries, an apparently endless extraction.

But as this book has sought to show, in the underseen, submerged, deliberately small Puerto Ricos, we know and claim ourselves not as items for sale, but as sovereign subjects, bodies of redress and reparation, mammals-in-relation within our "sea of islands," those who will not pay any more prices nor sell any more souls.[2] We know ourselves as free. As though engaged with you in a *Mujeres que Abrazan la Mar*'s circle of intentions, the following closing words reflect on some of the ways in which the offerings that this book brought together, might translate today onto Puerto Rico's collective *así sea, así será*.

In chapter 1, while discussing Betances's *Confederación Antillana* dream, I aimed to provide a nuanced consideration of the Puerto Rican anticolonial movements' overarching faith in the nation-state as the necessary outcome—whatever its conditions—of decolonization.[3] This attachment was quite understandable, as I further discussed in chapter 3, when considering the historical context (1920s–1930s), both locally and internationally, in which the modern anticolonial tradition took hold in Puerto Rico. However, even before that moment, and certainly since, the historical evidence also offers multiple reasons to pause.

First, the contents of this book clearly show a great diversity of alternative, affective offerings for Puerto Rico's decolonization that do not position the nation-state as an objective or litmus test for their emancipatory impulses. They claim our sovereignty as that which is not to come and be bestowed, but rather, as always already embodied and practiced in the liquid homeland of our relations: Betances's affective and archipelagic "federation *of* nations, not federation *as* nation" (see Vergerio 2021) (chapter 1); Capetillo's anarcho-feminist abolition of state and property in favor of cooperatives, free love, workers' autonomy, and women's emancipation (chapter 2); Albizu Campos's radical gesture of refusal, dignity, and love (chapter 3); the archipelagic collaboration between activist and artistic collectives on multiple fronts (ecological, political, bodily, regional) despite, or openly against, the state (chapter 4); and a multiplicity of artistic productions, interventions, and pulsations that reimagine our lives beyond and, for the most part, against the state, both local and federal (chapters 4 and 5).

Moreover, as *Amigxs del MAR* eloquently affirmed when celebrating the *Playas Pa'l Pueblo* camp's triumph (see chapter 4), most of the forms of oppression and exploitation that the "files" in this book's archive defy have as their source the nation-state itself—Teresa Hernández's PRUSA (see chapter 5), characterized as it is by a juridical and oppressive condensation of capitalist interests, ecocide, patriarchy, racism, and queerphobia. Even in the "anomalous" case of Puerto Rico, the ELA's "weak state" (or stateless nation, as Albizu Campos would have preferred to call it) has been strong enough to cause unremitting and dramatic harm, both in tandem with, and independently of, the US state. Certainly, the onslaught of Puerto Rico's corrupt maneuvers, insularist ideology, regional obliviousness, repressive apparatuses, and complicity with the regime of power in all its forms, has been deadly, both literally and symbolically (see, especially, the Introduction and chapters 3 and 4). There is thus little, if any, evidence that "ascending" to the status of a formal, independent nation-state would ensure our decolonization, emancipation, and regional integration, especially if such a project is pursued without reparatory justice or significant transformations, both ideologically and materially, of what "nation-state" means in the present moment.[4]

Thirdly, beyond what this limited book includes, the instances of under-seen forms of Puerto Rican decolonial sovereignty are multitudinous. While I provide some examples in notes throughout *Affect, Archive, Archipelago*, here I ask you to recall (or imagine) Puerto Rico's 2019 *Verano Boricua*: its limitations notwithstanding, the movement was horizontal, diverse, creative, joyful, "leader-full," sovereign, and archipelagic.[5] I also ask you to remember (or imagine) that when the hour of need irrupts most dramatically—our memory from 2017 still near—it is this archipelagic patchwork of affective, sovereign relations that, quite literally, saves us. No nation-state, corporation, "private-public alliance," or institution has done for us what we, surviving mammals of love and water, have.

If, following Yarimar Bonilla's argument in *Non-Sovereign Futures* (2015) concerning the "non-sovereign"[6] Francophone Caribbean, we can interpret the contemporary Puerto Rican scenario (post–2016 PROMESA, 2017 María, and 2019 *Verano Boricua*) as experiencing a seismic political-imaginative reorganization capable of either radically transforming what the "nation-state" means for us,[7] or abandoning it altogether as the only emancipatory political horizon, then our creative errantry, in Glissant's sense, should be ciphered on the kinds of archipelagic, sovereign practices explored in this book.[8] That is, against power and the insularist ideology, we must continue walking-swimming our islands as laboratories of emancipation, as Aponte Alsina's "experimental island" metaphor. Such reclaiming of our land- and seascapes is moved by the simultaneous conviction that they have always already been related *and* that they are always in need of more Relation.

As *Affect, Archive, Archipelago* notes throughout, and especially in chapters 1 and 4, one of the areas in which we are in urgent need of more archipelagic, Caribbean relations is in nurturing Puerto Rico's inclusion, participation, and collaboration with regional struggles for reparations.[9] The imperial nation-states—both in Europe and North America—should, and must, be held accountable for their historical role in unleashing and perpetuating Puerto Rico's and the Caribbean's continuous exploitation for their own benefit.

No current project for Puerto Rico's decolonization should overlook a concomitant demand that the US Congress—and the Spanish State—agree to reparations.

In the meantime, we must support the work in Puerto Rico advanced most especially by *Comuna Caribe* (see chapter 4) in collaboration with collectives working toward reparative justice across the Caribbean, as well as with the Caribbean Community's (CARICOM's) Reparations Commission, chaired by Sir Hilary Beckles.[10] Recall from chapter 4, however, that for Puerto Rico to collaborate with CARICOM's Commission, it needs to continue engaging in creative forms of sovereignty, as the US Congress prohibits the archipelago's formal membership in CARICOM. To do so, we should heed lessons gathered from the affective and archipelagic relations and archival "files" explored throughout this book. In what follows, I provide some possible alternatives.

Coalitional efforts across the political and activist decolonial spectrum in Puerto Rico could start by launching a truly participatory process to draft reparatory justice plans, which would of course include monetary compensation to descendants of the enslaved, killed, and displaced, but could also deepen even further our diverse sovereignties and archipelagic relations. Joining *Comuna Caribe*'s and *Frente Ciudadano por la Auditoría de la Deuda*'s ongoing collaboration with *Jubileo Sur Américas* (see chapter 4) is essential, especially as it concerns making debt cancellation a form of reparation, which is also consigned in the CARICOM's Commission's *Ten Point Plan*.

Terms to demand as part of possible reparations plans could also include the following:

1. financing ecological repair and mitigation efforts led by collectives such as *Amigxs del MAR* and local communities on our coasts;
2. the sensible and comprehensive cleanup of militarized lands;
3. the endowment of all farmlands to the multiple groups working on sustainable agriculture in Puerto Rico;
4. unrestricted funding for on-the-ground communitarian-artistic-bodily collectives with an established record of working toward diverse Puerto Rican sovereignties (see the Introduction and chapter 4 for some examples);
5. dedicated support to Puerto Rican banking co-ops (*Cooperativas de Ahorro y Crédito*) to fund collaborations with activist collectives and projects characterized by economies of solidarity,[11] as well as for the creation of production and consumer co-ops for food, health, and the arts, in the tradition of Luisa Capetillo (see chapter 2) and early twentieth-century Puerto Rican and Caribbean anarchism; and
6. the creation of maritime transportation co-ops within and beyond the Puerto Rican archipelago, in connection with the wider Caribbean region.

In addition to addressing states themselves, reparatory efforts, which are not exempt—nor should they be—from debates concerning the terms,[12] include demands on educational (such as universities), cultural (such as museums), and religious (such as the Catholic and Protestant Churches) institutions that reaped profits from genocide, enslavement, sexual predation, and the plantation-tourism machine in the Caribbean region. One such regional case concerns the recent agreement between the University of the West Indies (UWI) and the University of Glasgow (UG):

> The terms of the agreement call for the University of Glasgow to provide £20 million to fund research to promote development initiatives to be jointly undertaken with The UWI over the next two decades. The sum of £20 million was the amount paid to slave owners as reparations by the British government when it abolished slavery in 1834. The agreement represents the first occasion on which a slavery-enriched British or European institution has apologized for its part in slavery and committed funds to facilitate a reparations programme. In this instance, the two universities have adopted a regional development approach to reparations.[13]

In Puerto Rico, we must seek collaborations with such efforts in the Anglophone Caribbean, which would certainly offer valuable insights regarding the identification, through historical research, of specific institutional instances to which we could jointly make reparatory justice demands. This process would also bring reparations more prominently to public debate in both Puerto Rico and the wider region. Organizations and individuals associated with activist collectives, artistic undertakings, and University of Puerto Rico's programs concerned with collective memory and archivism, for example, might fruitfully consider devoting some of their decolonial efforts to such an endeavor.

There is one last word of love I wish to offer on this book's underseen cartography. Insofar as the communitarian-artistic-bodily sovereignties explored in *Affect, Archive Arhipelago*'s part II are not predicated upon the kinds of heroic, revolutionary metanarratives underpinning the thought and work of the figures discussed in part I, and to the extent that they are eminently and deliberately embodied, collective, horizontal, small, and ephemeral, they have tended to be either ignored as part of Puerto Rico's political struggles or discarded as inconsequential, minor episodes. In contrast, this book has attempted to offer a passionate defense of the enormous political and imaginative significance of smallness, ephemerality, horizontal organization, collective action, and bodily sensations and affections.

To that, I now add that the potency of these affective archival instances—as much as that of Betances's "failed" revolution and *Confederación Antillana*,

Capetillo's "failed" anarcho-feminist project, and Albizu Campos's "failed" struggle for national liberation—lies in their "affective and subjective transformations," as Yarimar Bonilla reminds us:

> The success or failure of social movements has most often been assessed through the evaluation of material outcomes . . . and other tangible and quantifiable metrics of success. However . . . even participants in "failed" or "disappointing" forms of social action are often transformed by their involvement. Political participation, even in a failed strike, conditions expectations of social struggle, shapes hopes and aspirations for the future, and influences the willingness to engage in collective action . . . the long-lasting effects of political struggle cannot be gauged through a simple measure of material and economic gains. Instead, they need to be more subtly rendered through a qualitative analysis of the affective and subjective transformations that characterize political life. (2015, 5)

It also lies, with Guillermo Rebollo Gil's moving observation, in their unforeseeable and unmeasurable effects:

> That world [the world envisioned in the instant of revolution], we could say, is an always, not in the sense that it remains unchanged over time but that the potential for a different world is always present in every single instance of revolutionary activity. That is what makes the instance worthwhile and worthy of repetition. Revolutionary instances are like chants in that way, quotidian strategies of remembrance for that which must never be forgotten. (2018, 68)

The arrogance with which some judge the incommensurable conditions against which decolonial, feminist, anti-racist, and queer thinkers, artists, and activists act, is only commensurate in degree to the dogged insistence on love and remembrance by the actors whom they dismiss. In this sense, every instance of our affective archive of Caribbean relations included in *Affect, Archive, Archipelago*, as well as in the infinite ones beyond it, holds a place in Glissant's "open boat," which sails, always, across our shared liquid homeland, in the stubborn, collective certitude of an emancipated time and space that has been, is, *and* will be.

NOTES

1. See BrandStudio's "'Una Isla, 78 Destinos'" (n.d.).
2. "Our sea of islands" is Tongan and Fijian writer and thinker Epeli Hau'ofa's (2008) counter to the insularist "belittlement" of islands.
3. I especially wish to recall here the discussion concerning the ways in which the nation-state ideal has tended to work *against* (rather than for) an archipelagic consciousness and practice in Puerto Rico that would respond to Betances's

confederacionista dream. Moreover, even if inadvertently, it has tended to entrench insularist ideology (see the Introduction).

4. Moreover, as Claire Vergerio (2021) has recently argued, the ongoing questioning of the hegemonic, Eurocentric narrative concerning the Westphalian nation-state, which "sought to make both the rise of the states-system and of global European power seem like a linear, inevitable, and laudable process," is essential in order to "open the way to envisioning an international order that could make space for a greater diversity of polities and restore some balance between the rights of states and the rights of other collectivities." General critiques of the concept of "nation" itself have also insisted on its intrinsically exclusionary character. See, for instance, Marx (2005), Etherington (2008), and Zúñiga Reyes (2018). For references offering similar critiques in the context of Puerto Rico, see chapter 1.

5. For textual and visual commentary on other such "leader-full" movements in the twenty-first century, see Jobin-Leeds and AgitArte's *When We Fight, We Win!* (2016), which includes the University of Puerto Rico's student strike of 2010–2011. References on the 2019 *Verano Boricua* are provided in the Introduction.

6. Note that Bonilla is deploying "sovereignty" strictly in its official, juridical sense.

7. This is, of course, a vast question exceeding the reach of *Affect, Archive, Archipelago*. But, at the very least, the transformation would entail that "the State [becomes] a space of distributive and cultural experimentation" (De Sousa Santos and Avritzer 2003, 70), capable of ensuring all forms of sovereignty and dignity, and of facilitating *economías solidarias* (economies of solidarity) at every turn, including mutual aid and coops (as Peter Ranis demands of the State in *Cooperatives Confront Capitalism* [2016]). It would also require a radical shift toward reparative, rather than repressive and punishing, justice (three such models of reparative justice are explored in Anna Celma's "Pueblos que anteponen la reparación al castigo" [2021]). At the same time, a transformed Puerto Rican nation-state must become archipelagic, orienting itself toward Caribbean relations in every sense of the word, as has been amply argued in this book.

8. It is both illuminating and necessary that we link these practices to similar ones across the Global South, and within internally colonized communities in the Global North. For this, an exploration of other conceptual and material constellations is of the essence. We can begin, for instance, by considering Erik Olin Wright's (2010) "real utopias." Acknowledging the constant possibility of error and ignorance, and after thoroughly investigating the capitalist world where real people must live, Wright wishes to examine, both empirically and theoretically, "the feasibility of radically different kinds of institutions and social relations that could potentially advance the democratic egalitarian goals historically associated with the idea of socialism" (1). His empirical grounding rests on the examination of examples such as participatory budgeting, worker-owned cooperatives, and the unconditional basic income model, while the theoretical proposals are distilled into three possible strategies for transformation within the existing capitalist society: (1) ruptural (defined on pp. 308–09), (2) interstitial (defined on p. 321), and (3) symbiotic (defined on p. 337). *Affect, Archive, Archipelago* contains examples of all these strategies. We can also consider the

"demodiversity" (De Sousa Santos and Avritzer 2003, 65) associated with participatory democracy. De Sousa Santos's *Democratizar la democracia* (2005) and Michael Menser's *We Decide!* (2018) are two excellent sources that, like Wright's, examine on-the-ground instances of participatory democracy, including participatory budgeting, workers and consumers cooperatives, civil networks, and a basic income guarantee. Avoiding idealization, these books provide careful analyses of both triumphs and shortcomings. Long-standing, international anarchist traditions of mutual aid and coops, exemplified in this book by Luisa Capetillo and her early twentieth-century comrades, are also essential references (for a general panorama, consult Colin Ward's *Anarchism: A Very Short Introduction* [2004]). Finally, as it concerns the US context—and, forcibly, Puerto Rico's situation—the ongoing radically democratic, abolitionist movement is fundamental (to start, consider Jeremy Scahill's interview with Ruth Wilson Gilmore [2020], as well as Angela Y. Davis's *Abolition Democracy* [2005]).

9. Candia Mitchell-Hall (2021) provides a general panorama on these efforts, while Claudia Rauhut offers more detailed analysis of the struggle for reparations' present status, overall focusing on the Anglophone Caribbean and, especially, on Jamaica, "a forerunner in the region" (2018, 141). For the most comprehensive analysis available on the struggle for reparations worldwide, see Ana Lucía Araujo's extraordinary *Reparations for Slavery and the Slave Trade* (2017). If concerned with the philosophical, theoretical, and moral nuances involved in the struggle for reparations, consider David Scott's ongoing reflections on "reparatory history" and the "irreparability" of enslavement, as explored in two of his lectures (2017 and 2018).

10. On the latter, see the Commission's *Ten Point Plan* (see www.caricom.org/caricom-ten-point-plan-for-reparatory-justice/), as well as Beckles's fundamental book, *Britain's Black Debt* (2013).

11. A recent, and most welcome, example is the agreement between the feminist organization *Matria* and the Jesús Obrero Cooperative (see *Primera Hora*'s news report, "Proyecto Matria y Jesús Obrero Cooperativa" [2021]).

12. For instance, in the US context, King, Navarro and Smith write: "Black movements for reparations for slavery continue to elide the fact that reparations, particularly when compensation is configured as land, requires the further consolidation of the US settler nation and affirms its authority to redistribute wealth and "Native land" as it sees fit. . . . Black politics that do not contest the very existence and idea of the United States present themselves as antagonistic to Indigenous survival and sovereignty. On the other hand, Black abolitionist politics that propose a move away from the very idea of the nation critique Native nations and their movements for sovereignty as overly invested in international, Western, and humanist models of governance that make survival untenable for stateless and nationless Black diasporic peoples" (2020, 7).

13. See UWI's press release, "£20 Million Caribbean Reparations Agreement" (2019). On its part, Deborah Barfield Berry's report, "The US Is Grappling with Its History of Slavery" (2019) contextualizes the struggle for reparations in the United States (as it concerns universities) within the Caribbean, and, specifically, in connection with the UWI–UG agreement and the work of the Antigua and Barbuda Reparations Support Commission.

Bibliography

Abadía-Rexach, Bárbara I. "Adolfina Villanueva Osorio, *Presente.*" *NACLA Report on the Americas*, 53, no. 2 (2021): 174–80, doi: 10.1080/10714839.2021.1923222.

Ackelsberg, Martha A. *Free Women of Spain: Anarchism and the Struggle for the Emancipation of Women*. Bloomington, IN: Indiana University Press, 1991.

Acosta-Belén, Edna. "Puerto Rican Women in Culture, History, and Society." In *The Puerto Rican Woman: Perspectives on Culture, History and Society*, 1–29. New York: Praeger Publishers, 1986.

Acosta Lespier, Ivonne. *La palabra como delito: Los discursos por los que condenaron a Pedro Albizu Campos, 1948–1950*. San Juan, Puerto Rico: Editorial Cultural, 2000.

Adorno, Pedro. "Un artista forjado a agua, sol y sereno (parte 1)." *Revista Cruce*.

Adorno, Pedro, and Cristina Vives from *Agua, Sol y Sereno*. Personal Interview. February 2, 2019.

"Agua, sol y sereno." *Mapa cultural del Puerto Rico contemporáneo*. 2009. www.mapacultural.files.wordpress.com/2009/11/ficha_aguasolysereno-revrev-print.pdf.

Agua, sol y sereno. Marea alta, marea baja. Scripts 1–7. 2002. Collection of Mareia Quintero, San Juan, Puerto Rico.

———. *Marea alta, marea baja.* Promotional material. 2002. Collection of *Agua, sol y sereno*. San Juan, Puerto Rico.

Albizu-Campos Meneses, Laura, and Mario A. Rodríguez León, eds. *Pedro Albizu Campos. Escritos.* San Juan, Puerto Rico: Publicaciones Puertorriqueñas, 2007.

Alegría Rampante. "El recipiente." *Se nos fue la mano*, composed by Eduardo Alegría. Discos Diáspora, 2015.

Alvarado León, Gerardo E. "El cambio climático amenaza las salinas de Cabo Rojo." *El Nuevo Día*. December 4, 2019. www.elnuevodia.com/noticias/locales/notas/el-cambio-climatico-amenaza-las-salinas-de-cabo-rojo/.

———. "Isla ¿sin playas?" *Centro de Periodismo Investigativo*. May 2017. www.periodismoinvestigativo.com/series/isla-sin-playas/.

Álvarez, José "Pepe." "Entrevista PEPOSA: Teresa Hernández." Instagram, uploaded by @hidranteee. January 29, 2021. www.instagram.com/tv/CKo-321pjaO/?utm_source=ig_web_copy_link.

Álvarez Curbelo, Silvia. "La Patria desde la tierra: Pedro Albizu Campos y el nacionalismo antillano." In *La nación puertorriqueña: Ensayos en torno Pedro Albizu Campos*, edited by Juan M. Carrión, Teresa C. Gracia Ruiz, and Carlos Rodríguez Fraticelli, 83–96. Río Piedras, Puerto Rico: Editorial de la Universidad de Puerto Rico, 1993.

———. *Un país del porvenir: El afán de modernidad en Puerto Rico, siglo XX*. San Juan, Puerto Rico: Ediciones Callejón, 2001.

Amigxs del MAR. "Antecedentes." *Travesía Libre*. www.travesialibre.wordpress.com/antecedentes/.

———. "Biografía." *Travesía Libre*. www.travesialibre.wordpress.com/oscar-lopez/.

———. "Convocatoria Artistas." *Travesía Libre*. www.travesialibre.wordpress.com/about/.

———. Facebook Page. www.facebook.com/amigxsdelmarpr/.

———. Facebook Post. March 16, 2015. www.facebook.com/amigxsdelmarpr/photos/a.1583536011873133/1701911813368885.

———. "Kayakeando por el Caribe por la libertad de Óscar López Rivera." *Travesíalibre*. 2012. www.travesialibre.wordpress.com.

Anckar, Dag. "Islandness or Smallness? A Comparative Look at Political Institutions in Small Island States." *Island Studies Journal* 1, no. 1 (2006): 43–54.

Anzaldúa, Gloria. *Borderlands/La Frontera: The New Mestiza*. San Francisco, CA: Aunt Lute Books, 1999.

Aponte Alsina, Marta. "Caminos de la sorpresa." *Angélica furiosa*. September 23, 2005. www.angelicafuriosa.blogspot.com/search?q=caminos+de+la+sorpresa.

———. "Historias íntimas, cuentos dispersos: palabras, tramas e identidades." *Angélica furiosa*. November 14, 2007. www.angelicafuriosa.blogspot.com/2008/04/historias-ntimas-cuentos-dispersos.html.

———. "La metáfora madre." *80grados*. March 8, 2013, www.80grados.net/la-metafora-madre/.

———. *La muerte feliz de William Carlos Williams*. Cayey, Puerto Rico: Sopa de Letras, 2015.

———. "La patria líquida." *80grados*. February 25, 2011. www.80grados.net/la-patria-liquida/.

———. "Madre del fuego: La identidad caribeña de William Carlos Williams." *Primera Cátedra Nilita Vientós Gastón del Programa de Estudio de Mujer y Género*. April 29, 2014. Estudios Generales, Universidad de Puerto Rico–Río Piedras.

———. *PR 3 Aguirre*. Cayey, Puerto Rico: Sopa de Letras, 2018.

———. "Principio Estrella." *Angélica furiosa*. May 1, 2021, www.angelicafuriosa.blogspot.com/2021/.

———. *Somos islas: Ensayos de camino*. Cabo Rojo, Puerto Rico: Editora Educación Emergente, 2015.

———. "The Pocket of a Migrant." In *One Month after Being Known in That Island: Caribbean Art Today*, edited by Yina Jiménez Suriel and Pablo Guardiola, 27–33. Sttutgart, Germany: Hatje Cantz, 2020.

———. "The Secret Island: A Literary Reading of Puerto Rico." *Angélica furiosa*. September 23, 2008, www.angelicafuriosa.blogspot.com/2008/09/somos-islas.html.

Aponte, Dolores. "La evolución del esplendor: Violencia y construcción de identidades en *Salve la Reina* de Teresa Hernández (comentarios desde el palco)." *Tinkuy: Boletín de investigación y debate*, no. 13 (2010): 25–36. Dialnet.

Araujo, Ana Lucía. *Reparations for Slavery and the Slave Trade: A Transnational and Comparative History*. London, UK: Bloomsbury, 2017.

Arpini, Adriana María. "Abolición, independencia y confederación. Los escritos de Ramón Emeterio Betances, 'El Antillano.'" *Cuyo. Anuario de Filosofía Argentina y Americana* 5 (2008): 119–44.

———. "Antillanismo y construcción de la nación. El pensamiento filosófico del Caribe hispánico en el siglo XIX." In *Unir lo diverso: Problemas y desafíos de la integración latinoamericana*, edited by Claudio Maíz, 63–84. Mendoza, Argentina: Facultad de Filosofía y Letras, Universidad Nacional de Cuyo, 2010.

———. "Dos propuestas constitucionales en el Caribe del siglo XIX." *Estudios de Filosofía Práctica e Historia de las Ideas* 11, no. 2 (2009): pp. 11–20.

———. "Ideas en el Caribe hispano durante el siglo XIX. El Antillanismo como ideal emancipatorio y de integración." *Revista en línea de la Maestría en Estudios Latinoamericanos* 3, no. 3 (2014): 1–20.

Arroyo, Jossiana. *Writing Secrecy in Caribbean Freemansory*. London, UK: Palgrave, 2013.

Atiles-Osoria, José. *Apuntes para abandonar el derecho: Estado de excepción colonial en Puerto Rico*. Cabo Rojo, Puerto Rico: Editora Educación Emergente, 2016.

———. *Jugando con el derecho: Movimientos anticoloniales puertorriqueños y la fuerza de la ley*. Cabo Rojo, Puerto Rico: Editora Educación Emergente, 2018.

———. *Profanaciones del Verano de 2019: Corrupción, frentes comunes y justicia decolonial*. Cabo Rojo, Puerto Rico: Editora Educación Emergente, 2020.

Atiles-Osoria, José, Jeffrey Herlihy-Mera, and Beatriz Llenín-Figueroa, eds. "Crisis." *Voces del Caribe* 11, nos. 1–2 (2019). www.vocesdelcaribe.org/volumen-11.

Avilés, Luis A. *Contra la tortura de los números*. Cabo Rojo, Puerto Rico: Editora Educación Emergente, 2019.

Ayala, César J., and Rafael Bernabe. "Political and Social Struggles in a New Colonial Context, 1900–1930." In *Puerto Rico in the American Century: A History since 1898*, 52–73. Chapel Hill, NC: University of North Carolina Press, 2007. JSTOR.

Azize, Yamila. *La mujer en la lucha*. San Juan, Puerto Rico: Editorial Cultural, 1985.

———. "Mujeres en lucha: Orígenes y evolución del movimiento feminista." In *La mujer en Puerto Rico: Ensayos de investigación*, 11–47. Río Piedras, Puerto Rico: Ediciones Huracán, 1987.

Baccus, Lauren. "A Pattern of Resistance: Subversive Dress and the Politics of Clothing in Caribbean Masquerade" [Video]. Los Angeles, CA: Textile Arts, 2020. www.textileartsla.org/recordings.

Baerga, María del Carmen, ed. *Género y trabajo: La industria de la aguja en Puerto Rico y el Caribe Hispánico*. San Juan, Puerto Rico: Editorial de la Universidad de Puerto Rico, 1995.

Baerga, Vanesa. "Bateyes: La frontera del conflicto." *Radio Ambulante*. February 7, 2015. www.radioambulante.org/extras/bateyes-la-frontera-del-conflicto.

———. *Negociaciones de sangre: Dinámicas racializantes en el Puerto Rico decimonónico*. Madrid, Spain: Iberoamericana, 2015.

———. "Routes to Whiteness, or How to Scrub Out the Stain: Hegemonic Masculinity and Racialization in Nineteenth-Century Puerto Rico." *Translating the Americas* 3 (2015): 109–47. doi: 10.3998/lacs.12338892.0003.004.

Balasopoulos, Antonis. "Nesologies: Island Form and Postcolonial Geopoetics." *Postcolonial Studies* 11, no. 1 (2008): 9–26. doi: 10.1080/13688790801971555.

Barreto, Maritza. "El estado de las playas de Puerto Rico Post-María." *ArcGIS StoryMaps*. August 25, 2021. www.storymaps.arcgis.com/stories/dfb5b1a22af6440b809cde3aac482b42.

———. "El estado de las playas de Puerto Rico Post-María (Grupo 2)." *ArcGIS StoryMaps*. February 10, 2021. www.storymaps.arcgis.com/stories/85620fe49e8a4b19b02a1d13303fc316.

Barthes, Roland. *Mythologies*. Translated by Annette Lavers. New York, NY: Hill and Wang, 1972. First published 1957.

Becerra, Claudia. *Versión del viaje*. San Juan, Puerto Rico: Folium, 2018.

Beckles, Sir Hilary. *Britain's Black Debt: Reparations for Caribbean Slavery and Native Genocide*. Kingston, Jamaica: University of West Indies Press, 2013.

———. "Irma-Maria: A Reparations Requiem for Caribbean Poverty." *The University of the West Indies Open Campus*. September 22, 2017. www.open.uwi.edu/irma-maria-reparations-requiem-caribbean-poverty.

Beer, Gillian. "Discourses of the Island." In *Literature and Science as Modes of Expression*, edited by Frederick Amrine, 1–28. Dordrecht, Netherlands: Kluwer Academic Publishers, 1989.

———. "Island Bounds." In *Islands in History and Representation*, edited by Rod Edmond and Vanessa Smith, 32–42. New York, NY and London, UK: Routledge, 2003. www.taylorfrancis.com/chapters/edit/10.4324/9781003060260-3/island-bounds-gillian-beer.

Benítez-Rojo, Antonio. *Archivo de los pueblos del mar*. Edited by Rita Molinero. San Juan, Puerto Rico: Ediciones Callejón, 2010.

———. *The Repeating Island: The Caribbean and the Postmodern Perspective*. Translated by James E. Maraniss. Durham, NC: Duke University Press, 1996.

Bermúdez-Ruiz, Johanna. "Sugar Pathways" [Video]. *Vimeo*. September 18, 2015. www.vimeo.com/ondemand/sugarpathways.

Berry, Deborah Barfield. "The US Is Grappling with Its History of Slavery. The Blueprint for Dealing with It? Some Say Brown University." *USA Today*. December 16, 2019. www.usatoday.com/in-depth/news/education/2019/12/16/slavery-reparations-brown-university-antigua-colleges-paying-up/4401725002/.

Beta-Local. "Ciclo de (re)lecturas: Otras montañas, las que andan sueltas bajo el agua." May 2021. www.betalocal.org/otras-montanas-las-que-andan-sueltas-bajo-el-agua/.

———. "Pin up #42: Pó Rodil y Teresa Hernández." October 10, 2019. www.betalocal.org/pin-up-42-po-rodil-y-teresa-hernandez-10-oct/.

Betances Alacán, Ramón Emeterio. *Las Antillas para los antillanos.* Edited by Carlos M. Rama. San Juan, Puerto Rico: Instituto de Cultura Puertorriqueña, 1975.

———. "Cartas a Lola." *Carta de Ramón Emeterio Betances a Lola Rodríguez de Tió en CMAT.* c. 011. Transcribed by Juan González Mendoza and Mario R. Cancel Sepúlveda, 2004. First published 1880. www.documentaliablog.files.wordpress.com/2018/06/betances_a_lola_16_4_1886.pdf.

———. "Carta dirigida al General Máximo Gómez." *Puerto Rico entre siglos.* 2015. First published 1888. www.puertoricoentresiglos.files.wordpress.com/2015/01/1164_betances_autonomismo.pdf.

———. *Ramón Emeterio Betances.* Edited by Haroldo Dilla and Emilio Godínez. Havana, Cuba: Casa de las Américas, 1984.

———. *Ramon Emeterio Betances: Obras completas. Volúmenes III: Escritos literarios; IV: Escritos políticos: Proclamas, discursos, estudios; X: Escritos políticos: Periodismo militante I (1866–1877); XI: Escritos políticos: Periodismo militante II (1878–1898).* Edited by Félix Ojeda Reyes and Paul Estrade. San Juan, Puerto Rico: ZOOMideal, 2017.

———. "Testamento de Ramón Emeterio Betances Alacán." In *Documentalia: Texto e imaginación histórica,* edited by Mario R. Cancel-Sepúlveda. www.documentaliablog.files.wordpress.com/2018/06/testamento_betances.pdf.

Biabiany, Minia. www.miniabiabiany.com.

Bird Carmona, Arturo. *Parejeros y desafiantes: La comunidad tabaquera de Puerta de Tierra de principio de siglo XX.* San Juan, Puerto Rico: Ediciones Huracán, 2008.

Bird-Soto, Nancy I. *Dissident Spirits: The Post-Insular Imprint in Puerto Rican/Diasporic Literature.* Bern, Switzerland: Peter Lang Publishing, 2018.

———. "Sobre los contratos sociales y la igualdad: Luisa Capetillo." In *Tono y expresión: Escritoras puertorriqueñas de la transición del siglo XIX al XX,* 174–220. PhD diss., University of Wisconsin–Madison, 2006.

Boletín Mercantil de Puerto Rico. "La falda-pantalón en nuestras calles." San Juan, Puerto Rico, 13 April 1911. *Chronicling America: Historic American Newspapers.* Library of Congress, www.chroniclingamerica.loc.gov/lccn/sn91099739/1911-04-13/ed-1/seq-2/.

Bonilla, Yarimar and Marisol LeBrón. *Aftershocks of Disaster: Puerto Rico before and after the Storm,* Chicago, IL: Haymarket Books, 2019.

Bonilla, Yarimar. *Non-Sovereign Futures: French Caribbean Politics in the Wake of Disenchantment.* Chicago, IL: University of Chicago Press, 2015.

———. "Postdisaster Futures: Hopeful Pessimism, Imperial Ruination, and *La futura cuir.*" *Small Axe* 24, no. 2 (July 2020): 147–62. doi: www.doi.org/10.1215/07990537-8604562.

———. "Trump's False Claims about Puerto Rico Are Insulting. But They Reveal a Deeper Truth." *The Washington Post*. September 14, 2018. www.washingtonpost.com/outlook/2018/09/14/trumps-false-claims-about-puerto-rico-are-insulting-they-reveal-deeper-truth/?noredirect=on&utm_term=.889fcc7ab85b.

Bonneuil, Christophe, and Jean-Baptise Fressoz. *The Shock of the Anthropocene: The Earth, History and Us*. Brooklyn, NY: Verso Books, 2017.

Bothwell González, Reece B. *Puerto Rico: Cien años de lucha política (índice de documentos Vol. I–IV)*. Río Piedras, Puerto Rico: Editorial Universitaria, 1979.

Bowles, Nellie. "Making a Crypto Utopia in Puerto Rico." *New York Times*. February 2, 2018. www.nytimes.com/2018/02/02/technology/cryptocurrency-puerto-rico.html.

Boyce-Davies, Carole. "Los mares esquizofrénicos y la transnación caribeña." *Chasqui. Revista Latinoamericana de Comunicación* 138 (2018): 13–27.

BrandStudio. "'Una Isla, 78 Destinos': La nueva campaña de la Compañía de Turismo para incentivar el turismo local." *El Nuevo Día*. n.d. www.elnuevodia.com/brandstudio/voy-turisteando/notas/una-isla-78-destinos-la-nueva-campana-de-la-compania-de-turismo-para-incentivar-el-turismo-local/.

Brathwaite, Edward Kamau. "Caribbean Culture: Two Paradigms." In *Missile and Capsule*, edited by Jurgen Martini, 9–54. Bremen, Germany: Universitat Bremen, 1983.

———. "Caribbean Man in Space and Time." In *Carifesta Forum: An Anthology of Twenty Caribbean Voices*, edited by John Hearne, 199–208. Kingston, Jamaica: Institute of Jamaica, 1976.

———. *ConVERSations with Nathaniel Mackey*. Staten Island, NY: We Press, 1999.

Brinklow, Laurie. "Stepping-Stones to the Edge: Artistic Expressions of Islandness in an Ocean of Islands." *Island Studies Journal* 8, no. 1 (2013): 39–54.

Briggs, Laura. *Reproducing Empire: Race, Sex, Science, and U.S. Imperialism on Puerto Rico*. Berkeley, CA: University of California Press, 2003.

Britton, Celia. "Philosophy, Poetics, Politics." *Callaloo* 36, no. 4 (2013): 841–47.

Brusi, Rima. "Críptidos." *Claridad*. February 13, 2018. www.claridadpuertorico.com/sera-otra-cosa-criptidos/.

Brusi, Rima, Isar Godreau, and Yarimar Bonilla. "When Disaster Comes for the University of Puerto Rico." *The Nation*. September 20, 2018. www.thenation.com/article/when-disaster-capitalism-comes-for-the-university-of-puerto-rico/.

Buscaglia Salgado, José F. "Las Antillas, nuevamente, 'entre imperios' y de cómo enfrentarse al insularismo racialista para alcanzar el objetivo de una confederación regional." *Revistas de Indias* 75, no. 263 (2015): 205–38.

———. "Race and the Constitutive Inequality of the Modern/Colonial Condition." In *Critical Terms in Caribbean and Latin American Thought: Historical and Institutional Trajectories*, edited by Yolanda Martínez-San Miguel, Ben Sifuentes-Jáuregui, and Marisa Belausteguigoitia, 109–24. New York, NY: Palgrave Macmillan, 2016.

Cabrejas Quintana, Mildred. "Sargazos en Antillas francesas. ¿Vector de decolonialidad?" In *Cambio Climático y sus impactos en el Gran Caribe*, edited by Jacqueline Laguardia Martínez, 141–66. Buenos Aires, Argentina: CLACSO, 2020. www

.biblioteca.clacso.edu.ar/clacso/gt/20200928053822/Cambio-climatico-impactos.pdf.
Campbell, John. "Islandness: Vulnerability and Resilience in Oceania." *Shima: The International Journal of Research into Island Cultures* 3, no. 1 (2009): 85–97. www.shimajournal.org/issues/v3n1/i.-Campbell-Shima-v3n1-85-97.pdf.
Cancel-Sepúlveda, Mario R. "Albizu Campos: Concepto de raza." *Puerto Rico entre siglos: Historiografía y cultura.* www.puertoricoentresiglos.wordpress.com/2010/01/27/albizu-concepto-de-raza/.
———. "Betances ante Hostos (y viceversa): Reflexiones en torno a una polémica." *80grados.* April 6, 2018. www.80grados.net/Betances-ante-Hostos-y-viceversa-reflexiones-en-torno-a-una-polemica/.
———. "El Puerto Rico del Ciclo Revolucionario Antillano: Segundo Ruiz Belvis y su generación (Parte 1)." *80grados.* August 10, 2018. www.80grados.net/el-puerto-rico-del-ciclo-revolucionario-antillano-segundo-ruiz-belvis-y-su-generacion-parte-1/.
———. "El Puerto Rico del Ciclo Revolucionario Antillano: Segundo Ruiz Belvis y su generación (Parte 2)." *80grados.* September 14, 2018. www.80grados.net/el-puerto-rico-del-ciclo-revolucionario-antillano-segundo-ruiz-belvis-y-masoneria-parte-2/.
———. "El separatismo independentista y las izquierdas en el contexto del siglo 19." *80grados.* January 22, 2018. www.80grados.net/el-separatismo-independentista-y-las-izquierdas-en-el-contexto-del-siglo-19/.
Cancel-Sepúlveda, Mario R., and José Anazagasty. *Porto Rico: Hecho en EEUU.* Cabo Rojo, Puerto Rico: Editora Educación Emergente, 2011.
Caraballo Cueto, José. "¿Qué causó la crisis de deuda?" *El Nuevo Día.* July 12, 2018. www.elnuevodia.com/opinion/columnas/quecausolacrisisdedeuda-columna-2434509/.
"CARICOM Ten Point Plan for Reparatory Justice." *Caricom: Caribbean Community.* n.d. www.caricom.org/caricom-ten-point-plan-for-reparatory-justice/.
Carreras, Carlos N. *Ramón Emeterio Betances, el antillano proscrito.* San Juan, Puerto Rico: Editorial Club de la Prensa, 1974.
Carrión, Juan Manuel. "Two Variants of Caribbean Nationalism: Marcus Garvey and Pedro Albizu Campos." *CENTRO Journal* 17, no. 1 (Spring 2015): 27–45. Academia.edu. www.academia.edu/7864781/Two_Variants_of_Caribbean_Nationalism.
Carrión, Juan Manuel, Teresa C. Gracia Ruiz, and Carlos Rodríguez Fraticelli. *La nación puertorriqueña: Ensayos en torno a Pedro Albizu Campos.* San Juan, Puerto Rico: Editorial de la Universidad de Puerto Rico, 1993.
Carson, Rachel. *The Sea around Us.* Oxford, UK: Oxford University Press, 1950. www.fadedpage.com/link.php?file=20190551-a5.pdf.
"Carta Autonómica de 1897 de Puerto Rico." *Lex Juris Puerto Rico.* 1897. www.lexjuris.com/LEXLEX/lexotras/lexcartaautonomica.htm.
Cassano, Franco. *Pensamiento meridiano.* Translated by Roberto Raschella. Buenos Aires, Argentina: Losada, 2004.
Cavallero, Luci, and Verónica Gago. *Una lectura feminista de la deuda: Vivas, libres y desendeudadas nos queremos.* Buenos Aires, Argentina: Fundación Luxemburgo,

2019. www.rosalux-ba.org/wp-content/uploads/2019/05/lectura-feminista-deuda-PANTALLAS.pdf.

Ceballos, Helen. Facebook Page. www.facebook.com/helen.ceballos.

Celma, Anna. "Pueblos que anteponen la reparación al castigo." *Pikara*. March 10, 2021. www.pikaramagazine.com/2021/03/pueblos-que-anteponen-la-reparacion-al-castigo/?fbclid=IwAR0QndOCWqpY9YGs-tfEDMV1r_NlOYFuJf5ciiqmE9bmfxhyHUd7BRycQ28.

Centro de Periodismo Investigativo. www.periodismoinvestigativo.com.

Chaar-Pérez, Khalila. "'A Revolution of Love:' Ramón Emeterio Betances, Anténor Firmin, and Affective Communities in the Caribbean." *The Global South* 7, no. 2 (2013): 11–36.

———. "Revolutionary Visions? Ramón Emeterio Betances, *Les deux Indiens*, and Haiti." *Small Axe* 24, no. 1 (2020): 44–52.

Chrichlow, Michaeline A. *Globalization and the Post-Creole Imagination: Notes on Feeling the Plantation*. Durham, NC: Duke University Press, 2009.

Cintrón Arbasetti, Joel. "Las leyes 20 y 22 crearon una casta de intermediarios que gestiona exenciones contributivas." *Centro de Periodismo Investigativo*. April 8, 2021. www.periodismoinvestigativo.com/2021/04/las-leyes-20-y-22-crearon-una-casta-de-intermediarios-que-gestiona-exenciones-contributivas/.

Cintrón Arbasetti, Joel, Carla Minet, Alex V. Hernández, and Jessica Stites. "Who Owns Puerto Rico's Debt, Exactly? We've Tracked Down 10 of the Biggest Vulture Firms." *Centro de Periodismo Investigativo* and *In These Times*. October 17, 2017. www.inthesetimes.com/features/puerto_rico_debt_bond_holders_vulture_funds_named.html.

Cintrón Ríos, María A. "El higienista social: Ramón Emeterio Betances y Alacán." *80grados*. April 23, 2020. www.80grados.net/el-higienista-social-ramon-emeterio-betances-y-alacan/.

Colectiva Feminista en Construcción (La Cole). Facebook Page. www.facebook.com/Colectiva.Feminista.PR/.

———. "¡No la debemos, no la pagamos!" *Scribd*. 2015. www.scribd.com/document/272021669/Boletin-No-la-debemos-no-la-pagamos?fbclid=IwAR1Xjq3SASSFhx6Hrb0iYgEEfPGu7AU43UeIW42rVKN5cbaMS2D8VYVeYD0.

Colectivo Ilé. www.colectivo-ile.org.

Comité Pro Niñez Dominico Haitiana. 2008. www.comiteproninezdominicohaitiana.blogspot.com.

Comuna Antilla. "Día de solidaridad internacional: Haití y Puerto Rico con Comuna Caribe." Facebook Post. December 20 2019. www.facebook.com/comunaantilla/videos/1013996852286862.

Comuna Caribe. Facebook Page. www.facebook.com/pages/category/Community/Comuna-Caribe-393502544171381/.

———. "Junto a la mar: Vivas y en resistencia." Facebook Post. October 12, 2020. www.facebook.com/watch/live/?v=351682209384864&ref=watch_permalink.

Concepción, Alma. "En el Río Piedras de los años 70: Un pequeño colectivo danzante." *80grados*. April 13, 2021. www.80grados.net/en-el-rio-piedras-de-los-anos-70-un-pequeno-colectivo-danzante/.

Contreras Capó, Vanesa from *Coalición 8M*. Personal Interview. April 20, 2021.
Corio, Alessandro. "The Living and the Poetic Intention: Glissant's Biopolitics of Literature." *Callaloo* 36, no. 4 (2013): 916–31.
Costa, Marithelma. "Del Paso de Anegada al hospital de Tortola." *80grados*. September 14, 2012. www.80grados.net/del-paso-de-anegada-al-hospital-de-tortola/.
———. "¿De qué color es la utopía?" *80grados*. February 1, 2011. www.80grados.net/¿de-que-color-es-la-utopia/.
———. "El kayak se rajó dos veces pero Tito no." *80grados*. July 6, 2012. www.80grados.net/el-kayak-se-rajo-dos-veces-pero-tito-no/.
———. "Islas, islas, islas." *80grados*. July 27, 2012. www.80grados.net/islas-islas-islas/.
———. "La Mano Poderosa y la Travesía de la Libertad." *80grados*. August 3, 2012. www.80grados.net/la-mano-poderosa-y-la-travesia-de-la-libertad/.
———. "Tito tocó tierra y no fue en Trinidad." *80grados*. June 29, 2012. www.80grados.net/tito-toco-tierra-y-no-fue-trinidad-la-travesia-admirable-de-tito-kayak/.
Cotto Morales, Liliana. *Desalambrar: Orígenes de los rescates de terreno en Puerto Rico y su pertinencia en los movimientos sociales contemporáneos*. San Juan, Puerto Rico: Editorial Tal Cual, 2006.
Cotto Quijano, Evaluz. "How the Triple Tax Exemption on Puerto Rico's Bonds Financed Its Territorial Status—and Helped Spark Its Debt Crisis." *Promarket*. September 11, 2018. www.promarket.org/triple-tax-exemption-puerto-ricos-bonds-financed-territorial-status-helped-spark-debt-crisis/.
Courtad, James C. "Appropriation of Culture and the Quest for a Voice in the Works of Luisa Capetillo." *Symposium* 70, no. 1 (January 2016): 24. EBSCOhost. www.search.ebscohost.com/login.aspx?direct=true&db=edb&AN=113745320&site=eds-live.
Crane, Ralph, and Fletcher, Lisa. *Island Genres, Genre Islands: Conceptualisation and Representation in Popular Fiction*. Lanham, MD: Rowman & Littlefield Publishers, 2018.
Cruz Soto, Marie. "The Making of Viequenses: Militarized Colonialism and Reproductive Rights." *Meridians: Feminism, Race, Transnationalism* 19 no. 2 (2020): 360–82. Project MUSE.
Cubero, Carlo A. *Caribbean Island Movements: Culebra's Transinsularities*. Lanham, MD: Rowman & Littlefield, 2017.
Curtin, Philip D. *The Rise and Fall of the Plantation Complex: Essays in Atlantic History*. Cambridge, UK: Cambridge University Press, 1998.
Dalleo, Raphael. "Regionalism, Imperialism, and Sovereignty: West Indies Federations and the Occupation of Haiti." *Small Axe* 24, no. 1 (2020): 61–68.
Dash, J. Michael. *The Other America: Caribbean Literature in a New World Context*. Charlottesville, VA: University Press of Virginia, 1998.
Daut, Marlene. "When France Extorted Haiti—the Greatest Heist in History." *The Conversation*. June 30, 2020. www.theconversation.com/when-france-extorted-haiti-the-greatest-heist-in-history-137949.

Dávila del Valle, Oscar G. "Presencia del ideario masónico en el proyecto revolucionario antillano de Ramón Emeterio Betances." *Nuevo Grupo de Servidores del Mundo en IberoAmérica.* 1989. www.ngsm.org/aleph/Hostos/masoneria_PR.html.

Dávila Marichal, José Manuel. "Estudio del nacionalismo revolucionario puertorriqueño a través de una fotografía." *Alborada: Revista interdisciplinaria de la Universidad de Puerto Rico en Utuado* 11, no. 1 (June 2015–May 2016): 37–46.

———. "Metamorfosis: De las hijas de la libertad al cuerpo de enfermeras de la república del Partido Nacionalista de Puerto Rico, 1932–1937." *Asociación Puertorriqueña de Investigación de Historia de las Mujeres.* March 6, 2014. www.senriquezseiders.blogspot.com/p/blog-page_17.html.

Dávila Santiago, Rubén. *Teatro obrero en Puerto Rico (1900–1920): Antología.* San Juan, Puerto Rico: Editorial Edil, 1985.

Davis, Angela Y. *Abolition Democracy: Beyond Empire, Prisons, and Torture.* New York, NY: Seven Stories Press, 2005.

Davis, Annalee. www.annaleedavis.com.

———. "Innerseeing versus Overseeing." *Place 2020–2021.* https://www.placewriting.co.uk/place-2021-blog/annalee-davis.

———. *Sobre el estar comprometida con un lugar pequeño / On Being Committed to a Small Place.* Edited by Miguel A. López. San José, Costa Rica: TEOR-*éTica*, 2019.

Davis, David Brion. *Inhuman Bondage: The Rise and Fall of Slavery in the New World.* Oxford, UK: Oxford University Press, 2008.

De Armas, Ramón. "La integración latinoamericana en la historiografía cubana: El caso de la Confederación Antillana." *Trocadero* 1, nos. 6–7 (1995): 219–30.

De Burgos, Julia. *Obra poética.* San Juan, Puerto Rico: Instituto de Cultura Puertorriqueña, 2016.

De Jesús, Anthony. "'I Have Endeavored to Seize the Beautiful Opportunity for Learning Offered Here: Pedro Albizu Campos at Harvard a Century Ago." *Latino Studies* 9 (2011): 473–85. doi: 10.1057/lst.2011.54.

De Jesús Salamán, Adriana. "Leyes 20 y 22 crean un 'Apartheid contributivo' Puerto Rico." *Noticel.* 1February 19, 2021. www.noticel.com/legislatura/ahora/economia/20210219/leyes-20-y-22-crean-un-apartheid-contributivo-puerto-rico/.

De Onís, Catalina M., Hilda Lloréns, and Ruth Santiago. *"¡Ustedes tienen que limpiar las cenizas e irse de Puerto Rico para siempre!": La lucha por la justicia ambiental, climática y energética como trasfondo del Verano de Revolución Boricua 2019.* Cabo Rojo, Puerto Rico: Editora Educación Emergente, 2020.

DeLoughrey, Elizabeth M. *Allegories of the Anthropocene.* Durham, NC: Duke University Press, 2019.

———. "Globalizing the Routes of Breadfruit and Other Bounties." *Journal of Colonialism and Colonial History* 8, no. 3 (2008): 1–31. www.english.ucla.edu/wp-content/uploads/DeLoughrey-Globalizing-the-Routes-of-Breadfruit-2008.pdf.

———. "Heavy Waters: Waste and Atlantic Modernity." *PMLA* 125, no. 3 (2010): 703–12.

———. "Island Ecologies and Caribbean Literatures." *Tijdschrift voor Economische en Sociale Geografie* 95, no. 3 (2004): 298–310.

---. "Radiation Ecologies and the Wars of Light." *Modern Fiction Studies* 55, no. 3 (2009): 468–98.

---. *Routes and Roots: Navigating Caribbean and Pacific Island Literatures*. Honolulu, Hawai'i: University of Hawai'i Press, 2007.

---. "Some Pitfalls of Caribbean Regionalism, Colonial Roots, and Migratory Routes." *Journal of Caribbean Literature* 3, no. 1 (2000): 35–55.

---. "The Myth of Isolates: Ecosystem Ecologies in the Nuclear Pacific." *Cultural Geographies* 20, no. 2 (2013): 167–84. JSTOR.

DeLoughrey, Elizabeth, Renée K. Gosson, and George B. Handley, eds. *Caribbean Literature and the Environment: Between Nature and Culture*. Charlottesville, VA: University of Virginia Press, 2005.

De Sousa Santos, Boaventura. *Democratizar la democracia. Los caminos de la democracia participativa*. Mexico, DF: Fondo de Cultura Económica, 2005.

De Sousa Santos, Boaventura, and Leonardo Avritzer. "Introducción: Para ampliar el canon democrático." In *Democratizar la democracia: Los caminos de la democracia participativa*, edited by Boaventura De Sousa Santos, 35–74. Mexico, DF: Fondo de Cultura Económica, 2003.

Díaz Quiñones, Arcadio. *El arte de bregar*. San Juan, Puerto Rico: Ediciones Callejón, 2000.

---. "'Isla de quimeras': Pedreira, Palés y Albizu." *Revista de Crítica Literaria Latinoamericana* 23, no. 45 (1997): 229–46. JSTOR.

---. *Sobre principios y finales (dos ensayos)*. San Juan, Puerto Rico: Fundación Puertorriqueña de las Humanidades, 2016.

Díaz Torres, Rafael R. "Erosión de costa elevada amenaza a comunidades e infraestructura en Puerto Rico." *Centro de Periodismo Investigativo*. May 24, 2021. www.periodismoinvestigativo.com/2021/05/erosion-de-costa-elevada-amenaza-a-comunidades-e-infraestructura-en-puerto-rico/.

Dick, Diane Lourdes. "U.S. Tax Imperialism." *American University Law Review* 65, no. 1 (2015): 1–86.

Domínguez, Daylet. "Imaginarios antillanos: Humboldt, Haití y la Confederación Africana en las Antillas." *Revista Iberoamericana* 84, no. 262 (2018): 45–63.

Dubois, Laurent. *Haiti: The Aftershocks of History*. New York, NY: Metropolitan Books, 2012.

Duchesne Winter, Juan. "Metafísica narrativa de la nación albizuista." In *La nación puertorriqueña: Ensayos en torno Pedro Albizu Campos*, edited by Juan M. Carrión, Teresa C. Gracia Ruiz, and Carlos Rodríguez Fraticelli, 83–96. Río Piedras, Puerto Rico: Editorial de la Universidad de Puerto Rico, 1993.

Duke, Eric D. *Building a Nation: Caribbean Federation in the Black Diaspora*. Gainesville, FL: University Press of Florida, 2016.

Echevarría, Ana M. "Performing Subversion: A Comparative Study of Caribbean Women Playwrights." PhD diss., Cornell University, 2000. ProQuest.

Eco, Umberto. "Sobre los islarios." *Revista de Occidente*, no. 342 (2009): 33–35.

Edmond, Rod, and Vanessa Smith, editors. *Islands in History and Representation*. London, UK: Routledge, 2003.

Espada, Mariah. "Influencers, Developers, Crypto Currency Tycoons: How Puerto Ricans Are Fighting Back against Using the Island as a Tax Haven." *TIME*. April 16, 2021. www.time.com/5955629/puerto-rico-tax-haven-opposition/.

Estrade, Paul. "El heraldo de la 'independencia absoluta.'" In *Pasión por la libertad: Actas del Coloquio Internacional "El independentismo puertorriqueño, de Betances a nuestros días,"* edited by Félix Ojeda Reyes and Paul Estrade, 3–13, San Juan, Puerto Rico: Editorial de la Universidad de Puerto Rico, 2000.

Etherington, John Robert. "Nationalism, Exclusion and Violence: A Territorial Approach." *Studies in Ethnicity and Nationalism* 7, no. 3 (2008): 24–44. doi: 10.1111/j.1754-9469.2007.tb00160.x.

Fanon, Frantz. *Black Skin, White Masks*. Translated by Charles Lam Markmann. New York, NY: Grove Press, 1967. First published 1952.

———. *The Wretched of the Earth*. Translated by Richard Philcox. New York, NY: Grove Press, 2004. First published 1963.

Federici, Silvia. *Caliban and the Witch: Women, Body and Primitive Accumulation*. New York, NY: Autonomedia, 2004.

Fernández Retamar, Roberto. *Todo Caliban*. San Juan, Puerto Rico: Ediciones Callejón, 2003.

Ferreira da Silva, Denise. "Reading the Dead: A Feminist Black Critique of Global Capital." In *Otherwise Worlds: Against Settler Colonialism and Anti-Blackness*, edited by Tiffany Lethabo King, Jenell Navarro, and Andrea Smith, 38–51. Durham, NC: Duke University Press, 2020.

———. *Toward a Global Idea of Race*. Minneapolis, MN: University of Minnesota Press, 2007.

Fiet, Lowell. *El teatro puertorriqueño reimaginado: Notas críticas sobre la creación dramática y el performance*. San Juan, Puerto Rico: Ediciones Callejón, 2004.

———. "New Tropicalisms: Performance on the Shifting Borders of Caribbean Disappearance." In *Performance in the Borderlands*, edited by Ramón H. Rivera-Servera and Harvey Young, 248–65. London, UK: Palgrave, 2011.

———. "Teresa 'Bravata.' 'Inciertas: espectáculo erosionado.'" *Claridad*. December 15, 2020. www.claridadpuertorico.com/teresa-bravata-inciertas-espectaculo-erosionado/.

Figueroa-Vásquez, Yomaira. *Decolonizing Diasporas: Radical Mappings of Afro-Atlantic Literatures*. Evanston, IL: Northwestern University Press, 2020.

Finamore, Daniel, ed. *Maritime History as World History: New Perspectives on Maritime History and Nautical Archaeology*. Salem, MA: Peabody Essex Museum and Gainesville, FL: University Press of Florida, 2004.

Finley, Chris. "Building Maroon Intellectual Communities." In *Otherwise Worlds: Against Settler Colonialism and Anti-Blackness*, edited by Tiffany Lethabo King, Jenell Navarro, and Andrea Smith, 362–70. Durham, NC: Duke University Press, 2020.

Flores Collazo, María Margarita. "(Des)memorias en torno a la esclavitud negra y la abolición: Puerto Rico, siglo XIX." *Cincinnati Romance Review* 30 (2011): 17–38.

Florido, Adrián. "Puerto Rico, Island of Racial Harmony?" *NPR*. April 24, 2020. www.npr.org/2020/04/23/842832544/puerto-rico-island-of-racial-harmony.

Font-Guzmán, Jacqueline N. *Experiencing Puerto Rican Citizenship and Cultural Nationalism*. London, UK: Palgrave, 2015.

Forsdick, Charles. "Late Glissant: History, 'World Literature,' and the Persistence of the Political," *Small Axe* 33 (2010): 121–34.

Frente Ciudadano por la Auditoría de la Deuda. Facebook Page. www.facebook.com/FrenteCiudadanoAuditoriaDeLaDeuda/.

Funes Monzote, Reinaldo. "El Gran Caribe. De las plantaciones al turismo." *RCC Perspectives*, no. 7 (2013): 17–24. JSTOR.

Gago, Verónica, Luci Cavallero, and Beatriz Ortiz Martínez. "Debt Is a War against Women's Autonomy." *Committee for the Abolition of Illegitimate Debt*. April 22, 2021. www.cadtm.org/Debt-Is-A-War-Against-Women-s-Autonomy.

Gallisá Muriente, Sofía. "Sofía Gallisá Muriente." www.hatoreina.com.

García, Ana María. *La operación* [Video]. YouTube, uploaded by Jean Vallejo, February 24, 2014. www.youtube.com/playlist?list=PLSFvl4lWGgT6dV7vVCuYz_bXALfVjGYEO. First published 1982.

García, Gervasio L. "La nación antillana: ¿Historia o ficción?" *Historia Social* 52 (2005): 35–58.

García, Gervasio L., and Ángel Quintero Rivera. *Desafío y solidaridad: Breve historia del movimiento obrero puertorriqueño*. San Juan, Puerto Rico: Ediciones Huracán, 1982.

García López, Gustavo. "The Multiple Layers of Environmental Injustice in Contexts of (Un)natural Disasters: The Case of Puerto Rico Post-Hurricane Maria." *Environmental Justice* 11, no. 3 (June 2018): 101–08, doi: 10.1089/env.2017.0045.

García-Muñiz, Humberto. "Boots, Boots, Boots: Intervention, Regional Security, and Militarization in the Caribbean, 1979–1986." San Juan, Puerto Rico: Caribbean Project for Justice and Peace, 1986.

———. "U.S. Military Installations in Puerto Rico: An Essay on Their Role and Purpose." *Caribbean Studies* 24, nos. 3–4 (1991): 79–97. JSTOR.

Garriga-López, Adriana. "Debt, Crisis, and Resurgence in Puerto Rico." *Small Axe* 24, no. 2 (July 1, 2020): 122–32. doi: www.doi.org/10.1215/07990537-8604538.

———. "Puerto Rico: The Future In Question." *Shima* 13, no. 2 (2019): 174–192. doi: 10.21463/shima.13.2.13.

———. "The Other Puerto Rico." *Social Text*. June 7, 2018. www.socialtextjournal.org/periscope_article/the-other-puerto-rico/.

Gaztambide Géigel, Antonio. "La invención del Caribe en el siglo XX. Las definiciones del Caribe como problema histórico y metodológico." In *Tan lejos de Dios . . . Ensayos sobre las relaciones del Caribe con Estados Unidos*, 29–58. San Juan, Puerto Rico: Ediciones Callejón, 2006.

———. "Nacionalismo, antillanismo e (hispano)americanismo en la era de las revoluciones," 1–22. St. Michael, Barbados: Association of Caribbean Historians, 2010.

———. *Tan lejos de Dios. . .: Ensayos sobre las relaciones del Caribe con Estados Unidos*. San Juan, Puerto Rico: Ediciones Callejón, 2006.

Gaztambide Géigel, Antonio, Juan González-Mendoza, and Mario R. Cancel-Sepúlveda, eds. *Cien años de sociedad: Los 98 del Gran Caribe*. San Juan, Puerto Rico: Ediciones Callejón, 2000.

Geirola, Gustavo. "Entrevista a Pedro Adorno." In *Arte y oficio del director teatral en América Latina: Caribe*, 165–94. Buenos Aires, Argentina and Los Angeles, CA: Editorial Argus-a, 2013. www.ctda.library.miami.edu/media/publications/geirola_Arte_y_oficio_castillo.pdf

Gibson, Carrie. *Empire's Crossroads: A History of the Caribbean from Columbus to the Present Day*. London, UK: Pan Macmillan, 2014.

Gillis, John R. *Islands of the Mind: How the Imagination Created the Atlantic World*. London, UK: Palgrave, 2004.

Girvan, Norman. "Constructing the Greater Caribbean." In *Pan-Caribbean Integration Beyond CARICOM*, edited by Patsy Lewis, Terri-Ann Gilbert-Roberts, Jessica Byron, 14–27. London, UK: Routledge, 2017.

Glissant, Édouard. *Caribbean Discourse: Selected Essays*. Translated by J. Michael Dash. Charlottesville, VA: University Press of Virginia, 1989.

———. "In Praise of the Different and of Difference." Translated by Celia Britton. *Callaloo* 36, no. 4 (2013): 856–62. Project MUSE. doi: 10.1353/cal.2013.0203.

———. *Poetics of Relation*. Translated by Betsy Wing. Ann Arbor, MI: University of Michigan Press, 1997. First published 1990 in French by Gallimard.

———. *Poetic Intention*. Translated by Nathalie Stephens and Anne Malena. Callicoon, NY: Nightboat Books, 2010. First published 1969.

———. *The Collected Poems*. Edited by Jeff Humphries, Translated by Jeff Humphries and Melissa Manolas. Minneapolis, MN: University of Minnesota Press, 2005. First published 1994.

———. *The Fourth Century*. Translated by Betsy Wing. Lincoln, NE: University of Nebraska Press, 2001. First published 1964.

———. *Tratado del Todo-Mundo*. Translated by María Teresa Gallego Urrutia. Barcelona, Spain: El Cobre Ediciones, 2006. First published 1997.

Global Action for Debt Cancellation. www.debtgwa.net.

Godreau Aubert, Ariadna. *Las propias: Apuntes para una pedagogía de las endeudadas*. Cabo Rojo, Puerto Rico: Editora Educación Emergente, 2018.

González Seligmann, Katerina. "Un-Nationalisms of the Federated Archipelago." *Small Axe* 24, no. 61 (2020): 69–77.

Gros, Frédéric. *Andar: Una filosofía*. Translated by Isabel González Gallarza. Paris, France: Titivillus, 2015.

Guerrero, Hilda from *Comuna Caribe* and *Mujeres que Abrazan la Mar*. Personal Interviews. April 14 and 21, 2021.

Gumbs, Alexis Pauline. *Undrowned: Black Feminist Lessons from Marine Mammals*. Chico, CA: AK Press, 2020.

Handley, George B. *New World Poetics: Nature and the Adamic Imagination of Whitman, Neruda, and Walcott*. Athens, GA: The University of Georgia Press, 2010.

Harris, Wilson. "Tradition and the West Indian Novel." In *The Unfinished Genesis of the Imagination. Selected Essays*, edited by Andrew Bundy, 140–51. London, UK and New York, NY: Routledge, 1999.

Hau'ofa, Epeli. *We Are the Ocean: Selected Works*. Honolulu, Hawai'i: University of Hawai'i Press, 2008.

Heller, Ben A. "Landscape, Femininity, and Caribbean Discourse." *MLN* 111, no. 2 (1996): 391–416. JSTOR.
Hernández-Adrián, Francisco-J. "Atlantic Nessologies: Image, Territory, Value." *ST&TCL* 30, no. 1 (2006): 20–43.
———. "Géneros y vanguardias insulares: Canarias y Cuba en el límite de dos repúblicas." *Hispanic Research Journal* 8, no. 2 (2007): 141–54.
Hernández, Teresa. "Alterada: Un proyecto intangible. Mirada a la práctica y gestión de una artista del escenario." MA diss., Universidad de Puerto Rico–Río Piedras, 2016.
———. *Bravata: El comienzo de un comienzo*. Fragment. Vimeo. August 26, 2019. www.vimeo.com/355940804.
———. "How Complex Being Is, or, The Complex of Being." In *Holy Terrors: Latin American Women Perform*, edited by Diana Taylor and Roselyn Constantino, translated by Marlène Ramírez-Cancio, 385–98. Durham, NC: Duke University Press, 2003.
———. "Lá-cubana." *Puerto Rico Review*, no. 3 (2018): 93–102.
———. Personal Interview. July 23, 2019.
———. "Teresa Hernández." Vimeo Page. www.vimeo.com/teresanoinc.
———. "Works." Digital Archives, Hemispheric Institute. n.d. https://hemisphericinstitute.org/en/hidvl-collections/itemlist/category/343-thernandez-works.html.
Hernández Pérez, Maribel. "Eliezer Molina es citado por la fiscalía tras protesta por construcción de piscina al borde de playa en Rincón." *Primera Hora*. June 2, 2021. www.primerahora.com/noticias/policia-tribunales/notas/eliezer-molina-es-citado-por-la-fiscalia-tras-protesta-por-construccion-de-piscina-al-borde-de-playa-en-rincon/.
Horne, Gerald. *The Apocalypse of Settler Colonialism: The Roots of Slavery, White Supremacy, and Capitalism in Seventeenth-Century North America and the Caribbean*. New York, NY: Monthly Review Press, 2018.
Hudson, Peter James. *Bankers and Empire: How Wall Street Colonized the Caribbean*. Chicago, IL: University of Chicago Press, 2017.
Hulme, Peter. "Shakespeare's Spanish *Tempest*: Colonial Sources, Postcolonial Readings," 1–11. Colchester, UK: University of Essex, 2002. www.repository.essex.ac.uk/2831/1/The_Spanish_Tempest.pdf.
International Consortium of Investigative Journalists. *Paradise Papers: Secrets of the Global Elite*. November 2, 2017. www.icij.org/investigations/paradise-papers/.
Irizarry, Roberto. "Desenterrando y mareando la memoria: El arte del recuerdo de *Agua, sol y sereno*," 37–55. Sargasso. Special Issue: Caribbean Theater and Cultural Performance, 2005. www.ufdc.ufl.edu/UF00096005/00016/67j.
"Islands Adrift." *Centro de Periodismo Investigativo*. April 11, 2018. www.periodismoinvestigativo.com/series/islands-adrift/.
James, C. L. R., ed. *American Civilization*. Oxford, UK: Blackwell Publishing, 1993.
———. *The Black Jacobins: Toussaint L'Ouverture and the San Domingo Revolution*. New York, NY: Vintage Books, 1989. First Published 1938.

———. *The Life of Captain Cipriani: An Account of British Government in the West Indies, with the Pamphlet The Case for West-Indian Self Government*. Durham, NC: Duke University Press, 2014.

Jiménez, Mónica. "Looking for a Way Forward in the Past: Lessons from the Puerto Rican Nationalist Party." In *Aftershocks of Disaster: Puerto Rico before and after the Storm*, edited by Yarimar Bonilla and Marisol LeBrón, 263–70. Chicago, IL: Haymarket, 2019.

Jiménez Muñoz, Gladys M. "'Race' and Class among *Nacionalista* Women in Interwar Puerto Rico: The Activism of Dominga de la Cruz Becerril and Trina Padilla de Sanz." *Caribbean Review of Gender Studies* 12 (2018): 168–98. Academia.edu. www.academia.edu/38024238/_Race_and_Class_among_Nacionalista_Women_in_Interwar_Puerto_Rico_The_Activism_of_Dominga_de_la_Cruz_Becerril_and_Trina_Padilla_de_Sanz_Gladys_M_Jiménez_Muñoz.

Jiménez Suriel, Yina and Pablo Guardiola, curators and eds. *One Month after Being Known in That Island: Caribbean Art Today*. Stutgart, Germany: Hatje Cantz, 2020.

Jiménez Suriel, Yina. "yinajimenezs." Instagram Page. www.instagram.com/yinajimenezs/?hl=en.

Jiménez-Vera, Cindy. *Islandia*. Bayamón, Puerto Rico: Ediciones Aguadulce, and San Juan, Puerto Rico: Disonante, 2017.

Jobin-Leeds, Greg, and AgitArte. *When We Fight, We Win!: Twenty-First-Century Social Movements and the Activists That Are Transforming Our World*. New York, NY and London, UK: The New Press, 2016.

Jones, Sam. "Aid, Cholera and Protest: Life in Haiti Five Years after the Earthquake." *The Guardian*. January 12, 2015, www.theguardian.com/global-development/2015/jan/12/haiti-earthquake-five-years-on-village-solidarite.

"José Ciénaga - Materna" [Video]. YouTube, uploaded by José Ciénaga. June 14, 2021. www.youtube.com/watch?v=pEuYm8BWNEw.

Jubileo Sur Américas. www.jubileosuramericas.net.

Jubileo Sur Américas. "Articulacion Caribe : 'La vida antes de la Deuda'" [Video]. YouTube. July 24, 2020. www.youtube.com/watch?v=nygnTtTIdY0.

Kamugisha, Aaron. *Beyond Coloniality: Citizenship and Freedom in the Caribbean Intellectual Tradition*. Bloomington, IN: Indiana University Press, 2019.

Kennedy, Cynthia M. "The Other White Gold: Salt, Slaves, the Turks and Caicos Islands, and British Colonialism." *The Historian* 69, no. 2 (2007): 215–30. JSTOR.

Kinane, Ian. *Theorising Literary Islands: The Island Trope in Contemporary Robinsonade Narratives*. Lanham, MD: Rowman & Littlefield Publishers, 2016.

King, Tiffany Lethabo, Jenell Navarro, and Andrea Smith, eds. *Otherwise Worlds: Against Settler Colonialism and Anti-Blackness*. Durham, NC: Duke University Press, 2020.

Klein, Bernhard, and Gesa Mackenthun, eds. *Sea Changes: Historicizing the Ocean*. London, UK and New York, NY: Routledge, 2004.

Klein, Naomi. *The Battle for Paradise: Puerto Rico Takes on the Disaster Capitalists*. Chicago, IL: Haymarket Books, 2018.

———. *The Shock Doctrine: The Rise of Disaster Capitalism*. New York, NY: Knopf, 2007.

Knight, Franklin W. "The Caribbean in the 1930s." In *General History of the Caribbean*, edited by Bridget Brereton, Teresita Martínez-Vergne, René A. Römer, and Blanca G. Silvestrini, 42–81. London, UK: Palgrave, 2003. doi: 10.1007/978-1-349-73773-4_3.

———. *The Caribbean. The Genesis of a Fragmented Nationalism*. 2011. Oxford, UK: Oxford University Press. First published 1978.

Lamba-Nieves, Deepak, Sergio M. Marxuach, and Rosanna Torres. "PROMESA: ¿Un experimento colonial fallido?" *Centro para una Nueva Economía*. June 30, 2021. www.grupocne.org/2021/06/30/cne-review-junio-2021/.

Lamour, Sabine. "Haiti: How Women Shake Up the Political World." *International Viewpoint*. February 7, 2020. www.internationalviewpoint.org/spip.php?article6394.

Langdon, Robyn, Emily Connaughton, and Max Coltheart. "The Fregoli Delusion: A Disorder of Person Identification and Tracking." *Topics in Cognitive Science* 6, no. 4 (October 2014): 615–31. Wiley Online Library. doi: 10.1111/tops.12108.

Langevin, Karen. "MAMÍFERAsola—Un performance de Karen Langevin—Mature" [Video]. Vimeo, uploaded by Museo de Arte Contemporáneo de Puerto Rico. February 20, 2021. www.vimeo.com/513871949.

LeBrón, Marisol. *Against Muerto Rico: Lessons from the Verano Boricua*. Translated by Beatriz Llenín-Figueroa. Cabo Rojo, Puerto Rico: Editora Educación Emergente, 2021.

———. *Policing Life and Death: Race, Violence, and Resistance in Puerto Rico*. Berkeley, CA: University of California Press, 2019.

Lebrón Ortiz, Pedro. *Filosofía del cimarronaje*. Cabo Rojo, Puerto Rico: Editora Educación Emergente, 2020.

Leeming, David A. *The World of Myth: An Anthology*. Oxford, UK: Oxford University Press, 2013.

Leonard, Scott, and Michael McClure, eds. *Myth and Knowing: An Introduction to World Mythology*. New York, NY: McGraw-Hill Education, 2003.

León, Osvaldo. "El Grito de los Excluidos." *América Latina en movimiento*. September 8, 1999. www.alainet.org/es/articulo/104204.

Lestringant, Frank. "Pensar por islas." *Revista de Ocidente* 342 (2009): 9–29.

Lethabo King, Tiffany, Jenell Navarro, and Andrea Smith. "Introduction. Beyond Incommensurability: Toward an Otherwise Stance on Black and Indigenous Relationality." In *Otherwise Worlds: Against Settler Colonialism and Anti-Blackness*, 1–26. Durham, NC: Duke University Press, 2020.

Levins Morales, Aurora and Ricardo. "DeCLARAción/tion." *Aurora Levins Morales*. www.auroralevinsmorales.com/declaracion.html.

Lewis, James. "An Island Characteristic: Derivative Vulnerabilities to Indigenous and Exogenous Hazards." *Shima: The International Journal of Research into Island Cultures* 3, no. 1 (2009): 3–15. www.shimajournal.org/issues/v3n1/d.-Lewis-Shima-v3n1-3-15.pdf.

Lewis, Martin W., and Kären E. Wigen. *The Myth of Continents: A Critique of Metageography*. Berkeley, CA: University of California Press, 1997.

Lewis, Patsy, Terri-Ann Gilbert-Roberts, and Jessica Byron. *Pan-Caribbean Integration Beyond CARICOM*. New York, NY and London, UK: Routledge, 2018.

Llenín-Figueroa, Beatriz. "'Armar una literatura de conexiones' en nuestra 'patria líquida': El contexto caribeño de la ensayística de Marta Aponte Alsina." *Caribbean Studies* 44, no. 1 (2016): 29–45.

———. "Conjuring Puerto Rico's Archipelagic, Decolonial Future." *Shima* 14, no. 2 (2020): 172–93. www.shimajournal.org/issues/v14n1/12.-Llenin-Figueroa-Shima-v14n1.pdf

———. "Descolonización, democracia radical y archipielagismo: Puerto Rico como islas-experimentos de emancipación." *Visitas al patio* 166, no. X (2019): xx–xx. www.revistas.unicartagena.edu.co/index.php/visitasalpatio/article/view/2439.

———. "En el principio fue el agua: Sobre *inciertas: espectáculo erosionado* de/con Teresa Hernández." *80grados*. January 2021, https://www.80grados.net/en-el-principio-fue-el-agua-sobre-inciertas-espectaculo-erosionado-de-con-teresa-hernandez/.

———. "Encarnando soberanías oceánicas: Luisa Capetillo y la tribuna en la calle." In *Amor y anarquía: Escritos de Luisa Capetillo* (rev. ed.), edited by Julio Ramos, 225–35. Cabo Rojo, Puerto Rico: Editora Educación Emergente 2021.

———. "'I Believe in the Future of Small Countries': Édouard Glissant's Small, Archipelagic Scale in Dialogue with Other Caribbean Writers." *Discourse: Journal for Theoretical Studies in Media and Culture* 36, no. 1 (2014): 87–111.

———. "Imagined Islands: A Caribbean Tidalectics." PhD diss., Duke University, 2012. www.dukespace.lib.duke.edu/dspace/bitstream/handle/10161/5420/LlennFigueroa_duke_0066D_11264.pdf?sequence=1.

———. "In the Beginning Was the Water: On *inciertas-eroded spectacle* by/with Teresa Hernández." *PREE* #7. May 2021. https://preelit.com/2021/05/13/4985/.

———. "Situar la crisis y ceremoniar su pago: Ensayo en cuatro actos." *Voces del Caribe* 11, nos. 1–2 (2019): 893–930, www.img1.wsimg.com/blobby/go/17d75147-ba5c-4e83-bc9f-efc947767190/downloads/11.4.pdf?ver=1621590613361.

———. "The Maroons Are Deathless. We Are Deathless." *Abusable Past*. July 20, 2019. www.radicalhistoryreview.org/abusablepast/?p=3145.

"Las Lolitas-Culminación Jornada Centenario 19 Nov 19" [Video]. YouTube, uploaded by Amalia García Padilla. November 20, 2019. www.youtu.be/Glo1XnPymw0.

López-Santiago, Ángel. "The Antillean League." *Transforming Anthropology* 26, no. 2 (2018): 181–94. doi: 10.1111/traa.12131.

Lorde, Audre. "A Litany for Survival." 1978. www.poetryfoundation.org/poems/147275/a-litany-for-survival.

"Los arrestos de Tito Kayak." *Noticel*. September 1, 2017. www.noticel.com/ahora/20170901/los-arrestos-de-tito-kayak/.

Loxley, Diana. *Problematic Shores: The Literature of Islands*. New York, NY: St Martin's Press, 1990.

Maldonado Denis, Manuel. "Las perspectivas del nacionalismo latinoamericano: El caso de Puerto Rico." *Revista mexicana de sociología* 38, no. 4 (1976): 799–810. JSTOR.

———. *The Emigration Dialectic: Puerto Rico and the USA*. New York, NY: International Publishers, 1980.

Mancke, Elizabeth. "Early Modern Expansion and the Politicization of Oceanic Space." *Geographical Review* 89, no. 2 (1999): 225–36.

———. "Oceanic Space and the Creation of a Global International System, 1450–1800." Finamore, 149–66.

Mardorossian, Carine M. "'Poetics of Landscape': Édouard Glissant's Creolized Ecologies." *Callaloo* 36, no. 4 (2013): 983–94.

Mari Narváez, Mari. "Vieques podría ir en una dirección maravillosamente buena. O podría desaparecer." *Claridad*. May 10, 2021. www.claridadpuertorico.com/vieques-podria-ir-en-una-direccion-maravillosamente-buena-o-podria-desaparecer.

Mariani Ríos, Ricardo. "Albizu y su concepción de 'raza.' Una perspectiva decolonial." *Horizontes Decoloniales* 2 (2016): 141–61. Academia.edu. www.academia.edu/25991345/Albizu_y_su_concepción_de_raza_una_perspectiva_decolonial.

Marqués, René. "En la popa hay un cuerpo reclinado." In *Cuentos puertorriqueños de hoy*, 135–52. Río Piedras, Puerto Rico: Editorial Cultural, 1959.

———. *La víspera del hombre*. Río Piedras, Puerto Rico: Editorial Cultural, 1959.

Martínez Lebrón, Amado. "Betances, un empresario sin Dios." *80grados*. June 5, 2015. www.80grados.net/betances-un-empresario-sin-dios/.

Martínez-San Miguel, Yolanda. "Cartografías pancaribeñas: Representaciones culturales de los enclaves caribeños en Puerto Rico y Estados Unidos." *Revista de Estudios Hispánicos* 25 (1998): 65–92.

———. "Comparatismo en el pluriverso." *80grados*. May 15, 2020. www.80grados.net/comparatismo-en-el-pluriverso/.

———. "Deconstructing Puerto Ricanness through Sexuality: Female Counternarratives on Puerto Rican Identity (1894–1934)." In *Puerto Rican Jam: Rethinking Colonialism and Nationalism*, edited by Frances Negrón-Muntaner and Ramón Grosfoguel, 127–39. Minneapolis, MN: University of Minnesota Press, 1997. JSTOR.

———. "Entre con/federaciones: Nicolás Guillén, Luis Palés Matos y Aimé Césaire." *80grados*. June 28, 2019. www.80grados.net/entre-con-federaciones/.

———. "West Indies/Caribe/Caribbean/Caraibes: fisuras del caribeñismo." *80grados*. November 2, 2018. www.80grados.net/west-indies-caribe-caribbean-caraibes-fisuras-del-caribenismo-notas-desde-miami/.

Martínez-San Miguel, Yolanda, and Katerina González Seligmann, eds. "Con-Federating the Archipelago: The *Confederación Antillana* and the West Indies Federation (Special Section)." *Small Axe* 24, no. 1 (March 1, 2020): 37–43. doi: 10.1215/07990537-8190541.

Martínez-San Miguel, Yolanda, and Michelle Stephens, eds. *Contemporary Archipelagic Thinking: Towards New Comparative Methodologies and Disciplinary Formations*. Lanham, MD: Rowman & Littlefield Publishers, 2020.

Martínez Tabares, Vivian. "Teresa Hernández: Artista de la acción, performera caribeña," 1–22. *Archivo Artea*. 2007. www.archivoartea.uclm.es/textos/teresa-hernandez-artista-de-la-accion-performera-caribena/.

Martorell, Deborah. "En peligro Las Salinas de Cabo Rojo por el cambio climático." *NotiCentro*. February 2021. www.wapa.tv/noticias/especiales/en-peligro-las-salinas-de-cabo-rojo-por-el-cambio-climatico_20131122499156.html.

Marx, Anthony W. *Faith in Nation: Exclusionary Origins of Nationalism*. Oxford, UK: Oxford University Press, 2005.

May Day 2021. "Reclamos del Movimiento Obrero." Adobe.com. www.indd.adobe.com/view/1cf32c84-7b5b-496e-9892-eb78e8e3ada6.

Mbembe, Achille. "The Power of the Archive and its Limits." *Refiguring the Archive*. Translated by Judith Inggs, edited by Carolyn Hamilton, Verne Harris, Michêle Pickover, Graeme Reid, Razia Saleh, and Jane Taylor, 19–26. Berlin, Germany: Kluwer Academic Publishers, 2002. www.sites.duke.edu/vms565s_01_f2014/files/2014/08/mbembe2002.pdf.

McMahon, Elizabeth, Carol Farbotko, Godfrey Baldacchino, Andrew Harwood, and Elaine Stratford. "Envisioning the Archipelago." *Island Studies Journal* 6, no. 2 (2011): 113–30. https://ro.uow.edu.au/scipapers/3062/.

Meléndez, Edwin, and Jennifer Hinojosa. "Estimates of Post-Hurricane María Exodus from Puerto Rico." *Center for Puerto Rican Studies*. October 2017. www.centropr.hunter.cuny.edu/research/data-center/research-briefs/estimates-post-hurricane-maria-exodus-puerto-rico.

Meléndez Badillo, Jorell. *The Lettered Barriada: Workers, Archival Power, and the Politics of Knowledge in Puerto Rico*. Durham, NC: Duke University Press, 2021.

———. *Voces libertarias: Orígenes del anarquismo en Puerto Rico*. Bloomington, IN: Secret Sailor Books, 2013.

Menser, Michael. *We Decide! Theories and Cases in Participatory Democracy*. Philadelphia, PA: Temple University Press, 2018.

Meyer, Gerald J. "Pedro Albizu Campos, Gilberto Concepción de Gracia, and Vito Marcantonio's Collaboration in the Cause of Puerto Rico's Independence." *CENTRO Journal* 23, no. 1 (2011): 86–123.

Mintz, Sidney W. *Sweetness and Power: The Place of Sugar in Modern History*. New York, NY: Penguin Books, 1986.

Mitchell-Hall, Candia. "Reconciliation and Reparations" [Video]. YouTube, uploaded by History UWIMona. March 24, 2021. www.youtube.com/watch?v=EjsdY9B_R8I.

Mooney, Henry, Joan Oriol Prats, David Rosenblatt, and Jason Christie. "Why Have Caribbean Countries Been so Indebted, and What Can They Do to Improve Outcomes?" *Inter-American Development Bank*. March 10, 2021. www.blogs.iadb.org/caribbean-dev-trends/en/why-have-caribbean-countries-been-so-indebted-and-what-can-they-do-to-improve-outcomes/.

Moten, Fred, and Stefano Harney. *The Undercommons: Fugitive Planning & Black Study*. New York, NY: Autonomedia, 2013.

Murdoch, H. Adlai. "Édouard Glissant's Creolized World Vision: From Resistance and Relation to *Opacité*." *Callaloo* 36, no. 4 (2013): 875–89.

"Nadia Huggins." 2021. www.nadiahuggins.com/info.

Nanan, Wendy. Facebook Page. www.facebook.com/WendyNananArtist/.
Naranjo Orovio, Consuelo, María Dolores González-Ripoll Navarro, and María Ruiz del Árbol Moro, eds. *El Caribe: Origen del mundo moderno.* Aranjuez, Spain: Doce Calles S. L., 2020. www.docecalles.com/wp-content/uploads/2020/03/El_Caribe_Origen_del_mundo_moderno.pdf.
Neate, Rupert. "Richest 1% Own Half the World's Wealth, Study Finds." *The Guardian.* November 14, 2017. www.theguardian.com/inequality/2017/nov/14/worlds-richest-wealth-credit-suisse.
Negrón, Mara. "El Caribe en la época de Babel: Entre grito y gemido." *Revista Iberoamericana* 75, no. 229 (2009): 945–62.
Negrón-Muntaner, Frances, ed. *None of the Above: Puerto Ricans in the Global Era.* London, UK: Palgrave, 2007.
———. ed. *Sovereign Acts: Contesting Colonialism across Indigenous Nations and Latinx America.* Tucson, AZ: The University of Arizona Press, 2017.
Niblett, Michael, and Kerstin Oloff, eds. *Perspectives on the "Other America." Comparative Approaches to Caribbean and Latin American Culture.* Amsterdam, Netherlands: Rodopi, 2009.
Nieves Falcón, Luis. *Un siglo de represión política en Puerto Rico: 1898–1998.* San Juan, Puerto Rico: Ediciones Puerto, 2009.
NoSiri/Emilia Beatriz. "emilixbeatriz." Instagram Page. www.instagram.com/emilixbeatriz/?hl=en
Núñez Santaliz. Kairiana. *Archivo Santaliz* [Multimedia performance]. April 8, 2021. Taller Libertá, Mayagüez, Puerto Rico.
———. "Bravata, o la mujer del cuchillo en la boca." *80grados.* July 5, 2019. www.80grados.net/bravata-o-la-mujer-del-cuchillo-en-la-boca/.
Ojeda Reyes, Félix. "Ramón Emeterio Betances, patriarca de la antillanía." In *Pasión por la libertad: Actas del Coloquio Internacional "El independentismo puertorriqueño, de Betances a nuestros días,"* edited by Félix Ojeda Reyes and Paul Estrade, 31–38. San Juan, Puerto Rico: Editorial de la Universidad de Puerto Rico, 2000.
O'Neil Lewis, J. "From West Indian Federation to Caribbean Economic Community." *Social and Economic* Studies 48, no. 4 (1999): 3–19.
Ortiz, María Elena, and Marsha Pierce, curators and eds. *The Other Side of Now: Foresight in Contemporary Caribbean Art.* Miami, FL: Pérez Art Museum (PAMM), 2019.
Pabón, Carlos. *Nación postmortem: Ensayos sobre los tiempos de insoportable ambigüedad.* San Juan, Puerto Rico: Ediciones Callejón, 2002.
"Pacific Plunder" [Series]. *The Guardian.* www.theguardian.com/world/series/pacific-plunder.
Padmore, George. "Federation: The Demise of an Idea." *Social and Economic Studies* 48, no. 4 (1999): 21–63.
Palenzuela, Nilo. *Encrucijadas de un insulario.* Santa Cruz de Tenerife, Spain: Ediciones Idea, 2006.
Palés Matos, Luis. *Fiel fugada: Antología poética de Luis Palés Matos.* Edited by Noel Luna. San Juan, Puerto Rico: Instituto de Cultura Puertorriqueña, 2008.

———. *Litoral: Reseña de una vida inútil*. San Juan, Puerto Rico: Folium, 2013.
Paquette, Robert L., and Mark M. Smith. *The Oxford Handbook of Slavery in the Americas*. Oxford, UK: Oxford University Press, 2016.
"Paradise Papers: Secrets of the Global Elite Is Stored and Updated in the International Consortium of Investigative Journalists." *International Consortium of Investigative Journalists*. November 5, 2017. www.icij.org/investigations/paradise-papers/.
Paralitici, José "Ché." *La represión contra el independentismo puertorriqueño: 1960–2010*. San Juan, Puerto Rico: Publicaciones Gaviota, 2011.
———. *Sentencia impuesta: 100 años de encarcelamientos por la independencia de Puerto Rico*. San Juan, Puerto Rico: Ediciones Puerto, 2004.
pastrana santiago, nibia. "Aquí había una isla (here was an island)." *nibia pastrana santiago*. 2019. www.nibiapastrana.com/habia.
———. "Our Island Here." *nibia pastrana santiago*. 2019. www.nibiapastrana.com/our-island.
Patke, Rajeev S. *Poetry and Islands: Materiality and the Creative Imagination*. Lanham, MD: Rowman & Littlefield Publishers, 2018.
Payne, Anthony. *The Political History of CARICOM*. Kingston, Jamaica: Ian Randle Publishers, 2008. First published 1980.
Pedreira, Antonio. *Insularismo: Ensayos de interpretación puertorriqueña*. Hato Rey, San Juan, Puerto Rico: C. M. A. Books Distributors, 1934.
Pedro, Alberto. *Mar nuestro/Manteca*. San Juan, Puerto Rico: Fragmento Imán Editores, 2003. First published 1997.
Peña Jordán, Teresa. "Luisa Capetillo: Una práctica del cuerpo, el pensamiento y la palabra." In *Amor y anarquía: Escritos de Luisa Capetillo* (rev. ed.), edited by Julio Ramos, 161–73. Río Piedras, Puerto Rico: Ediciones Huracán, 2021.
Pérez Jiménez, Cristina. "Puerto Rican Colonialism, Caribbean Radicalism, and *Pueblos Hispanos*'s Inter-Nationalist Alliance." *Small Axe* 23, no. 3 (2019): 50–68. Project Muse.
Picó, Fernando. *1898: La guerra después de la guerra*. Río Piedras, Puerto Rico: Ediciones Huracán, 1987.
———. *Historia general de Puerto Rico*. Río Piedras, Puerto Rico: Ediciones Huracán, 2008.
Picó Vidal, Isabel. "Apuntes preliminares para el estudio mujer puertorriqueña y su participación en las luchas sociales de principios del siglo XX." In *La mujer en América Latina*, edited by Carmen Elú de Lei, 98–113. Publisher City, State: Publisher Location, 1975.
Piñera, Virgilio. "Isla." *Zenda: Autores, libros y compañía*. November 25, 2017. www.zendalibros.com/5-poemas-virgilio-pinera/.
———. "La isla en peso." In *Virgilio Piñera*, edited by Teresa Cristófani Barreto, xx–xx. Publisher City, State: Publisher Name, 1995. www.fflch.usp.br/sitesint/virgilio/isla.html. First published 1942.
Platón, Lydia. "Tendiendo afectos: *inciertas-espectáculo erosionado* de Teresa Hernández." *80grados*. December 18, 2020.

Power, Margaret. "Nacionalismo en una nación colonizada: El Partido Nacionalista y Puerto Rico." *Memorias. Revista Digital de Historia y Arqueología del Caribe* (May 2013): 119–37.

———. "Women, Gender, and the Puerto Rican Nationalist Party." In *Gendering Nationalism*, edited by John Mulholland, Nicola Montagna, and Erin Sanders-McDonagh, 129–43. London, UK: Palgrave, 2018. doi: .

Powers, Christopher. *4645*. Cabo Rojo, Puerto Rico: Editora Educación Emergente, 2020.

Prinsen, Gerard, and Séverine Blaise. "An Emerging 'Islandian' Sovereignty of Non-Self-Governing Islands." *International Journal* 72, no. 1 (March 2017): 56–78. doi: 10.1177/0020702017693260

"Protestan en Ocean Park para exigir apertura de playas." *Noticel.* May 16, 2020.

"Proyecto Matria y Jesús Obrero Cooperativa crean proyecto de empoderamiento." *Primera Hora.* May 29, 2021.

"Puerto Rico." *LittleSis.* www.littlesis.org/search?q=puerto+rico

Pugh, Jonathan. "Island Movements: Thinking with the Archipelago." *Island Studies Journal* 8, no. 1 (2013): 9–24.

"Puntos de partida". *Ivoox*, uploaded by Amigos de Radio Vieques. April 19, 2021.

Quintero Rivera, Ángel. *Conflictos de clase y política en Puerto Rico.* Río Piedras, Puerto Rico: Ediciones Huracán, 1978.

Quintero Rivera, Mareia. "Cartografías culturales de entre siglos: Arte y política en las décadas de 1990 y 2000." In *Historia de Puerto Rico*, edited by Luis González Vale and María Dolores Luque, 683–720. Madrid, Spain: Editorial Doce Calles, 2012. Online edition, 1–51. www.smjegupr.net/wp-content/uploads/2013/02/Quintero-Cartograf%C3%ADas-culturales-del-entresiglos.pdf

Quiñones Maldonado, Francisco. "Roban vestuario de Albizu Campos en Lares." *Jornadapr.* September 22, 2018. www.jornadapr.com/noticias/policiacas/1641/roban-vestuario-de-albizu-campos-en-lares/

Raban, Jonathan, ed. *The Oxford Book of the Sea.* Oxford, UK: Oxford University Press, 1992.

Rama, Carlos M. *La idea de la Federación Antillana en los independentistas puertorriqueños del siglo XIX.* San José, Costa Rica: Ediciones Librería Internacional, 1971.

———. "Ramón Emeterio Betances y América Latina." In *La Independencia de las Antillas y Ramón Emeterio Betances*, 133–38. San Juan, Puerto Rico: Instituto de Cultura Puertorriqueña, 1980.

Ramírez Padilla, Luis A. *Sal, sangre y sudor: Memorias históricas de las Salinas de Cabo Rojo.* Cabo Rojo, Puerto Rico: Ediciones CCPSAI, 2012.

Ramos, Aarón Gamaliel. *Islas migajas: Los países no independientes del Caribe contemporáneo.* San Juan, Puerto Rico: Travesier & Leduc Editores, 2016.

Ramos, Julio, ed. *Amor y anarquía: Los escritos de Luisa Capetillo.* Río Piedras, Puerto Rico: Ediciones Huracán, 1992.

———, ed. *Amor y anarquía: Escritos de Luisa Capetillo* (rev. ed.). Cabo Rojo, Puerto Rico: Editora Educación Emergente, 2021.

———. "Entrevista a Norma Valle Ferrer sobre Luisa Capetillo." In *Amor y anarquía: Escritos de Luisa Capetillo* (rev. ed.), edited by Julio Ramos, 153–60. Cabo Rojo, Puerto Rico: Editora Educación Emergente, 2021.

Ramos Escobar, José L. "Génesis y desarrollo del teatro popular en Puerto Rico." *Assaig de teatre*, no. 36 (2003): 85–96.

Ramos Malavé, Natalia. "Abrazan la mar y la justicia en Piñones." *Todas*. May 1, 2019. www.todaspr.com/abrazan-la-mar-y-la-justicia-en-pinones/

Ramos Mattei, Andrés. *Betances en el ciclo revolucionario antillano: 1867–1875*. San Juan, Puerto Rico: Instituto de Cultura Puertorriqueña, 1987.

Ramos Rubén, Sabrina. *Mangle rojo*. San Juan, Puerto Rico: La secta de los perros, 2017.

Randall, Margaret. *El pueblo no sólo es testigo: La historia de Dominga*. Río Piedras, Puerto Rico: Ediciones Huracán, 1979.

Ranis, Peter. *Cooperatives Confront Capitalism: Challenging the Neoliberal Economy*. London, UK: Zed Books, 2016.

Rauhut, Claudia. "Caribbean Activism for Slavery Reparations: An Overview." In *Practices of Resistance in the Caribbean: Narratives, Aesthetics and Politics*, edited by Wiebke Beushausen, Miriam Brandel, Joseph Farquharson, Marius Littschwager, Annika McPherson, and Julia Roth, 137–50. New York, NY and London, UK: Routledge, 2018. doi: 10.4324/9781315222721.

Rebollo Gil, Guillermo. *Writing Puerto Rico: Our Decolonial Moment*. London, UK: Palgrave, 2018.

Rediker, Marcus. *The Slave Ship: A Human History*. London, UK: Penguin Books, 2007.

Revista Cruce 4, no. 1 (February 14, 2018). Edición especial María. www.issuu.com/revistacruce/docs/crucevol1_feb11.

———. 4, no. 2 (March 1, 2018). Edición especial María. www.issuu.com/revistacruce/docs/crucevol2_feb18.

Revista étnica. https://www.revistaetnica.com

"revoluciona." *Editora Educación Emergente*.https://www.portal.editoraemergente.com/revoluciona/

Reyes Cruz, Mariolga. "Por quiénes esperamos." *80grados*. February 2, 2018. www.80grados.net/por-quienes-esperamos/

Reyes Franco, Marina, curator. *El momento del yagrumo*. San Juan, Puerto Rico: Museo de Arte Contemporáneo de Puerto Rico (MACPR), 2021.

Reynolds, Ruth M. "Ruth M. Reynolds archives." *CENTRO: Center for Puerto Rican Studies*.

Rice, Andrew, and Luis Valentín Ortiz. "The McKinsey Way to Save an Island. Why Is a Bankrupt Puerto Rico Spending More Than a Billion Dollars on Expert Advice?" *New York Magazine*. April 17, 2019. www.nymag.com/intelligencer/2019/04/mckinsey-in-puerto-rico.html

Ríos Villarini, Nadja. "Interview with Rosa Luisa Márquez." *Radio Universidad de Puerto Rico*. March 30, 2014.

———. "Ritmos que unen islas: Calipso y drones entre Puerto Rico e Islas Vírgenes Americanas." *Revista Umbral*. 2016.

———. "Vieques, ¡manos arriba!" [Video]. YouTube, uploaded by Sirsaca. May 16, 2020. https://www.youtube.com/watch?v=_Nl2Xn1rn2w.
Rivera Berruz, Stephanie. "Writing to Be Heard: Recovering the Philosophy of Luisa Capetillo." *Essays in Philosophy* 19, no. 1 (2018): 1–18. doi: 10.7710/1526-0569.1595.
Rivera Ramos, Efrén. "La construcción legal del colonialismo de los Estados Unidos: Los Casos Insulares (1901–1922)." *El otro Derecho* 22, no. 8 (1998).
Roberts, Brian Russell. *Borderwaters: Amid the Archipelagic States of America*. Durham, NC: Duke University Press, 2021.
Roberts, Brian Russell, and Michelle Stephens, eds. *Archipelagic American Studies*. Durham, NC: Duke University Press, 2017.
Robinson, Cedric. *Black Marxism: The Making of the Black Radical Tradition*. Chapel Hill, NC: University of North Carolina Press, 2005.
Robles, Elizabeth. "Notas II: De(s)generar." *Revista Cruce* (March 2021): 66–73. https://issuu.com/revistacruce/docs/asunto_1.
Rodríguez Bagué, Arnaldo. "Archipelagic Performance #1 (v.1)." *En el matorral*. n.d. www.enelmatorral.wordpress.com/portfolio/archipelagic-performance-1-v-1/
———. "BRAVATA, Caribbean Feminist Performance: Oceanic Decolonial Ruination after Hurricane María." Unpublished manuscript, 2020.
Rodríguez, Jorge. "*Marea alta, marea baja*. Teatro acuático en el Escambrón." *El Vocero*. (November 28, 2002): E9–E10.
Rodríguez, Martha. "Campaña Continental." *Chasqui*, no. 40 (199): 80–83. www.repositorio.flacsoandes.edu.ec/bitstream/10469/14535/1/REXTN-Ch40-24-Rodriguez.pdf
Rodríguez-Silva, Ileana M. *Silencing Race: Disentangling Blackness, Colonialism, and National Identities in Puerto Rico*. London, UK: Palgrave, 2012.
Rodríguez Vázquez, José Juan. *El sueño que no cesa: La nación deseada en el debate intelectual y político puertorriqueño, 1920–1940*. San Juan, Puerto Rico: Ediciones Callejón, 2004.
Rolón Collazo, Lissette. "Querida L., Te abraza L. (Parte del *Epistolario Boricuir*)." In *Amor y anarquía: Escritos de Luisa Capetillo* (rev. ed.), edited by Julio Ramos 249–54. Cabo Rojo, Puerto Rico: Editora Educación Emergente, 2021.
Romero-Cesareo, Ivette. "Whose Legacy?: Voicing Women's Rights from the 1870s to the 1930s." *Callaloo* 17, no. 3 (1994): 770–89. JSTOR.
Romeu Toro, Carmen Ana. "Luisa Capetillo: Anarquista y espiritista puertorriqueña." In *Amor y anarquía: Escritos de Luisa Capetillo* (rev. ed.), edited by Julio Ramos 203–13. Cabo Rojo, Puerto Rico: Editora Educación Emergente, 2021.
Rosa, Luis Othoniel. "La inteligencia y lo ingobernable." In *Amor y anarquía: Escritos de Luisa Capetillo* (rev. ed.), edited by Julio Ramos 236–42. Cabo Rojo, Puerto Rico: Editora Educación Emergente, 2021.
Rosado, Marisa. *Las llamas de la aurora. Acercamiento a la biografía de Pedro Albizu Campos*. San Juan, Puerto Rico: Ediciones Puerto, 2009. First published 1992.
Rosario, Melissa Lynn. "Ephemeral Spaces, Undying Dreams: Social Justice Struggles in Contemporary Puerto Rico." PhD diss., Cornell University, 2013.

Roy-Féquière, Magali. *Women, Creole Identity, and Intellectual Life in Early Twentieth-Century Puerto Rico*. Philadelphia, PA: Temple University Press, 2004.

Salvemos Jauca. Facebook Page. www.facebook.com/playajauca/

Sánchez, Andrés Agustín. "Entre asimilistas y autonomistas. El republicanismo español y el debate en torno a la concesión de un régimen autonómico a las Antillas (1868–1898)." *Caribbean Studies* 30, no. 1 (2002): 135–68. JSTOR.

Sánchez-Rivera, Rachell. "Imágenes y representaciones de la prensa puertorriqueña: Control de natalidad, esterilización y anticonceptivos en *El Mundo*, *El Imparcial* y *Claridad* (1943–1974)." *De raíz diversa: Revista especializada en Estudios Latinoamericanos* 4, no. 7 (2017): 101–35.

Sánchez Robayna, Andrés. "Breve mapa de islas comparadas." *Revista de Occidente*, no. 342 (2009): 127–38.

San Miguel, Pedro L. "Visiones históricas del Caribe: Entre la mirada imperial y las resistencias de los subalternos." In *Los desvaríos de Ti Noel: Ensayos sobre la producción del saber en el Caribe*, xx–xx. San Juan, Puerto Rico: Ediciones Vértigo, 2004.

Santiago-Ortiz, Aurora. "Mapping Collaboration as Resistance to Neoliberalism: A Case Study of Participatory Action Research in Puerto Rico." *Tracce Urbane* 4, no. 8 (2020): 269–89, doi: 10.13133/2532-6562_4.8.17220.

Santiago-Valles, Kelvin. "'Our Race Today [Is] the Only Hope for the World': An African Spaniard as Chieftain of the Struggle against 'Sugar Slavery' in Puerto Rico, 1926–1934." *Caribbean Studies* 35, no. 1 (2007): 107–40. JSTOR.

Santory Jorge, Anayra. *Nada es igual: Bocetos del país que nos acontece*. Cabo Rojo, Puerto Rico: Editora Educación Emergente, 2018.

Santory Jorge, Anayra, and Mareia Quintero Rivera. *Antología del pensamiento crítico puertorriqueño contemporáneo*. Buenos Aires, Argentina: CLACSO, 2019.

Scahill, Jeremy. "Ruth Wilson Gilmore Makes the Case for Abolition." *The Intercept*. June 10, 2020. www.theintercept.com/2020/06/10/ruth-wilson-gilmore-makes-the-case-for-abolition/

Scott, David. *Conscripts of Modernity: The Tragedy of Colonial Enlightenment*. Durham, NC: Duke University Press, 2004.

———. "New World Slavery as Irreparable Evil." *Research Center for Material Culture*. November 1, 2018. www.materialculture.nl/en/events/new-world-slavery-irreparable-evil.

———. "On the Moral Justification of Reparation for New World Slavery" [Video]. Vimeo, uploaded by IsabelCastro and GuilhermeHoffmann. 2017. www.vimeo.com/203099024

———. "The Re-Enchantment of Humanism: An Interview with Sylvia Wynter." *Small Axe* 8 (2000): 119–207.

Seascapes Poetics. 2021. www.seascapepoetics.com

Senate of Puerto Rico. *P. del S. 32*. January 2, 2021. San Juan, Puerto Rico.

———. *P. del S. 43*. January 2, 2021. San Juan, Puerto Rico.

Senior, Oliver. "Meditation on Yellow." In *Gardening in the Tropics*, 11–18. Ontario, Canada: Insomniac Press, 2005.

Shaffer, Kirwin R. *Black Flag Boricuas: Anarchism, Antiauthoritarianism, and the Left in Puerto Rico, 1897–1921*. Champaign, IL: University of Illinois Press, 2013.

———. "By Dynamite, Sabotage, Revolution, and the Pen: Violence in Caribbean Anarchist Fiction, 1890s–1920s." *NWIG: New West Indian Guide* 83, nos. 1–2 (2009): 5–38. JSTOR.

Smith, Andrea. "Sovereignty as Deferred Genocide." In *Otherwise Worlds: Against Settler Colonialism and Anti-Blackness*, edited by Tiffany Lethabo King, Jenell Navarro, and Andrea Smith, 118–32. Durham, NC: Duke University Press, 2020.

Solá-Santiago, Frances. "What Logan Paul's Move to Puerto Rico Means—Beyond the Tax Breaks." *Refinery29*. May 3, 2021. www.refinery29.com/en-us/2021/05/10391555/logan-paul-moving-puerto-rico-millionaires-tax-break.

Sosa Pascual, Omaya, Ana Campoy, and Mike Weissenstein. "Los muertos de María." *Centro de Periodismo Investigativo*. n.d. www.losmuertosdemaria.com

Sotomayor, Aurea María. "La imaginería nacionalista: de la historia al relato." In *La nación puertorriqueña: Ensayos en torno Pedro Albizu Campos*, edited by Juan M. Carrión, Teresa C. Gracia Ruiz, and Carlos Rodríguez Fraticelli, 251–76. Río Piedras, Puerto Rico: Editorial de la Universidad de Puerto Rico, 1993.

Steinberg, Philip E. *The Social Construction of the Ocean*. Cambridge, UK: Cambridge University Press, 2001.

Stiglitz, Joseph, and Martín Guzmán. "From Bad to Worse for Puerto Rico." *Project Syndicate*. February 28, 2017.

Stratford, Elaine, Godfrey Baldacchino, Elizabeth McMahon, Carol Farbotko, and Andrew Harwood. "Envisioning the Archipelago." *Island Studies Journal* 6, no. 2 (2011): 113–30.

Suárez Findlay, Eileen J. *Imposing Decency: The Politics of Sexuality and Race in Puerto Rico, 1870–1920*. Durham, NC: Duke University Press, 1999.

Suárez Santiago, Zuan. "Una mirada a la participación política de la mujer por la independencia de Puerto Rico a través del Partido Nacionalista." *Documentalia: texto e imaginación histórica*. May 2016. www.documentaliablog.files.wordpress.com/2016/05/suarez_santiago_mujeres.pdf

Susler, Jan. "Puerto Rican Political Prisoners in U.S. Prisons." In *Puerto Rico under Colonial Rule: Political Persecution and the Quest for Human Rights*, edited by Ramón Bosque-Pérez and José Javier Colón Morera, 119–38. Albany, NY: State University of New York Press, 2006. *People's Law Office*. www.peopleslawoffice.com/wp-content/uploads/2012/02/Puerto-Rican-Prisoners-_201203281858.pdf

Tate, Shirley Anne, and Ian Law. *Caribbean Racisms: Connections and Complexities in the Racialization of the Caribbean Region*. London, UK: Palgrave Macmillan, 2015.

Tavárez Vales, Amarilis. *Larga jornada en el trópico*. San Juan, Puerto Rico: Instituto de Cultura Puertorriqueña, 2015.

Taylor, Diana, and Roselyn Costantino, eds. *Holy Terrors: Latin American Women Perform*. Durham, NC: Duke University Press, 2003.

Teatreros Ambulantes and Bread and Puppet Theater. *La pasión y muerte de Adolfina Villanueva*. 1989. www.hemisphericinstitute.org/en/hidvl-collections/item/1172-rlmarquez-adolfina.html

Teatro Público and Instituto de Cultura Puertorriqueña. "Mujeres del teatro puertorriqueño, episodio 2: Viveca Vázquez y Teresa Hernández." Facebook. March 8, 2021. www.facebook.com/267199020049032/videos/1326690814360925/?__so__=watchlist&__rv__=video_home_www_playlist_video_list.

The Madison Daily Leader. "Porto Rican Belle Fails to Create Popularity in Pantaloon Dress." Madison, SD. July 5, 1912. Chronicling America: Historic American Newspapers. Library of Congress. www.chroniclingamerica.loc.gov/lccn/sn99062034/1912-07-05/ed-1/seq-3/

The Richmond Palladium and Sun-Telegram. "Trouserettes the Latest in Gotham." Richmond, IN. July 1, 1912. Chronicling America: Historic American Newspapers. Library of Congress. www.chroniclingamerica.loc.gov/lccn/sn86058226/1912-07-01/ed-1/seq-8/

Thompson, Lanny. *Imperial Archipelago: Representation and Rule in the Insular Territories under U.S. Dominion after 1898.* Honolulu, Hawaiʻi: University of Hawaiʻi Press, 2010.

Tirado Avilés, Amílcar. "Notas sobre el desarrollo de la industria del tabaco en Puerto Rico y su impacto en la mujer puertorriqueña: 1898–1920." *Centro (Boletín del Centro de Estudios Puertorriqueños)* 2, no. 7 (Winter 1989–1990): 19–29.

Tormos-Aponte, Fernando. "The Politics of Survival in Puerto Rico: The Balance of Forces in the Wake of Hurricane María." *Alternautas.* November 16, 2018. www.alternautas.net/blog/2018/11/16/the-politics-of-survival-in-puerto-rico-the-balance-of-forces-in-the-wake-of-hurricane-mara.

Toro, Ana Teresa. "Puerto Rico, atrapado en el tiempo." *El País.* April 9, 2021. www.elpais.com/eps/2021-04-10/puerto-rico-atrapado-en-el-tiempo.html

Torres, J. Benjamín. *Pedro Albizu Campos: Obras escogidas 1923–1936 Tomo I.* San Juan, Puerto Rico: Editorial Jelofe, 1975.

———. *Pedro Albizu Campos: Obras escogidas 1923–1936 Tomo II.* San Juan, Puerto Rico: Editorial Jelofe, 1975.

———. *Pedro Albizu Campos: Obras escogidas 1923–1936 Tomo III.* San Juan, Puerto Rico: Editorial Jelofe, 1975.

Torres Gotay, Benjamín. "Bob Rabin, el bostoniano que nunca se quiso ir de Vieques." *El Nuevo Día.* May 26, 2021. www.torresgotayentrevista.elnuevodia.com/e/s2-ep-11-bob-rabin-el-bostoniano-que-nunca-se-quiso-ir-de-vieques/

Torres-Saillant, Silvio. "Conocimiento, legitimidad y el sueño de unidad caribeña." *Cuadernos de Literatura,* no. 30 (2011): pp. 21–39.

———. *An Intellectual History of the Caribbean.* London, UK: Palgrave, 2006.

Trigo, María de los Ángeles. *Los Estados Unidos y la PROMESA para Puerto Rico: Un análisis de la Ley para la Supervisión, Administración y Estabilidad Económica de Puerto Rico.* San Juan, Puerto Rico: América en Libros, 2018.

Tucker, Richard P. *Insatiable Appetite: The United States and the Ecological Degradation of the Tropical World.* Lanham, MD: Rowman & Littlefield Publishers, 2007.

University of Puerto Rico, Mayagüez Campus. Sea Grant Puerto Rico. www.seagrantpr.org/

University of the West Indies (UWI). "£20 Million Caribbean Reparations Agreement." *The University of the West Indies Campus News*. August 2, 2019. www.sta.uwi.edu/news/releases/release.asp?id=21947

Uriarte Centeno, Vanessa from *Amigxs del MAR*. Personal Interviews. January 10, 2019 and April 19, 2021.

Valdés, Vanessa K. "The Road of Social Progress: Revolutions and Resistance in the 1936 Lectures of Dantès Bellegarde." In *Racialized Visions: Haiti and the Hispanic Caribbean*, XX–XX. Albany, NY: State University of New York Press, 2020. ProQuest.

Valle Ferrer, Norma. *Luisa Capetillo: Historia de una mujer proscrita*. San Juan, Puerto Rico: Editorial Cultural, 1990.

Vargas Canales, Margarita Aurora. "La revuelta también vino de la caña: El caso de Puerto Rico." *Latinoamérica. Revista de Estudios Latinoamericanos*, no. 50 (2010). Scielo.

Vázquez, Viveca. *Coreografía del error: CONDUCTA*. San Juan, Puerto Rico: Museo de Arte Contemporáneo de Puerto Rico, 2013.

———. "Las playas son nuestras." [Video]. YouTube, uploaded by Arnaldo Rodríguez Bagué. January 11, 2018, . First published 1989. https://youtu.be/tMKG9pY7FZ8

———. "Terreno: Antecedentes del evento *Rompeforma*, cavilación sobre el cuerpo hacia la danza experimental en Puerto Rico." *Umbral*, no. 12 (October 2016): 77–103. Revistas UPR.

Vázquez Vera, Efraín. "Las relaciones oficiales de Puerto Rico con el Caribe." *Gloobalhoy* 14, no. 15 (2005).

Vega, Ana Lydia. *Encancaranublado y otros cuentos de naufragio*. San Juan, Puerto Rico: Editorial Antillana, 1982.

———. "Mi país es el mar." In *Mirada de doble filo*, 21–25. San Juan, Puerto Rico: Editorial de la Universidad de Puerto Rico, 2008.

———. *Mirada de doble filo*. San Juan, Puerto Rico: Editorial de la Universidad de Puerto Rico, 2008.

Venegas Delgado, Hernán. "La Confederación Antillana: Realidad y esperanza." *Caribbean Studies* 27, no. 1.2 (1994): 118–127.

"Verano Boricua/ #RickyRenunica." *Puerto Rico Syllabus*. n.d. puertoricosyllabus.wordpress.com/verano-boricua-rickyrenunica/.

Vergerio, Claire. "Beyond the Nation-State." *Boston Review*. May 27, 2021. www.bostonreview.net/politics/claire-vergerio-beyond-nation-state

Vidal Rodríguez, Rayza. "El teatro de Luisa Capetillo. Signos para un espectador popular." PhD diss., Universidad de Puerto Rico–Río Piedras, 2016.

"Vieques and the Promise to Build Back Better." *La Brega* from *WNYC Studios*. February 24, 2021. https://www.wnycstudios.org/podcasts/la-brega/articles/vieques-and-promise-build-back-better.

Vilches Norat, Vanessa. "El inquieto reflexionar de Teresa Hernández, sobre *Nada que ver*." *Claridad*. December 2006, 21–27.

———. "El mar de los pelícanos." *Claridad*. August 14–17, 2016, 19.

———. *Geografías de lo perdido*. San Juan, Puerto Rico: Ediciones Callejón, 2018.

———. "Mar de fondo." *Claridad*. May 19, 2020.

Villanueva, Joaquín, and Marisol Lebrón. "The Decolonial Geographies of Puerto Rico's 2019 Summer Protests: A Forum." *Society and Space*. n.d. www.societyandspace.org/forums/the-decolonial-geographies-of-puerto-ricos-2019-summer-protests-a-forum

Villanueva, Víctor. "Colonial Memory and the Crime of Rhetoric: Pedro Albizu Campos." *College English* 71, no. 6 (2009): 630–38.

Vueltabajo Teatro. Facebook Page. www.facebook.com/vueltabajoteatro

"Vultures in Puerto Rico." *Hedge Clippers*. n.d. www.hedgeclippers.org/rogues-gallery-vultures-in-puerto-rico/

Walcott, Derek. "The Sea Is History." *Poets.org*. 2007. www.poets.org/poem/sea-history

———. *Tiepolo's Hound*. New York, NY: Farrar, Straus and Giroux, 2000.

———. *What the Twilight Says: Essays*. New York, NY: Farrar, Straus and Giroux, 1998.

Walker, Lara, and translator. "Introduction." In *Absolute Equality: An Early Feminist Perspective*, 5–162. Houston, TX: Arte Público Press, 2009.

Ward, Colin. *Anarchism: A Very Short Introduction*. Oxford, UK: Oxford University Press, 2004.

Weiss, Laura, Marisol Lebrón, and Michelle Chase. *Eye of the Storm*. NACLA Report on the Americas 50, no. 2 (2018).

Wiedorn, Michael. "Glissant's *Philosophie de la Relation*: 'I Have Spoken the Chaos of Writing in the Ardor of the Poem." *Callaloo* 36, no. 4 (2013): 902–15.

Williams, Eric. *Capitalism and Slavery*. Chapel Hill, NC: University of North Carolina Press, 1994. First published 1944.

"World's Richest 0.1% Have Boosted Their Wealth by as Much as Poorest Half." *The Guardian*. December 14, 2017. www.theguardian.com/inequality/2017/dec/14/world-richest-increased-wealth-same-amount-as-poorest-half.

Wright, Erik Olin. *Envisioning Real Utopias*. London, UK: Verso, 2010.

Wynter, Sylvia. "Novel and History, Plot and Plantation." *Savacou* 5 (1971): 95–102.

———. "Sambos and Minstrels." *Social Text*, no. 1 (1979): 149–56. JSTOR.

———. "The Ceremony Must Be Found: After Humanism." *boundary 2* 12, no. 3 (1984): 19–70. JSTOR.

———. "The Pope Must Have Been Drunk, the King of Castile a Madman: Culture as Actuality, and the Caribbean Rethinking Modernity." In *The Reordening of Culture: Latin America, the Caribbean and Canada*, edited by Alvina Ruprecht and Cecilia Taiana, 17–41. Ottawa, Canada: Carleton University Press, 1995.

Zambrana, Rocío. *Colonial Debts: The Case of Puerto Rico*. Durham, NC: Duke University Press, 2021.

———. "Introduction: On Debt, Blame, and Responsibility: Feminist Resistance in the Colony of Puerto Rico." *Critical Times* 4, no. 1 (April 1, 2021): 125–29, doi: 10.1215/26410478-8855275

Zúñiga Reyes, Danghelly Giovanna. "Nación, identidad y ciudadanía: Del ejercicio de inclusión al de exclusión." *CS*, no. 2 (2018): 165–80.

Index

Page references for figures are italicized.

abolition and abolitionism, 61, 70n12, 73n28;
   and abolitionist movement, 226nn8,12;
   indemnity for, 46, 117;
   and Puerto Rico's Abolition Act (1873), 200–201;
   of slavery, 46–47, 69n7, 117;
   of state and property, 220
   See also Betances, Ramón Emeterio
ACircPR, 28
   See also communitarian-artistic-bodily sovereignties
activism, 38n58, 61, 87, 141, 168, 176n26, 179n44
   See also communitarian-artistic-bodily sovereignties
Adorno, Pedro, 142–48
   See also Agua, Sol y Sereno (ASYS)
Afro-Puerto Rican, 87, 107, 120, 127, 136n40, 151, 163, 166, 167, 206, 213
Afro-Caribbean/Antillean, 114, 115, 135nn34,37, 167, 174n2
affect and "affectability," xv–xvi, xixn2, 24
affective archive of Caribbean relations, xvii–xviii, 6, 9–11, 14, 24–29, 38n59, 41, 51–52, 75, 95, 105, 108, 139, 152, 156, 170, 174n9, 185, 210, 224
   See also communitarian-artistic-bodily sovereignties
AgitArte, 28, 157
   See also communitarian-artistic-bodily sovereignties
Agua, Sol y Sereno (ASYS), xviii, 28, 139, 141, 142–43, *145*, 146–47;
   founding members of, 142–43;
   as tidal theater, xvii, 142, 148;
   use of *cabezudos* by, 143, 152, 170;
   use of *zancudos* by, 143, 152
   See also Adorno, Pedro; *Marea alta, marea baja*
Albizu Campos, Pedro, xviii, 35n40, 41, 50, 51, 53, 63, 75, 79–82, 92, 95, 99n7, 105–137, *126*, 176n21, 177n30, 201, 219–220, 224;
   as Afro-Puerto Rican anticolonial leader, 107, 127;
   and Catholicism, 114–15, 119, 121, 127, 135n37;
   and command of the voice, 126–27, 128–29;
   and *Confederación Antillana*; 108–109; 111–12;

258　　　　　　　　　　　　Index

and Haiti, 109–111, 133n16;
and the performative quality of his politics, 125–27;
persecution and torture suffered by, 107, 131n9, 133n20, 136n43, 137n45;
views on the Antilles and Antillean history, 108–111; 113–14;
views on Iberoamerican Republics, 109–111, 116, 119–20, 135n34;
views on islands and archipelagos, 111–13;
views on Puerto Rican nation and nationality, 107, 114–21;
views on race, 114–20, 133n15, 134n26, 135nn33–34;
views on Spain and the Spanish empire, 35n40, 110, 113–118, 127, 130n2, 134n30;
views on the United States and the US empire, 63, 105–108, 110–14, 116, 119–21, 127;
views on women and gender, 35n40, 79, 92, 104n32, 116, 120–124
See also nationalism; *Partido Nacionalista* (PN)
Alvarado Burgos, Miosoti, 203;
as *la mujer del güiro*, 204–206, 209;
as *mujer marejada*, 206
See also Hernández, Teresa
American Communist Party, 125, 137n43
See also Partido Nacionalista (PN)
Amigxs del MAR (AMAR), xvii, xviii, 33n30, 139, 141–142, 148–158, *152*, 163, 165, *166*, 167, 172, 174n3, 175nn10,12,17, 177nn27,29, 220, 222;
and *derecho a permanecer*, 158;
and *derecho a regresar*, 158;
and ecosocialism, 150;
and *manatiburón*, 149, 157;
and *Las playas son del pueblo*, xvii, 150–152, 220;
and *Las playas son nuestras*, 150, 174n9;

and struggle for the protection and restoration of Puerto Rico's bodies of water, 150, 152, 156;
views on Caribbean region, 149–150, 152–154, 158, 172;
views on gender and race, 150, 156
See also de Jesús Mercado, Alberto (Tito Kayak); kayak; Uriarte Centeno, Vanessa
Anamú (Puerto Rican theater collective), 187
anarchism, 77, 85, 89, 98–99n4, 102n22, 114, 137n43, 169, 217n34, 222, 226n8
See also Capetillo, Luisa
anticolonialism, 9, 34n36, 35n40, 80, 95, 107, 110, 112, 114, 121, 130n6, 132n9, 176n19, 180n55, 201, 220
See also Albizu Campos, Pedro; Betances, Ramón Emeterio; nationalism
Antigua and Barbuda Reparations Support Commission, 226n13
See also reparations
Antilles and Antilleans, 8, 25, 46–49, 55–59, 68n3, 69n8, 110–12, 153, 156, 159, 199
Aponte Alsina, Marta, xvi, xviii, 2–14, 24–25, 30n4, 32n19, 36n44, 52, 66, 110, 186, 202, 210, 213, 221;
and "experimental island," 13–14, 25, 221;
and *historias íntimas* (intimate histories), 6, 10;
and *patria líquida* (liquid homeland), xvi, 5, 10–11;
and tradition, 11–13
apoyo mutuo. *See* mutual aid
archipelago and archipelagos, xixn2, xv, xvii, 1, 2, 5, 8, 10, 11, 14, 18, 20, 21, 23, 24, 25, 27, 30n4, 33n25, 35n41, 47nn2,4–5, 48, 49, 52, 53, 54, 56, 57, 63, 73n31, 101n14, 106, 107, 109, 115, 116, 118, 124, 133n16, 148, 154, 155, 157, 161, 162, 165, 166, 169,

170, 174n9, 177n28, 179n48, 184, 186, 196, 200, 201, 204, 205, 210, 215n15, 216nn22,27, 222;
and archipelagic archive, 8, 27;
and archipelagic condition, xvii, 8, 34n37, 156, 181;
and archipelagic connections/relations/collaborations, 10, 29n3, 56, 113, 146, 158, 162, 168, 177n26, 198, 220, 221, 222, 225n7;
and archipelagic consciousness, 24, 111, 125, 224n3;
and archipelagic decolonization, 9, 38n53, 95, 107, 142;
and archipelagic geography, 3, 5, 30n4, 41, 43, 71n20, 75, 150, 158, 196, 205;
and archipelagic horizons, xviii;
and archipelagic imaginary/imagination/dream/poetics, 6, 27, 43, 72n27, 163, 181;
and archipelagic (political) thought and practice/praxis, 2, 9, 25, 26, 30n4, 39n63, 62, 101, 105, 108, 113, 185, 210;
and archipelagic region, 3, 17, 31n5, 112, 135n34, 139;
and archipelagic travel, 49, 71n20, 86, 200;
and archipelagic understanding of sovereignty, 27, 147, 221, 222;
and archipelagic working-class, 85
island and islands archive, 24–26
Archivo Santaliz (live arts piece by Kairiana Núñez Santaliz), 215n15
Ariel (book by José Enrique Rodó). *See arielismo*
arielismo, 108, 114–15
See also Albizu Campos, Pedro
artivist groups and collectives, 142, 170
See also communitarian-artistic-bodily sovereignties
Asamblea de los Pueblos del Caribe, 159

See also Comuna Caribe (CC); Guerrero, Hilda
austerity, 21–22, 172;
and its greater impact on marginalized and vulnerable populations, 21;
and Puerto Rico as "austerity laboratory," 22
See also the debt; neoliberal and neoliberalism
autonomistas, 63, 132n12
See also Betances, Ramón Emeterio
Ayuda Legal Puerto Rico, 28, 157
See also communitarian-artistic-bodily sovereignties

El Bastión, 28
See also communitarian-artistic-bodily sovereignties
bateyes, 161, 178n37
See also Comuna Caribe (CC); Dominican Republic
Becerra, Claudia, 30n4
Beckles, Sir Hilary, 23, 222
See also reparations
becoming other, 25, 203
Bellegarde, Dantès, 133n16
See also Haiti
Bemba PR, 28
See also communitarian-artistic-bodily sovereignties
Benítez Rojo, Antonio, 30n4
Beta-Local, 28
See also communitarian-artistic-bodily sovereignties
Betances, Ramón Emeterio, xvi, xviii, 41, 43–73, *64*, 75, 76, 77, 79, 80, 81, 95, 105, 106, 107, 108, 109, 110, 111, 113, 114, 115, 117, 118, 123, 124, 125, 132n12, 137n43, 143, 152, 153, 156, 159, 163, 172, 173, 182, 200, 201, 212, 213, 219, 220, 223, 224n3;
and affective dream, 45–49;
and Anti-Black racism, 61–62, 72n25;
and *El Antillano*, 55;

and *Las Antillas para los Antillanos*, 44, 58;
and armed revolution, 46, 49, 54, 63, 118;
and commitment to archipelagic political practice, 52, 62, 63;
and *Confederación Antillana* (Antillean Confederation) (AC), xvi, 18, 43–49, 54–57, 62, 68n3–4, 72n23, 111, 136, 156, 163, 220, 223, 225;
and French Republicanism, 47, 49, 52, 60, 70n15, 71n21;
and Haiti, 45, 47, 48, 53, 57–61, 71n18, 72n225;
and participation in *Sociedad Secreta Abolicionista*, 61;
and *revolución del amor*, 61–65;
views on the Antilles and Antillean history, 46–49, 55, 56, 58–59, 62, 68n3, 69n8;
views on independence, 43, 44, 46–51, 53–54, 57–59;
views on islands and archipelagos, 54–57;
views on leadership and liberation, 62, 201;
views on Puerto Rican revolution and nation-building, 49–54;
views on race, 59, 61–62, 71n22, 72n27, 73n29
See also Confederación Antillana (Antillean Confederation-AC)
Biabiany, Minia, 31n4
Black, 17, 57, 60, *64*, 72n25, 111, 115, 120, 158, 166, 179n48, 206
Boal, Augusto, 143
the body, bodily, and embodied/embodying, xv, xvi, xvii, xviii, xxii, 1, 14, 20, 24, 25, 26, 27, 29, 41, 44, 50, 55, 65, 75, 76, 79, 83, 84, 85, 86, 89, 91, 96, 100n8, 105, 108, 109, 119, 120, 124, 125, 129, 131n9, 139, 143, 146, 147, 148, 153, 155, 156, 165, 170, 171, 175n17, 180n55, 181, 182, 184, 185, 186, 189, 190, 191, 192, 194, 195, 197, 198, 203, 209, 212, 218n42, 220, 223
See also affective archive of Caribbean relations; Albizu Campos, Pedro; Capetillo, Luisa; communitarian-artistic-bodily sovereignties; Hernández, Teresa
Boquerón, Cabo Rojo, 44, 66, 76
See also Betances, Ramón Emeterio
Brathwaite, Kamau, 30n4
Bread and Puppet Theatre (US theater collective), 143, 179n48
de Burgos, Julia, 30n4, 125, 213

CABE, 28
See also communitarian-artistic-bodily sovereignties; queer
Cadetes de la República, 125
See also Albizu Campos, Pedro; *Partido Nacionalista* (PN)
calypso music, 38n59, 156
Canales, Blanca, 131n9, 136n40
See also Albizu Campos, Pedro; nationalism; *Partido Nacionalista* (PN)
La Candelaria (Colombian theater collective), 143
Capetillo, Luisa, xvi, xviii, 35, 41, 50, 63, 75–104, *90*, 103n30, 105, 106, 107, 108, 114, 122, 124, 125, 137n43, 141, 168, 172, 181, 191, 192, 194, 195, 216n26, 219, 220, 222, 224, 226n8;
and anarchofeminism, 77, 81, 85, 102n22, 107, 108, 114, 168, 195, 220, 224;
archipelagic geo- and biography of, 75;
and the body, 35, 75, 76, 83, 86, 91, 93, 195;
and claiming her voice, 79, 80, 89, 95;
coastal/littoral situatedness of, 75, 77, 78;
and *espiritismo*, 77, 78, 99n4;
and feminism, 91–97;
oceanic sensibility of, 76, 95;

and performative embodiment of her
work, 76, 78–79, 124;
as political organizer and performer,
78, 85–87, 89;
as reader at tobacco factories, 78,
86–88;
as sewing worker, 78, 87;
and "sovereign life," 76, 85, 96;
and transg/dressing, xvi, 83, 84, 89, 91,
101n15, 181, 191, 192, 194, 195;
as writer, 75, 78–81, 84, 89;
views on education, 79, 81, 92;
views on motherhood, 92–93, 104n31;
views on reading and writing, 77,
79, 82;
views on same-sex desire, 92;
views on sex work, 92, 103n30;
views on socialism, 98n4, 137n43;
views on womanhood, 80, 82–84, 91,
92–94
See also anarchism; feminism and
feminist/s; Hernández, Teresa
capitalism and capitalist, xixn5, 15, 16,
18, 28, 33nn24,28, 37n50, 47, 53,
69n8, 80, 81, 89, 93, 116, 142, 158,
159, 161, 175n11, 179n48, 181, 185,
190, 191, 199, 209, 220, 225n8;
See also neoliberal and neoliberalism
carpeteo, 131n9
See also anticolonialism; nationalism
Carta Autonómica (1987), 63,
73n32, 118
See also Albizu Campos, Pedro
Casa Pueblo (Adjuntas), 27, 143
See also communitarian-artistic-bodily
sovereignties
Caribbean region and regionalism, xviii,
xxn10, 11, 27, 30n4, 31n5, 34n35,
37n50, 48, 54, 58, 109, 112, 113, 114,
116, 125, 130n3, 154, 158, 163, 166,
181, 199, 200, 201, 202, 222, 223
CARICOM, 159, 222, 226n10
Ceballos, Helen, 30n4
Centro de Periodismo Investigativo, 22,
35n42, 36n47, 161, 178n43

Césaire, Aimé, 46, 107, 132n14
See also négritude
cimarronear, 52;
and maroon, 52, 179n48
clothing/dress performative-political,
83–84, 89, 91, 125, 128, 137n45,
182, 184, 191, 194;
See also Albizu Campos, Pedro;
Capetillo, Luisa; Hernández, Teresa
Coalición 8M (C8M), xviii, 28, 139,
141, 142, *166*, 167–70;
and *Alacena Feminista*, 168;
and animal rights, xvii, 169;
and intersectional, coalitional
struggle, 169;
and May Day in Puerto Rico, 169,
176n24;
views on women and gender, 167–69;
and Women's Day in Puerto Rico, 167;
See also feminism and feminist/s;
Contreras Capó, Vanesa
Coalición Playas pa'l Pueblo, 151, *152*;
See also Amigxs del MAR (AMAR);
Uriarte Centeno, Vanessa
the coast and coastal, xixn5, 3, 5, 8, 11,
20, 30n4, 35n41, 36n44, 44, 55, 66,
71n22, 75, 76, 77, 84, 91, 96, 139,
146, 150, 151, 157–58, 163, 166,
171, 172, 174nn1,5, 175nn11,14,
177nn28,30, 181, 196, 197, 215n11,
218n36, 203, 204, 206
*Colectiva Feminista en Construcción
(La Cole)*, 28, 180n54, 161, 162, 168,
169, 178–79n44
See also feminism and feminist/s
Colectivo Ilé, 28, 135n35, 174n3
See also communitarian-artistic-bodily
sovereignties; racism
collective, horizontal organization, 139,
150, 221, 223
See also Verano Boricua 2019
colonialism and colonization, xixn9, 6,
7, 11, 18, 52, 53, 105, 106, 107, 108,
113, 115, 136n43, 162, 167, 174n2,
189, 199

Columbus Square (*Plaza Colón*), San Juan, 177–78n33, 192, *193*, 194;
See also Comuna Caribe (CC); Hernández, Teresa
Comité Pro-Niñez Dominico Haitiana. See Comuna Caribe (CC)
Commonwealth of Puerto Rico. See *Estado Libre Asociado* (ELA)
communitarian-artistic-bodily sovereignties, xix, 25–29, 95, 124, 139, 141, 170, 187, 222, 223
Comuna Caribe (CC), xvii–xviii, 139, 141–142, 158–63, *160*, 174n3, 177n33, 222;
  and affirmation of multiple sovereignties, 163;
  and Dominican Republic, 158–61;
  and efforts to link Puerto Rico to the Caribbean, 159, 161, 222;
  and Haiti, 158–63, *164*, 165, 177n33, 178nn36–38;
  and *Haití y Puerto Rico: deuda y reparaciones* campaign, 157, 161, 162, 177n33, 178n36;
  and struggle for reparations, 162, 177n33, 222
  See also Dominican Republic; *Frente Ciudadano por la Auditoría de la Deuda*; Guerrero, Hilda; Haiti
Concepción de Gracia, Gilberto, 124
  See also *Partido Independentista Puertorriqueño (PIP)*
Confederación Antillana (Antillean Confederation-AC), xvi, 18, 44–49, 51–52, 57, 62–63, 72n23, 73n33, 136n41, 220, 223;
  as archipelagic political dream and project, 45, 52, 54–57;
  See also Albizu Campos, Pedro; Betances, Ramón Emeterio
Construyamos Otro Acuerdo (Puerto Rican activist collective), 28
  See also communitarian-artistic-bodily sovereignties; the debt; *La Junta*; neoliberal and neoliberalism; PROMESA law
Contreras Capó, Vanesa, 168–69, 179n44, 180n54
  See also *Coalición 8M* (C8M)
co-ops (cooperatives), 220, 222, 225–26nn7–8
criollismo, 108
  See also *arielismo*; *Generación del 30*
criollo elites. See neocolonial elites
crisis in Puerto Rico, 20–24
Cruzada del Ideal, 101n16
  See also anarchism; Capetillo, Luisa
de la Cruz Becerril, Dominga, 87, 136n40
  See also nationalism; *Partido Nacionalista* (PN)
cryptoutopia, 24, 37n52
Cuba, 44, 45, 46, 48–50, 53, 58, 59, 70n13, 71n18, 87, 89, 108, 109, 110, 114, 115, 131n9, 158
  See also Albizu Campos, Pedro; Betances, Ramón Emeterio; Capetillo, Luisa
Culebra, 18, 34n37, 35n41, 55, 133n19, 142, 155–56, 174–75n10, 176n24, 177n30, 197, 204, 205, *206*;
  and bidirectional migration with US Virgin Islands, 155–56;
  displacement from, 35n41;
  militarization of, 18;
  political struggles in, 155
  See also Albizu Campos, Pedro; *Amigxs del MAR* (AMAR); Betances, Ramón Emeterio; displacement; kayak; neocolonial and neocolonialism; United States of America (US); US Virgin Islands
Curaçao, 55
  See also Betances, Ramón Emeterio

Davis, Annalee, 29n1, 31n4
the debt, 21, 28n5, 36n46, 162, 179n44;
  in the Caribbean, 24, 161;
  and *endeudamiento*, 20, 179n45;

and *Global Action for Debt Cancellation*, 180n52;
in Puerto Rico, 20–24; 162, 178–79nn43–44, 215n15
See also Comuna Caribe (CC); *Frente Ciudadano por la Auditoría de la Deuda*; neoliberal and neoliberalism; PROMESA law; reparations
decolonization, xvii, xviii, 24–25, 27, 38n53, 111, 121, 124, 149, 168, 220–22
dependency and dependent economy, 17, 27, 53
Díaz Quiñones, Arcadio, 38n56, 70n16, 122, 134n26
disaster, 22–23, 28, 37n50, 57, 185, 202; and "disaster imperialism," 23, 37n50
See also Hurricane Irma, Hurricane María
displacement, 3, 20, 35–36nn41–42, 69n8, 158, 162, 177n30;
and *destierro*, 133n19
See also Culebra; Vieques
Dominican Republic (DR), 44, 45, 46, 48, 53, 58, 66, 71n22, 109, 110, 111, 114, 156, 157, 158, 161, 177n27, 178nn36–37
See also Comuna Caribe (CC); Albizu Campos, Pedro; Betances, Ramón Emeterio; Guerrero, Hilda

echolocation and echolocating, xvi, xixn7, 3, 14, 30n4, 41, 55, 56, 63, 77, 126, 139, 185, 190, 195, 206, 210
See also Gumbs, Alexis Pauline
Editora Educación Emergente, 28, 98n2
See also communitarian-artistic-bodily sovereignties
Editorial Casa Cuna, 28
See also communitarian-artistic-bodily sovereignties; queer
emancipation, 39n63, 41, 43, 102, 103n30, 115, 139, 142, 220, 221
Empresas Padilla (Cabo Rojo), 182, 201, 205

See also Hernández, Teresa; sea salt
Escambrón Beach (Puerto Rico), 144, 170
See also Agua, Sol y Sereno (ASYS); *Marea alta, marea baja*
Espicy Nipples, 28
See also communitarian-artistic-bodily sovereignties; queer
Estado Libre Asociado (ELA), 18, 20, 23, 34n36, 132nn11–12, 191, 204
eugenics in Puerto Rico, 18–20
See also United States of America (US)

Fanon, Frantz, 33n31, 46, 51
Federación Libre de Trabajadores (FLT), 102
Federación de Maestros y Maestras de Puerto Rico (FMPR), 28
See also communitarian-artistic-bodily sovereignties
feminism and feminist/s, 35n40, 75, 77, 78, 79, 81, 83–85, 87, 91–95, 101–102n20, 107, 108, 122, 124, 161, 168–70, 174n3, 178n38, 179n44, 195, 210, 220, 224, 226;
and *andando la calle sola*, 180n50;
in Puerto Rico, 101–102n20
See also Capetillo, Luisa; *Coalición 8M* (C8M); *Colectiva Feminista en Construcción (La Cole)*; Hernández, Teresa; *Matria*; *Mujeres que Abrazan la Mar* (MAM); *Partido Nacionalista* (PN)
Fernández-Retamar, Roberto, 133n22
Ferreira da Silva, Denise, xvii, xixn2, 5, 7, 24–27
Fiestas de la Calle San Sebastián, 143
See also Agua, Sol y Sereno (ASYS)
Fiscal Oversight and Management Board (FOMB). *See La Junta*
from within, 3, 5, 38n53, 215n12
Freemasons and Freemasonry, 45, 71n20
See also Betances, Ramón Emeterio

Frente Ciudadano por la Auditoría de la Deuda, 28, 161, 178n43, 191, 222
  See also communitarian-artistic-bodily sovereignties; the debt; *La Junta*; neoliberal and neoliberalism; PROMESA law; reparations

Gallisá, Carlos, 131n9
  See also anticolonialism
Gallisá Muriente, Sofía, 30n4, 214n11
Garvey, Marcus, 107
Generación del 30, 19, 100n8, 115;
  as criollo political-intellectual circles, 111, 127
  See also criollismo; Pedreira, Antonio S.
Glissant, Édouard, xvi, xviii, xixn2, 2–3, 5–14, 19, 24–25, 30n4, 31nn8,10, 32nn12,15,21, 52, 60, 141–42, 173, 186, 188, 210, 213, 221, 224;
  and detour (deterritorialization), 7, 11, 13, 32n15;
  and errantry, 221;
  and opacity, 5, 7, 11;
  and the open boat, 6–7, 224;
  and *Poetics of Relation/Rélation*, 3–9, 186;
  and retour (reterritorialization), 7, 13
  and the rhizome, 5;
  and the spiral, 3, 5, 31n6;
  and the trace, 5, 31n10, 173, 210
Gómez, Máximo, 45
La Goyco, 28
  See also communitarian-artistic-bodily sovereignties
El Grito de Lares (1868), 50, 54, 117, 134n27, 137n45
  See also Betances, Ramón Emeterio
Le Group d'Appui aux Repatriés et Réfugiés (GARR), 161
  See also *Comuna Caribe* (CC); Haiti
Guardiola, Pablo, 30n4
Guerrero, Hilda, 141, 158–59, *160*, 162–63, 165–66, 174n2, 178–79n44, 179nn45–46;

and *500 años de resistencia indígena y popular*, 158, 174n3;
and *Grito de los Excluidos*, 159, 167, 174n3;
  See also *Comuna Caribe* (CC); *Mujeres que Abrazan la Mar* (MAM)
Guillén, Nicolás, 115
Gumbs, Alexis Pauline, xvi, xixn3, 29, 32n13, 149, 169;
  and school of dolphins, xvi

Haiti, 43, 45, 47, 48, 53, 57–61, 71nn18,22, 72nn24–25, 109–111, 114, 132n14, 133n16, 157, 158–63, *164*, 165, 177n33, 178nn36–38;
  US occupation of, 71n18, 132n14, 136n41;
  See also Albizu Campos, Pedro; Betances, Ramón Emeterio; *Comuna Caribe* (CC)
Haitian Revolution, 59, 72nn24–25, 115
El Hangar, 28
  See also communitarian-artistic-bodily sovereignties
Hauʻofa, Epeli, 224n2;
  and "sea of islands," 220
Hernández, Teresa, xvii, xviii, 84, 139, 147, 178n33, 181–218, *183*, *193*, *206*, *207*, *208*, 220
  and *(a)parecer* (2014), 178, 181, 189, 191, 192, *193*, 194, 210;
  and archipelagic art/practice, 181, 185, 186, 196, 198, 205, 209, 210;
  and becoming nonhuman, 181, 209, 210, 211;
  and *bravata*, xvii, 184, 195–198, 205–209, 211;
  and *Bravata: el comienzo de un comienzo* (2018–2019) in Santurce and Vieques, 182, *183*, 184, 197;
  and *bravata: encuesta a domicilio* (2020-ongoing), 197, 198, 218n40;
  and *Bravatas: sal, sargazo y cansancio* (2018-ongoing), 181, 189, 195;
  as *la enjaulada*, 191, 192, 217n29;

Index 265

as *la erizada*, 191, 203, 205, 207–208, *208*, 209, 218n41;
and *inciertas: espectáculo erosionado* (2020), 197, *206*, *207*, *208*;
as *la mujer de la cola*, 191, 192, *193*, 210;
as *la mujer de la concha*, 182, 184, 191, 209, 210;
as *la mujer del corazón*, 191, 192;
as *la mujer del cuchillo*, 182, *183*, 184, 191, 197, 198, 204, 206, 211, 214n2, 214n11;
as *mujer marejada*, 207;
as *la mujer de la sal*, 182, 191;
as *la mujer del sillón*, 190, 191, *207*;
and *producciones teresa no inc.*, 214n10;
and PRUSA, 189, 216n24, 220;
and scenic presences, 185, 186, 190;
and scenic writing, 84, 185;
as transdisciplinary, experimental artist, 181, 185–188;
views on the body, 182, 184–186, 189–191, 194, 195, 198, 209;
views on objects, 185, 186, 189–191;
views on smallness, 186, 210;
views on space, 185, 188, 191, 195, 198;
views on survival, 190, 195, 201–203, 205, 210;
views on uncertainty, 195, 196
See also Capetillo; Luisa; feminism and feminist/s; *Empresas Padilla*; performance; sargasso; sea salt; Vieques
History versus histories, 3, 6–10, 14, 24, 63
See also Aponte Alsina, Marta; Glissant, Édouard
de Hostos, Eugenio María, 45, 48, 51, 59, 119
See also Betances, Ramón Emeterio
Huggins, Nadia, 31n4
Humboldt, Alexander von, 69n9
Hurricane Irma, 23, 37n49

Hurricane María, 23, 35n41, 36n47, 37nn48–51, 157, 162, 165, 177n28, 196, 197, 209, 221
Hurricane San Ciriaco, 106

Iberoamerican and Iberoamericanism, 109–112, 116, 120, 135n33;
Puerto Rico as, 109, 116
See also Albizu Campos, Pedro
IDEBAJO (Salinas), 27
See also communitarian-artistic-bodily sovereignties
industrialization, 16, 18, 20, 69n8;
"by invitation" in Puerto Rico, 20
See also capitalism and capitalist
Insular Cases, 18, 34n36
See also colonialism and colonization; neocolonial and neocolonialism; United States of America (US)
insularist ideology, 9, 15, 17, 19, 22–24, 31n7, 33n24, 221, 225n3
See also insularity
insularity, 2–3, 9, 15, 18–20, 23–24, 31n4, 33n25, 35n40, 37n52, 54, 57, 111–13
See also insularist ideology
island and islands, xvii, xxii, 1–2, 5, 8–9, 11, 13–15, 17–20, 23–24, 26, 29, 33n4, 34n33, 35nn37,41, 37nn49–50, 39n63, 44–45, 47–48, 52–57, 76, 105, 113, 127, 128, 141–142, 153, 155–156, 184, 196, 204–205, 208, 209–210, 215n12, 219–222;
affirmation of, 205, 219;
feminization of, 15, 19;
as fiscal paradise, 17;
as isolated/ing, 56;
as laboratory of/for decolonization and liberation against power, 24, 221;
as laboratory of/for power, 14–15, 18, 24, 35n37, 37n48;
militarization of, 18;
as negation, 13, 24, 215n12;
small scale of, 5;
as tomb, 20, 24;

uses of, 15, 33n25;
  as women's bodies, 15, 20
  See also archipelago and archipelagos
island and archipelago studies, 2
Isla Verde, Carolina, 27, 151, 170, 171–72
  See also Amigxs del MAR (AMAR); Laguerre, Enrique; Uriarte Centeno, Vanessa

Jamaica, 45, 48, 55, 68n3, 226n9
James, C.L.R., 33n31
Jauca Bay, Santa Isabel, 177n29
de Jesús Mercado, Alberto (Tito Kayak), 149, 152–55, 157, 175n11, 176n21
  See also Amigxs del Mar (AMAR); kayak
Jiménez Suriel, Yina, 30n4
Jiménez Vera, Cindy, 30n4
Jones Act, 87, 156
Jubileo Sur Américas, 159, 161–62, 178nn34,42,44, 222
  See also Comuna Caribe (CC); *Frente Ciudadano por la Auditoría de la Deuda*; Guerrero, Hilda; reparations
La Junta, 21–22, 36n46, 172
  See also the debt; neoliberal and neoliberalism; PROMESA law

kayak, 153–55, 170
  See also Amigxs del MAR (AMAR); de Jesús Mercado, Alberto (Tito Kayak)
Kilómetro 0, 28
  See also communitarian-artistic-bodily sovereignties

Laguerre, Enrique, 151, 175n14
Langevin, Karen, xixn3
Laws #20 and #22, 35n42, 177n30
  See also capitalism and capitalist; displacement; neoliberal and neoliberalism
Law #53. *See Ley de la Mordaza*
Lebrón, Lolita, 131n9, 137n45, 217n31

  See also Hernández, Teresa; nationalism; *Partido Nacionalista* (PN)
Levins Morales, Aurora and Ricardo, 26
Ley de Moratoria de Construcción en la Zona Costanera de Puerto Rico, 157
  See also Santiago, María de Lourdes
Ley de la Mordaza, 131n9
  See also Albizu Campos, Pedro; Muñoz Marín, Luis; nationalism
Ley de la Zona Costanera de Puerto Rico, 157, 174n4
  See also Santiago, María de Lourdes
Loíza, 151, 157, 163, 171–72, 174n1, 175n12, 179n48, 197, 206, *207*, 211–12;
  and the *Pocita de Piñones*, 142, 165, 167, 170, 171–72, 174n1
  See also Guerrero, Hilda; Hernández, Teresa; *Mujeres que Abrazan la Mar* (MAM); Villanueva, Adolfina
López Rivera, Óscar, 28, 131n9, 152–53
  See also Amigxs del MAR (AMAR); anticolonialism
L'Ouverture, Toussaint, 58, 59
  See also Haiti
Luperón, Gregorio, 45

Maceo, Antonio, 45, 68n3
El Maestro (theatrical piece by Nelson Rivera), 127, 137n47
  See also Albizu Campos, Pedro
Malayerba (Ecuadorian theater collective), 143
la mar, xvii, 141–42, 152, 155–57, 165–67, 170
  See also Comuna Caribe (CC); Guerrero, Hilda; *Mujeres que Abrazan la Mar* (MAM)
Marcantonio, Vito, 124
  See also American Communist Party; *Partido Nacionalista* (PN)
Mari Brás, Juan, 131n9
  See also anticolonialism
Mari Pesquera, Santiago, 131n9

See also anticolonialism
Marichal, Tere, 187
Marea alta, marea baja, 144–48, 153, 174n5, 175n17;
  the beach and sand in, 144, 146–47;
  as collective creation, 147;
  the cosmic in, 31n6, 146, 148;
  submarine unity in, 55, 146
  See also Adorno, Pedro; *Agua, Sol y Sereno* (ASYS)
Mar nuestro/Manteca (play by Alberto Pedro), 34n33
Marqués, René, 34n33, 175n14
Martí, José, 45, 48, 59, 62, 119, 163
Matria, 28, 226n11
  See also communitarian-artistic-bodily sovereignties; feminism and feminist/s
misogyny, 28, 124
El momento del yagrumo (exhibition curated by Marina Reyes Franco), 30n4, 39n61
Movimiento de mujeres dominico-haitianas (MUDHA), 161;
  See also Comuna Caribe (CC); Dominican Republic
Movimiento Victoria Ciudadana (MVC), 136n42, 204
Mujeres que Abrazan la Mar (MAM), xvii–xviii, 139, 141, 142, *160*, 163, *164*, 165–67, *166*, 172, 174n5, 220;
  and *así sea, así será*, 172, 220;
  and *la mar sana*, xvii, 165;
  and *mística*, 167;
  struggle to defend and protect Puerto Rican beaches and coastal communities, 163;
  views on the body, 163, 165;
  views on women and gender, 163, 165, 167;
  See also feminism and feminist/s; Guerrero, Hilda; *Pocita de Piñones*
Muñoz Marín, Luis, 20, 23, 121, 127, 131nn8–9, 132n12

  See also Estado Libre Asociado (ELA); *Ley de la mordaza*; *Partido Popular Democrático* (PPD)
mutual aid, 28, 168, 225n7, 226n8
myth of racial harmony in Puerto Rico, 119, 135n34

Nanan, Wendy, 31n4
nationalism, 60, 80, 92, 95, 105, 108, 110, 113, 115, 116, 121–25, 130n6, 131n9, 135n37, 201;
  US and Puerto Rican violent repression of, 131n9;
  See also Albizu Campos, Pedro; anticolonialism; *Partido Nacionalista* (PN)
nation-state, xviii, 27, 39n63, 51–54, 58, 63, 71n18, 72n25, 77, 121, 220–21, 224n3, 225nn4,7
  See also Albizu Campos, Pedro; anticolonialism; Betances, Ramón Emeterio; *Partido Nacionalista* (PN)
négritude, 115, 134n26
neocolonial elites, 19, 77, 106, 189, 200, 219
neocolonial and neocolonialism, 18, 20, 24, 34n36, 35nn40,42, 53, 108, 114, 127, 131n9, 132n12, 187, 198
neoliberal and neoliberalism, 16, 18, 21, 28, 141, 158, 159, 174n3, 187–89, 204;
  and privatization, 17, 20, 22, 37n51, 150, 177nn28–29, 163, 188
  See also capitalism and capitalist; *La Junta*; Rosselló, Pedro; power
NoSiri/Emilia Beatriz, 30n4, 39n61

ocean and oceanic, xxii, 7, 15, 17, 30n4, 31n7, 76, 95, 129, 147, 171, 172, 182, 202, 203, 209, 210, 212;
  See also Capetillo, Luisa; the coast and coastal; Glissant, Édouard; *la mar*; the sea
Ocean Park Beach (Puerto Rico), 165, *166*, 170, 211

See also Amigxs del MAR (AMAR);
  Coalición 8M (C8M); Mujeres que
  Abrazan la Mar (MAM)
Ojeda Ríos, Filiberto, 107, 131n9,
  137n45
  See also anticolonialism
The Other Side of Now: Foresight
  in Contemporary Caribbean Art
  (curated exhibition by María Elena
  Ortiz and Marsha Pierce), 30n4
overpopulation, 19, 35n39
  See also eugenics in Puerto Rico

Padilla de Sanz, Trina, 136n40
  See also nationalism; Partido
  Nacionalista (PN)
Palés Matos, Luis, 13, 30n4, 101n14,
  115, 134n26, 195, 203, 207, 218n37
  See also Generación del 30;
  Hernández, Teresa
Pan-Africanism, 134n26
Papel Machete (Puerto Rican
  transdisciplinary artistic
  collective), 187
  See also communitarian-artistic-bodily
  sovereignties
participatory action research, 38n60
participatory budgeting, 225–26n8
  See also anarchism; co-ops
  (cooperatives)
participatory democracy, 25, 150, 157,
  163, 168–69, 222, 226n8
  See also anarchism; co-ops
  (cooperatives)
partidas sediciosas (seditious
  groups), 106
Partido Independentista Puertorriqueño
  (PIP), 35n42, 124, 136n42
Partido Nacionalista (PN), 52, 80, 82,
  105, 107–109, 111, 112, 113–115,
  122–125, 126, 132n11, 134n30,
  136nn40,42–43, 137nn45–46, 201;
  and Declaración de principios (1922),
  108–109, 111, 115;
  politics of dress in the, 125;

and Programa político, social y
  económico del Partido Nacionalista
  de Puerto Rico (1930), 111;
and staging and symbolic practices,
  125, 136n46;
views on public education, 122;
views on women and gender, 122–23;
women's active participation in, 123,
  136n40
  See also Albizu Campos, Pedro;
  anticolonialism
Partido Nuevo Progresista (PNP),
  xxn10, 52, 188, 204
  See also Rosselló, Ricardo; Rosselló,
  Pedro
Partido Popular Democrático (PPD),
  xxn10, 20, 52, 127, 132n12, 204
  See also Estado Libre Asociado (ELA);
  Muñoz Marín, Luis
Partido del Pueblo Trabajador (PPT),
  136n42
Partido Socialista Puertorriqueño
  (PSP), 136n42
Partido Unión, 80, 127
La pasión y muerte de Adolfina
  Villanueva (theatrical piece by Los
  teatreros ambulantes and Bread and
  Puppet Theatre), 179n48
pastrana santiago, nibia, 30n4
patria (homeland), 44, 47n4, 49, 52,
  55, 57, 66, 67, 80, 116–17, 121,
  167, 168;
  fathers of the, 80, 117;
  Albizu Campos's views on,
  116–17, 121;
  Betances's views on, 47n4, 49, 52,
  55, 57;
  Capetillo's views on, 80
  See also anticolonialism; nationalism;
  nation-state; Partido Nacionalista
  (PN)
patriarchy, 16, 44, 62–65, 83–84, 91, 94,
  122, 159, 174, 220
Pedreira, Antonio S., 19–20, 34n33,
  35n40, 122, 134n26

See also Generación del 30;
neocolonial elites
performance, xviii, xixn3, 2, 25, 28,
29n3, 30n4, 62, 82, 88–89, 91,
100n13, 101n15, 125–126, 139,
142, 174n5, 178n33, 181, 185, 189,
191–92, 194–95, 197, 198, 203, 212,
214n4, 217n30;
piece, xviii, 25, 178n33, 181, – 189,
192, 195, 197, 203;
as struggle, 82, 89, 142;
as political, 29n3, 89, 91, 139, 142,
181, 191
See also Capetillo, Luisa; Hernández,
Teresa
performative interventions as political/
activist actions, xviii, 144, 194
See also Agua, Sol y Sereno (ASYS);
Hernández, Teresa
performative/embodied writing, xviii,
10, 75, 78–79, 84
See also Capetillo, Luisa
Pétion, Alexandre, 47, 50, 58–60, 73n30
See also Betances, Ramón Emeterio;
Haiti
Picó, Fernando, 106, 130n2, 213
Piñera, Virgilio, 34n33
Pisotón (Puerto Rican dance collective),
187–88
plantation and plantation system, xixn9,
4, 7, 16, 18, 25, 29, 35n42, 106,
200, 223
See also capitalism and capitalist;
colonialism and colonization; slavery
Playuela, Aguadilla, 27
political/activist actions as performative
interventions, xviii, 82, 91, 95,
152–55
See also Amigxs del MAR (AMAR);
Capetillo, Luisa; de Jesús Mercado,
Alberto (Tito Kayak)
poetics, xvii, 2, 5–8, 10–11, 14, 25,
31n8, 32n21, 185, 201;
and Caribbean, 10;
as imagination, 5–6, 14, 25, 185;

as intuition, 5, 25–27, 78, 185;
as speculation, 201
See also Ferreira da Silva, Denise;
Glissant, Édouard
population control. *See* eugenics in
Puerto Rico
power (as name for capitalist-
patriarchal-racist-coloniality), 15
PROMESA law, 20–21, 36nn45–46,
197, 216n27, 221
See also the debt; *La Junta*; neoliberal
and neoliberalism; United States of
America (US)
Pueblos Hispanos, 125

queer, xvii, 83, 103n29, 167, 224

Rabin, Robert, 156, 176n26
See also Vieques
racism and struggle against, 17, 33n31,
48, 72n25, 100, 119–20, 124, 178n36,
179n48, 220
racialization dynamics in Puerto Rico,
72n27
Ramos Rubén, Sabrina, 30n4
recuperación justa (just recovery), 157
See also Amigxs del MAR (AMAR);
Ayuda Legal Puerto Rico
reformistas, 63, 73n28
See also Betances, Ramón Emeterio
rescate de tierra (land rescue), 148,
174n8
See also Villanueva, Adolfina
reparations, xviii, 23, 37n50, 53,
71nn18–19, 134n30, 139, 141–42,
157, 159, 161–62, 170, 177n33,
221–23, 226n9;
and reparatory justice, xvii, 52–54, 63,
221–23;
Caribbean struggle for, xviii, 23, 54,
63, 221, 226n9;
David Scott's reflections on, 130n6,
178n33, 226n9;
debt cancellation as a form of, 142,
161, 177n33;

and institutions, 223;
terms to demand in Puerto Rico as part of possible, 157, 162, 222
See also Comuna Caribe (CC); *Frente Ciudadano por la Auditoría de la Deuda*
Reynolds, Ruth Mary, *126*, 136n40, 137n45
See also nationalism; *Partido Nacionalista* (PN)
Rodríguez de Tió, Lola, 44, 63, 66, 73n32
See also Betances, Ramón Emeterio
Rosado Torres, Arnaldo Darío, 131n9
See also anticolonialism
Rosselló, Pedro, 159, 174n3, 177n32, 188, 216n20;
and *mano dura contra el crimen*, 188;
militarization of Puerto Rico by, 216n20, 189;
neoliberal regime of, 174n3, 189, 204;
and *obra que se ve*, 189;
and *pensar en grande*, 189
See also neoliberal and neoliberalism; *Partido Nuevo Progresista* (PNP)
Rosselló, Ricardo, 33n24, 188, 191
See also Partido Nuevo Progresista (PNP); *Verano Boricua 2019*
Ruiz Belvis, Segundo, 44, 61
See also Betances, Ramón Emeterio

sacrifice, 50–51, 53, 108, 119, 121–22;
Albizu Campos's views on, 108, 119, 121–22;
Betances's views on, 50–51
See also Partido Nacionalista (PN)
salinas (Cabo Rojo) (salt ponds) and *salineros* (sea salt workers), 200–202
See also Empresas Padilla; Hernández, Teresa; sea salt
Sanes, David, 144, 147, 148, 175n17
See also Vieques; United States of America (US)
Santaliz, Pedro (Pedrito), 187
Santiago, María de Lourdes, 35n42, 157

See also Ley de Moratoria de Construcción en la Zona Costanera de Puerto Rico; *Ley de la Zona Costanera de Puerto Rico*; *Partido Independentista Puertorriqueño* (PIP)
sargasso, 12–13, 33n22, 181, 182, 189, 198, 202–203, 204, 205, 208, 209, 218n36;
and Sargasso Sea, 12–13
See also Aponte Alsina, Marta; Hernández, Teresa; the sea
Seascape Poetics (virtual exhibition curated by Bettina Pérez Martínez), 30n4
Schumann, Peter, 143
Se Acabaron las Promesas (Puerto Rican activist collective), 28
See also the debt; *La Junta*; neoliberal and neoliberalism; PROMESA law
the sea, xviii, 3, 5–10, 12, 17, 18, 20, 30, 31n5, 32n14, 34n33, 44, 75, 76, 78, 96, 128, 141, 146, 149, 150, 152, 154, 182, 184, 190, 196, 198, 200, 202, 205, 208–210, 211, 213;
Amigxs del MAR (AMAR)'s relation to, 149, 150, 152, 154;
Aponte Alsina's views on, 9, 10;
Capetillo's views on, 76, 78;
Glissant's views on, 3, 6, 7;
Hernández's relation to, 182, 184, 190, 196, 198, 200, 202, 205, 208–210, 211, 213;
exploitation of, 17, 199;
insularist ideology's figuration of, 3;
in *Marea alta, marea baja*, 144, 146–48;
Mujeres que Abrazan la Mar (MAM)'s relation to, 165;
Pedreira's views on, 19, 20;
and rising sea levels, xvii, 211;
traumatic relation to, 17, 18, 34n33, 166–67
See also la mar; ocean and oceanic
sea salt, 182, 184, 198, 199–202, 205, 206, 209, 214n5

See also Empresas Padilla; Hernández, Teresa; *salinas* (Cabo Rojo); slavery
self-government, 53, 73n32, 80, 132
  See also anticolonialism; nationalism; sovereignty and sovereignties
slavery, 6, 7, 25, 33n27, 46, 47, 53, 114, 117, 118, 120, 146, 200;
  and enslavement, xixn9, 5, 17, 34n31, 113, 166, 167, 184, 199, 223, 226n9;
  and genocide, 17, 113, 167, 223;
  and the slave trade, 6, 7
  See also abolition and abolitionism; capitalism and capitalist; Caribbean; colonialism and colonization; racism and the struggle against
smallness, xxii, 3, 8, 11, 54, 186, 210, 214n10, 215n13, 223;
  and "small countries," 5, 8
  See also Glissant, Édouard; Hernández, Teresa
Solidarité Fanm Ayisyèn (SOFA), 161
  See also Comuna Caribe (CC); Haiti
La Sombrilla Cuir (Puerto Rican activist collective), 28
  See also communitarian-artistic-bodily sovereignties
Soto Arriví, Carlos Enrique, 131n9
  See also anticolonialism
sovereignty and sovereignties, xvii–xviii, 8, 14, 25–27, 35n40, 39n63, 41, 52, 64, 75, 83, 111, 121, 124, 139, 143, 147, 154, 162, 167–69, 177n28, 185, 220–22, 225nn6–7;
  as bodily, 75, 83, 139;
  as multiple, xvii, 25–27, 41, 75, 162;
  as opaque, 27;
  as other, 27
  See also communitarian-artistic-bodily sovereignties
Spain, 45–48, 53, 73n32, 77, 106, 111, 113, 114, 115–20, 132n12, 134n30;
  and Spanish empire, 34n34, 35n40, 45–46, 49, 63, 71n20, 109, 114, 118, 120

See also Albizu Campos, Pedro; Betances, Ramón Emeterio; reparations
St. Thomas, 45, 48, 55–56, 68n3, 156
  See also Betances, Ramón Emeterio
student movements and strikes, 28, 38n57, 175n17, 216n28, 225n5
  See also communitarian-artistic-bodily sovereignties
study as autonomous, revolutionary practice, 77, 88, 122;
  art as a means to, 198
  See also Capetillo, Luisa; Gumbs, Alexis Pauline; Hernández, Teresa
submarine connections, histories, memory, and relations, xvi, 10, 11, 29, 55, 95, 124, 146, 152, 156, 175n17, 178n33
sugar and sugarcane, 16, 18, 184, 199, 200
  See also colonialism and colonization; plantation and plantation system; slavery

El tajo del alacrán (Puerto Rican theater collective), 187
Tallaboa, Peñuelas, 27
Taller Libertá. *See Vueltabajo Teatro*
Taller de Otra Cosa (Puerto Rican live arts collective), 28, 188, 216n19
  See also Hernández, Teresa; Vázquez, Viveca
Taller Salud (Puerto Rican activist collective), 28
Tavárez Vales, Amarilis, 30n4
Los teatreros ambulantes (Puerto Rican theater collective), 143, 187
Teatro Pregones (Puerto Rican theater collective), 143
Teatro Rodante de la UPR (Puerto Rican theater collective), 215n14
Teatro del Sesenta (Puerto Rican theater collective), 187
The Tempest (play by William Shakespeare), 114, 133n22

Index

teología de la liberación (liberation theology), 135n37
Tito Kayak. *See* Alberto de Jesús Mercado
tobacco factories and industry, 25, 78, 86, 87–88, 101nn18–19;
and archipelagic institution of reading, 87–89;
and *despalilladoras* (strippers), 87;
and women, 87–88, 102n20;
and the working-class, 87–88, 102n20
See also Capetillo, Luisa
tourism, 16, 17, 219, 223;
and Puerto Rico's Tourism Office, 219
tribuna (stand or platform), 85, 86, 88, 104n32, 105, 107, 126, 128, 206
See also Albizu Campos, Pedro; Capetillo, Luisa; *Partido Nacionalista* (PN)

unconditional basic income model, 225n8
See also anarchism
underseeing and underseen, 6, 10, 26, 29n1, 41, 43, 63, 105, 139, 141, 181, 185, 194, 201, 205, 208, 219, 221, 223
United States of America (US), 18, 21, 35n42, 49, 52, 53, 69n10, 73n31, 77, 81, 107–109, 111–14, 116, 119–20, 121, 124, 130n4, 131n9, 132n12, 133n16, 134n30, 135n34, 153, 162, 204, 218n41, 226n13;
and US empire, 20, 35n38, 48, 49, 87, 107, 109, 113, 116, 120;
and US militarization of Puerto Rico, 113, 73n31;
and US Navy, 148, 149, 156, 175n10, 176n24
Unión Independiente de los Trabajadores de la Sal, 201
University of Glasgow (UG), 223
See also reparations
University of Puerto Rico (UPR), x, 22, 28, 32n19, 33n30, 38n57, 133n16,
135n35, 175nn12,17, 180n54, 191, 215n14, 216n28, 223, 225n5
University of the West Indies (UWI), 223
See also reparations
Uriarte Centeno, Vanessa, 149–51, 153–54, 157–58, 165–66, 175n12, 177n27
See also Amigxs del MAR (AMAR)
US Virgin Islands, 45, 48, 156
See also Betances, Ramón Emeterio; Culebra; Vieques

Vázquez, Viveca, 174n9, 179n48, 188, 216n19
See also Hernández, Teresa; *Pisotón*
Vega, Ana Lydia, 13, 17, 30n4
Venezuela, 55, 153
Verano Boricua 2019 (Puerto Rico's summer 2019 rebellion), xviii, 28, 33n24, 53, 101n17, 155, 175n11, 206, 221, 225n5
See also communitarian-artistic-bodily sovereignties
Vieques, 18, 27, 34n37, 35n41, 55, 86, 113, 133nn18–19, 142, 148–149, 155–156, 158, 162, 172, 175n10, 176nn24–25, 177n30, 182, *183*, 184, 190, 195, 197, 198, 202, 204–205, *206*, 209;
Albizu Campos's views on, 113, 133n18, 177n30;
bidirectional migration with US Virgin Islands, 155–156;
displacement from, 35n41, 158, 177n30;
Hernández's work in, 182, *183*, 184, 190, 195, 197, 198, 202, 204–205, *206*, 209;
lack of public hospital in, 155, 172, 176n24;
militarization of, 18, 34n37, 148–149, 156
See also Albizu Campos, Pedro; *Amigxs del MAR* (AMAR); Betances,

Ramón Emeterio; displacement; Hernández, Teresa; kayak; neocolonial and neocolonialism; United States of America (US); US Virgin Islands
Village Solidarité, 161
   See also Comuna Caribe (CC); Haiti
Villanueva, Adolfina, 179n48
   See also Loíza; *rescate de tierra*; *Los teatreros ambulantes*; Vázquez, Viveca
Vilches Norat, Vanessa, 30n4
Vueltabajo Teatro (Puerto Rican theater collective), 28, 30n4, 187
   See also communitarian-artistic-bodily sovereignties

walk and walking, xvi, xxii, xixn5, 1, 5–7, 11, 25, 29n1, 65–66, 83, 96–97, 170, 173, 180n50, 182, 186, 198, 204–205, 211, 212
   See also Capetillo, Luisa; Glissant, Édouard; Hernández, Teresa
walk-swim and walking-swimming, xvi–xvii, 1, 2, 6, 29, 41, 43, 128, 139, 141, 155, 170, 181, 221
West Indies Federation, 18, 51, 109, 115, 132n14
   See also Confederación Antillana (Antillean Confederation-AC)
White and whiteness, xv, 24, 59, 81, 106, 115, 116, 119, 127, 189, 192
White supremacy, 17, 72n25, 174n2
Women's Day in Puerto Rico. *See Coalición 8M* (C8M)
working-class, 17, 85–88, 99n4, 102nn20,22, 104n32, 106, 107, 122, 148, 169, 175n11, 176n24, 206; and Puerto Rican women, 102n20, 104n32
Wright, Erik Olin, 225n8
Wynter, Sylvia, 33n31

Yemayá, 142, 167
yola. *See* kayak
Yuyachkani (Peruvian theater collective), 143

zona marítimo-terrestre (maritime land zone), 157
   See also Amigxs del MAR (AMAR); the coast and coastal; displacement; *Ley de Moratoria de Construcción en la Zona Costanera de Puerto Rico*; *Ley de la Zona Costanera de Puerto Rico*; Santiago, María de Lourdes

About the Author

Beatriz Llenín-Figueroa is a companion, partner, comrade, friend, nerd, writer, editor, translator, and animal and live arts apprentice. Having completed a PhD from the Program in Literature at Duke University, she worked as an adjunct professor at the University of Puerto Rico in Mayagüez and Río Piedras for almost a decade. Presently, she is an "independent" writer and scholar who stands for Puerto Rican and Caribbean emancipations. Her creative, intellectual, and political lives revolve around the relations between Puerto Rican and Caribbean archipelagos; islands, seas, and coasts; experimental and street theater and performance; and multiple, embodied forms of sovereignty. Some of her creative writing has been published in the collection *Puerto Islas: crónicas, crisis, amor* (2018). She works as associate editor for the small independent Puerto Rican press, *Editora Educación Emergente*, and as freelance editor and translator.